THE AMERICAN YAWP

THE AMERICAN YAWP

A Massively Collaborative Open U.S. History Textbook

VOL. 2: SINCE 1877

EDITED BY JOSEPH L. LOCKE AND BEN WRIGHT

STANFORD UNIVERSITY PRESS • STANFORD, CALIFORNIA

Printed in the United States of America on acid-free, archival-quality paper

Library of Congress Cataloging-in-Publication Data

Names: Locke, Joseph L., editor. | Wright, Ben, editor.
Title: The American yawp : a massively collaborative open U.S. history textbook /
    edited by Joseph L. Locke and Ben Wright.
Description: Stanford, California : Stanford University Press, 2019. |
    Includes bibliographical references and index.
Identifiers: LCCN 2018015206 (print) | LCCN 2018017638 (ebook) |
    ISBN 9781503608139 (e-book) | ISBN 9781503606715 | ISBN 9781503606715
    (v. 1 :pbk. :alk. paper) | ISBN 9781503606883(v. 2 :pbk. :alk. paper) |
    ISBN 9781503608139(v. 1 :ebook) | ISBN 9781503608146(v. 2 :ebook)
Subjects: LCSH: United States—History—Textbooks.
Classification: LCC E178.1 (ebook) | LCC E178.1 .A493673 2019 (print) |
    DDC 973—dc23
LC record available at https://lccn.loc.gov/2018015206

Bruce Lundquist
Typeset by Newgen in Sabon LT 11/15
Cover illustration: Detail from "Victory!" by M.F. Tobin, c. 1884. Source: Susan H.
Douglas Political Americana Collection, Division of Rare and Manuscript Collections,
Cornell University Library.

Yawp \yôp\ *n*: 1: a raucous noise 2: rough vigorous language

"I sound my barbaric yawp over the roofs of the world."

Walt Whitman, 1854

Contents

Preface

We are the heirs of our history. Our communities, our politics, our culture: it is all a product of the past. As William Faulkner wrote, "The past is never dead. It's not even past."[1] To understand who we are, we must therefore understand our history.

Civil rights march from Selma to Montgomery, Alabama, in 1965. Library of Congress.

But what *is* history? What does it mean to study the past? History can never be the simple memorizing of names and dates (how would we even know what names and dates are worth studying?). It is too complex a task and too dynamic a process to be reduced to that. It must be something more because, in a sense, it is we who give life to the past. Historians ask historical questions, weigh evidence from primary sources (material produced in the era under study), grapple with rival interpretations, and argue for their conclusions. History, then, is our ongoing conversation about the past.

Every generation must write its own history. Old conclusions—say, about the motives of European explorers or the realities of life on slave plantations—fall before new evidence and new outlooks. Names of leaders and dates of events may not change, but the weight we give them and the context with which we frame them invariably evolves. History is a conversation between the past and the present. To understand a global society, we must explore a history of transnational forces. To understand the lived experiences of ordinary Americans, we must look beyond the elites who framed older textbooks and listen to the poor and disadvantaged from all generations.

But why study history in the first place? History can cultivate essential and relevant—or, in more utilitarian terms, "marketable"—skills: careful reading, creative thinking, and clear communication. Many are familiar with a famous quote of philosopher George Santayana: "Those who fail to learn from history are doomed to repeat it."[2] The role of history in shaping current events is more complicated than this quote implies, but Santayana was right in arguing that history offers important lessons. The historical sensibility yields perspective and context and broader awareness. It liberates us from our narrow experiences and pulls us into, in the words of historian Peter Stearns, "the laboratory of human experience."[3] Perhaps a better way to articulate the importance of studying history would be, "Those who fail to understand their history will fail to understand themselves."

Historical interpretation is never wholly subjective: it requires method, rigor, and perspective. The open nature of historical discourse does not mean that all arguments—and certainly not all "opinions"—about the past are equally valid. Some are simply wrong. And yet good historical questions will not always have easy answers. Asking "When did Christopher Columbus first sail across the Atlantic?" will tell us far less than "What inspired Columbus to attempt his voyage?" or "How did Native Americans interpret the arrival of Europeans?" Crafting answers to these questions reveals far greater insights into our history.

But how can any textbook encapsulate American history? Should it organize around certain themes or surrender to the impossibility of synthesis and retreat toward generality? In the oft-cited lines of the American poet Walt Whitman, we found as good an organizing principle as any other: "I too am not a bit tamed—I too am untranslatable," he wrote, "I sound my barbaric yawp over the roofs of the world."[4] Long before Whitman and long after, Americans have sung something collectively amid the deafening roar of their many individual voices. Here we find both chorus and cacophony together, as one. This textbook therefore offers the story of that barbaric, untranslatable American yawp by constructing a coherent and accessible narrative from all the best of recent historical scholarship. Without losing sight of politics and power, it incorporates transnational perspectives, integrates diverse voices, recovers narratives of resistance, and explores the complex process of cultural creation. It looks for America in crowded slave cabins, bustling markets, congested tenements, and marbled halls. It navigates between maternity wards, prisons, streets, bars, and boardrooms. Whitman's America, like ours, cut across the narrow boundaries that can strangle narratives of American history.

We have produced *The American Yawp* to help guide students in their encounter with American history. *The American Yawp* is a collaboratively built, open American history textbook designed for general readers and college-level history courses. Over three hundred academic historians—scholars and experienced college-level instructors—have come together and freely volunteered their expertise to help democratize the American past for twenty-first century readers. The project is freely accessible online at www.AmericanYawp.com, and in addition to providing a peer review of the text, Stanford University Press has partnered with *The American Yawp* to publish a low-cost print edition. Furthermore, *The American Yawp* remains an evolving, collaborative text: you are encouraged to help us improve by offering comments on our feedback page, available through AmericanYawp.com.

The American Yawp is a fully open resource: you are encouraged to use it, download it, distribute it, and modify it as you see fit. The project is formally operated under a Creative Commons Attribution-Share Alike 4.0 International (CC-BY-SA) License and is designed to meet the standards of a "Free Cultural Work." We are happy to share it and we hope you will do the same.

Joseph Locke & Ben Wright, editors

A Note on Updates

The American Yawp was designed to capture the cutting edge of historical scholarship.

It is, above all else, a collaborative project, and we follow the advice of content experts. On our website, scholars provide detailed feedback on our content. We have received hundreds of smart, helpful suggestions from trained, academic historians. Each summer, we have made small changes based on this feedback. This print edition incorporates some of the updates that had appeared online before January 2023.

Most of our changes have been minor. Several chapters have new names. For example, we now begin the text with "Indigenous America." Some changes are more substantial. Our discussion of the New Deal, for instance, has changed considerably to reflect new perspectives on how Americans reckoned with the Great Depression. Moreover, we have updated the text to reflect our own momentous times. Our final chapter, on the "Recent Past," now includes discussions of the COVID-19 pandemic, the Black Lives Matter movement, the January 6 insurrection, and more. We do not believe these changes are substantial enough to merit a new edition, but we nevertheless want to ensure that print readers have access to these updates. A comprehensive list of our annual updates is available online at http://americanyawp.com/text/updates.

History, as we write in our text, is an ongoing conversation between the present and the past. *The American Yawp* remains committed to capturing the current state of that conversation.

NOTES TO PREFACE

1. William Faulkner, *Requiem for a Nun* (New York: Random House, 1954), 73.

2. George Santayana, *The Life of Reason: Or the Phases of Human Progress, Volume I* (New York: Scribner, 1905), 284.

3. Peter N. Stearns, "Why Study History," *American Historical Association* (July 11, 2008). https://www.historians.org/about-aha-and-membership/aha-history-and-archives/archives/why-study-history-(1998.

4. Walt Whitman, *Leaves of Grass* (Brooklyn: Rome, 1855), 55.

THE AMERICAN YAWP

16

Capital and Labor

I. Introduction

The Great Railroad Strike of 1877 heralded a new era of labor conflict in the United States. That year, mired in the stagnant economy that followed the bursting of the railroads' financial bubble in 1873, rail lines slashed workers' wages (even, workers complained, as they reaped enormous subsidies and paid shareholders lucrative stock dividends). Workers struck from Baltimore to St. Louis, shutting down railroad traffic—the nation's economic lifeblood—across the country.

Panicked business leaders and friendly political officials reacted quickly. When local police forces would not or could not suppress the strikes, governors called out state militias to break them and restore rail service. Many strikers destroyed rail property rather than allow militias to reopen the rails. The protests approached a class war. The governor of Maryland deployed the state's militia. In Baltimore, the militia fired into a crowd of striking workers, killing eleven and wounding many more. Strikes convulsed towns and cities across Pennsylvania. The head of the Pennsylvania Railroad, Thomas Andrew Scott, suggested that if workers

A Maryland National Guard unit fires upon strikers during the Great Railroad Strike of 1877. *Harper's Weekly*, via Wikimedia.

were unhappy with their wages, they should be given "a rifle diet for a few days and see how they like that kind of bread."[1] Law enforcement in Pittsburgh refused to put down the protests, so the governor called out the state militia, who killed twenty strikers with bayonets and rifle fire. A month of chaos erupted. Strikers set fire to the city, destroying dozens of buildings, over a hundred engines, and over a thousand cars. In Reading, strikers destroyed rail property and an angry crowd bombarded militiamen with rocks and bottles. The militia fired into the crowd, killing ten. A general strike erupted in St. Louis, and strikers seized rail depots and declared for the eight-hour day and the abolition of child labor. Federal troops and vigilantes fought their way into the depot, killing eighteen and breaking the strike. Rail lines were shut down all across neighboring Illinois, where coal miners struck in sympathy, tens of thousands gathered to protest under the aegis of the Workingmen's Party, and twenty protesters were killed in Chicago by special police and militiamen.

Courts, police, and state militias suppressed the strikes, but it was federal troops that finally defeated them. When Pennsylvania militiamen were unable to contain the strikes, federal troops stepped in. When militia in West Virginia refused to break the strike, federal troops broke it instead. On the orders of the president, American soldiers were deployed all across northern rail lines. Soldiers moved from town to town, suppressing protests and reopening rail lines. Six weeks after it had begun, the strike had been crushed. Nearly 100 Americans died in "The Great Upheaval." Workers destroyed nearly $40 million worth of property. The strike galvanized the country. It convinced laborers of the need for institutionalized unions, persuaded businesses of the need for even greater political influence and government aid, and foretold a half century of labor conflict in the United States.[2]

II. The March of Capital

Growing labor unrest accompanied industrialization. The greatest strikes first hit the railroads only because no other industry had so effectively marshaled together capital, government support, and bureaucratic management. Many workers perceived their new powerlessness in the coming industrial order. Skills mattered less and less in an industrialized, mass-producing economy, and their strength as individuals seemed ever smaller and more insignificant when companies grew in size and power and managers grew flush with wealth and influence. Long hours, dangerous working conditions, and the difficulty of supporting a family on

meager and unpredictable wages compelled armies of labor to organize and battle against the power of capital.

John Pierpont Morgan with two friends, c. 1907. Library of Congress.

The post–Civil War era saw revolutions in American industry. Technological innovations and national investments slashed the costs of production and distribution. New administrative frameworks sustained the weight of vast firms. National credit agencies eased the uncertainties surrounding rapid movement of capital among investors, manufacturers, and retailers. Plummeting transportation and communication costs opened new national media, which advertising agencies used to nationalize various products.

By the turn of the century, corporate leaders and wealthy industrialists embraced the new principles of scientific management, or Taylorism, after its noted proponent, Frederick Taylor. The precision of steel parts, the harnessing of electricity, the innovations of machine tools, and the mass markets wrought by the railroads offered new avenues for efficiency. To match the demands of the machine age, Taylor said, firms needed a scientific organization of production. He urged all manufacturers to increase efficiency by subdividing tasks. Rather than having thirty mechanics individually making thirty machines, for instance, a manufacturer could assign thirty laborers to perform thirty distinct tasks. Such a shift would not only make workers as interchangeable as the parts they were using, it would also dramatically speed up the process of production. If managed by trained experts, specific tasks could be done quicker and more efficiently. Taylorism increased the scale and scope of manufacturing and allowed for the flowering of mass production. Building on the use of interchangeable parts in Civil War–era weapons manufacturing, American firms advanced mass production techniques and technologies. Singer sewing machines, Chicago packers' "disassembly" lines, McCormick grain reapers, Duke cigarette rollers: all realized unprecedented efficiencies and achieved unheard-of levels of production that propelled their companies into the forefront of American business. Henry Ford made the assembly line famous, allowing the production of automobiles to skyrocket as their cost plummeted, but various American firms had been paving the way for decades.[3]

Cyrus McCormick had overseen the construction of mechanical reapers (used for harvesting wheat) for decades. He had relied on skilled blacksmiths, skilled machinists, and skilled woodworkers to handcraft horse-drawn machines. But production was slow and the machines were expensive. The reapers still enabled massive efficiency gains in grain farming, but their high cost and slow production times put them out of reach of most American wheat farmers. But then, in 1880, McCormick hired a production manager who had overseen the manufacturing of Colt firearms to transform his system of production. The Chicago plant introduced new jigs, steel gauges, and pattern machines that could make precise duplicates of new, interchangeable parts. The company had produced twenty-one thousand machines in 1880. It made twice as many in

Glazier Stove Company, moulding room, Chelsea, Michigan, c. 1900–1910. Library of Congress.

1885, and by 1889, less than a decade later, it was producing over one hundred thousand a year.[4]

Industrialization and mass production pushed the United States into the forefront of the world. The American economy had lagged behind Britain, Germany, and France as recently as the 1860s, but by 1900 the United States was the world's leading manufacturing nation. Thirteen years later, by 1913, the United States produced one third of the world's industrial output—more than Britain, France, and Germany combined.[5]

Firms such as McCormick's realized massive economies of scale: after accounting for their initial massive investments in machines and marketing, each additional product lost the company relatively little in production costs. The bigger the production, then, the bigger the profits. New industrial companies therefore hungered for markets to keep their high-volume production facilities operating. Retailers and advertisers sustained the large markets needed for mass production, and corporate bureaucracies meanwhile allowed for the management of giant new firms. A new class of managers—comprising what one prominent economic historian called the "visible hand"—operated between the worlds of workers and owners and ensured the efficient operation and administration of mass production and mass distribution. Even more important to the growth and maintenance of these new companies, however, were the legal creations used to protect investors and sustain the power of massed capital.[6]

The costs of mass production were prohibitive for all but the very wealthiest individuals, and, even then, the risks would be too great to bear individually. The corporation itself was ages old, but the actual right to incorporate had generally been reserved for public works projects or government-sponsored monopolies. After the Civil War, however, the corporation, using new state incorporation laws passed during the Market Revolution of the early nineteenth century, became a legal mechanism for nearly any enterprise to marshal vast amounts of capital while limiting the liability of shareholders. By washing their hands of legal and financial obligations while still retaining the right to profit massively, investors flooded corporations with the capital needed to industrialize.

But a competitive marketplace threatened the promise of investments. Once the efficiency gains of mass production were realized, profit margins could be undone by cutthroat competition, which kept costs low as price cutting sank into profits. Companies rose and fell—and investors suffered losses—as manufacturing firms struggled to maintain supremacy in their particular industries. Economies of scale were a double-edged sword: while additional production provided immense profits, the high fixed costs of operating expensive factories dictated that even modest losses from selling underpriced goods were preferable to not selling profitably priced goods at all. And as market share was won and lost, profits proved unstable. American industrial firms tried everything to avoid competition: they formed informal pools and trusts, they entered price-fixing agreements, they divided markets, and, when blocked by antitrust laws and renegade price cutting, merged into consolidations. Rather than suffer from ruinous competition, firms combined and bypassed it altogether.

Between 1895 and 1904, and peaking between 1898 and 1902, a wave of mergers rocked the American economy. Competition melted away in what is known as "the great merger movement." In nine years, four thousand companies—nearly 20 percent of the American economy—were folded into rival firms. In nearly every major industry, newly consolidated firms such as General Electric and DuPont utterly dominated their market. Forty-one separate consolidations each controlled over 70 percent of the market in their respective industries. In 1901, financier J. P. Morgan oversaw the formation of United States Steel, built from eight leading steel companies. Industrialization was built on steel, and one firm—the world's first billion-dollar company—controlled the market. Monopoly had arrived.[7]

III. The Rise of Inequality

Industrial capitalism realized the greatest advances in efficiency and productivity that the world had ever seen. Massive new companies marshaled capital on an unprecedented scale and provided enormous profits that created unheard-of fortunes. But it also created millions of low-paid, unskilled, unreliable jobs with long hours and dangerous working conditions. The notion of a glittering world of wealth and technological innovation masking massive social inequities and deep-seated corruption gave the era its most common label, the Gilded Age, which drew from the title of an 1873 satirical novel written by Mark Twain and Charles Dudley Warner. Industrial capitalism confronted Gilded Age Americans with unprecedented inequalities. The sudden appearance of the extreme wealth of industrial and financial leaders alongside the crippling squalor of the urban and rural poor shocked Americans. "This association of poverty with progress is the great enigma of our times," economist Henry George wrote in his 1879 bestseller, *Progress and Poverty*.[8]

The great financial and industrial titans, the so-called robber barons, including railroad operators such as Cornelius Vanderbilt, oilmen such

The Breakers, Vanderbilt residence, Newport, R.I., c. 1904. Library of Congress.

as J. D. Rockefeller, steel magnates such as Andrew Carnegie, and bankers such as J. P. Morgan, won fortunes that, adjusted for inflation, are still among the largest the nation has ever seen. According to various measurements, in 1890 the wealthiest 1 percent of Americans owned one fourth of the nation's assets; the top 10 percent owned over 70 percent. And inequality only accelerated. By 1900, the richest 10 percent controlled perhaps 90 percent of the nation's wealth.[9]

As these vast and unprecedented new fortunes accumulated among a small number of wealthy Americans, new ideas arose to bestow moral legitimacy upon them. In 1859, British naturalist Charles Darwin published his theory of evolution through natural selection in his *On the Origin of Species*. It was not until the 1870s, however, that those theories gained widespread traction among biologists, naturalists, and other scientists in the United States and, in turn, challenged the social, political, and religious beliefs of many Americans. One of Darwin's greatest popularizers, the British sociologist and biologist Herbert Spencer, applied Darwin's theories to society and popularized the phrase *survival of the fittest*. The fittest, Spencer said, would demonstrate their superiority through economic success, while state welfare and private charity would lead to social degeneration—it would encourage the survival of the weak.[10]

"There must be complete surrender to the law of natural selection," the *Baltimore Sun* journalist H. L. Mencken wrote in 1907. "All growth must occur at the top. The strong must grow stronger, and that they may

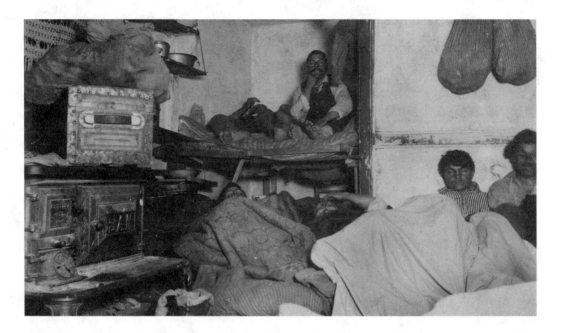

Jacob A. Riis, "Five Cents a Spot," unauthorized immigration lodgings in a Bayard Street tenement, New York City, c. 1890. Library of Congress.

do so, they must waste no strength in the vain task of trying to uplift the weak."[11] By the time Mencken wrote those words, the ideas of social Darwinism had spread among wealthy Americans and their defenders. Social Darwinism identified a natural order that extended from the laws of the cosmos to the workings of industrial society. All species and all societies, including modern humans, the theory went, were governed by a relentless competitive struggle for survival. The inequality of outcomes was to be not merely tolerated but encouraged and celebrated. It signified the progress of species and societies. Spencer's major work, *Synthetic Philosophy*, sold nearly four hundred thousand copies in the United States by the time of his death in 1903. Gilded Age industrial elites, such as steel magnate Andrew Carnegie, inventor Thomas Edison, and Standard Oil's John D. Rockefeller, were among Spencer's prominent followers. Other American thinkers, such as Yale's William Graham Sumner, echoed his ideas. Sumner said, "Before the tribunal of nature a man has no more right to life than a rattlesnake; he has no more right to liberty than any wild beast; his right to pursuit of happiness is nothing but a license to maintain the struggle for existence."[12]

But not all so eagerly welcomed inequalities. The spectacular growth of the U.S. economy and the ensuing inequalities in living conditions and incomes confounded many Americans. But as industrial capitalism overtook the nation, it achieved political protections. Although both major political parties facilitated the rise of big business and used state power to support the interests of capital against labor, big business looked primarily to the Republican Party.

The Republican Party had risen as an antislavery faction committed to "free labor," but it was also an ardent supporter of American business. Abraham Lincoln had been a corporate lawyer who defended railroads, and during the Civil War the Republican national government took advantage of the wartime absence of southern Democrats to push through a pro-business agenda. The Republican congress gave millions of acres and dollars to railroad companies. Republicans became the party of business, and they dominated American politics throughout the Gilded Age and the first several decades of the twentieth century. Of the sixteen presidential elections between the Civil War and the Great Depression, Republican candidates won all but four. Republicans controlled the Senate in twenty-seven out of thirty-two sessions in the same period. Republican dominance maintained a high protective tariff, an import tax designed to shield American businesses from foreign competition. Southern planters had opposed this policy before the war but now could do nothing to stop it. It provided the protective foundation for a new American industrial order, while Spencer's social Darwinism provided moral justification for national policies that minimized government interference in the economy for anything other than the protection and support of business.

IV. The Labor Movement

The ideas of social Darwinism attracted little support among the mass of American industrial laborers. American workers toiled in difficult jobs for long hours and little pay. Mechanization and mass production threw skilled laborers into unskilled positions. Industrial work ebbed and flowed with the economy. The typical industrial laborer could expect to be unemployed one month out of the year. They labored sixty hours a week and could still expect their annual income to fall below the poverty line. Among the working poor, wives and children were forced into the labor market to compensate. Crowded cities, meanwhile, failed to accommodate growing urban populations and skyrocketing rents trapped families in crowded slums.

Strikes ruptured American industry throughout the late nineteenth and early twentieth centuries. Workers seeking higher wages, shorter hours, and safer working conditions had struck throughout the antebellum era, but organized unions were fleeting and transitory. The Civil War and

Lawrence Textile Strike, 1912. Library of Congress.

Reconstruction seemed to briefly distract the nation from the plight of labor, but the end of the sectional crisis and the explosive growth of big business, unprecedented fortunes, and a vast industrial workforce in the last quarter of the nineteenth century sparked the rise of a vast American labor movement.

The failure of the Great Railroad Strike of 1877 convinced workers of the need to organize. Union memberships began to climb. The Knights of Labor enjoyed considerable success in the early 1880s, due in part to its efforts to unite skilled and unskilled workers. It welcomed all laborers, including women (the Knights only barred lawyers, bankers, and liquor dealers). By 1886, the Knights had over seven hundred thousand members. The Knights envisioned a cooperative producer-centered society that rewarded labor, not capital, but, despite their sweeping vision, the Knights focused on practical gains that could be won through the organization of workers into local unions.[13]

In Marshall, Texas, in the spring of 1886, one of Jay Gould's rail companies fired a Knights of Labor member for attending a union meeting. His local union walked off the job, and soon others joined. From Texas and Arkansas into Missouri, Kansas, and Illinois, nearly two hundred thousand workers struck against Gould's rail lines. Gould hired strikebreakers and the Pinkerton Detective Agency, a kind of private security contractor, to suppress the strikes and get the rails moving again. Political leaders helped him, and state militias were called in support of

An 1892 cover of *Harper's Weekly* depicting the Homestead Riot showed Pinkerton men who had surrendered to the steel mill workers navigating a gauntlet of violent strikers. W. P. Snyder (artist) after a photograph by Dabbs, "The Homestead Riot," 1892. Library of Congress.

Gould's companies. The Texas governor called out the Texas Rangers. Workers countered by destroying property, only winning them negative headlines and for many justifying the use of strikebreakers and militiamen. The strike broke, briefly undermining the Knights of Labor, but the organization regrouped and set its eyes on a national campaign for the eight-hour day.[14]

The campaign for an eight-hour day, long a rallying cry that united American laborers, culminated in a national strike on May 1, 1886. Somewhere between three hundred thousand and five hundred thousand workers struck across the country.

In Chicago, police forces killed several workers while breaking up protesters at the McCormick reaper works. Labor leaders and radicals called for a protest at Haymarket Square the following day, which police also proceeded to break up. But as they did, a bomb exploded and killed seven policemen. Police fired into the crowd, killing four. The deaths of the Chicago policemen sparked outrage across the nation, and the sensationalization of the Haymarket Riot helped many Americans to associate unionism with radicalism. Eight Chicago anarchists were arrested and, despite no direct evidence implicating them in the bombing, were charged and found guilty of conspiracy. Four were hanged (and one died by suicide before he could be executed). Membership in the Knights had peaked earlier that year but fell rapidly after Haymarket; the group became associated with violence and radicalism. The national movement for an eight-hour day collapsed.[15]

The American Federation of Labor (AFL) emerged as a conservative alternative to the vision of the Knights of Labor. An alliance of craft unions (unions composed of skilled workers), the AFL rejected the Knights' expansive vision of a "producerist" economy and advocated "pure and simple trade unionism," a program that aimed for practical gains (higher wages, fewer hours, and safer conditions) through a conservative approach that tried to avoid strikes. But workers continued to strike.

In 1892, the Amalgamated Association of Iron and Steel Workers struck at one of Carnegie's steel mills in Homestead, Pennsylvania. After repeated wage cuts, workers shut the plant down and occupied the mill. The plant's operator, Henry Clay Frick, immediately called in hundreds of Pinkerton detectives, but the steel workers fought back. The Pinkertons tried to land by river and were besieged by the striking steel workers. After several hours of pitched battle, the Pinkertons surrendered, ran a bloody gauntlet of workers, and were kicked out of the mill grounds. But the Pennsylvania governor called the state militia, broke the strike, and reopened the mill. The union was essentially destroyed in the aftermath.[16]

Still, despite repeated failure, strikes continued to roll across the industrial landscape. In 1894, workers in George Pullman's Pullman car factories struck when he cut wages by a quarter but kept rents and utilities in his company town constant. The American Railway Union (ARU), led by Eugene Debs, launched a sympathy strike: the ARU would refuse to handle any Pullman cars on any rail line anywhere in the country. Thousands of workers struck and national railroad traffic ground to a halt. Unlike in nearly every other major strike, the governor of Illinois sympathized with workers and refused to dispatch the state militia. It didn't matter. In July, President Grover Cleveland dispatched thousands of American soldiers to break the strike, and a federal court issued a preemptive injunction against Debs and the union's leadership. The strike violated the injunction, and Debs was arrested and imprisoned. The strike evaporated without its leadership. Jail radicalized Debs, proving to him that political and judicial leaders were merely tools for capital in its struggle against labor.[17] But it wasn't just Debs. In 1905, the degrading conditions of industrial labor sparked strikes across the country. The

final two decades of the nineteenth century saw over twenty thousand strikes and lockouts in the United States. Industrial laborers struggled to carve for themselves a piece of the prosperity lifting investors and a rapidly expanding middle class into unprecedented standards of living. But workers were not the only ones struggling to stay afloat in industrial America. American farmers also lashed out against the inequalities of the Gilded Age and denounced political corruption for enabling economic theft.

Two women strikers on a picket line during the "Uprising of the 20,000," garment workers' strike, New York City, 1910. Library of Congress.

V. The Populist Movement

"Wall Street owns the country," the Populist leader Mary Elizabeth Lease told dispossessed farmers around 1890. "It is no longer a government of the people, by the people, and for the people, but a government of Wall Street, by Wall Street, and for Wall Street." Farmers, who remained a majority of the American population through the first decade of the twentieth century, were hit especially hard by industrialization. The expanding markets and technological improvements that increased efficiency also decreased commodity prices. Commercialization of agriculture put farmers in the hands of bankers, railroads, and various economic intermediaries. As the decades passed, more and more farmers fell ever further into debt, lost their land, and were forced to enter the industrial workforce or, especially in the South, became landless farmworkers.

The rise of industrial giants reshaped the American countryside and the Americans who called it home. Railroad spur lines, telegraph lines, and credit crept into farming communities and linked rural Americans, who still made up a majority of the country's population, with towns, regional cities, American financial centers in Chicago and New York, and, eventually, London and the world's financial markets. Meanwhile, improved farm machinery, easy credit, and the latest consumer goods flooded the countryside. But new connections and new conveniences came at a price.

Farmers had always been dependent on the whims of the weather and local markets. But now they staked their financial security on a national economic system subject to rapid price swings, rampant speculation, and limited regulation. Frustrated American farmers attempted to reshape the fundamental structures of the nation's political and economic systems, systems they believed enriched parasitic bankers and industrial monopolists at the expense of the many laboring farmers who fed the nation by producing its many crops and farm goods. Their dissatisfaction with an erratic and impersonal system put many of them at the forefront of what would become perhaps the most serious challenge to the established political economy of Gilded Age America. Farmers organized and launched their challenge first through the cooperatives of the Farmers' Alliance and later through the politics of the People's (or Populist) Party.

Mass production and business consolidations spawned giant corporations that monopolized nearly every sector of the U.S. economy in the decades after the Civil War. In contrast, the economic power of the individual farmer sank into oblivion. Threatened by ever-plummeting commodity prices and ever-rising indebtedness, Texas agrarians met in Lampasas, Texas, in 1877 and organized the first Farmers' Alliance to restore some economic power to farmers as they dealt with railroads, merchants, and bankers. If big business relied on its numerical strength to exert its economic will, why shouldn't farmers unite to counter that power? They could share machinery, bargain from wholesalers, and negotiate higher prices for their crops. Over the following years, organizers spread from town to town across the former Confederacy, the Midwest, and the Great Plains, holding evangelical-style camp meetings, distribut-

The banner of the first Texas Farmers' Alliance. Source: N. A. Dunning (ed.), *Farmers' Alliance History and Agricultural Digest* (Washington, DC: Alliance Publishing Co., 1891), iv.

ing pamphlets, and establishing over one thousand alliance newspapers. As the alliance spread, so too did its near-religious vision of the nation's future as a "cooperative commonwealth" that would protect the interests of the many from the predatory greed of the few. At its peak, the Farmers' Alliance claimed 1,500,000 members meeting in 40,000 local sub-alliances.[18]

The alliance's most innovative programs were a series of farmers' cooperatives that enabled farmers to negotiate higher prices for their crops and lower prices for the goods they purchased. These cooperatives spread across the South between 1886 and 1892 and claimed more than a million members at their high point. While most failed financially, these "philanthropic monopolies," as one alliance speaker termed them, inspired farmers to look to large-scale organization to cope with their economic difficulties.[19] But cooperation was only part of the alliance message.

In the South, alliance-backed Democratic candidates won four governorships and forty-eight congressional seats in 1890.[20] But at a time when falling prices and rising debts conspired against the survival of family farmers, the two political parties seemed incapable of representing the needs of poor farmers. And so alliance members organized a political party—the People's Party, or the Populists, as they came to be known.

The Populists attracted supporters across the nation by appealing to those convinced that there were deep flaws in the political economy of Gilded Age America, flaws that both political parties refused to address. Veterans of earlier fights for currency reform, disaffected industrial laborers, proponents of the benevolent socialism of Edward Bellamy's popular *Looking Backward*, and the champions of Henry George's farmer-friendly "single-tax" proposal joined alliance members in the new party. The Populists nominated former Civil War general James B. Weaver as their presidential candidate at the party's first national convention in Omaha, Nebraska, on July 4, 1892.[21]

At that meeting the party adopted a platform that crystallized the alliance's cooperate program into a coherent political vision. The platform's preamble, written by longtime political iconoclast and Minnesota populist Ignatius Donnelly, warned that "the fruits of the toil of millions [had been] boldly stolen to build up colossal fortunes for a few."[22] Taken as a whole, the Omaha Platform and the larger Populist movement sought to counter the scale and power of monopolistic capitalism with a strong, engaged, and modern federal government. The platform proposed an unprecedented expansion of federal power. It advocated nationalizing the country's railroad and telegraph systems to ensure that essential services would be run in the best interests of the people. In an attempt to deal with the lack of currency available to farmers, it advocated postal savings banks to protect depositors and extend credit. It called for the establishment of a network of federally managed warehouses—called subtreasuries—which would extend government loans to farmers who stored crops in the warehouses as they awaited higher market prices. To save debtors it promoted an inflationary monetary policy by monetizing silver. Direct election of senators and the secret ballot would ensure that this federal government would serve the interest of the people rather than entrenched partisan interests, and a graduated income tax would protect Americans from the establishment of an American aristocracy. Combined, these efforts would, Populists believed, help shift economic and political power back toward the nation's producing classes.

In the Populists' first national election campaign in 1892, Weaver received over one million votes (and twenty-two electoral votes), a truly startling performance that signaled a bright future for the Populists. And when the Panic of 1893 sparked the worst economic depression the nation had ever yet seen, the Populist movement won further credibility and gained even more ground. Kansas Populist Mary Lease, one of the movement's most fervent speakers, famously, and perhaps apocryphally, called on farmers to "raise less corn and more Hell." Populist stump speakers crossed the country, speaking with righteous indignation, blaming the greed of business elites and corrupt party politicians for causing the crisis fueling America's widening inequality. Southern orators like Texas's James "Cyclone" Davis and Georgian firebrand Tom Watson stumped across the South decrying the abuses of northern capitalists and the Democratic Party. Pamphlets such as W. H. Harvey's *Coin's Financial School* and Henry D. Lloyd's *Wealth Against Commonwealth* provided Populist answers to the age's many perceived problems. The faltering economy combined with the Populists' extensive organizing. In the 1894 elections, Populists elected six senators and seven representatives to Congress.[23]

The Populist movement, however, still faced substantial obstacles, especially in the South. The failure of alliance-backed Democrats to live up to their campaign promises drove some southerners to break with the party of their forefathers and join the Populists. Many, however, were unwilling to take what was, for southerners, a radical step. Southern Democrats, for their part, responded to the Populist challenge with electoral fraud and racial demagoguery. Both severely limited Populist gains. The alliance struggled to balance the pervasive white supremacy of the American South with their call for a grand union of the producing class. American racial attitudes—and their virulent southern strain—simply proved too formidable. Democrats race-baited Populists, and Populists capitulated. The Colored Farmers' Alliance, which had formed as a segregated sister organization to the southern alliance and had as many as 250,000 members at its peak, fell prey to racial and class-based hostility. The group went into rapid decline in 1891 when faced with the violent white repression of a number of Colored Farmers' Alliance–sponsored cotton picker strikes. Racial mistrust and division remained the rule, even among Populists, and even in North Carolina, where a political marriage of convenience between Populists and Republicans resulted in the election of Populist Marion Butler to the Senate. Populists opposed Democratic corruption, but this did not necessarily make them champions of interracial democracy. As Butler explained to an audience in Edgecombe County, "We are in favor of white supremacy, but we are not in favor of cheating and fraud to get it."[24]

By the middle of the 1890s, Populism had exploded in popularity. The first major political force to tap into the vast discomfort of many

Americans with the disruptions wrought by industrial capitalism, the Populist Party seemed poised to capture political victory. And yet, even as Populism gained national traction, the movement was stumbling. The party's often divided leadership found it difficult to shepherd what remained a diverse and loosely organized coalition of reformers toward unified political action. The Omaha platform was a radical document, and some state party leaders selectively embraced its reforms. More importantly, the institutionalized parties were still too strong, and the Democrats loomed, ready to swallow Populist frustrations and inaugurate a new era of American politics.

VI. William Jennings Bryan and the Politics of Gold

William Jennings Bryan (March 19, 1860–July 26, 1925) accomplished many different things in his life: he was a skilled orator, a Nebraska congressman, a three-time presidential candidate, U.S. secretary of state under Woodrow Wilson, and a lawyer who supported prohibition and opposed Darwinism (most notably in the 1925 Scopes Monkey Trial). In terms of his political career, he won national renown for his attack on the gold standard and his tireless promotion of free silver and policies for the benefit of the average American. Although Bryan was unsuccessful in winning the presidency, he forever altered the course of American political history.[25]

William Jennings Bryan, 1896. Library of Congress.

Bryan was born in Salem, Illinois, in 1860 to a devout family with a strong passion for law, politics, and public speaking. At twenty, he attended Union Law College in Chicago and passed the bar shortly thereafter. After his marriage to Mary Baird in Illinois, Bryan and his young family relocated to Nebraska, where he won a reputation among the state's Democratic Party leaders as an extraordinary orator. Bryan later won recognition as one of the greatest speakers in American history.

When economic depressions struck the Midwest in the late 1880s, despairing farmers faced low crop prices and found few politicians on their side. While many rallied to the Populist cause, Bryan worked from within the Democratic Party, using the strength of his oratory. After delivering one speech, he told his wife, "Last night I found that I had a power over the audience. I could move them as I chose. I have more than usual power as a speaker. . . . God grant that I may use it wisely."[26] He soon won election to the House of Representatives, where he served for two terms. Although he lost a bid to join the Senate, Bryan turned his attention to a higher position: the presidency of the United States. There, he believed he could change the country by defending farmers and urban laborers against the corruptions of big business.

In 1895–1896, Bryan launched a national speaking tour in which he promoted the free coinage of silver. He believed that bimetallism, by inflating American currency, could alleviate farmers' debts. In contrast, Republicans championed the gold standard and a flat money supply. American monetary standards became a leading campaign issue. Then, in July 1896, the Democratic Party's national convention met to choose their presidential nominee in the upcoming election. The party platform asserted that the gold standard was "not only un-American but anti-American." Bryan spoke last at the convention. He astounded his listeners. At the conclusion of his stirring speech, he declared, "Having behind us the commercial interests and the laboring interests and all the toiling masses, we shall answer their demands for a gold standard by saying to them, you shall not press down upon the brow of labor this crown of thorns. You shall not crucify mankind upon a cross of gold."[27] After a few seconds of stunned silence, the convention went wild. Some wept, many shouted, and the band began to play "For He's a Jolly Good Fellow." Bryan received the 1896 Democratic presidential nomination.

The Republicans ran William McKinley, an economic conservative who championed business interests and the gold standard. Bryan crisscrossed the country spreading the silver gospel. The election drew

Conservative William McKinley promised prosperity to ordinary Americans through his "sound money" initiative, a policy he ran on during his election campaigns in 1896 and again in 1900. This election poster touts McKinley's gold standard policy as bringing "Prosperity at Home, Prestige Abroad." "Prosperity at home, prestige abroad," [between 1895 and 1900]. Library of Congress.

enormous attention and much emotion. According to Bryan's wife, he received two thousand letters of support every day that year, an enormous amount for any politician, let alone one not currently in office. Yet Bryan could not defeat McKinley. The pro-business Republicans outspent Bryan's campaign fivefold. A notably high 79.3 percent of eligible American voters cast ballots, and turnout averaged 90 percent in areas supportive of Bryan, but Republicans swayed the population-dense Northeast and Great Lakes region and stymied the Democrats.[28]

In early 1900, Congress passed the Gold Standard Act, which put the country on the gold standard, effectively ending the debate over the nation's monetary policy. Bryan sought the presidency again in 1900 but was again defeated, as he would be yet again in 1908.

Bryan was among the most influential losers in American political history. When the agrarian wing of the Democratic Party nominated the Nebraska congressman in 1896, Bryan's fiery condemnation of northeastern financial interests and his impassioned calls for "free and unlimited coinage of silver" co-opted popular Populist issues. The Democrats stood ready to siphon off a large proportion of the Populists' political support. When the People's Party held its own convention two weeks later, the party's moderate wing, in a fiercely contested move, overrode

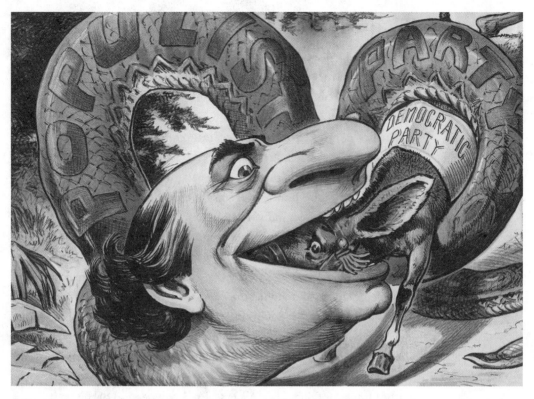

William Jennings Bryan espoused Populist politics while working within the two-party system as a Democrat. Republicans characterized this as a kind of hijacking by Bryan, arguing that the Democratic Party was now a party of a radical faction of Populists. The pro-Republican magazine *Judge* rendered this perspective in a political cartoon showing Bryan (representing Populism writ large) as a huge serpent swallowing a bucking mule (representing the Democratic Party). Political cartoon, *Judge*, 1896. Wikimedia.

the objections of more ideologically pure Populists and nominated Bryan as the Populist candidate as well. This strategy of temporary "fusion" fatally fractured the movement and the party. Populist energy moved from the radical-yet-still-weak People's Party to the more moderate-yet-powerful Democratic Party. And although at first glance the Populist movement appears to have been a failure—its minor electoral gains were short-lived, it did little to dislodge the entrenched two-party system, and the Populist dream of a cooperative commonwealth never took shape—in terms of lasting impact, the Populist Party proved the most significant third-party movement in American history. The agrarian revolt established the roots of later reform, and the majority of policies outlined within the Omaha Platform would eventually be put into law over the following decades under the management of middle-class reformers. In large measure, the Populist vision laid the intellectual groundwork for the coming progressive movement.[29]

VII. The Socialists

American socialists carried on the Populists' radical tradition by uniting farmers and workers in a sustained, decades-long political struggle to reorder American economic life. Socialists argued that wealth and power were consolidated in the hands of too few individuals, that monopolies and trusts controlled too much of the economy, and that owners and investors grew rich while the workers who produced their wealth, despite massive productivity gains and rising national wealth, still suffered from low pay, long hours, and unsafe working conditions. Karl Marx had described the new industrial economy as a worldwide class struggle between the wealthy bourgeoisie, who owned the means of production, such as factories and farms, and the proletariat, factory workers and tenant farmers who worked only for the wealth of others. According to Eugene Debs, socialists sought "the overthrow of the capitalist system and the emancipation of the working class from wage slavery."[30] Under an imagined socialist cooperative commonwealth, the means of production would be owned collectively, ensuring that all men and women received a fair wage for their labor. According to socialist organizer and newspaper editor Oscar Ameringer, socialists wanted "ownership of the trust by the government, and the ownership of the government by the people."[31]

American socialist leader Eugene Victor Debs, 1912. Library of Congress.

The socialist movement drew from a diverse constituency. Party membership was open to all regardless of race, gender, class, ethnicity, or religion. Many prominent Americans, such as Helen Keller, Upton Sin-

clair, and Jack London, became socialists. They were joined by masses of American laborers from across the United States: factory workers, miners, railroad builders, tenant farmers, and small farmers all united under the red flag of socialism. Many united with labor leader William D. "Big Bill" Haywood and other radicals in 1905 to form the Industrial Workers of the World (IWW), the "Wobblies," a radical and confrontational union that welcomed all workers, regardless of race or gender.[32] Others turned to politics.

The Socialist Party of America (SPA), founded in 1901, carried on the American third-party political tradition. Socialist mayors were elected in thirty-three cities and towns, from Berkeley, California, to Schenectady, New York, and two socialists—Victor Berger from Wisconsin and Meyer London from New York—won congressional seats. All told, over one thousand socialist candidates won various American political offices. Julius A. Wayland, editor of the socialist newspaper *Appeal to Reason*, proclaimed that "socialism is coming. It's coming like a prairie fire and nothing can stop it . . . you can feel it in the air."[33] By 1913 there were 150,000 members of the Socialist Party and, in 1912, Eugene V. Debs, the Indiana-born Socialist Party candidate for president, received almost one million votes, or 6 percent of the total.[34]

Over the following years, however, the embrace of many socialist policies by progressive reformers, internal ideological and tactical disagreements, a failure to dissuade most Americans of the perceived incompatibility between socialism and American values, and, especially, government oppression and censorship, particularly during and after World War I, ultimately sank the party. Like the Populists, however, socialists had tapped into a deep well of discontent, and their energy and organizing filtered out into American culture and American politics.

VIII. Conclusion

The march of capital transformed patterns of American life. While some enjoyed unprecedented levels of wealth, and an ever-growing slice of middle-class workers won an ever more comfortable standard of living, vast numbers of farmers lost their land and a growing industrial working class struggled to earn wages sufficient to support themselves and their families. Industrial capitalism brought wealth and it brought poverty; it created owners and investors and it created employees. But whether winners or losers in the new economy, all Americans reckoned in some way with their new industrial world.

IX. Reference Material

This chapter was edited by Joseph Locke, with content contributions by Andrew C. Baker, Nicholas Blood, Justin Clark, Dan Du, Caroline Bunnell Harris, David Hochfelder Scott Libson, Joseph Locke, Leah Richier, Matthew Simmons, Kate Sohasky, Joseph Super, and Kaylynn Washnock.

Recommended citation: Andrew C. Baker et al., "Capital and Labor," Joseph Locke, ed., in *The American Yawp*, eds. Joseph Locke and Ben Wright (Stanford, CA: Stanford University Press, 2019).

NOTES TO CHAPTER 16

1. David T. Burbank, *Reign of the Rabble: The St. Louis General Strike of 1877* (New York: Kelley, 1966), 11.

2. Robert V. Bruce, *1877: Year of Violence* (New York: Dee, 1957); Philip S. Foner, *The Great Labor Uprising of 1877* (New York: Monad Press, 1977); David Omar Stowell, ed., *The Great Strikes of 1877* (Champaign: University of Illinois Press, 2008).

3. Alfred D. Chandler Jr., *The Visible Hand: The Managerial Revolution in American Business* (Cambridge, MA: Belknap Press, 1977); David A. Hounshell, *From the American System to Mass Production, 1800–1932* (Baltimore: Johns Hopkins University Press, 1984).

4. Hounshell, *From the American System*, 153–188.

5. Alfred D. Chandler Jr., *Scale and Scope: The Dynamics of Industrial Capitalism* (Cambridge, MA: Harvard University Press, 1990), 52.

6. Chandler, *Visible Hand*.

7. Naomi R. Lamoreaux, *The Great Merger Movement in American Business, 1895–1904* (New York: Cambridge University Press, 1985).

8. See especially Edward O'Donnell, *Henry George and the Crisis of Inequality: Progress and Poverty in the Gilded Age* (New York: Columbia University Press, 2015), 41–45.

9. Michael McGerr, *A Fierce Discontent: The Rise and Fall of the Progressive Movement in America, 1870–1920* (New York: Free Press, 2003).

10. Richard Hofstadter, *Social Darwinism in American Thought* (Boston: Beacon Books, 1955).

11. Henry Louis Mencken, *The Philosophy of Friedrich Nietzsche* (Boston: Luce, 1908), 102–103.

12. William Graham Sumner, *Earth-Hunger, and Other Essays*, ed. Albert Galloway Keller (New Haven, CT: Yale University Press, 1913), 234.

13. Leon Fink, *Workingmen's Democracy: The Knights of Labor and American Politics* (Urbana: University of Illinois Press, 1983).

14. Ruth A. Allen, *The Great Southwest Strike* (Austin: University of Texas Press, 1942).

15. James R. Green, *Death in the Haymarket: A Story of Chicago, the First Labor Movement and the Bombing That Divided Gilded Age America*. New York: Pantheon Books, 2006.

16. Paul Krause, *The Battle for Homestead, 1890–1892: Politics, Culture, and Steel* (Pittsburgh, PA: University of Pittsburgh Press, 1992).

17. Almont Lindsey, *The Pullman Strike: The Story of a Unique Experiment and of a Great Labor Upheaval* (Chicago: University of Chicago Press, 1943).

18. Historians of the Populists have produced a large number of excellent histories. See especially Lawrence Goodwyn, *Democratic Promise: The Populist Moment in America* (New York: Oxford University Press, 1976); and Charles Postel, *The Populist Vision* (New York: Oxford University Press, 2009).

19. Lawrence Goodwyn argued that the Populists' "cooperative vision" was the central element in their hopes of a "democratic economy." Goodwyn, *Democratic Promise*, 54.

20. John Donald Hicks, *The Populist Revolt: A History of the Farmers' Alliance and the People's Party* (Minneapolis: University of Minnesota Press, 1931), 178.

21. Ibid., 236.

22. Edward McPherson, *A Handbook of Politics for 1892* (Washington, DC: Chapman, 1892), 269.

23. Hicks, *Populist Revolt*, 321–339.

24. Postel, *Populist Vision*, 197.

25. For William Jennings Bryan, see especially Michael Kazin, *A Godly Hero: The Life of William Jennings Bryan* (New York: Knopf, 2006).

26. Ibid., 25.

27. Richard Franklin Bensel, *Passion and Preferences: William Jennings Bryan and the 1896 Democratic Convention* (Cambridge, UK: Cambridge University Press, 2008), 232.

28. Lyn Ragsdale, *Vital Statistics on the Presidency* (Washington, DC: Congressional Quarterly Press, 1998), 132–138.

29. Elizabeth Sanders, *The Roots of Reform: Farmers, Workers, and the American State, 1877–1917* (Chicago: University of Chicago Press, 1999).

30. Eugene V. Debs, "The Socialist Party and the Working Class," *International Socialist Review* (September 1904).

31. Oscar Ameringer, *Socialism: What It Is and How to Get It* (Milwaukee, WI: Political Action, 1911), 31.

32. Philip S. Foner, *The Industrial Workers of the World 1905–1917* (New York: International Publishers, 1965).

33. R. Laurence Moore, *European Socialists and the American Promised Land* (New York: Oxford University Press, 1970), 214.

34. Nick Salvatore, *Eugene V. Debs, Citizen and Socialist* (Chicago: University of Illinois Press, 1983).

RECOMMENDED READING

Beckert, Sven. *Monied Metropolis: New York City and the Consolidation of the American Bourgeoisie, 1850–1896.* Cambridge, UK: Cambridge University Press, 2001.

Benson, Susan Porter. *Counter Cultures: Saleswomen, Managers, and Customers in American Department Stores, 1890–1940.* Champaign: University of Illinois Press, 1986.

Cameron, Ardis. *Radicals of the Worst Sort: Laboring Women in Lawrence, Massachusetts, 1860–1912.* Champaign: University of Illinois Press, 1993.

Chambers, John W. *The Tyranny of Change: America in the Progressive Era, 1890–1920*, 2nd ed. New Brunswick, NJ: Rutgers University Press, 2000.

Chandler, Alfred D., Jr., *The Visible Hand: The Managerial Revolution in American Business*. Cambridge, MA: Belknap Press, 1977.

Chandler, Alfred D., Jr. *Scale and Scope: The Dynamics of Industrial Capitalism*. Cambridge, MA: Harvard University Press, 1990.

Cronon, William. *Nature's Metropolis: Chicago and the Great West*. New York: Norton, 1991.

Edwards, Rebecca. *New Spirits: Americans in the Gilded Age, 1865–1905*. New York: Oxford University Press, 2005.

Enstad, Nan. *Ladies of Labor, Girls of Adventure: Working Women, Popular Culture, and Labor Politics at the Turn of the Twentieth Century*. New York: Columbia University Press, 1999.

Fink, Leon. *Workingmen's Democracy: The Knights of Labor and American Politics*. Chicago: University of Illinois Press, 1993.

Goodwyn, Lawrence. *Democratic Promise: The Populist Moment in America*. New York: Oxford University Press, 1976.

Green, James. *Death in the Haymarket: A Story of Chicago, the First Labor Movement, and the Bombing That Divided Gilded Age America*. New York City: Pantheon Books, 2006.

Greene, Julie. *Pure and Simple Politics: The American Federation of Labor and Political Activism, 1881–1917*. New York: Cambridge University Press, 1998.

Hofstadter, Richard. *Social Darwinism in American Thought*. Philadelphia: University of Pennsylvania Press, 1944.

Johnson, Kimberley S. *Governing the American State: Congress and the New Federalism, 1877–1929*. Princeton, NJ: Princeton University Press, 2006.

Kazin, Michael. *A Godly Hero: The Life of William Jennings Bryan*. New York: Knopf, 2006.

Kessler-Harris, Alice. *Out to Work: A History of Wage-Earning Women in the United States*. New York: Oxford University Press, 1982.

Krause, Paul. *The Battle for Homestead, 1880–1892: Politics, Culture, and Steel*. Pittsburgh, PA: University of Pittsburgh Press, 1992.

Lamoreaux, Naomi R. *The Great Merger Movement in American Business, 1895–1904*. New York: Cambridge University Press, 1985.

McMath, Robert C., Jr. *American Populism: A Social History, 1877–1898*. New York: Hill and Wang, 1993.

Montgomery, David. *The Fall of the House of Labor: The Workplace, the State, and American Labor Activism, 1865–1925*. New York: Cambridge University Press, 1988.

Painter, Nell Irvin. *Standing at Armageddon: The United States, 1877–1919*. New York: Norton, 1987.

Postel, Charles. *The Populist Vision*. New York: Oxford University Press, 2009.

Sanders, Elizabeth. *Roots of Reform: Farmers, Workers, and the American State, 1877–1917*. Chicago: University of Chicago Press, 1999.

Trachtenberg, Alan. *The Incorporation of America: Culture and Society in the Gilded Age*. New York: Hill and Wang, 1982.

17

Conquering the West

I. Introduction

Native Americans long dominated the vastness of the American West. Linked culturally and geographically by trade, travel, and warfare, various Indigenous groups controlled most of the continent west of the Mississippi River deep into the nineteenth century. Spanish, French, British, and later American traders had integrated themselves into many regional economies, and American emigrants pushed ever westward, but no imperial power had yet achieved anything approximating political or military control over the great bulk of the continent. But then the Civil War came and went and decoupled the West from the question of slavery just as the United States industrialized and laid down rails and pushed its ever-expanding population ever farther west.

Indigenous Americans have lived in North America for over ten millennia and, into the late nineteenth century, perhaps as many as 250,000 Native people still inhabited the American West.[1] But then unending waves of American settlers, the American military, and the unstoppable

Curtis, *Navajo Riders in Canyon de Chelly*, c. 1904. Library of Congress.

onrush of American capital conquered all. Often in violation of it's own treaties, the United States removed Native groups to ever-shrinking reservations, incorporated the West first as territories and then as states, and, for the first time in its history, controlled the enormity of land between the two oceans.

The history of the late-nineteenth-century West is not a simple story. What some touted as a triumph—the westward expansion of American authority—was for others a tragedy. The West contained many peoples and many places, and their intertwined histories marked a pivotal transformation in the history of the United States.

II. Post–Civil War Westward Migration

In the decades after the Civil War, American settlers poured across the Mississippi River in record numbers. No longer simply crossing over the continent for new imagined Edens in California or Oregon, they settled now in the vast heart of the continent.

Many of the first American migrants had come to the West in search of quick profits during the midcentury gold and silver rushes. As in the California rush of 1848–1849, droves of prospectors poured in after precious-metal strikes in Colorado in 1858, Nevada in 1859, Idaho in 1860, Montana in 1863, and the Black Hills in 1874. While women often performed housework that allowed mining families to subsist in often difficult conditions, a significant portion of the mining workforce were single men without families dependent on service industries in nearby towns and cities. There, working-class women worked in shops, saloons, boardinghouses, and brothels. Many of these ancillary operations profited from the mining boom: as failed prospectors found, the rush itself often generated more wealth than the mines. The gold that left Colorado in the first seven years after the Pikes Peak gold strike—estimated at $25.5 million—was, for instance, less than half of what outside parties had invested in the fever. The 100,000-plus migrants who settled in the Rocky Mountains were ultimately more valuable to the region's development than the gold they came to find.[2]

Others came to the Plains to extract the hides of the great bison herds. Millions of animals had roamed the Plains, but their tough leather supplied industrial belting in eastern factories and raw material for the booming clothing industry. Specialized teams took down and skinned the herds. The infamous American bison slaughter peaked in the early 1870s. The number of American bison plummeted from over ten million

While bison supplied leather for America's booming clothing industry, the skulls of the animals also provided a key ingredient in fertilizer. This 1870s photograph illustrates the massive number of bison killed for these and other reasons (including sport) in the second half of the nineteenth century. Photograph of a pile of American bison skulls waiting to be ground for fertilizer, 1870s. Wikimedia.

at midcentury to only a few hundred by the early 1880s. The expansion of the railroads allowed ranching to replace the bison with cattle on the American grasslands.[3]

The nearly seventy thousand members of the Church of Jesus Christ of Latter-Day Saints (more commonly called Mormons) who migrated west between 1846 and 1868 were similar to other Americans traveling west on the overland trails. They faced many of the same problems, but unlike most other American migrants, Mormons were fleeing from religious persecution.

Many historians view Mormonism as a "uniquely American faith," not just because it was founded by Joseph Smith in New York in the 1830s, but because of its optimistic and future-oriented tenets. Mormons believed that Americans were exceptional—chosen by God to spread truth across the world and to build utopia, a New Jerusalem in North

America. However, many Americans were suspicious of the Latter-Day Saint movement and its unusual rituals, especially the practice of polygamy, and most Mormons found it difficult to practice their faith in the eastern United States. Thus began a series of migrations in the midnineteenth century, first to Illinois, then Missouri and Nebraska, and finally into Utah Territory.

Once in the west, Mormon settlements served as important supply points for other emigrants heading on to California and Oregon. Brigham Young, the leader of the Church after the death of Joseph Smith, was appointed governor of the Utah Territory by the federal government in 1850. He encouraged Mormon residents of the territory to engage in agricultural pursuits and be cautious of the outsiders who arrived as the mining and railroad industries developed in the region.[4]

It was land, ultimately, that drew the most migrants to the West. Family farms were the backbone of the agricultural economy that expanded in the West after the Civil War. In 1862, northerners in Congress passed the Homestead Act, which allowed male citizens (or those who declared their intent to become citizens) to claim federally owned lands in the West. Settlers could head west, choose a 160-acre surveyed section of land, file a claim, and begin "improving" the land by plowing fields, building houses and barns, or digging wells, and, after five years of living on the land, could apply for the official title deed to the land. Hundreds of thousands of Americans used the Homestead Act to acquire land. The treeless plains that had been considered unfit for settlement became the new agricultural mecca for land-hungry Americans.[5]

The Homestead Act excluded married women from filing claims because they were considered the legal dependents of their husbands. Some unmarried women filed claims on their own, but single farmers (male or female) were hard-pressed to run a farm and they were a small minority. Most farm households adopted traditional divisions of labor: men worked in the fields and women managed the home and kept the family fed. Both were essential.[6]

Migrants sometimes found in homesteads a self-sufficiency denied at home. Second or third sons who did not inherit land in Scandinavia, for instance, founded farm communities in Minnesota, Dakota, and other Midwestern territories in the 1860s. Boosters encouraged emigration by advertising the semiarid Plains as, for instance, "a flowery meadow of great fertility clothed in nutritious grasses, and watered by numerous streams."[7] Western populations exploded. The Plains were transformed. In 1860, for example, Kansas had about 10,000 farms; in 1880 it had

239,000. Texas saw enormous population growth. The federal government counted 200,000 people in Texas in 1850, 1,600,000 in 1880, and 3,000,000 in 1900, making it the sixth most populous state in the nation.

III. The Indian Wars and Federal Peace Policies

The "Indian wars," so mythologized in western folklore, were a series of seemingly sporadic, localized, and often brief engagements between U.S. military forces and various Native American groups. More sustained and equally impactful conflicts were economic and cultural. New patterns of American settlement, railroad construction, and material extraction clashed with the vast and cyclical movement across the Great Plains to hunt buffalo, raid enemies, and trade goods. Thomas Jefferson's old dream that Indian groups might live isolated in the West was, in the face of American expansion, no longer a viable reality. Political, economic, and even humanitarian concerns intensified American efforts to isolate Native Americans on reservations. Although removal had long been a part of federal Indian policy, following the Civil War the U.S. government redoubled its efforts. If treaties and other forms of persistent coercion would not work, federal officials pushed for more drastic measures: after the Civil War, coordinated military action by celebrity Civil War generals such as William Sherman and William Sheridan exploited and exacerbated local conflicts sparked by illegal business ventures and settler incursions. Against the threat of confinement and the extinction of traditional ways of life, Native Americans battled the American army and the encroaching lines of American settlement.

In one of the earliest western engagements, in 1862, while the Civil War still consumed the United States, tensions erupted between the Dakota Nation and white settlers in Minnesota and the Dakota Territory. The 1850 U.S. census recorded a white population of about 6,000 in Minnesota; eight years later, when it became a state, it was more than 150,000.[8] The illegal influx of American farmers pushed the Dakota to the breaking point. Hunting became unsustainable and those Dakota who had taken up farming found only poverty. The federal Indian agent refused to disburse promised food. Many starved. Andrew Myrick, a trader at the agency, refused to sell food on credit. "If they are hungry," he is alleged to have said, "let them eat grass or their own dung."[9] Then, on August 17, 1862, four young men of the Santees, a Dakota band, killed five white settlers near the Redwood Agency, an American administrative office. In the face of an inevitable American retaliation, and over

Buffalo Soldiers, the nickname given to African-American cavalrymen by the Native Americans they fought, were the first peacetime, all-Black regiments in the regular U.S. Army. These soldiers regularly confronted racial prejudice from other Army members and civilians but were an essential part of American victories during the Indian Wars of the late nineteenth and early twentieth centuries. "[Buffalo soldiers of the 25th Infantry, some wearing buffalo robes, Ft. Keogh, Montana] / Chr. Barthelmess, photographer, Fort Keogh, Montana," 1890. Library of Congress.

the protests of many members, the tribe chose war. On the following day, Dakota warriors attacked settlements near the Agency. They killed thirty-one men, women, and children (including Myrick, whose mouth was found filled with grass). They then ambushed a U.S. military detachment at Redwood Ferry, killing twenty-three. The governor of Minnesota called up militia and several thousand Americans waged war against the Indigenous insurgents. Fighting broke out at New Ulm, Fort Ridgely, and Birch Coulee, but the Americans broke Indigenous resistance at the Battle of Wood Lake on September 23, ending the so-called Dakota War.[10]

More than two thousand Dakota had been taken prisoner during the fighting. Many were tried at federal forts for murder, rape, and other atrocities, in a kind of legalistic choreography that conveyed American ideas of Native guilt and white innocence. Military tribunals convicted 303 Dakota and sentenced them to hang. At the last minute, President Lincoln commuted all but thirty-eight of the sentences. Minnesota settlers and government officials insisted not only that the Dakota lose much of their reservation lands and be removed farther west, but that those who had fled be hunted down and placed on reservations as well. The American military gave chase and, on September 3, 1863, after a year of attrition, American military units surrounded a large encampment of Dakota. American troops killed an estimated three hundred men, women, and children. Dozens more were taken prisoner. Troops spent the next two days burning winter food and supply stores to starve out the Dakota resistance, which continued to insist on Dakota sovereignty and treaty rights.

Farther south, settlers inflamed tensions in Colorado. In 1851, the first Treaty of Fort Laramie had secured right-of-way access for Americans passing through on their way to California and Oregon. But a gold rush in 1858 drew approximately 100,000 white gold seekers, and they demanded new treaties be made with local Indigenous groups to secure land rights in the newly created Colorado Territory. Cheyenne bands splintered over the possibility of signing a new treaty that would confine them to a reservation. Settlers, already wary of raids by powerful groups of Cheyennes, Arapahos, and Comanches, meanwhile read in their local newspapers sensationalist accounts of the uprising in Minnesota. Militia leader John M. Chivington warned settlers in the summer of 1864 that the Cheyenne were dangerous, urged war, and promised a swift military victory. Sporadic fighting broke out. The aged Cheyenne chief Black Kettle, believing that a peace treaty would be best for his people, traveled to Denver to arrange for peace talks. He and his followers traveled toward Fort Lyon in accordance with government instructions, but on November 29, 1864, Chivington ordered his seven hundred militiamen to move on the Cheyenne camp near Fort Lyon at Sand Creek. The Cheyenne tried to declare their peaceful intentions but Chivington's militia cut them down. It was a slaughter. Chivington's men killed two hundred men, women, and children.[11]

The Sand Creek Massacre was a national scandal, alternately condemned and applauded. As settler incursions continued to provoke conflict, Americans pushed for a new "peace policy." Congress, confronted with these tragedies and further violence, authorized in 1868 the creation of an Indian Peace Commission. The commission's study of Native Americans decried prior American policy and galvanized support for reformers. After the inauguration of Ulysses S. Grant the following spring, Congress allied with prominent philanthropists to create the Board of Indian Commissioners, a permanent advisory body to oversee Indigenous affairs and prevent the further outbreak of violence. The board effectively Christianized American Indian policy. Much of the reservation system was handed over to Protestant churches, which were tasked with finding agents and missionaries to manage reservation life. Congress hoped that

Tom Torlino, a member of the Navajo Nation, entered the Carlisle Indian School, a Native American boarding school founded by the United States government in 1879, on October 21, 1882, and departed on August 28, 1886. Torlino's student file contained photographs from 1882 and 1885. Carlisle Indian School Digital Resource Center.

religiously minded men might fare better at creating just assimilation policies and persuading Native Americans to accept them. Historian Francis Paul Prucha believed that this attempt at a new "peace policy . . . might just have properly been labelled the 'religious policy.'"[12]

Many female Christian missionaries played a central role in cultural reeducation programs that attempted to not only instill Protestant religion but also impose traditional American gender roles and family structures. They endeavored to replace Indigenous peoples' tribal social units with small, patriarchal households. Women's labor became a contentious issue because few tribes divided labor according to the gender norms of middle- and upper-class Americans. Fieldwork, the traditional domain of white males, was primarily performed by Native women, who also usually controlled the products of their labor, if not the land that was worked, giving them status in society as laborers and food providers. For missionaries, the goal was to get Native women to leave the fields and engage in more proper "women's" work—housework. Christian missionaries performed much as secular federal agents had. Few American agents could meet Native Americans on their own terms. Most Americans viewed Indigenous peoples on reservations as lazy and thought of Indigenous cultures as inferior to their own. The views of J. L. Broaddus, appointed to oversee several small tribes on the Hoopa Valley reservation in California, are illustrative: in his annual report to the Commissioner of Indian Affairs for 1875, he wrote, "The great majority of them are idle, listless, careless, and improvident. They seem to take no thought about provision for the future, and many of them would not work at all if they were not compelled to do so. They would rather live upon the roots and acorns gathered by their women than to work for flour and beef."[13]

If the Indigenous peoples could not be forced through kindness to change their ways, most Americans agreed that it was acceptable to use force, which Native groups resisted. In Texas and the Southern Plains, the Comanche, the Kiowa, and their allies had wielded enormous influence. The Comanche in particular controlled huge swaths of territory and raided vast areas, inspiring terror from the Rocky Mountains to the interior of northern Mexico to the Texas Gulf Coast. But after the Civil War, the U.S. military refocused its attention on the Southern Plains.

The American military first sent messengers to the Plains to find the elusive Comanche bands and ask them to come to peace negotiations at Medicine Lodge Creek in the fall of 1867. But terms were muddled: American officials believed that Comanche bands had accepted reservation life, while Comanche leaders believed they were guaranteed vast lands for buffalo hunting. Comanche bands used designated reservation lands as a base from which to collect supplies and federal annuity goods while continuing to hunt, trade, and raid American settlements in Texas.

Confronted with renewed Comanche raiding, particularly by the famed war leader Quanah Parker, the U.S. military finally proclaimed that all Indigenous peoples who were not settled on the reservation by the fall of 1874 would be considered "hostile." The Red River War began when many Comanche bands refused to resettle and the American military launched expeditions into the Plains to subdue them, culminating in the defeat of the remaining roaming bands in the canyonlands of the Texas Panhandle. Cold and hungry, with their way of life already decimated by soldiers, settlers, cattlemen, and railroads, the last free Comanche bands were moved to the reservation at Fort Sill, in what is now southwestern Oklahoma.[14]

On the northern Plains, the Sioux people had yet to fully surrender. Following the military defeats of 1862, many bands had signed treaties with the United States and drifted into the Red Cloud and Spotted Tail agencies to collect rations and annuities, but many continued to resist American encroachment, particularly during Red Cloud's War, a rare victory for the Plains people that resulted in the Treaty of 1868 and created the Great Sioux Reservation. Then, in 1874, an American expedition to the Black Hills of South Dakota discovered gold. White prospectors flooded the territory. Caring very little about Indigenous rights and very much about getting rich, they brought the Sioux situation again to its breaking point. Aware that U.S. citizens were violating treaty provisions, but unwilling to prevent them from searching for gold, federal officials pressured the western Sioux to sign a new treaty that would transfer control of the Black Hills to the United States while General Philip Sheridan quietly moved U.S. troops into the region. Initial clashes between U.S. troops and Sioux warriors resulted in several Sioux victories that, combined with the visions of Sitting Bull, who had dreamed of an even more triumphant victory, attracted Sioux bands who had already signed treaties but now joined to fight.[15]

In late June 1876, a division of the 7th Cavalry Regiment led by Lieutenant Colonel George Armstrong Custer was sent up a trail into the Black Hills as an advance guard for a larger force. Custer's men approached a camp along a river known to the Sioux as Greasy Grass but marked on Custer's map as Little Bighorn, and they found that the influx of "treaty" Sioux as well as aggrieved Cheyenne and other allies had swelled the population of the village far beyond Custer's estimation. Custer's 7th Cavalry was vastly outnumbered, and he and 268 of his men were killed.[16]

Custer's fall shocked the nation. Cries for a swift American response filled the public sphere, and military expeditions were sent out to crush Native resistance. The Sioux splintered off into the wilderness and began a campaign of intermittent resistance but, outnumbered and suffering after a long, hungry winter, Crazy Horse led a band of Oglala Sioux to surrender in May 1877. Other bands gradually followed until finally, in July 1881, Sitting Bull and his followers at last laid down their weapons and came to the reservation. Indigenous powers had been defeated. The Plains, it seemed, had been pacified.

IV. Beyond the Plains

Plains peoples were not the only ones who suffered as a result of American expansion. Groups like the Utes and Paiutes were pushed out of the Rocky Mountains by U.S. expansion into Colorado and away from the northern Great Basin by the expanding Mormon population in Utah Territory in the 1850s and 1860s. Faced with a shrinking territorial base, members of these two groups often joined the U.S. military in its campaigns in the southwest against other powerful Native groups like the Hopi, the Zuni, the Jicarilla Apache, and especially the Navajo, whose population of at least ten thousand engaged in both farming and sheep herding on some of the most valuable lands acquired by the United States after the Mexican War.

Conflicts between the U.S. military, American settlers, and Native nations increased throughout the 1850s. By 1862, General James Carleton began searching for a reservation where he could remove the Navajo and end their threat to U.S. expansion in the Southwest. Carleton selected a dry, almost treeless site in the Bosque Redondo Valley, three hundred miles from the Navajo homeland.

In April 1863, Carleton gave orders to Colonel Kit Carson to round up the entire Navajo population and escort them to Bosque Redondo. Those who resisted would be shot. Thus began a period of Navajo history called the Long Walk, which remains deeply important to Navajo people today. The Long Walk was not a single event but a series of forced marches to the reservation at Bosque Redondo between August 1863 and December 1866. Conditions at Bosque Redondo were horrible. Provisions provided by the U.S. Army were not only inadequate but often spoiled; disease was rampant, and thousands of Navajos died.

By 1868, it had become clear that life at the reservation was unsustainable. General William Tecumseh Sherman visited the reservation and wrote of the inhumane situation in which the Navajo were essentially kept as prisoners, but lack of cost-effectiveness was the main reason Sherman recommended that the Navajo be returned to their homeland in the West. On June 1, 1868, the Navajo signed the Treaty of Bosque Redondo, an unprecedented treaty in the history of U.S.-native relations in which the Navajo were able to return from the reservation to their homeland.

The attacks on Native nations in California and the Pacific Northwest received significantly less attention than the dramatic conquest of the Plains, but Native peoples in these regions also experienced violence, population decline, and territorial loss. For example, in 1872, the California/Oregon border erupted in violence when the Modoc people left the reservation of the Klamath Nation, onto which they had been forced, and returned to their homelands in an area known as Lost River. Americans had settled the region after Modoc removal several years before, and they complained bitterly of the Natives' return. The U.S. military arrived when fifty-two remaining Modoc warriors, led by Kintpuash, known to settlers as Captain Jack, refused to return to the reservation and holed up in defensive positions along the state border. They fought a guerrilla war for eleven months in which at least two hundred U.S. troops were killed before they were finally forced to surrender. Despite appeals from settlers acquainted with the Modoc, the federal government hanged Kintpuash and three other leaders in a highly choreographed and publicized public execution.[17] Four years later, in the Pacific Northwest, a branch of the Nez Perce (who, generations earlier, had aided Lewis and Clark in their famous journey to the Pacific Ocean) refused to be moved to a reservation and, under the leadership of Hin-mah-too-yah-lat-kekt, known to settlers and American readers as Chief Joseph, attempted to flee to Canada but were pursued by the U.S. Cavalry. The outnumbered Nez Perce battled across a thousand miles and were attacked nearly two dozen times before they succumbed to hunger and exhaustion, surrendered, were imprisoned, and removed to a reservation in Indian Territory. The flight of the Nez Perce captured the attention of the United States, and a transcript of Chief Joseph's surrender, as allegedly recorded by a U.S. Army officer, became a landmark of American rhetoric. "Hear me, my chiefs," Joseph was supposed to have said, "I am tired. My heart is sick and sad. From where the sun now stands, I will fight no more forever." Chief Joseph used his celebrity, and, after several years, negotiated his people's relocation to a reservation nearer to their historic home.[18]

The treaties that had been signed with numerous Native nations in California in the 1850s were never ratified by the Senate. Over one hundred distinct Native groups lived in California before the Spanish and American conquests, but by 1880, the Native population of California had collapsed from about 150,000 on the eve of the gold rush to a little less than 20,000. A few reservation areas were eventually set up by the U.S. government to collect what remained of the Native population, but most were dispersed throughout California. This was partly the result of state laws from the 1850s that allowed white Californians to obtain both Native children and adults as "apprentice" laborers by merely bringing the desired laborer before a judge and promising to feed, clothe, and eventually release them after a period of "service" that ranged from ten to twenty years. Thousands of California's Natives were thus pressed into a form of slave labor that supported the growing mining, agricultural, railroad, and cattle industries.

V. Western Economic Expansion: Railroads and Cattle

Aside from agriculture and the extraction of natural resources—such as timber and precious metals—two major industries fueled the new western economy: ranching and railroads. Both developed in connection with each

Railroads made the settlement and growth of the West possible. By the late nineteenth century, maps of the Midwest were filled with advertisements touting how quickly a traveler could traverse the country. The *Environment and Society* Portal, a digital project from the Rachel Carson Center for Environment and Society, a joint initiative of LMU Munich and the Deutsches Museum.

other, accelerated the inrush of settlers displacing Native peoples out, and shaped the collective American memory of the post–Civil War "Wild West."

As one booster put it, "the West is purely a railroad enterprise." No economic enterprise rivaled the railroads in scale, scope, or sheer impact. No other businesses had attracted such enormous sums of capital, and no other ventures ever received such lavish government subsidies (business historian Alfred Chandler called the railroads the "first modern business enterprise").[19] By "annihilating time and space"—by connecting the vastness of the continent—the railroads transformed the United States and made the American West.

No railroad enterprise so captured the American imagination—or federal support—as the transcontinental railroad. The transcontinental railroad crossed western plains and mountains and linked the West Coast with the rail networks of the eastern United States. Constructed from the west by the Central Pacific and from the east by the Union Pacific, the two roads were linked in Utah in 1869 to great national fanfare. But such a herculean task was not easy, and national legislators threw enormous subsidies at railroad companies, a part of the Republican Party platform since 1856. The 1862 Pacific Railroad Act gave bonds of between $16,000 and $48,000 for each mile of construction and provided vast land grants to railroad companies. Between 1850 and 1871 alone, railroad companies received more than 175,000,000 acres of public land, an area larger than the state of Texas. Investors reaped enormous profits. As one congressional opponent put it in the 1870s, "If there be profit, the corporations may take it; if there be loss, the Government must bear it."[20]

If railroads attracted unparalleled subsidies and investments, they also created enormous labor demands. By 1880, approximately four hundred thousand men—or nearly 2.5 percent of the nation's entire workforce—labored in the railroad industry. Much of the work was dangerous and low-paying, and companies relied heavily on immigrant labor to build tracks. Companies employed Irish workers in the early nineteenth century and Chinese workers in the late nineteenth century. By 1880, over two hundred thousand Chinese migrants lived in the United States. Once the rails were laid, companies still needed a large workforce to keep the trains running. Much railroad work was dangerous, but perhaps the most hazardous work was done by brakemen. Before the advent of automatic braking, an engineer would blow the "down brake" whistle and brakemen would scramble to the top of the moving train, regardless of the weather conditions, and run from car to car manually turning brakes. Speed was necessary, and any slip could be fatal. Brakemen were also responsible for coupling the cars, attaching them together with a large pin. It was easy to lose a hand or finger and even a slight mistake could cause cars to collide.[21]

The railroads boomed. In 1850, there were 9,000 miles of railroads in the United States. In 1900 there were 190,000, including several transcontinental lines.[22] To manage these vast networks of freight and passenger lines, companies converged rails at hub cities. Of all the Midwestern and western cities that blossomed from the bridging of western resources and eastern capital in the late nineteenth century, Chicago was the most spectacular. It grew from two hundred inhabitants in 1833 to over a million by 1890. By 1893 it and the region from which it drew were completely transformed. The World's Columbian Exposition that year trumpeted the city's progress and broader technological progress, with typical Gilded Age ostentation. A huge, gleaming (but temporary) "White City" was built in neoclassical style to house all the features of the fair and cater to the needs of the visitors who arrived from all over the world. Highlighted in the title of this world's fair were the changes that had overtaken North

America since Columbus made landfall four centuries earlier. Chicago became the most important western hub and served as the gateway between the farm and ranch country of the Great Plains and eastern markets. Railroads brought cattle from Texas to Chicago for slaughter, where they were then processed into packaged meats and shipped by refrigerated rail to New York City and other eastern cities. Such hubs became the central nodes in a rapid-transit economy that increasingly spread across the entire continent linking goods and people together in a new national network.

This national network created the fabled cattle drives of the 1860s and 1870s. The first cattle drives across the central Plains began soon after the Civil War. Railroads created the market for ranching, and for the few years after the war that railroads connected eastern markets with important market hubs such as Chicago, but had yet to reach Texas ranchlands, ranchers began driving cattle north, out of the Lone Star state, to major railroad terminuses in Kansas, Missouri, and Nebraska. Ranchers used well-worn trails, such as the Chisholm Trail, for drives, but conflicts arose with Native Americans in the Indian Territory and farmers in Kansas who disliked the intrusion of large and environmentally destructive herds onto their own

This photochrom print (a new technology in the late nineteenth century that colorized images from a black-and-white negative) depicts a cattle round-up in Cimarron, a crossroads of the late nineteenth-century cattle drives. Detroit Photographic Co., "Colorado. 'Round up' on the Cimarron," c. 1898. Library of Congress.

hunting, ranching, and farming lands. Other trails, such as the Western Trail, the Goodnight-Loving Trail, and the Shawnee Trail, were therefore blazed.

Cattle drives were difficult tasks for the crews of men who managed the herds. Historians estimate the number of men who worked as cowboys in the late-nineteenth century to be between twelve thousand and forty thousand. Perhaps a fourth were African American, and more were likely Mexican or Mexican American. Much about the American cowboys evolved from Mexican *vaqueros*: cowboys adopted Mexican practices, gear, and terms such as *rodeo*, *bronco*, and *lasso*.

While most cattle drivers were men, there are at least sixteen verifiable accounts of women participating in the drives. Some, like Molly Dyer Goodnight, accompanied their husbands. Others, like Lizzie Johnson Williams, helped drive their own herds. Williams made at least three known trips with her herds up the Chisholm Trail.

Many cowboys hoped one day to become ranch owners themselves, but employment was insecure and wages were low. Beginners could expect to earn around $20–$25 per month, and those with years of expe-

Cowboys like the one pictured here worked the drives that supplied Chicago and other midwestern cities with the necessary cattle to supply and help grow the meatpacking industry. Their work was obsolete by the turn of the century, yet their image lived on through vaudeville shows and films that romanticized life in the West. John C. H. Grabill, "The Cow Boy," c. 1888. Library of Congress.

rience might earn $40–$45. Trail bosses could earn over $50 per month. And it was tough work. On a cattle drive, cowboys worked long hours and faced extremes of heat and cold and intense blowing dust. They subsisted on limited diets with irregular supplies.[23]

But if workers of cattle earned low wages, owners and investors could receive riches. At the end of the Civil War, a steer worth $4 in Texas could fetch $40 in Kansas. Although profits slowly leveled off, large profits could still be made. And yet, by the 1880s, the great cattle drives were largely done. The railroads had created them, and the railroads ended them: railroad lines pushed into Texas and made the great drives obsolete. But ranching still brought profits and the Plains were better suited for grazing than for agriculture, and western ranchers continued supplying beef for national markets.

Ranching was just one of many western industries that depended on the railroads. By linking the Plains with national markets and rapidly moving people and goods, the railroads made the modern American West.

VI. The Allotment Era and Resistance in the Native West

As the rails moved into the West, and more and more Americans followed, the situation for Native groups deteriorated even further. Treaties negotiated between the United States and Native groups had typically promised that if tribes agreed to move to specific reservation lands, they would hold those lands collectively. But as American westward migration mounted and open lands closed, white settlers began to argue that Native people had more than their fair share of land, that the reservations were too big, that Native people were using the land "inefficiently," and that they still preferred nomadic hunting instead of intensive farming and ranching.

By the 1880s, Americans increasingly championed legislation to allow the transfer of Indigenous lands to farmers and ranchers, while many argued that allotting land to individual Native Americans, rather than to tribes, would encourage American-style agriculture and finally put Indigenous peoples who had previously resisted the efforts of missionaries and federal officials on the path to "civilization."

Passed by Congress on February 8, 1887, the Dawes General Allotment Act splintered Native American reservations into individual family homesteads. Each head of a Native family was to be allotted 160 acres, the typical size of a claim that any settler could establish on federal lands under the provisions of the Homestead Act. Single individuals over age eighteen would receive an eighty-acre allotment, and orphaned children received forty acres.

A four-year timeline was established for Indigenous peoples to make their allotment selections. If at the end of that time no selection had been made, the act authorized the secretary of the interior to appoint an agent to make selections for the remaining tribal members. Allegedly to protect Native Americans from being swindled by unscrupulous land speculators, all allotments were to be held in trust—they could not be sold by allottees—for twenty-five years. Lands that remained unclaimed by tribal members after allotment would revert to federal control and be sold to American settlers.[24]

Americans touted the Dawes Act as an uplifting humanitarian reform, but it upended Native lifestyles and left Native nations without sovereignty over their lands. The act claimed that to protect Native property rights, it was necessary to extend "the protection of the laws of the United States . . . over the Indians." Tribal governments and legal principles could be superseded, or dissolved and replaced, by U.S. laws. Under the terms of the Dawes Act, Native groups struggled to hold on to some measure of tribal sovereignty.

The stresses of conquest unsettled generations of Native Americans. Many took comfort from the words of prophets and holy men. In Nevada, on January 1, 1889, Northern Paiute prophet Wovoka experienced a great revelation. He had traveled, he said, from his earthly home in western Nevada to heaven and returned during a solar eclipse to prophesy to his people. "You must not hurt anybody or do harm to anyone. You must not fight. Do right always," he allegedly exhorted. And they must, he said, participate in a religious ceremony that came to be known as the Ghost Dance. If the people lived justly and danced the Ghost Dance, Wovoka said, their ancestors would rise from the dead, droughts would dissipate, the whites in the West would vanish, and the buffalo would once again roam the Plains.[25]

Native American prophets had often confronted American imperial power. Some prophets, including Wovoka, incorporated Christian elements like heaven and a Messiah figure into indigenous spiritual traditions. And so, though it was far from unique, Wovoka's prophecy nevertheless caught on quickly and spread beyond the Paiutes. From across the West, members of the Arapaho, Bannock, Cheyenne, and Shoshone nations, among others, adopted the Ghost Dance religion. Perhaps the most avid Ghost Dancers—and certainly the most famous—were the Lakota Sioux.

The Lakota were in dire straits. South Dakota, formed out of land that belonged by treaty to the Lakota, became a state in 1889. White homesteaders poured in, reservations were carved up and diminished, starvation set in, corrupt federal agents cut food rations, and drought

Red Cloud and American Horse—two of the most renowned Oglala chiefs—are seen clasping hands in front of a tipi on the Pine Ridge Reservation in South Dakota. Both men served as delegates to Washington, D.C., after years of actively fighting the American government. John C. Grabill, "'Red Cloud and American Horse.' The two most noted chiefs now living," 1891. Library of Congress.

hit the Plains. Many Lakota feared a future as the landless subjects of a growing American empire when a delegation of eleven men, led by Kicking Bear, joined Ghost Dance pilgrims on the rails westward to Nevada and returned to spread the revival in the Dakotas.

The energy and message of the revivals frightened settlers and Indian agents. Newly arrived Pine Ridge agent Daniel Royer sent fearful dispatches to Washington and the press, urging a military crackdown. Newspapers, meanwhile, sensationalized the Ghost Dance.[26] Agents began arresting Lakota leaders. Chief Sitting Bull and several others, were killed in December 1890 during a botched arrest, convincing many bands to flee the reservations to join fugitive bands farther west, where Lakota adherents of the Ghost Dance preached that the Ghost Dancers would be immune to bullets.

Two weeks later, an American cavalry unit intercepted a band of 350 Lakota, including over 100 women and children under Chief Spotted Elk (later known as Bigfoot), seeking refuge at the Pine Ridge Agency. They were escorted to Wounded Knee Creek, where they camped for the night. The following morning, December 29, the American cavalrymen entered the camp to disarm Spotted Elk's band. Tensions flared, a

Burial of the dead after the massacre of Wounded Knee. U.S. soldiers putting Native Americans in a common grave; some corpses are frozen in different positions. South Dakota. 1891. Library of Congress.

shot was fired, and a skirmish became a massacre. The Americans fired their heavy weaponry indiscriminately into the camp. Two dozen cavalrymen had been killed by the Lakotas' concealed weapons or by friendly fire, but when the guns went silent, between 150 and 300 Native men, women, and children were dead.[27]

Wounded Knee marked the end of sustained, armed Native American resistance on the Plains. Individuals continued to resist the pressures of assimilation and preserve traditional cultural practices, but sustained military defeats, the loss of sovereignty over land and resources, and the onset of crippling poverty on the reservations marked the final decades of the nineteenth century as a particularly dark era for America's western tribes. But for Americans, it became mythical.

VII. Rodeos, Wild West Shows, and the Mythic American West

"The American West" conjures visions of tipis, cabins, cowboys, Native Americans, farm wives in sunbonnets, and outlaws with six-shooters. Such images pervade American culture, but they are as old as the West

American frontierswoman and professional scout Martha Jane Canary was better known to America as Calamity Jane. A figure in western folklore during her life and after, Calamity Jane was a central character in many of the increasingly popular novels and films that romanticized western life in the twentieth century. "[Martha Canary, 1852–1903, ("Calamity Jane"), full-length portrait, seated with rifle as General Crook's scout]," c. 1895. Library of Congress.

itself: novels, rodeos, and Wild West shows mythologized the American West throughout the post–Civil War era.

In the 1860s, Americans devoured dime novels that embellished the lives of real-life individuals such as Calamity Jane and Billy the Kid. Owen Wister's novels, especially *The Virginian*, established the character of the cowboy as a gritty stoic with a rough exterior but the courage and heroism needed to rescue people from train robbers, Native Americans, and cattle rustlers. Such images were later reinforced when the emergence of rodeo added to popular conceptions of the American West. Rodeos began as small roping and riding contests among cowboys in towns near ranches or at camps at the end of the cattle trails. In Pecos, Texas, on July 4, 1883, cowboys from two ranches, the Hash Knife and the W Ranch, competed in roping and riding contests as a way to settle an argument; this event is recognized by historians of the West as the first real rodeo. Casual contests evolved into planned celebrations. Many were scheduled around national holidays, such as Independence Day, or during traditional roundup times in the spring and fall. Early rodeos took place in open grassy areas—not arenas—and included calf and steer roping and roughstock events such as bronc riding. They gained popularity

I AM COMING

William Frederick "Buffalo Bill" Cody helped commercialize the cowboy lifestyle, building a mythology around life in the Old West that produced big bucks for men like Cody. Courier Lithography Company, "Buffalo Bill Cody," 1900. Wikimedia.

and soon dedicated rodeo circuits developed. Although about 90 percent of rodeo contestants were men, women helped popularize the rodeo and several popular female bronc riders, such as Bertha Kaepernick, entered men's events, until around 1916 when women's competitive participation was curtailed. Americans also experienced the "Wild West"—the mythical West imagined in so many dime novels—by attending traveling Wild West shows, arguably the unofficial national entertainment of the United States from the 1880s to the 1910s. Wildly popular across the country, the shows traveled throughout the eastern United States and even across Europe and showcased what was already a mythic frontier life. William Frederick "Buffalo Bill" Cody was the first to recognize the broad national appeal of the stock "characters" of the American West—cowboys, "Indians," sharpshooters, cavalrymen, and rangers—and put them all together into a single massive traveling extravaganza. Operating out of Omaha, Nebraska, Buffalo Bill launched his touring show in 1883. Cody himself shunned the word *show*, fearing that it implied an exaggeration or misrepresentation of the West. He instead called his production "Buffalo Bill's Wild West." He employed real cowboys and Native Americans in his productions. But it was still, of course, a show. It was entertainment, little different in its broad outlines from contemporary theater. Storylines depicted westward migration, life on the Plains, and Indigenous attacks, all punctuated by "cowboy fun": bucking broncos, roping cattle, and sharpshooting contests.[28]

Buffalo Bill, joined by shrewd business partners skilled in marketing, turned his shows into a sensation. But he was not alone. Gordon William "Pawnee Bill" Lillie, another popular Wild West showman, got his start in 1886 when Cody employed him as an interpreter for Pawnee members of the show. Lillie went on to create his own production in 1888, "Pawnee Bill's Historic Wild West." He was Cody's only real competitor in the business until 1908, when the two men combined their shows to create a new extravaganza, "Buffalo Bill's Wild West and Pawnee Bill's Great Far East" (most people called it the "Two Bills Show"). It was an unparalleled spectacle. The cast included American cowboys, Mexican *vaqueros*, Native Americans, Russian Cossacks, Japanese acrobats, and an Australian aboriginal.

Cody and Lillie knew that Native Americans fascinated audiences in the United States and Europe, and both featured them prominently in their Wild West shows. Most Americans believed that Native cultures were disappearing or had already, and felt a sense of urgency to see their dances, hear their song, and be captivated by their bareback riding skills and their elaborate buckskin and feather attire. The shows certainly veiled the true cultural and historic value of so many Native demonstrations, and the Native performers were curiosities to white Americans, but the shows were one of the few ways for many Native Americans to make a living in the late nineteenth century.

In an attempt to appeal to women, Cody recruited Annie Oakley, a female sharpshooter who thrilled onlookers with her many stunts. Billed as "Little Sure Shot," she shot apples off her poodle's head and the ash from her husband's cigar, clenched trustingly between his teeth. Gordon Lillie's wife, May Manning Lillie, also became a skilled shot and performed as "World's Greatest Lady Horseback Shot." Female sharpshooters were Wild West show staples. As many as eighty toured the country at the shows' peak. But if such acts challenged expected Victorian gender roles, female performers were typically careful to blunt criticism by maintaining their feminine identity—for example, by riding sidesaddle and wearing full skirts and corsets—during their acts.

The western "cowboys and Indians" mystique, perpetuated in novels, rodeos, and Wild West shows, was rooted in romantic nostalgia and, perhaps, in the anxieties that many felt in the late nineteenth century's new seemingly "soft" industrial world of factory and office work. The mythical cowboy's "aggressive masculinity" was the seemingly perfect antidote for middle- and upper-class, city-dwelling Americans who feared they "had become over-civilized" and longed for what Theodore Roosevelt called the "strenuous life." Roosevelt himself, a scion of a wealthy New York family and later a popular American president, turned a brief tenure as a failed Dakota ranch owner into a potent part of his political image. Americans looked longingly to the West, whose romance would continue to pull at generations of Americans.

VIII. The West as History: The Turner Thesis

In 1893, the American Historical Association met during that year's World's Columbian Exposition in Chicago. The young Wisconsin historian Frederick Jackson Turner presented his "frontier thesis," one of the most influential theories of American history, in his essay "The Significance of the Frontier in American History."

American anthropologist and ethnographer Frances Densmore records the Blackfoot chief Mountain Chief in 1916 for the Bureau of American Ethnology. Library of Congress.

Turner looked back at the historical changes in the West and saw, instead of a tsunami of war and plunder and industry, waves of "civilization" that washed across the continent. A frontier line "between savagery and civilization" had moved west from the earliest English settlements in Massachusetts and Virginia across the Appalachians to the Mississippi and finally across the Plains to California and Oregon. Turner invited

his audience to "stand at Cumberland Gap [the famous pass through the Appalachian Mountains], and watch the procession of civilization, marching single file—the buffalo following the trail to the salt springs, the Native American, the fur trader and hunter, the cattle-raiser, the pioneer farmer—and the frontier has passed by."[29]

Americans, Turner said, had been forced by necessity to build a rough-hewn civilization out of the frontier, giving the nation its exceptional hustle and its democratic spirit and distinguishing North America from the stale monarchies of Europe. Moreover, the *style* of history Turner called for was democratic as well, arguing that the work of ordinary people (in this case, pioneers) deserved the same study as that of great statesmen. Such was a novel approach in 1893.

But Turner looked ominously to the future. The Census Bureau in 1890 had declared the frontier closed. There was no longer a discernible line running north to south that, Turner said, any longer divided civilization from savagery. Turner worried for the United States' future: what would become of the nation without the safety valve of the frontier? It was a common sentiment. Theodore Roosevelt wrote to Turner that his essay "put into shape a good deal of thought that has been floating around rather loosely."[30]

The history of the West was made by many persons and peoples. Turner's thesis was rife with faults, not only in its bald Anglo-Saxon chauvinism—in which nonwhites fell before the march of "civilization" and Chinese and Mexican immigrants were invisible—but in its utter inability to appreciate the impact of technology and government subsidies and large-scale economic enterprises alongside the work of hardy pioneers. Still, Turner's thesis held an almost canonical position among historians for much of the twentieth century and, more importantly, captured Americans' enduring romanticization of the West and the simplification of a long and complicated story into a march of progress.

IX. Reference Material

This chapter was edited by Lauren Brand, with content contributions by Lauren Brand, Carole Butcher, Josh Garrett-Davis, Tracey Hanshew, Lindsay Stallones Marshall, Nick Roland, David Schley, Emma Teitelman, and Alyce Webb.

Recommended citation: Lauren Brand et al., "Conquering the West," Lauren Brand, ed., in *The American Yawp*, eds. Joseph Locke and Ben Wright (Stanford, CA: Stanford University Press, 2019).

NOTES TO CHAPTER 17

1. Based on U.S. Census figures from 1900. See, for instance, Donald Lee Parman, *Indians and the American West in the Twentieth Century* (Bloomington: Indiana University Press, 1994), ix.

2. Rodman W. Paul, *The Mining Frontiers of the West, 1848–1880* (New York: Holt, Rinehart and Winston, 1963); Richard Lingenfelter, *The Hard Rock Miners* (Berkeley: University of California Press, 1979).

3. Richard White, *It's Your Misfortune and None of My Own: A New History of the American West* (Norman: University of Oklahoma Press, 1991), 216–220.

4. Matthew Bowman, *The Mormon People: The Making of an American Faith* (New York: Random House, 2012).

5. White, *It's Your Misfortune*, 142–148; Patricia Nelson Limerick, *The Legacy of Conquest: The Unbroken Past of the American West* (New York: Norton, 1987), 161–162.

6. White, *It's Your Misfortune*; Limerick, *Legacy of Conquest*.

7. John D. Hicks, *The Populist Revolt: A History of the Farmers' Alliance and the People's Party* (Minneapolis: University of Minnesota Press, 1931), 6.

8. Robert Utley, *The Indian Frontier 1846–1890* (Albuquerque: University of New Mexico Press, 1984), 76.

9. Mary Butler Renville, *A Thrilling Narrative of Indian Captivity: Dispatches from the Dakota War* (Lincoln: University of Nebraska Press, 2012), 268n188.

10. Jeffrey Ostler, *The Plains Sioux and U.S. Colonialism from Lewis and Clark to Wounded Knee* (New York: Cambridge University Press, 2004).

11. Elliott West, *The Contested Plains: Indians, Goldseekers, and the Rush to Colorado* (Lawrence: Kansas University Press, 1998).

12. Francis Paul Prucha, *The Great Father: The United States Government and the American Indians* (Lincoln: University of Nebraska Press, 1995), 482.

13. Bureau of Indian Affairs, *Annual Report of the Commissioner of Indian Affairs to the Secretary of the Interior* (Washington, DC: U.S. Government Printing Office, 1875), 221.

14. For the Comanche, see especially Pekka Hämäläinen, *The Comanche Empire* (New Haven, CT: Yale University Press, 2008).

15. Ostler, *The Plains Sioux and U.S. Colonialism*.

16. Utley, *The Indian Frontier*.

17. Boyd Cothran, *Remembering the Modoc War: Redemptive Violence and the Making of American Innocence* (Chapel Hill: University of North Carolina Press, 2014).

18. *Report of the Secretary of War, Being Part of the Message and Documents Communicated to the Two Houses of Congress, Beginning of the Second Session of the Forty-Fifth Congress. Volume I* (Washington, DC: U.S. Government Printing Office, 1877), 630.

19. Alfred D. Chandler Jr., *The Visible Hand: The Managerial Revolution in American Business* (Cambridge, MA: Belknap Press, 1977).

20. Richard White, *Railroaded: The Transcontinentals and the Making of Modern America* (New York: Norton, 2011), 107.

21. Walter Licht, *Working on the Railroad: The Organization of Work in the Nineteenth Century* (Princeton, NJ: Princeton University Press, 2014), chap. 5.

22. John F. Stover, *The Routledge Historical Atlas of the American Railroads* (New York: Routledge, 1999), 15, 17, 39, 49.

23. Richard W. Slatta, *Cowboys of the Americas* (New Haven, CT: Yale University Press, 1994).

24. Limerick, *Legacy of Conquest*, 195–199; White, *It's Your Misfortune*, 115.

25. On the Ghost Dance Religion, see especially Louis S. Warren, *God's Red Son: The Ghost Dance Religion and the Making of Modern America* (New York: Basic, 2017).

26. See, for instance, Oliver Knight, *Following the Indian Wars* (Norman: University of Oklahoma Press, 1960).

27. Dee Brown, *Bury My Heart at Wounded Knee: An Indian History of the American West* (New York: Holt, Rinehart and Winston, 1970).

28. Joy S. Kasson, *Buffalo Bill's Wild West: Celebrity, Memory, and Popular History* (New York: Macmillan, 2001).

29. Frederick Jackson Turner, *The Frontier in American History* (New York: Holt, 1921), 12.

30. Kasson, *Buffalo Bill's Wild West*, 117.

RECOMMENDED READING

Aarim, Najia. *Chinese Immigrants, African Americans, and Racial Anxiety in the United States, 1848–1882.* Champaign: University of Illinois Press, 2006.

Andrews, Thomas. *Killing for Coal: America's Deadliest Labor War.* Cambridge, MA: Harvard University Press, 2009.

Brown, Dee. *Bury My Heart at Wounded Knee: An Indian History of the American West.* New York: Holt, Rinehart and Winston, 1970.

Cahill, Cathleen. *Federal Fathers and Mothers: A Social History of the United States Indian Service, 1869–1933.* Chapel Hill: University of North Carolina Press, 2011.

Cronon, William. *Nature's Metropolis: Chicago and the Great West.* New York: Norton, 1991.

Estes, Nick. *Our History is the Future: Standing Rock Versus the Dakota Access Pipeline, and the Long Tradition of Indigenous Resistance.* New York: Verso, 2019.

Gordan, Linda. *The Great Arizona Orphan Abduction.* Cambridge, MA: Harvard University Press, 1999.

Hämäläinen, Pekka. *The Comanche Empire.* New Haven, CT: Yale University Press, 2008.

Hine, Robert V. *The American West: A New Interpretive History.* New Haven, CT: Yale University Press, 2000.

Huhndorf, Shari M. *Going Native: Indians in the American Cultural Imagination.* Ithaca, NY: Cornell University Press, 2001.

Isenberg, Andrew C. *The Destruction of the Bison: An Environmental History, 1750–1920.* Cambridge, UK: Cambridge University Press, 2000.

Jacobs, Margaret D. *White Mother to a Dark Race: Settler Colonialism, Maternalism, and the Removal of Indigenous Children in the American West and Australia, 1880–1940*. Lincoln: University of Nebraska Press, 2009.

Johnson, Benjamin Heber. *Revolution in Texas: How a Forgotten Rebellion and Its Bloody Suppression Turned Mexicans into Americans*. New Haven, CT: Yale University Press, 2003.

Kelman, Ari. *A Misplaced Massacre: Struggling over the Memory of Sand Creek*. Cambridge, MA: Harvard University Press, 2013.

Krech, Shepard. *The Ecological Indian: Myth and History*. New York: Norton, 1999.

Limerick, Patricia Nelson. *The Legacy of Conquest: The Unbroken Past of the American West*. New York: Norton, 1987.

Marks, Paula Mitchell. *In a Barren Land: American Indian Dispossession and Survival*. New York: Morrow, 1998.

Montejano, David. *Anglos and Mexicans in the Making of Texas, 1836–1986*. Austin: University of Texas Press, 1987.

Pascoe, Peggy. *Relations of Rescue: The Search for Female Moral Authority in the American West, 1874–1939*. New York: Oxford University Press, 1990.

Prucha, Francis Paul. *The Great Father: The United States Government and the American Indians*. Lincoln: University of Nebraska Press, 1984.

Schulten, Susan. *The Geographical Imagination in America, 1880–1950*. Chicago: University of Chicago Press, 2001.

Shah, Nayan. *Stranger Intimacy: Contesting Race, Sexuality, and the Law in the North American West*. Berkeley: University of California Press, 2011.

Smith, Henry Nash. *Virgin Land: The American West as Symbol and Myth*. New York: Vintage Books, 1957.

Taylor, Quintard. *In Search of the Racial Frontier: African Americans in the American West, 1528–1990*. New York: Norton, 1999.

Warren, Louis S. *Buffalo Bill's America: William Cody and the Wild West Show*. New York: Knopf, 2005.

White, Richard. *"It's Your Misfortune and None of My Own": A New History of the American West*. Norman: University of Oklahoma Press, 1991.

18

Life in Industrial America

I. Introduction

When British author Rudyard Kipling visited Chicago in 1889, he described a city captivated by technology and blinded by greed. He described a rushed and crowded city, a "huge wilderness" with "scores of miles of these terrible streets" and their "hundred thousand of these terrible people." "The show impressed me with a great horror," he wrote. "There was no color in the street and no beauty—only a maze of wire ropes overhead and dirty stone flagging under foot." He took a cab "and the cabman said that these things were the proof of progress." Kipling visited a "gilded and mirrored" hotel "crammed with people talking about money, and spitting about everywhere." He visited extravagant churches and spoke with their congregants. "I listened to people who said that the mere fact of spiking down strips of iron to wood, and getting a steam and iron thing to run along them was progress, that the telephone was

Mulberry Street, New York City, c. 1900. Library of Congress.

Wabash Avenue,
Chicago,
c. 1907. Library
of Congress.

progress, and the network of wires overhead was progress. They repeated their statements again and again." Kipling said American newspapers report "that the snarling together of telegraph-wires, the heaving up of houses, and the making of money is progress."[1]

Chicago embodied the triumph of American industrialization. Its meatpacking industry typified the sweeping changes occurring in American life. The last decades of the nineteenth century, a new era for big business, saw the formation of large corporations, run by trained bureaucrats and salaried managers, doing national and international business. Chicago, for instance, became America's butcher. The Chicago meat processing industry, a cartel of five firms, produced four fifths of the meat bought by American consumers. Kipling described in intimate detail the Union Stock Yards, the nation's largest meat processing zone, a square mile just southwest of the city whose pens and slaughterhouses linked the city's vast agricultural hinterland to the nation's dinner tables. "Once having seen them," he concluded, "you will never forget the sight." Like other notable Chicago industries, such as agricultural machinery and steel production, the meatpacking industry was closely tied to urbanization and immigration. In 1850, Chicago had a population of about thirty thousand. Twenty years later, it had three hundred thousand. Nothing could stop the city's growth. The Great Chicago Fire leveled 3.5 square miles and left a third of its residents homeless in 1871, but the city quickly recovered and resumed its spectacular growth. By the turn of the twentieth century, the city was home to 1.7 million people.

Chicago's explosive growth reflected national trends. In 1870, a quarter of the nation's population lived in towns or cities with populations greater than 2,500. By 1920, a majority did. But if many who flocked to Chicago and other American cities came from rural America, many others emigrated from overseas. Mirroring national immigration patterns, Chicago's newcomers had at first come mostly from Germany, the British Isles, and Scandinavia, but, by 1890, Poles, Italians, Czechs, Hungarians, Lithuanians, and others from southern and eastern Europe made up a majority of new immigrants. Chicago, like many other American industrial cities, was also an immigrant city. In 1900, nearly 80 percent of Chicago's population was either foreign-born or the children of foreign-born immigrants.[2]

Kipling visited Chicago just as new industrial modes of production revolutionized the United States. The rise of cities, the evolution of American immigration, the transformation of American labor, the further making of a mass culture, the creation of great concentrated wealth, the growth of vast city slums, the conquest of the West, the emergence of a middle class, the problem of poverty, the triumph of big business, widening inequalities, battles between capital and labor, the final destruction of independent farming, breakthrough technologies, environmental destruction: industrialization created a new America.

II. Industrialization and Technological Innovation

The railroads created the first great concentrations of capital, spawned the first massive corporations, made the first of the vast fortunes that would define the Gilded Age, unleashed labor demands that united thousands of farmers and immigrants, and linked many towns and cities. National railroad mileage tripled in the twenty years after the outbreak of the Civil War, and tripled again over the four decades that followed. Railroads impelled the creation of uniform time zones across the country, gave industrialists access to remote markets, and opened the American West. Railroad companies were the nation's largest businesses. Their vast national operations demanded the creation of innovative new corporate organization, advanced management techniques, and vast sums of capital. Their huge expenditures spurred countless industries and attracted droves of laborers. And as they crisscrossed the nation, they created a national market, a truly national economy, and, seemingly, a new national culture.[3]

The railroads were not natural creations. Their vast capital requirements required the use of incorporation, a legal innovation that protected shareholders from losses. Enormous amounts of government support followed. Federal, state, and local governments offered unrivaled handouts to create the national rail networks. Lincoln's Republican Party—which dominated government policy during the Civil War and Reconstruction—passed legislation granting vast subsidies. Hundreds of millions of acres of land and millions of dollars' worth of government bonds were freely given to build the great transcontinental railroads and the innumerable trunk lines that quickly annihilated the vast geographic barriers that had so long sheltered American cities from one another.

As railroad construction drove economic development, new means of production spawned new systems of labor. Many wage earners had traditionally seen factory work as a temporary stepping-stone to attaining their own small businesses or farms. After the war, however, new

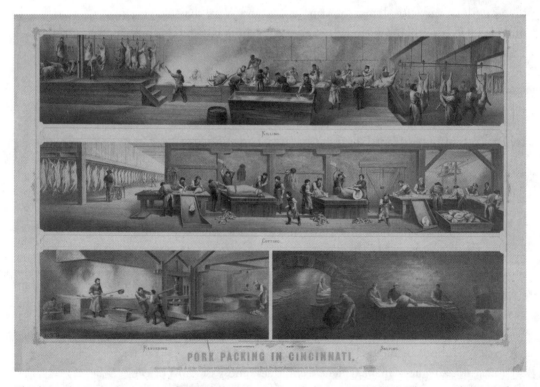

This print shows the four stages of pork packing in nineteenth-century Cincinnati. This centralization of production made meatpacking an innovative industry, one of great interest to industrialists of all ilks. In fact, this chromo-lithograph was exhibited by the Cincinnati Pork Packers' Association at the International Exposition in Vienna, Austria. 1873. Wikimedia.

technology and greater mechanization meant fewer and fewer workers could legitimately aspire to economic independence. Stronger and more organized labor unions formed to fight for a growing, more-permanent working class. At the same time, the growing scale of economic enterprises increasingly disconnected owners from their employees and day-to-day business operations. To handle their vast new operations, owners turned to managers. Educated bureaucrats swelled the ranks of an emerging middle class.

Industrialization also remade much of American life outside the workplace. Rapidly growing industrialized cities knit together urban consumers and rural producers into a single, integrated national market. Food production and consumption, for instance, were utterly nationalized. Chicago's stockyards seemingly tied it all together. Between 1866 and 1886, ranchers drove a million head of cattle annually overland from Texas ranches to railroad depots in Kansas for shipment by rail to Chicago. After travelling through modern "disassembly lines," the animals left the adjoining slaughterhouses as slabs of meat to be packed into refrigerated rail cars and sent to butcher shops across the continent. By 1885, a handful of large-scale industrial meatpackers in Chicago were producing nearly five hundred million pounds of "dressed" beef annually.[4] The new scale of industrialized meat production transformed the landscape. Buffalo herds, grasslands, and old-growth forests gave way to cattle, corn, and wheat. Chicago became the Gateway City, a crossroads connecting American agricultural goods, capital markets in New York and London, and consumers from all corners of the United States.

Technological innovation accompanied economic development. For April Fool's Day in 1878, the New York *Daily Graphic* published a fictitious interview with the celebrated inventor Thomas A. Edison. The piece described the "biggest invention of the age"—a new Edison machine that could create forty different kinds of food and drink out of only air, water, and dirt. "Meat will no longer be killed and vegetables no longer grown, except by savages," Edison promised. The machine would end "famine and pauperism." And all for $5 or $6 per machine! The story was a joke, of course, but Edison nevertheless received inquiries from readers wondering when the food machine would be ready for the market. Americans had apparently witnessed such startling technological advances—advances that would have seemed far-fetched mere years earlier—that the Edison food machine seemed entirely plausible.[5]

In September 1878, Edison announced a new and ambitious line of research and development—electric power and lighting. The scientific principles behind dynamos and electric motors—the conversion of mechanical energy to electrical power, and vice versa—were long known, but Edison applied the age's bureaucratic and commercial ethos to the problem. Far from a lone inventor gripped by inspiration toiling in isolation, Edison advanced the model of commercially minded management of research and development. Edison folded his two identities, business manager and inventor, together. He called his Menlo Park research laboratory an "invention factory" and promised to turn out "a minor invention every ten days and a big thing every six months or so." He brought his fully equipped Menlo Park research laboratory and the skilled machinists and scientists he employed to bear on the problem of building an electric power system—and commercializing it.

By late fall 1879, Edison exhibited his system of power generation and electrical light for reporters and investors. Then he scaled up production. He sold generators to businesses. By the middle of 1883, Edison had overseen construction of 330 plants powering over sixty thousand lamps in factories, offices, printing houses, hotels, and theaters around the world. He convinced municipal officials to build central power stations and run power lines. New York's Pearl Street central station opened in September 1882 and powered a square mile of downtown Manhattan. Electricity revolutionized the world. It not only illuminated the night, it powered the Second Industrial Revolution. Factories could operate anywhere at any hour. Electric rail cars allowed for cities to build out and electric elevators allowed for them to build up.

Economic advances, technological innovation, social and cultural evolution, demographic changes: the United States was a nation transformed. Industry boosted productivity, railroads connected the nation, more and more Americans labored for wages, new bureaucratic occupations created a vast "white collar" middle class, and unprecedented fortunes rewarded the owners of capital. These revolutionary changes, of course, would not occur without conflict or consequence (see Chapter 16), but they demonstrated the profound transformations remaking the nation. Change was not confined to economics alone. Change gripped the lives of everyday Americans and fundamentally reshaped American culture.[6]

III. Immigration and Urbanization

Industry pulled ever more Americans into cities. Manufacturing needed the labor pool and the infrastructure. America's urban population in-

State Street, south from Lake Street, Chicago, Illinois, c. 1900–1910. Library of Congress.

creased sevenfold in the half century after the Civil War. Soon the United States had more large cities than any country in the world. The 1920 U.S. census revealed that, for the first time, a majority of Americans lived in urban areas. Much of that urban growth came from the millions of immigrants pouring into the nation. Between 1870 and 1920, over twenty-five million immigrants arrived in the United States.

By the turn of the twentieth century, new immigrant groups such as Italians, Poles, and Eastern European Jews made up a larger percentage of arrivals than the Irish and Germans. The specific reasons that immigrants left their particular countries and the reasons they came to the United States (what historians call *push* and *pull factors*) varied. For example, a young husband and wife living in Sweden in the 1880s and unable to purchase farmland might read an advertisement for inexpensive land in the American Midwest and immigrate to the United States to begin a new life. A young Italian man might simply hope to labor in a steel factory long enough to save up enough money to return home and purchase land for a family. A Russian Jewish family persecuted in European pogroms might look to the United States as a sanctuary. Or perhaps a Japanese migrant might hear of fertile farming land on the West Coast and choose to sail for California. But if many factors pushed people away from their home countries, by far the most important factor drawing immigrants was economics. Immigrants came to the United States looking for work.

Industrial capitalism was the most important factor that drew immigrants to the United States between 1880 and 1920. Immigrant workers labored in large industrial complexes producing goods such as steel, textiles, and food products, replacing smaller and more local workshops. The influx of immigrants, alongside a large movement of Americans from the countryside to the city, helped propel the rapid growth of cities like New York, Pittsburgh, Cleveland, Milwaukee, and St. Louis. By 1890, immigrants and their children accounted for roughly 60 percent of the population in most large northern cities (and sometimes as high as 80 or 90 percent). Many immigrants, especially from Italy and the Balkans, always intended to return home with enough money to purchase land. But what about those who stayed? Did the new arrivals assimilate together in the American melting pot—becoming just like those already in the United States—or did they retain, and sometimes even strengthen, their traditional ethnic identities? The answer lies somewhere in between. Immigrants from specific countries—and often even specific communities— often clustered together in ethnic neighborhoods. They formed vibrant organizations and societies, such as Italian workmen's clubs, Eastern European Jewish mutual aid societies, and Polish Catholic churches, to ease the transition to their new American home. Immigrant communities published newspapers in dozens of languages and purchased spaces to keep their arts, languages, and traditions alive. And from these foundations they facilitated even more immigration: after staking out a claim to some corner of American life, they wrote home and encouraged others to follow them (historians call this *chain migration*).

Many cities' politics adapted to immigrant populations. The infamous urban political machines often operated as a kind of mutual aid society. New York City's Democratic Party machine, popularly known as Tammany Hall, drew the greatest ire from critics and seemed to embody all of the worst of city machines, but it also responded to immigrant needs. In 1903, journalist William Riordon published a book, *Plunkitt of Tammany Hall*, which chronicled the activities of ward heeler George Washington Plunkitt. Plunkitt elaborately explained to Riordon the difference between "honest graft" and "dishonest graft": "I made my pile in politics, but, at the same time, I served the organization and got more big improvements for New York City than any other livin' man." While exposing corruption, Riordon also revealed the hard work Plunkitt undertook on behalf of his largely immigrant constituency. On a typical day, Riordon wrote, Plunkitt was awakened at two a.m. to bail out a saloonkeeper who stayed open too late, was awakened again at six a.m. because of a fire in the neighborhood and spent time finding lodgings for the families displaced by the fire, and, after spending the rest of the morning in court to secure the release of several of his constituents, found jobs for four unemployed men, attended an Italian funeral, visited a church social, and dropped in on a Jewish wedding. He returned home at midnight.[7]

Tammany Hall's corruption, especially under the reign of William "Boss" Tweed, was legendary, but the public works projects that funded Tammany Hall's graft also provided essential infrastructure and public services for the city's rapidly expanding population. Water, sewer, and gas lines; schools, hospitals, civic buildings, and museums; police and fire departments; roads, parks (notably Central Park), and bridges (notably the Brooklyn Bridge): all could, in whole or in part, be credited to Tammany's reign. Still, machine politics could never be enough. As the urban population exploded, many immigrants found themselves trapped in crowded, crime-ridden slums. Americans eventually took notice of this urban crisis and proposed municipal reforms but also grew concerned about the declining quality of life in rural areas.

While cities boomed, rural worlds languished. Some Americans scoffed at rural backwardness and reveled in the countryside's decay, but many romanticized the countryside, celebrated rural life, and wondered what had been lost in the cities. Sociologist Kenyon Butterfield, concerned by the sprawling nature of industrial cities and suburbs, regretted the eroding social position of rural citizens and farmers: "Agriculture does not hold the same relative rank among our industries that it did in former years." Butterfield saw "the farm problem" as part of "the whole question of democratic civilization."[8] He and many others thought the rise of the cities and the fall of the countryside threatened traditional American values. Many proposed conservation. Liberty Hyde Bailey, a botanist and rural scholar selected by Theodore Roosevelt to chair a federal Commission on Country Life in 1907, believed that rural places and industrial cities were linked: "Every agricultural question is a city question."[9]

Many longed for a middle path between the cities and the country. New suburban communities on the outskirts of American cities defined themselves in opposition to urban crowding. Americans contemplated the complicated relationships between rural places, suburban living, and urban spaces. Los Angeles became a model for the suburban development of rural places. Dana Barlett, a social reformer in Los Angeles, noted that the city, stretching across dozens of small towns, was "a better city" because of its residential identity as a "city of homes."[10] This language was seized upon by many suburbs that hoped to avoid both urban sprawl and rural decay. In Glendora, one of these small towns on the outskirts of Los Angeles, local leaders were "loath as anyone to see it become cosmopolitan." Instead, in order to have Glendora "grow along the lines necessary to have it remain an enjoyable city of homes," they needed to "bestir ourselves to direct its growth" by encouraging not industry or agriculture but residential development.[11]

IV. The New South and the Problem of Race

"There was a South of slavery and secession," *Atlanta Constitution* editor Henry Grady proclaimed in an 1886 speech in New York. "That South is dead."[12] Grady captured the sentiment of many white southern business and political leaders who imagined a New South that could turn its back to the past by embracing industrialization and diversified agriculture. He promoted the region's economic possibilities and mutual future prosperity through an alliance of northern capital and southern labor. Grady and other New South boosters hoped to shape the region's economy in the North's image. They wanted industry and they wanted infrastructure. But the past could not be escaped. Economically and socially, the "New South" would still be much like the old.

A "New South" seemed an obvious need. The Confederacy's failed insurrection wreaked havoc on the southern economy and crippled southern prestige. Property was destroyed. Lives were lost. Political power vanished. And four million enslaved Americans—representing the wealth and power of the antebellum white South—threw off their chains and walked proudly forward into freedom.

Emancipation unsettled the southern social order. When Reconstruction regimes attempted to grant freedpeople full citizenship rights, anxious whites struck back. From their fear, anger, and resentment they lashed out, not only in organized terrorist organizations such as the Ku Klux Klan but in political corruption, economic exploitation, and violent intimidation. White southerners took back control of state and local governments and used their reclaimed power to disenfranchise African Americans and pass "Jim Crow" laws segregating schools, transportation, employment, and various public and private facilities. The

reestablishment of white supremacy after the "redemption" of the South from Reconstruction contradicted proclamations of a "New" South. Perhaps nothing harked so forcefully back to the barbaric southern past than the wave of lynchings—the extralegal murder of individuals by vigilantes—that washed across the South after Reconstruction. Whether for actual crimes or fabricated crimes or for no crimes at all, white mobs murdered roughly five thousand African Americans between the 1880s and the 1950s.

Lynching was not just murder, it was a ritual rich with symbolism. Victims were not simply hanged, they were mutilated, burned alive, and shot. Lynchings could become carnivals, public spectacles attended by thousands of eager spectators. Rail lines ran special cars to accommodate the rush of participants. Vendors sold goods and keepsakes. Perpetrators posed for photos and collected mementos. And it was increasingly common. One notorious example occurred in Georgia in 1899. Accused of killing his white employer and raping the man's wife, Sam Hose was captured by a mob and taken to the town of Newnan. Word of the impending lynching quickly spread, and specially chartered passenger trains brought some four thousand visitors from Atlanta to witness the

The ambitions of Atlanta, seen in the construction of such grand buildings as the Kimball House Hotel, reflected the larger regional aspirations of the so-called New South. 1890. Wikimedia.

gruesome affair. Members of the mob tortured Hose for about an hour. They sliced off pieces of his body as he screamed in agony. Then they poured a can of kerosene over his body and burned him alive.[13]

At the barbaric height of southern lynching, in the last years of the nineteenth century, southerners lynched two to three African Americans every week. In general, lynchings were most frequent in the Cotton Belt of the Lower South, where southern Black people were most numerous and where the majority worked as tenant farmers and field hands on the cotton farms of white landowners. The states of Mississippi and Georgia had the greatest number of recorded lynchings: from 1880 to 1930, Mississippi lynch mobs killed over five hundred African Americans; Georgia mobs murdered more than four hundred.

Throughout the late nineteenth and early twentieth centuries, a number of prominent southerners openly supported lynching, arguing that it was a necessary evil to punish Black rapists and deter others. In the late 1890s, Georgia newspaper columnist and noted women's rights activist Rebecca Latimer Felton—who would later become the first woman to serve in the U.S. Senate—endorsed such extrajudicial killings. She said, "If it takes lynching to protect women's dearest possession from drunken, ravening beasts, then I say lynch a thousand a week."[14] When opponents argued that lynching violated victims' constitutional rights, South Carolina governor Coleman Blease angrily responded, "Whenever the Constitution comes between me and the virtue of the white women of South Carolina, I say to hell with the Constitution."[15]

Black activists and white allies worked to outlaw lynching. Ida B. Wells, an African American woman born in the last years of slavery and a pioneering anti-lynching advocate, lost three friends to a lynch mob in Memphis, Tennessee, in 1892. That year, Wells published *Southern Horrors: Lynch Law in All Its Phases*, a groundbreaking work that documented the South's lynching culture and exposed the myth of the Black rapist.[16] The Tuskegee Institute and the NAACP both compiled and publicized lists of every reported lynching in the United States. In 1918, Representative Leonidas Dyer of Missouri introduced federal anti-lynching legislation that would have made local counties where lynchings took place legally liable for such killings. Throughout the early 1920s, the Dyer Bill was the subject of heated political debate, but, fiercely opposed by southern congressmen and unable to win enough northern champions, the proposed bill was never enacted.

Lynching was not the only form of racial violence that survived Reconstruction. White political violence continued to follow African Amer-

This photograph captures the lynching of Laura and Lawrence Nelson, a mother and son, on May 25, 1911, in Okemah, Oklahoma. In response to national attention, the local white newspaper in Okemah simply wrote, "While the general sentiment is adverse to the method, it is generally thought that the negroes got what would have been due them under due process of law." Wikimedia.

ican political participation and labor organization, however severely circumscribed. When the Populist insurgency created new opportunities for Black political activism, white Democrats responded with terror. In North Carolina, Populists and Republicans "fused" together and won stunning electoral gains in 1896. Shocked white Democrats formed "Red Shirt" groups—paramilitary organizations dedicated to eradicating Black political participation and restoring Democratic rule through violence and intimidation. Launching a self-described "white supremacy campaign" of violence and intimidation against Black voters and officeholders during the 1898 state elections, the Red Shirts effectively took back state government. But municipal elections were not held that year in Wilmington, where Fusionists controlled city government. After manning armed barricades blocking Black voters from entering the town to vote in the state elections, the Red Shirts drafted a "White Declaration of Independence," which declared "that that we will no longer be ruled and will never again be ruled, by men of African origin." Four hundred fifty-seven white Democrats signed the document. They also issued a twelve-hour ultimatum that the editor of the city's Black daily paper flee the city.

The editor left, but it wasn't enough. Twelve hours later, hundreds of Red Shirts raided the city's armory and ransacked the newspaper office anyway. The mob swelled and turned on the city's Black neighborhood, destroying homes and businesses and opening fire on any Black person they found. Dozens were killed and hundreds more fled the city. The mob then forced the mayor, the city's aldermen, and the police chief, at gunpoint, to immediately resign. To ensure their gains, the Democrats rounded up prominent Fusionists, placed them on railroad cars, and, under armed guard, sent them out of the state. The mob installed and swore in their own replacements. It was a full-blown coup.

Lynching and organized terror campaigns were only the violent worst of the South's racial world. Discrimination in employment and housing and the legal segregation of public and private life also reflected the rise of a new Jim Crow South. So-called Jim Crow laws legalized what custom had long dictated. Southern states and municipalities enforced racial segregation in public places and in private lives. Separate coach laws were some of the first such laws to appear, beginning in Tennessee in the 1880s. Soon schools, stores, theaters, restaurants, bathrooms, and nearly every other part of public life were segregated. So too were social lives. The sin of racial mixing, critics said, had to be heavily guarded against. Marriage laws regulated against interracial couples, and white men, ever anxious of relationships between Black men and white women, passed miscegenation laws and justified lynching as an appropriate extralegal tool to police the racial divide.

In politics, de facto limitations of Black voting had suppressed Black voters since Reconstruction. Whites stuffed ballot boxes and intimidated Black voters with physical and economic threats. And then, from roughly 1890 to 1908, southern states implemented de jure, or legal, disfranchisement. They passed laws requiring voters to pass literacy tests (which could be judged arbitrarily) and pay poll taxes (which hit poor whites and poor Blacks alike), effectively denying Black men the franchise that was supposed to have been guaranteed by the Fifteenth Amendment. Those responsible for such laws posed as reformers and justified voting restrictions as for the public good, a way to clean up politics by purging corrupt African Americans from the voting rolls.

With white supremacy secured, prominent white southerners looked outward for support. New South boosters hoped to confront post-Reconstruction uncertainties by rebuilding the South's economy and convincing the nation that the South could be more than an economically backward, race-obsessed backwater. And as they did, they began to retell the history of the recent past. A kind of civic religion known as the "Lost Cause" glorified the Confederacy and romanticized the Old South. White southerners looked forward while simultaneously harking back to a mythic imagined past inhabited by contented and loyal slaves, benevolent and generous masters, chivalric and honorable men, and pure and faithful southern belles. Secession, they said, had little to do with the institution of slavery, and soldiers fought only for home and honor, not the continued ownership of human beings. The New South, then, would be built physically with new technologies, new investments, and new industries, but undergirded by political and social custom.

Henry Grady might have declared the Confederate South dead, but its memory pervaded the thoughts and actions of white southerners. Lost Cause champions overtook the South. Women's groups, such as the United Daughters of the Confederacy, joined with Confederate veterans to preserve a pro-Confederate past. They built Confederate monuments and celebrated Confederate veterans on Memorial Day. Across the South, towns erected statues of General Robert E. Lee and other Confederate figures. By the turn of the twentieth century, the idealized Lost Cause past was entrenched not only in the South but across the country. In 1905, for instance, North Carolinian Thomas F. Dixon published a novel, *The Clansman*, which depicted the Ku Klux Klan as heroic defenders of the South against the corruption of African American and northern "carpetbag" misrule during Reconstruction. In 1915, acclaimed film director David W. Griffith adapted Dixon's novel into the groundbreaking blockbuster film, *Birth of a Nation*. (The film almost singlehandedly rejuvenated the Ku Klux Klan.) The romanticized version of the antebellum South and the distorted version of Reconstruction dominated popular imagination.[17]

While Lost Cause defenders mythologized their past, New South boosters struggled to wrench the South into the modern world. The railroads became their focus. The region had lagged behind the North in the railroad building boom of the midnineteenth century, and postwar expansion facilitated connections between the most rural segments of the population and the region's rising urban areas. Boosters campaigned for the construction of new hard-surfaced roads as well, arguing that improved roads would further increase the flow of goods and people and entice northern businesses to relocate to the region. The rising popularity of the automobile after the turn of the century only increased pressure for the construction of reliable roads between cities, towns, county seats, and the vast farmlands of the South.

Along with new transportation networks, New South boosters continued to promote industrial growth. The region witnessed the rise of various manufacturing industries, predominantly textiles, tobacco, furniture, and steel. While agriculture—cotton in particular—remained the mainstay of the region's economy, these new industries provided new wealth for owners, new investments for the region, and new opportunities for the exploding number of landless farmers to finally flee the land. Industries offered low-paying jobs but also opportunity for rural poor who could no longer sustain themselves through subsistence farming. Men, women, and children all moved into wage work. At the turn of the twentieth century, nearly one fourth of southern mill workers were children aged six to sixteen.

In most cases, as in most aspects of life in the New South, new factory jobs were racially segregated. Better-paying jobs were reserved for whites, while the most dangerous, labor-intensive, dirtiest, and lowest-paying positions were relegated to African Americans. African American women, shut out of most industries, found employment most often as domestic help for white families. As poor as white southern mill workers were, southern Black people were poorer. Some white mill workers could even afford to pay for domestic help in caring for young children, cleaning houses, doing laundry, and cooking meals. Mill villages that grew up alongside factories were whites-only, and African American families were pushed to the outer perimeter of the settlements.

That a "New South" emerged in the decades between Reconstruction and World War I is debatable. If measured by industrial output and railroad construction, the New South was a reality but if measured relative to the rest of the nation, it was a limited one. If measured in terms of racial discrimination, however, the New South looked much like the Old. Boosters such as Henry Grady said the South was done with racial questions but lynching and segregation and the institutionalization of Jim Crow exposed the South's lingering racial obsessions. Meanwhile, most southerners still toiled in agriculture and still lived in poverty. Industrial development and expanding infrastructure, rather than re-creating the South, coexisted easily with white supremacy and an impoverished agricultural economy. The trains came, factories were built, and capital was invested, but the region remained mired in poverty and racial apartheid. Much of the "New South," then, was anything but new.

V. Gender, Religion, and Culture

In 1905, Standard Oil tycoon John D. Rockefeller donated $100,000 (about $2.5 million today) to the American Board of Commissioners for

Foreign Missions. Rockefeller was the richest man in America but also one of the most hated and mistrusted. Even admirers conceded that he achieved his wealth through often illegal and usually immoral business practices. Journalist Ida Tarbell had made waves describing Standard Oil's long-standing ruthlessness and predilections for political corruption. Clergymen, led by reformer Washington Gladden, fiercely protested the donation. A decade earlier, Gladden had asked of such donations, "Is this clean money? Can any man, can any institution, knowing its origin, touch it without being defiled?" Gladden said, "In the cool brutality with which properties are wrecked, securities destroyed, and people by the hundreds robbed of their little all to build up the fortunes of the multi-millionaires, we have an appalling revelation of the kind of monster that a human being may become."[18]

Despite widespread criticism, the board accepted Rockefeller's donation. Board president Samuel Capen did not defend Rockefeller, arguing that the gift was charitable and the board could not assess the origin of every donation, but the dispute shook Capen. Was a corporate background incompatible with a religious organization? The "tainted

Visitors to the Columbian Exposition of 1893 took in the view of the Court of Honor from the roof of the Manufacturers Building. Art Institute of Chicago, via Wikimedia.

money debate" reflected questions about the proper relationship between religion and capitalism. With rising income inequality, would religious groups be forced to support either the elite or the disempowered? What was moral in the new industrial United States? And what obligations did wealth bring? Steel magnate Andrew Carnegie popularized the idea of a "gospel of wealth" in an 1889 article, claiming that "the true antidote for the temporary unequal distribution of wealth" was the moral obligation of the rich to give to charity.[19] Farmers and labor organizers, meanwhile, argued that God had blessed the weak and that new Gilded Age fortunes and corporate management were inherently immoral. As time passed, American churches increasingly adapted themselves to the new industrial order. Even Gladden came to accept donations from the so-called robber barons, such as the Baptist John D. Rockefeller, who increasingly touted the morality of business.

Secular knowledge-seeking and Gilded Age dollars increasingly muscled out the traditional role of religion in American higher education as well. The Gilded Age elite funneled their fortunes into new elite private institutions. The Morrill Land Grants of 1862 and 1890 subsidized new schools that emphasized practical knowledge in science, engineering, and agriculture. The 1890 Act also provided for Black colleges in states with segregated universities, nine years after Booker T. Washington founded the Tuskegee Institute in Alabama, a model of Black vocational education that Washington championed across the South and much of the country. Daniel Coit Gilman, meanwhile, borrowed the models of research-based graduate education from German universities—a popular destination for elite Americans who studied abroad—when he presided over the newly established Johns Hopkins University in 1876. At Harvard, educational reformer Charles William Eliot advocated for and modeled for the nation the replacement of a strictly guided classical curriculum with a more open-ended and practical-minded elective system. At the same time, women occupied a larger and larger percentage of American college students, either as students at separate women's colleges or, increasingly, at co-educational institutions. Such trends, in many ways, mirrored emerging social and cultural forces in America, and women's greater presence in American life—as typified by higher education—became sites for public discussion over the fate of traditional American masculinity.[20]

The economic and social changes of the late nineteenth and early twentieth centuries—including increased urbanization, immigration, advancements in science and technology, patterns of consumption and the new availability of goods, and new awareness of economic, racial, and gender inequalities—challenged traditional gender norms. At the same time, urban spaces and shifting cultural and social values presented new opportunities to challenge traditional gender and sexual norms. Many women, carrying on a campaign that stretched long into the past, vied for equal rights. They became activists: they targeted municipal reforms, launched labor rights campaigns, and, above all, bolstered the suffrage movement.

Urbanization and immigration fueled anxieties that old social mores were being subverted and that old forms of social and moral policing were increasingly inadequate. The anonymity of urban spaces presented an opportunity in particular for female sexuality and for male and female sexual experimentation along a spectrum of orientations and gender identities. Anxiety over female sexuality reflected generational tensions and differences, as well as racial and class ones. As young women pushed back against social mores through premarital sexual exploration and expression, social welfare experts and moral reformers labeled such girls feeble-minded, believing even that such unfeminine behavior could be symptomatic of clinical insanity rather than free-willed expression. Generational differences exacerbated the social and familial tensions provoked by shifting gender norms. Youths challenged the norms of their parents' generations by donning new fashions and enjoying the delights

Amusement-hungry Americans flocked to new entertainments at the turn of the twentieth century. In this early-twentieth-century photograph, visitors enjoy Luna Park, one of the original amusement parks on Brooklyn's famous Coney Island. Visitors to Coney Island's Luna Park, c. 1910–1915. Library of Congress.

of the city. Women's fashion loosed its physical constraints: corsets relaxed and hemlines rose. The newfound physical freedom enabled by looser dress was also mimicked in the pursuit of other freedoms.

While many women worked to liberate themselves, many, sometimes simultaneously, worked to uplift others. Women's work against alcohol propelled temperance into one of the foremost moral reforms of the period. Middle-class, typically Protestant women based their assault on alcohol on the basis of their feminine virtue, Christian sentiment, and their protective role in the family and home. Others, like Jane Addams and settlement house workers, sought to impart a middle-class education on immigrant and working-class women through the establishment of settlement homes. Other reformers touted a "scientific motherhood": the new science of hygiene was deployed as a method of both social uplift and moralizing, particularly of working-class and immigrant women.

Women vocalized new discontents through literature. Charlotte Perkins Gilman's short story "The Yellow Wallpaper" attacked the "naturalness" of feminine domesticity and critiqued Victorian psychological remedies administered to women, such as the "rest cure." Kate Chopin's *The Awakening*, set in the American South, likewise criticized the domestic and familial role ascribed to women by society and gave expression to feelings of malaise, desperation, and desire. Such literature directly challenged the status quo of the Victorian era's constructions of femininity and feminine virtue, as well as established feminine roles.

While many men worried about female activism, they worried too about their own masculinity. To anxious observers, industrial capitalism was withering American manhood. Rather than working on farms and in factories, where young men formed physical muscle and spiritual grit, new generations of workers labored behind desks, wore white collars, and, in the words of Supreme Court Justice Oliver Wendell Holmes, appeared "black-coated, stiff-jointed, soft-muscled, [and] paste-complexioned."[21] Neurologist George Beard even coined a medical term, *neurasthenia*, for a new emasculated condition that was marked by depression, indigestion, hypochondria, and extreme nervousness. The philosopher William James called it "Americanitis." Academics increasingly warned that America had become a nation of emasculated men.

Churches too worried about feminization. Women had always comprised a clear majority of church memberships in the United States, but now the theologian Washington Gladden said, "A preponderance of female influence in the Church or anywhere else in society is unnatural and injurious." Many feared that the feminized church had feminized Christ himself. Rather than a rough-hewn carpenter, Jesus had been made "mushy" and "sweetly effeminate," in the words of Walter Rauschenbusch. Advocates of a so-called muscular Christianity sought to stiffen young men's backbones by putting them back in touch with their primal manliness. Pulling from contemporary developmental theory, they believed that young men ought to evolve as civilization evolved, advancing from primitive nature-dwelling to modern industrial enlightenment. To facilitate "primitive" encounters with nature, muscular Christians founded summer camps and outdoor boys' clubs like the Woodcraft Indians, the Sons of Daniel Boone, and the Boy Brigades—all precursors of the Boy Scouts. Other champions of muscular Christianity, such as the newly formed Young Men's Christian Association, built gymnasiums, often attached to churches, where youths could strengthen their bodies as well as their spirits. It was a Young Men's Christian Association (YMCA) leader who coined the term *bodybuilding*, and others invented the sports of basketball and volleyball.[22]

Muscular Christianity, though, was about even more than building strong bodies and minds. Many advocates also ardently championed Western imperialism, cheering on attempts to civilize non-Western peoples. Gilded Age men were encouraged to embrace a particular vision of

Taken a few years after the publication of "The Yellow Wallpaper," this portrait photograph shows activist Charlotte Perkins Gilman's feminine poise and respectability even as she sought massive change for women's place in society. An outspoken supporter of women's rights, Gilman wrote short stories, novels, and poetry that challenged the supposedly "natural" inferiority of women. Wikimedia.

masculinity connected intimately with the rising tides of nationalism, militarism, and imperialism. Contemporary ideals of American masculinity at the turn of the century developed in concert with the United States' imperial and militaristic endeavors in the West and abroad. During the Spanish-American War in 1898, Teddy Roosevelt and his Rough Riders embodied the idealized image of the tall, strong, virile, and fit American man that simultaneously epitomized the ideals of power that informed the United States' imperial agenda. Roosevelt and others like him believed a reinvigorated masculinity would preserve the American race's superiority against foreign foes and the effeminizing effects of overcivilization.

But while many fretted about traditional American life, others lost themselves in new forms of mass culture. Vaudeville signaled new cultural worlds. A unique variety of popular entertainments, these traveling circuit shows first appeared during the Civil War and peaked between 1880 and 1920. Vaudeville shows featured comedians, musicians, actors, jugglers, and other talents that could captivate an audience. Unlike earlier rowdy acts meant for a male audience that included alcohol, vaudeville was considered family-friendly, "polite" entertainment, though the acts involved offensive ethnic and racial caricatures of African Americans and recent immigrants. Vaudeville performances were often small and quirky, though venues such as the renowned Palace Theatre in New York City signaled true stardom for many performers. Popular entertainers such as silent film star Charlie Chaplin and magician Harry Houdini made names for themselves on the vaudeville circuit. But if live entertainment still captivated audiences, others looked to entirely new technologies.

By the turn of the century, two technologies pioneered by Edison—the phonograph and motion pictures—stood ready to revolutionize leisure and help create the mass entertainment culture of the twentieth century. The phonograph was the first reliable device capable of recording and reproducing sound. But it was more than that. The phonograph could create multiple copies of recordings, sparking a great expansion of the market for popular music. Although the phonograph was a technical success, Edison at first had trouble developing commercial applications for it. He thought it might be used for dictation, recording audio letters, preserving speeches and dying words of great men, producing talking clocks, or teaching elocution. He did not anticipate that its greatest use would be in the field of mass entertainment, but Edison's sales agents soon reported that many phonographs were being used for just that, es-

Designers of the 1893 Columbian Exposition in Chicago built the White City in a neoclassical architectural style. The integrated design of buildings, walkways, and landscapes propelled the burgeoning City Beautiful movement. The Fair itself was a huge success, bringing more than twenty-seven million people to Chicago and helping to establish the ideology of American exceptionalism. Wikimedia.

pecially in so-called phonograph parlors, where customers could pay a nickel to hear a piece of music. By the turn of the century, Americans were purchasing phonographs for home use. Entertainment became the phonograph's major market.

Inspired by the success of the phonograph as an entertainment device, Edison decided in 1888 to develop "an instrument which does for the Eye what the phonograph does for the Ear." In 1888, he patented the concept of motion pictures. In 1889, he innovated the rolling of film. By 1891, he was exhibiting a motion-picture camera (a *kinetograph*) and a viewer (a *kinetoscope*). By 1894, the Edison Company had produced about seventy-five films suitable for sale and viewing. They could be viewed through a small eyepiece in an arcade or parlor. They were short, typically about three minutes long. Many of the early films depicted athletic feats and competitions. One 1894 film, for example, showed a six-round boxing match. The catalog description gave a sense of the appeal it had for male viewers: "Full of hard fighting, clever hits, punches, leads, dodges, body blows and some slugging." Other early kinetoscope subjects included Indian dances, nature and outdoor scenes, re-creations of historical events, and humorous skits. By 1896, the Edison Vitascope could project film, shifting audiences away from arcades and pulling them into theaters. Edison's film catalog meanwhile grew in sophistication. He sent filmmakers to distant and exotic locales like Japan and China. Long-form fictional films created a demand for "movie stars," such as the glamorous Mary Pickford, the swashbuckling Douglas Fairbanks, the acrobatic comedian Buster Keaton, who began to appear in the popular imagination beginning around 1910. Alongside professional boxing and baseball, the film industry was creating the modern culture of celebrity that would characterize twentieth-century mass entertainment.[23]

VI. Conclusion

After enduring four bloody years of warfare and a strained, decade-long effort to reconstruct the defeated South, the United States abandoned itself to industrial development. Businesses expanded in scale and scope. The nature of labor shifted. A middle class rose. Wealth concentrated. Immigrants crowded into the cities, which grew upward and outward. The Jim Crow South stripped away the vestiges of Reconstruction, and New South boosters papered over the scars. Industrialists hunted profits. Evangelists appealed to people's morals. Consumers lost themselves in new goods and new technologies. Women emerging into new urban spaces embraced new social possibilities. In all of its many facets, by the turn of the twentieth century, the United States had been radically transformed. And the transformations continued to ripple outward into the West and overseas, and inward into radical protest and progressive reforms. For Americans at the twilight of the nineteenth century and the dawn of the twentieth, a bold new world loomed.

VII. Reference Material

This chapter was edited by David Hochfelder, with content contributions by Jacob Betz, David Hochfelder, Gerard Koeppel, Scott Libson, Kyle Livie, Paul Matzko, Isabella Morales, Andrew Robichaud, Kate Sohasky, Joseph Super, Susan Thomas, Shawn Varghese, Kaylynn Washnock, and Kevin Young.

Recommended citation: Jacob Betz et al., "Life in Industrial America," David Hochfelder, ed., in *The American Yawp*, eds. Joseph Locke and Ben Wright (Stanford, CA: Stanford University Press, 2019).

NOTES TO CHAPTER 18

1. Rudyard Kipling, *The Works of Rudyard Kipling, Volume II* (New York: Doubleday, 1899), 141.

2. For the transformation of Chicago, see William Cronon's defining work, *Nature's Metropolis: Chicago and the West* (New York: Norton, 1991).

3. See Richard White, *Railroaded: The Transcontinentals and the Making of Modern America* (New York: Norton, 2011).

4. Cronon, *Nature's Metropolis*, 239.

5. David Hochfelder, "Edison and the Age of Invention," in *A Companion to the Reconstruction Presidents 1865–1881*, ed. Edward O. Frantz (Chichester, UK: Blackwell, 2014), 499.

6. Ibid., 499–517.

7. William L. Riordon, *Plunkitt of Tammany Hall: A Series of Very Plain Talks on Very Practical Politics* (New York: McClure, Phillips, 1905).

8. Kenyon L. Butterfield, *Chapters in Rural Progress* (Chicago: University of Chicago Press, 1908), 15.

9. L. H. Bailey, *The Harvest of the Year to the Tiller of the Soil* (New York: Macmillan, 1927), 60.

10. Oscar Osburn Winther, "The Rise of Metropolitan Los Angeles, 1870–1900," *Huntington Library Quarterly* 10 (August 1947): 391–405.

11. "Chamber Meeting," Glendora *Gleaner*, September 28, 1923.

12. Henry Grady, *The Complete Orations and Speeches of Henry Grady*, ed. Edwin DuBois Shurter (New York: Hinds, Noble and Eldredge, 1910), 7.

13. William Fitzhugh Brundage, *Lynching in the New South: Georgia and Virginia, 1880–1930* (Champaign: University of Illinois Press, 1993), 82–84.

14. Grace Elizabeth Hale, *Making Whiteness: The Culture of Segregation in the South, 1890–1940* (New York: Pantheon Books, 1998), 201.

15. Jacquelyn Dowd Hall, *Revolt Against Chivalry: Jessie Daniel Ames and the Women's Campaign Against Lynching* (New York: Columbia University Press, 1993), 195.

16. Ida B. Wells, *Crusade for Justice: The Autobiography of Ida B. Wells* (Chicago: University of Chicago Press, 1970).

17. Charles Reagan Wilson, *Baptized in Blood: The Religion of the Lost Cause, 1865–1920* (Athens: University of Georgia Press, 1980).

18. Washington Gladden, *The New Idolatry and Other Discussions* (New York: McClure, Phillips, 1905), 21.

19. Andrew Carnegie, "Wealth," *North American Review* 391 (June 1889): 656, 660.

20. George M. Marsden, *The Soul of the American University: From Protestant Establishment to Established Nonbelief* (New York: Oxford University Press, 1994); Julie A. Reuben, *The Making of the Modern University: Intellectual*

Transformation and the Marginalization of Morality (Chicago: University of Chicago Press, 1996); John R. Thelin, *A History of American Higher Education*, 3rd edition (Baltimore: Johns Hopkins University Press, 2019).

21. Michael S. Kimmel, *Manhood in America: A Cultural History* (New York: Oxford University Press, 2006), 41.

22. Norman Vance, *The Sinews of the Spirit: The Ideal of Christian Manliness in Victorian Literature and Religious Thought* (New York: Cambridge University Press, 1985).

23. Hochfelder, "Edison and the Age of Invention," 499–517.

RECOMMENDED READING

Ayers, Edward. *The Promise of the New South*. New York: Oxford University Press, 1992.

Beckert, Sven. *Monied Metropolis: New York City and the Consolidation of the American Bourgeoisie, 1850–1896*. Cambridge, UK: Cambridge University Press, 2001.

Bederman, Gail. *Manliness and Civilization: A Cultural History of Gender and Race in the United States, 1880–1917*. Chicago: University of Chicago Press, 1995.

Blight, David. *Race and Reunion: The Civil War in American Memory*. Cambridge, MA: Harvard University Press, 2001.

Briggs, Laura. "The Race of Hysteria: 'Overcivilization' and the 'Savage' Woman in Late Nineteenth-Century Obstetrics and Gynecology." *American Quarterly* 52 (June 2000). 246–273.

Chauncey, George. *Gay New York: Gender, Urban Culture, and the Making of the Gay Male World, 1890–1940*. New York: Basic Books, 1995.

Cole, Stephanie, and Natalie J. Ring, eds. *The Folly of Jim Crow: Rethinking the Segregated South*. College Station: Texas A&M University Press, 2012.

Cott, Nancy. *The Grounding of Modern Feminism*. New Haven, CT: Yale University Press, 1987.

Cronon, William. *Nature's Metropolis: Chicago and the Great West*. New York: Norton, 1991.

Edwards, Rebecca. *New Spirits: Americans in the Gilded Age, 1865–1905*. New York: Oxford University Press, 2005.

Gilmore, Glenda Elizabeth. *Gender and Jim Crow: Women and the Politics of White Supremacy in North Carolina, 1896–1920*. Chapel Hill: University of North Carolina Press, 1996.

Gutman, Herbert. *Work, Culture and Society in Industrializing America: Essays in American Working-Class and Social History*. New York: Knopf, 1976.

Hale, Grace Elizabeth. *Making Whiteness: The Culture of Segregation in the South, 1890–1940*. New York: Pantheon Books, 1998.

Hicks, Cheryl. *Talk with You Like a Woman: African American Women, Justice, and Reform in New York, 1890–1935*. Chapel Hill: University of North Carolina Press, 2010.

Kasson, John F. *Amusing the Million: Coney Island at the Turn of the Century*. New York: Hill and Wang, 1978.

Leach, William. *Land of Desire: Merchants, Power, and the Rise of a New American Culture.* New York: Random House, 1993.

Lears, T. J. Jackson. *No Place of Grace: Antimodernism and the Transformation of American Culture, 1880–1920.* Chicago: University of Chicago Press, 1981.

Odem, Mary. *Delinquent Daughters: Protecting and Policing Adolescent Female Sexuality in the United States, 1885–1920.* Chapel Hill: University of North Carolina Press, 1995.

Peiss, Kathy. *Cheap Amusements. Working Women and Leisure in Turn-of-the-Century New York.* Philadelphia: Temple University Press, 1986.

Peiss, Kathy. *Hope in a Jar: The Making of America's Beauty Culture.* Philadelphia: University of Pennsylvania Press, 1999.

Putney, Clifford. *Manhood and Sports in Protestant America, 1880–1920.* Cambridge, MA: Harvard University Press, 2001.

Silber, Nina. *The Romance of Reunion: Northerners and the South, 1865–1900.* Chapel Hill: University of North Carolina Press, 1997.

Strouse, Jean. *Alice James: A Biography.* New York: Houghton Mifflin, 1980.

Trachtenberg, Alan. *The Incorporation of America: Culture and Society in the Gilded Age.* New York: Hill and Wang, 2007.

Woodward, C. Vann. *Origins of the New South, 1877–1913.* Baton Rouge: LSU Press, 1951.

19

American Empire

I. Introduction

The word *empire* might conjure images of ancient Rome, the Persian Empire, or the British Empire—powers that depended variously on military conquest, colonization, occupation, or direct resource exploitation—but empires can take many forms and imperial processes can occur in many contexts. One hundred years after the United States won its independence from the British Empire, had it become an empire of its own?

In the decades after the American Civil War, the United States exerted itself in the service of American interests around the world. In the Pacific, Latin America, and the Middle East, and most explicitly in the Spanish-American War and under the foreign policy of Theodore Roosevelt and William Howard Taft, the United States expanded on a long history of exploration, trade, and cultural exchange to practice something that looked remarkably like empire. The question of American imperialism,

A political cartoon in *Puck* magazine on January 25, 1899, captures the mindset of American imperialists. Library of Congress.

then, seeks to understand not only direct American interventions in such places as Cuba, the Philippines, Hawaii, Guam, and Puerto Rico, but also the deeper history of American engagement with the wider world and the subsequent ways in which American economic, political, and cultural power has shaped the actions, choices, and possibilities of other groups and nations.

Meanwhile, as the United States asserted itself abroad, it acquired increasingly higher numbers of foreign peoples at home. European and Asian immigrants poured into the United States. In a sense, imperialism and immigration raised similar questions about American identity: Who was an "American," and who wasn't? What were the nation's obligations to foreign powers and foreign peoples? And how accessible—and how fluid—should American identity be for newcomers? All such questions confronted late-nineteenth-century Americans with unprecedented urgency.

II. Patterns of American Interventions

American interventions in Mexico, China, and the Middle East reflected the United States' new eagerness to intervene in foreign governments to protect American economic interests abroad.

The United States had long been involved in Pacific commerce. American ships had been traveling to China, for instance, since 1784. As a percentage of total American foreign trade, Asian trade remained comparatively small, and yet the idea that Asian markets were vital to American commerce affected American policy and, when those markets were threatened, prompted interventions.[1] In 1899, secretary of state John Hay articulated the Open Door Policy, which called for all Western powers to have equal access to Chinese markets. Hay feared that other imperial powers—Japan, Great Britain, Germany, France, Italy, and Russia—planned to carve China into spheres of influence. It was in the economic interest of American business to maintain China for free trade. The following year, in 1900, American troops joined a multinational force that intervened to prevent the closing of trade by putting down the Boxer Rebellion, a movement opposed to foreign businesses and missionaries operating in China. President McKinley sent the U.S. Army without consulting Congress, setting a precedent for U.S. presidents to order American troops to action around the world under their executive powers.[2]

The United States was not only ready to intervene in foreign affairs to preserve foreign markets, it was willing to take territory. The United States acquired its first Pacific territories with the Guano Islands Act of 1856. Guano—collected bird excrement—was a popular fertilizer integral to industrial farming. The act authorized and encouraged Americans to venture into the seas and claim islands with guano deposits for the United States. These acquisitions were the first insular, unincorporated territories of the United States: they were neither part of a state nor a federal district, and they were not on the path to ever attain such a status. The act, though little known, offered a precedent for future American acquisitions.[3]

Merchants, of course, weren't the only American travelers in the Pacific. Christian missionaries soon followed explorers and traders. The first American missionaries arrived in Hawaii in 1820 and China in 1830, for example. Missionaries, though, often worked alongside business interests, and American missionaries in Hawaii, for instance, obtained large tracts of land and started lucrative sugar plantations. During the nineteenth century, Hawaii was ruled by an oligarchy based on the sugar companies, together known as the "Big Five." This white American (*haole*) elite was extremely powerful, but they still operated outside the formal expression of American state power.[4]

As many Americans looked for empire across the Pacific, others looked to Latin America. The United States, long a participant in an increasingly complex network of economic, social, and cultural interactions in Latin America, entered the late nineteenth century with a new aggressive and interventionist attitude toward its southern neighbors.

American capitalists invested enormous sums of money in Mexico during the late nineteenth and early twentieth centuries, during the long reign of the corrupt yet stable regime of the modernization-hungry president Porfirio Diaz. But in 1910 the Mexican people revolted against Díaz, ending his authoritarian regime but also his friendliness toward the business interests of the United States. In the midst of the terrible destruction wrought by the fighting, Americans with investment interests pleaded for governmental help. But the U.S. government tried to control events and politics that could not be controlled. More and more American businessmen called for military intervention. When the brutal strongman Victoriano Huerta executed the revolutionary, democratically elected president Francisco Madero in 1913, newly inaugurated American president Woodrow Wilson put pressure on Mexico's new regime.

Wilson refused to recognize the new government and demanded that Huerta step aside and allow free elections to take place. Huerta refused.[5]

When Mexican forces mistakenly arrested American sailors in the port city of Tampico in April 1914, Wilson saw the opportunity to apply additional pressure on Huerta. Huerta refused to make amends, and Wilson therefore asked Congress for authority to use force against Mexico. But even before Congress could respond, Wilson invaded and took the port city of Veracruz to prevent, he said, a German shipment of arms from reaching Huerta's forces. The Huerta government fell in July 1914, and the American occupation lasted until November, when Venustiano Carranza, a rival of Huerta, took power. When Wilson threw American support behind Carranza, and not his more radical and now-rival Pancho Villa, Villa and several hundred supporters attacked American interests and raided the town of Columbus, New Mexico, in March 1916, and killed over a dozen soldiers and civilians. Wilson ordered a punitive expedition of several thousand soldiers led by General John J. "Blackjack" Pershing to enter northern Mexico and capture Villa. But Villa eluded Pershing for nearly a year and, in 1917, with war in Europe looming and great injury done to U.S.-Mexican relations, Pershing left Mexico.[6]

The United States' actions during the Mexican Revolution reflected long-standing American policy that justified interventionist actions in Latin American politics because of their potential bearing on the United States: on citizens, on shared territorial borders, and, perhaps most significantly, on economic investments. This example highlights the role of geography, or perhaps proximity, in the pursuit of imperial outcomes. But American interactions in more distant locations, in the Middle East, for instance, look quite different.

In 1867, Mark Twain traveled to the Middle East as part of a large tour group of Americans. In his satirical travelogue, *The Innocents Abroad*, he wrote, "The people [of the Middle East] stared at us everywhere, and we [Americans] stared at them. We generally made them feel rather small, too, before we got done with them, because we bore down on them with America's greatness until we crushed them."[7] When Americans later intervened in the Middle East, they would do so convinced of their own superiority.

The U.S. government had traditionally had little contact with the Middle East. Trade was limited, too limited for an economic relationship to be deemed vital to the national interest, but treaties were nevertheless signed between the U.S. and powers in the Middle East. Still, the majority of American involvement in the Middle East prior to World War I came not in the form of trade but in education, science, and humanitarian aid. American missionaries led the way. The first Protestant missionaries had arrived in 1819. Soon the American Board of Commissioners for Foreign Missions and the boards of missions of the Reformed Church of America became dominant in missionary enterprises. Missions were established in almost every country of the Middle East, and even though their efforts resulted in relatively few converts, missionaries helped establish hospitals and schools, and their work laid the foundation for the establishment of Western-style universities, such as Robert College in Istanbul, Turkey (1863), the American University of Beirut (1866), and the American University of Cairo (1919).[8]

III. 1898

Although the United States had a long history of international economic, military, and cultural engagement that stretched back deep into the eighteenth century, the Spanish-American and Philippine-American Wars (1898–1902) marked a crucial turning point in American interventions abroad. In pursuing war with Spain, and then engaging in counterrevolutionary conflict in the Philippines, the United States expanded the scope and strength of its global reach. Over the next two decades, the United States would become increasingly involved in international politics, particularly in Latin America. These new conflicts and ensuing territorial problems forced Americans to confront the ideological elements of imperialism. Should the United States act as an empire? Or were foreign interventions and the taking of territory antithetical to its founding democratic ideals? What exactly would be the relationship between the United States and its territories? And could colonial subjects be successfully and safely incorporated into the body politic as American citizens? The Spanish-American and Philippine-American Wars brought these questions, which had always lurked behind discussions of American expansion, out into the open.

In 1898, Americans began in earnest to turn their attention southward to problems plaguing their neighbor Cuba. Since the middle of the nineteenth century, Cubans had tried unsuccessfully again and again to gain independence from Spain. The latest uprising, and the one that would prove fatal to Spain's colonial designs, began in 1895 and was still raging in the winter of 1898. By that time, in an attempt to crush the

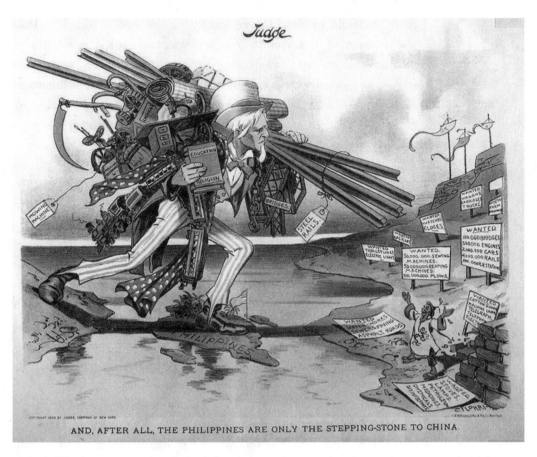

Judge

AND, AFTER ALL, THE PHILIPPINES ARE ONLY THE STEPPING-STONE TO CHINA.

In this political cartoon, Uncle Sam, loaded with the implements of modern civilization, uses the Philippines as a stepping-stone to cross the Pacific to China, which excitedly awaits Sam's arrival. Such cartoons captured Americans' growing infatuation with imperialist and expansionist policies. c. 1900–1902. Wikimedia.

uprising, Spanish general Valeriano Weyler y Nicolau had been conducting a policy of reconcentration—forcing Cubans living in certain cities to relocate en masse to military camps—for about two years. Prominent newspaper publishers sensationalized Spanish atrocities. Cubans in the United States and their allies raised cries of *Cuba Libre!* And while the U.S. government proclaimed a wish to avoid armed conflict with Spain, President McKinley became increasingly concerned about the safety of American lives and property in Cuba. He ordered the battleship *Maine* to Havana harbor in January 1898.

The *Maine* sat undisturbed in the harbor for about two weeks. Then, on the evening of February 15, a titanic explosion tore open the ship and sent it to the bottom of the ocean. Three quarters of the ship's 354 occupants died. A naval board of inquiry immediately began an investigation to ascertain the cause of the explosion, but the loudest Americans had already decided that Spanish treachery was to blame. Capitalizing on the outrage, "yellow journals"—newspapers that promoted sensational stories, notoriously at the cost of accuracy—such as William Randolph Hearst's *New York Journal* called for war with Spain. When urgent negotiations failed to produce a mutually agreeable settlement, Congress officially declared war on April 25.

Although America's war effort began haphazardly, Spain's decaying military crumbled. Military victories for the United States came quickly. In the Pacific, on May 1, Commodore George Dewey engaged the Spanish fleet outside Manila, the capital of the Philippines (another Spanish colonial possession), destroyed it, and proceeded to blockade Manila harbor. Two months later, American troops took Cuba's San Juan Heights in what would become the most well-known battle of the war, winning fame not for regular soldiers but for the irregular, especially Theodore Roosevelt and his Rough Riders. Roosevelt had been the assistant secretary of the navy but had resigned his position in order to see action in the war. His actions in Cuba made him a national celebrity. As disease began to eat away at American troops, the Spanish suffered the loss of Santiago de Cuba on July 17, effectively ending the war. The two nations agreed to a cease-fire on August 12 and formally signed the Treaty of Paris in December. The terms of the treaty stipulated, among other things, that the United States would acquire Spain's former holdings of Guam, Puerto Rico, and the Philippines.

Secretary of state John Hay memorably referred to the conflict as a "splendid little war," and at the time it certainly appeared that way. Fewer than four hundred Americans died in battle in a war that lasted about fifteen weeks. Contemporaries celebrated American victories as the providential act of God. The influential Brooklyn minister Lyman Abbott, for instance, declared that Americans were "an elect people of God" and saw divine providence in Dewey's victory at Manila.[9] Some, such as Senator Albert J. Beveridge of Indiana, took matters one step further, seeing in American victory an opportunity for imperialism. In Beveridge's view, America had a "mission to perform" and a "duty to discharge" around the world.[10] What Beveridge envisioned was nothing less than an American empire.

But the question of whether the United States *should* become an empire was sharply debated across the nation in the aftermath of the Spanish-American War and the acquisition of Hawaii in July 1898. At the behest of American businessmen who had overthrown the Hawaiian

This 1914 political cartoon shows embodiments of colonies and territories before and after American interventions. The differences are obvious and exaggerated, with the top figures described as "oppressed" by the weight of industrial slavery until America "rescued" them, turning them into the respectable and successful businessmen seen on the bottom half. Those who claimed that American imperialism brought civilization and prosperity to destitute peoples used such visuals to support their cause. Wikimedia.

monarchy, the United States annexed the Hawaiian Islands and their rich plantations. Between Hawaii and a number of former Spanish possessions, many Americans coveted the economic and political advantages that increased territory would bring. Those opposed to expansion, however, worried that imperial ambitions did not accord with the nation's founding ideals. American actions in the Philippines brought all of these discussions to a head.

The Philippines were an afterthought of the Spanish-American War, but when the smoke cleared, the United States found itself in possession of a key foothold in the Pacific. After Dewey's victory over the Spanish fleet in the Battle of Manila Bay, conversations about how to proceed occupied the attentions of President McKinley, political leaders from both parties, and the popular press. American and Philippine forces (under the leadership of Emilio Aguinaldo) were in communication: Would the Americans offer their support to the Filipinos and their ongoing efforts against the Spanish? Or would the Americans replace the Spanish as a colonial occupying force? American forces were instructed to secure Manila without allowing Philippine forces to enter the Walled

City (the seat of the Spanish colonial government), hinting, perhaps, at things to come. Americans wondered what would happen next. Perhaps a good many ordinary Americans shared the bewildered sentiments of Mr. Dooley, the fictional Irish-American barkeeper whom humorist Finley Peter Dunne used to satirize American life: "I don't know what to do with th' Ph'lippeens anny more thin I did las' summer, befure I heerd tell iv thim. . . . We can't sell thim, we can't ate thim, an' we can't throw thim into the th' alley whin no wan is lookin'."[11]

As debates about American imperialism continued against the backdrop of an upcoming presidential election, tensions in the Philippines escalated. Emilio Aguinaldo was inaugurated as president of the First Philippine Republic (or Malolos Republic) in late January 1899; fighting between American and Philippine forces began in early February; and in April 1899, Congress ratified the 1898 Treaty of Paris, which concluded the Spanish-American War and gave Spain $20 million in exchange for the Philippine Islands.[12]

Like the Cubans, Filipinos had waged a long war against their Spanish colonizers. The United States could have given them the independence they had long fought for, but, instead, at the behest of President William McKinley, the United States occupied the islands and from 1899 to 1902 waged a bloody series of conflicts against Filipino insurrectionists that cost far more lives than the war with Spain. Under the leadership of Emilio Aguinaldo, Filipinos who had fought for freedom against the Spanish now fought for freedom against the very nation that had claimed to have liberated them from Spanish tyranny.[13]

The Philippine Insurrection, or the Philippine-American War, was a brutal conflict of occupation and insurgency. Contemporaries compared the guerrilla-style warfare in challenging and unfamiliar terrain to the American experiences in the so-called Indian Wars of the late nineteenth century. Many commented on its brutality and the uncertain mission of American troops. An April 1899 dispatch from a *Harper's Weekly* correspondent began, "A week has passed—a week of fighting and marching, of jungles and rivers, of incident and adventure so varied and of so rapid transition that to sit down to write about it makes one feel as if he were trying to describe a dream where time, space, and all the logical sequences of ordinary life are upset in the unrelenting brutality of war."[14] John Bass described his experiences in detail, and his reportage, combined with accounts that came directly from soldiers, helped shape public knowledge about the war. Reports of cruelty on both sides and a few high-profile military investigations ensured continued public attention to events across the Pacific.

Amid fighting to secure the Philippine Islands, the federal government sent two Philippine Commissions to assess the situation in the islands and make recommendations for a civilian colonial government. A civilian administration, with William H. Taft as the first governor-general (1901–1903), was established with military support. Although President Theodore Roosevelt declared the war to be over in 1902, resistance and occasional fighting continued into the second decade of the twentieth century.[15]

Debates about American imperialism dominated headlines and tapped into core ideas about American identity and the proper role of the United States in the larger world. Should a former colony, established on the principles of freedom, liberty, and sovereignty, become a colonizer itself? What was imperialism, anyway? Many framed the Filipino conflict as a Protestant, civilizing mission. Others framed American imperialism in the Philippines as nothing new, as simply the extension of a never-ending westward American expansion. It was simply destiny. Some

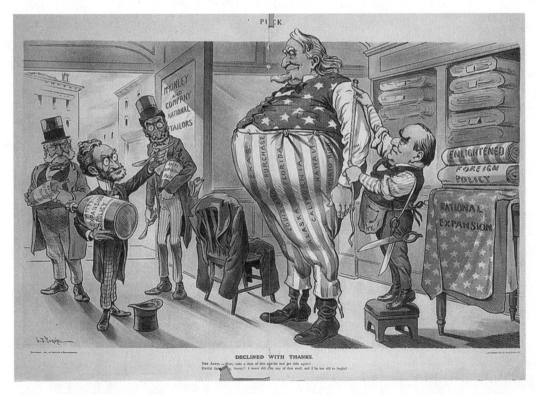

In this 1900 political cartoon, President McKinley measures an obese Uncle Sam for larger clothing, while anti-expansionists like Joseph Pulitzer unsuccessfully offer him a weight-loss elixir. As the nation increased its imperialistic presence and mission, many worried that America would grow too big for its own good. Wikimedia.

saw imperialism as a way to reenergize the nation by asserting national authority and power around the globe. Others baldly recognized the opportunities the Philippine Islands presented for access to Asian markets. But critics grew loud. The American Anti-Imperialist League, founded in 1899 and populated by such prominent Americans as Mark Twain, Andrew Carnegie, and Jane Addams, protested American imperial actions and articulated a platform that decried foreign subjugation and upheld the rights of all to self-governance. Still others embraced anti-imperialist stances because of concerns about immigration and American racial identity, afraid that American purity stood imperiled by contact with strange and foreign peoples. For whatever reason, however, the onset or acceleration of imperialism was a controversial and landmark moment in American history. America had become a preeminent force in the world.

IV. Theodore Roosevelt and American Imperialism

Under the leadership of President Theodore Roosevelt, the United States emerged from the nineteenth century with ambitious designs on global power through military might, territorial expansion, and economic influence. Though the Spanish-American War had begun under the administration of William McKinley, Roosevelt—the hero of San Juan Hill, assistant secretary of the navy, vice president, and president—was arguably the most visible and influential proponent of American imperialism at the turn of the century. Roosevelt's emphasis on developing the American navy, and on Latin America as a key strategic area of U.S. foreign policy, would have long-term consequences.

In return for Roosevelt's support of the Republican nominee, William McKinley, in the 1896 presidential election, McKinley appointed Roosevelt as assistant secretary of the navy. The head of the department, John Long, had a competent but lackadaisical managerial style that allowed Roosevelt a great deal of freedom which he used to network with such luminaries as military theorists Alfred Thayer Mahan and naval officer George Dewey and politicians such as Henry Cabot Lodge and William Howard Taft. During his tenure he oversaw the construction of new battleships and the implementation of new technology and laid the groundwork for new shipyards, all with the goal of projecting America's power across the oceans. Roosevelt wanted to expand American influence. For instance, he advocated for the annexation of Hawaii for several reasons: it was within the American sphere of influence, it would deny

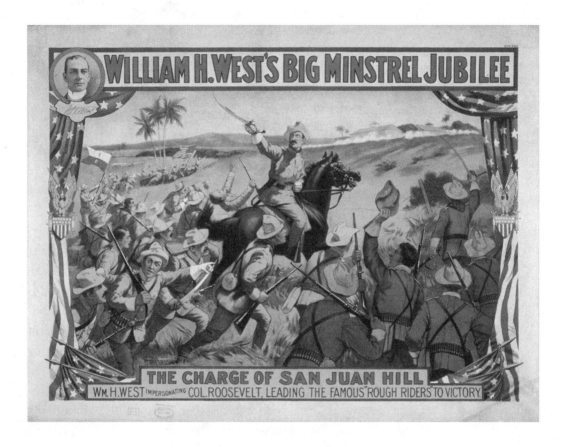

Japanese expansion and limit potential threats to the West Coast, it had an excellent port for battleships at Pearl Harbor, and it would act as a fueling station on the way to pivotal markets in Asia.[16]

Roosevelt, after winning headlines in the war, ran as vice president under McKinley and rose to the presidency after McKinley's assassination by the anarchist Leon Czolgosz in 1901. Among his many interventions in American life, Roosevelt acted with vigor to expand the military, bolstering naval power especially, to protect and promote American interests abroad. This included the construction of eleven battleships between 1904 and 1907. Alfred Thayer Mahan's naval theories, described in his *The Influence of Sea Power upon History*, influenced Roosevelt a great deal. In contrast to theories that advocated for commerce raiding, coastal defense, and small "brown water" ships, the imperative to control the sea required battleships and a "blue water" navy that could engage and win decisive battles with rival fleets. As president, Roosevelt continued the policies he established as assistant secretary of the navy and expanded the U.S. fleet. The mission of the Great White Fleet,

Teddy Roosevelt, a politician turned soldier, gained fame after he and his Rough Riders took San Juan Hill. Images like this poster praised Roosevelt and the battle as Americans celebrated a "splendid little war." 1899. Wikimedia.

sixteen all-white battleships that sailed around the world between 1907 and 1909, exemplified America's new power.[17]

Roosevelt insisted that the "big stick" and the persuasive power of the U.S. military could ensure U.S. hegemony over strategically important regions in the Western Hemisphere. The United States used military intervention in various circumstances to further its objectives, but it did not have the ability or the inclination to militarily impose its will on the entirety of South and Central America. The United States therefore more often used informal methods of empire, such as so-called dollar diplomacy, to assert dominance over the hemisphere.

The United States actively intervened again and again in Latin America. Throughout his time in office, Roosevelt exerted U.S. control over Cuba (even after it gained formal independence in 1902) and Puerto Rico, and he deployed naval forces to ensure Panama's independence from Colombia in 1903 in order to acquire a U.S. Canal Zone. Furthermore, Roosevelt pronounced the Roosevelt Corollary to the Monroe Doctrine in 1904, proclaiming U.S. police power in the Caribbean. As articulated by President James Monroe in his annual address to Congress in 1823, the United States would treat any military intervention in Latin America by a European power as a threat to American security. Roosevelt reaffirmed the Monroe Doctrine and expanded it by declaring that the United States had the right to preemptive action through intervention in any Latin American nation in order to correct administrative and fiscal deficiencies.[18]

Roosevelt's policy justified numerous and repeated police actions in "dysfunctional" Caribbean and Latin American countries by U.S. Marines and naval forces and enabled the founding of the naval base at Guantanamo Bay, Cuba. This approach is sometimes referred to as gunboat diplomacy, wherein naval forces and Marines land in a national capital to protect American and Western personnel, temporarily seize control of the government, and dictate policies friendly to American business, such as the repayment of foreign loans. For example, in 1905 Roosevelt sent the Marines to occupy the Dominican Republic and established financial supervision over the Dominican government. Imperialists often framed such actions as almost humanitarian. They celebrated white Anglo-Saxon societies such as those found in the United States and the British Empire as advanced practitioners of nation-building and civilization, helping to uplift debtor nations in Latin America that lacked the manly qualities of discipline and self-control. Roosevelt, for instance, preached that it was the "manly duty" of the United States to exercise an international police power in the Caribbean and to spread the benefits of Anglo-Saxon civilization to inferior states populated by inferior peoples. The president's language, for instance, contrasted debtor nations' "impotence" with the United States' civilizing influence, belying new ideas that associated self-restraint and social stability with Anglo-Saxon manliness.[19]

Dollar diplomacy offered a less costly method of empire and avoided the troubles of military occupation. Washington worked with bankers to provide loans to Latin American nations in exchange for some level of control over their national fiscal affairs. Roosevelt first implemented dollar diplomacy on a vast scale, while Presidents Taft and Wilson continued the practice in various forms during their own administrations. All confronted instability in Latin America. Rising debts to European and American bankers allowed for the inroads of modern life but destabilized much of the region. Bankers, beginning with financial houses in London and New York, saw Latin America as an opportunity for investment. Lenders took advantage of the region's newly formed governments' need for cash and exacted punishing interest rates on massive loans, which were then sold off in pieces on the secondary bond market. American economic interests were now closely aligned with the region but also further undermined by the chronic instability of the region's newly formed governments, which were often plagued by mismanagement, civil wars, and military coups in the decades following their independence. Turnover in regimes interfered with the repayment of loans, as new governments often repudiated the national debt or forced a renegotiation with suddenly powerless lenders.[20]

Creditors could not force settlements of loans until they successfully lobbied their own governments to get involved and forcibly collect debts. The Roosevelt administration did not want to deny the Europeans' rightful demands of repayment of debt, but it also did not want to encourage European policies of conquest in the hemisphere as part of that debt collection. U.S. policy makers and military strategists within the Roosevelt administration determined that this European practice of military intervention posed a serious threat to American interests in the region. Roosevelt reasoned that the United States must create and maintain fiscal and political stability within strategically important nations in Latin America, particularly those affecting routes to and from the proposed Panama Canal. As a result, U.S. policy makers considered intervention in places like Cuba and the Dominican Republic a necessity to ensure security around the region.[21]

The Monroe Doctrine provided the Roosevelt administration with a diplomatic and international legal tradition through which it could assert a U.S. right and obligation to intervene in the hemisphere. The Roosevelt Corollary to the Monroe Doctrine asserted that the United States wished to promote stable, prosperous states in Latin America that could live up to their political and financial obligations. Roosevelt declared that "wrongdoing, or an impotence which results in a general loosening of the ties of civilized society, may finally require intervention by some civilized nation, and in the Western Hemisphere the United States cannot ignore this duty."[22] President Monroe declared what Europeans could not do in the Western Hemisphere; Roosevelt inverted his doctrine to legitimize direct U.S. intervention in the region.[23]

Though aggressive and bellicose, Roosevelt did not necessarily advocate expansion by military force. In fact, the president insisted that in dealings with the Latin American nations, he did not seek national glory or expansion of territory and believed that war or intervention should be a last resort when resolving conflicts with problematic governments. According to Roosevelt, such actions were necessary to maintain "order and civilization."[24] Then again, Roosevelt certainly believed in using military power to protect national interests and spheres of influence when absolutely necessary. He also believed that the American sphere included not only Hawaii and the Caribbean but also much of the Pacific. When Japanese victories over Russia threatened the regional balance of power, he sponsored peace talks between Russian and Japanese leaders, earning him a Nobel Peace Prize in 1906.

V. Women and Imperialism

Debates over American imperialism revolved around more than just politics and economics and national self-interest. They also included notions of humanitarianism, morality, religion, and ideas of "civilization." And they included significant participation by American women.

In the fall of 1903, Margaret McLeod, age twenty-one, originally of Boston, found herself in Australia on family business and in need of income. Fortuitously, she made the acquaintance of Alexander MacWillie, the top salesman for the H. J. Heinz Company, who happened to be looking for a young lady to serve as a "demonstrator" of Heinz products to potential consumers. McLeod proved to be such an attractive purveyor of India relish and baked beans that she accompanied MacWillie on the rest of his tour of Australia and continued on to South Africa,

With much satisfaction, Columbia puts on her "Easter Bonnet," a hat shaped like a warship and labeled *World Power*. By 1901, when this political cartoon was published, Americans felt confident in their country's position as a world leader. Wikimedia.

India, and Japan. Wherever she went, this "dainty young girl with golden hair in white cap and tucker" drew attention to Heinz's products, but, in a much larger sense, she was also projecting an image of middle-class American domesticity, of pure womanhood. Heinz saw itself not only as purveying economical and healthful foodstuffs—it was bringing the blessings of civilization to the world.[25]

When commentators, such as Theodore Roosevelt in his speech on "the strenuous life," spoke about America's overseas ventures, they generally gave the impression that this was a strictly masculine enterprise—the work of soldiers, sailors, government officials, explorers, businessmen, and scientists. But in fact, U.S. imperialism, which focused as much on economic and cultural influence as on military or political power, offered a range of opportunities for white, middle-class, Christian women. In addition to working as representatives of American business, women could serve as missionaries, teachers, and medical professionals, and as artists and writers they were inspired by and helped transmit ideas about imperialism.

Moreover, the rhetoric of civilization that underlay imperialism was itself a highly gendered concept. According to the racial theory of the day, humans progressed through hierarchical stages of civilization in an orderly, linear fashion. Only Europeans and Americans had attained the highest level of civilization, which was superficially marked by whiteness but also included an industrial economy and a gender division in which men and women had diverging but complementary roles. Social and technological progress had freed women of the burdens of physical labor and elevated them to a position of moral and spiritual authority. White women thus potentially had important roles to play in U.S. imperialism, both as symbols of the benefits of American civilization and as vehicles for the transmission of American values.[26]

Civilization, while often cloaked in the language of morality and Christianity, was very much an economic concept. The stages of civilization were primarily marked by their economic character (hunter-gatherer, agricultural, industrial), and the consumption of industrially produced commodities was seen as a key moment in the progress of "savages" toward civilized life. Over the course of the nineteenth century, women in the West, for instance, had become closely associated with consumption, particularly of those commodities used in the domestic sphere. Thus it must have seemed natural for Alexander MacWillie to hire Margaret McLeod to "demonstrate" ketchup and chili sauce at the same time as she "demonstrated" white, middle-class domesticity. By adopting the use of such progressive products in their homes, consumers could potentially absorb even the virtues of American civilization.[27]

In some ways, women's work in support of imperialism can be seen as an extension of the kind of activities many of them were already engaged in among working-class, immigrant, and Native American communities in the United States. Many white women felt that they had a duty to spread the benefits of Christian civilization to those less fortunate than themselves. American overseas ventures, then, merely expanded the scope of these activities—literally, in that the geographical range of possibilities encompassed practically the entire globe, and figuratively, in that imperialism significantly raised the stakes of women's work. No longer only responsible for shaping the next generation of American citizens, white women now had a crucial role to play in the maintenance of civilization itself. They too would help determine whether civilization would continue to progress.

Of course, not all women were active supporters of U.S. imperialism. Many actively opposed it. Although the most prominent public voices against imperialism were male, women made up a large proportion of the membership of organizations like the Anti-Imperialist League. For white women like Jane Addams and Josephine Shaw Lowell, anti-imperialist activism was an outgrowth of their work in opposition to violence and in support of democracy. Black female activists, meanwhile, generally viewed imperialism as a form of racial antagonism and drew parallels between the treatments of African Americans at home and, for example, Filipinos abroad. Indeed, Ida B. Wells viewed her anti-lynching campaign as a kind of anti-imperialist activism.

VI. Immigration

For Americans at the turn of the century, imperialism and immigration were two sides of the same coin. The involvement of American women with imperialist and anti-imperialist activity demonstrates how foreign policy concerns were brought home and became, in a sense, domesticated. It is also no coincidence that many of the women involved in both imperialist and anti-imperialist organizations were also concerned with the plight of new arrivals to the United States. Industrialization, imperialism, and immigration were all linked. Imperialism had at its core a desire for markets for American goods, and those goods were increasingly manufactured by immigrant labor. This sense of growing dependence on "others" as producers and consumers, along with doubts about their capability of assimilation into the mainstream of white, Protestant American society, caused a great deal of anxiety among native-born Americans.

Between 1870 and 1920, over twenty-five million immigrants arrived in the United States. This migration was largely a continuation of a process begun before the Civil War, though by the turn of the twentieth century, new groups such as Italians, Poles, and Eastern European Jews made up a larger percentage of the arrivals while Irish and German numbers began to dwindle.

Although the growing U.S. economy needed large numbers of immigrant workers for its factories and mills, many Americans reacted negatively to the arrival of so many immigrants. Nativists opposed mass immigration for various reasons. Some felt that the new arrivals were unfit for American democracy, and that Irish or Italian immigrants used violence or bribery to corrupt municipal governments. Others (often earlier immigrants themselves) worried that the arrival of even more immigrants would result in fewer jobs and lower wages. Such fears combined and resulted in anti-Chinese protests on the West Coast in the 1870s. Still others worried that immigrants brought with them radical ideas such as socialism and communism. These fears multiplied after the Chicago Hay-

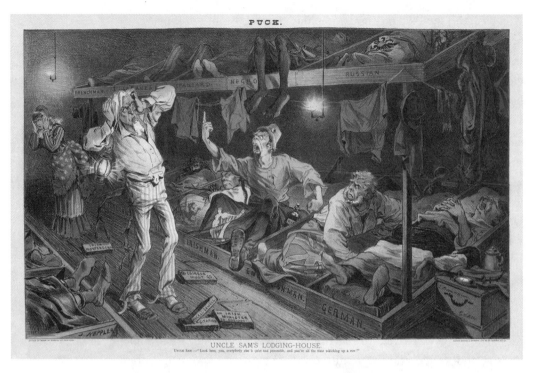

Nativist sentiment intensified in the late nineteenth century as immigrants streamed into American cities. "Uncle Sam's Lodging House," published in 1882, conveys this anti-immigrant attitude, with caricatured representations of Europeans, Asians, and African Americans creating a chaotic scene. Wikimedia.

market affair in 1886, in which immigrants were accused of killing police officers in a bomb blast.[28]

In September 1876, Franklin Benjamin Sanborn, a member of the Massachusetts Board of State Charities, gave an address in support of the introduction of regulatory federal immigration legislation at an interstate conference of charity officials in Saratoga, New York. Immigration might bring some benefits, but "it also introduces disease, ignorance, crime, pauperism and idleness." Sanborn thus advocated federal action to stop "indiscriminate and unregulated immigration."[29]

Sanborn's address was aimed at restricting only the immigration of paupers from Europe to the East Coast, but the idea of immigration restrictions was common across the United States in the late nineteenth century, when many variously feared that the influx of foreigners would undermine the racial, economic, and moral integrity of American society. From the 1870s to the 1920s, the federal government passed a series of laws limiting or discontinuing the immigration of particular groups, and the United States remained committed to regulating the kind of im-

migrants who would join American society. To critics, regulations legiti-
mized racism, class bias, and ethnic prejudice as formal national policy.

The first move for federal immigration control came from California, where racial hostility toward Chinese immigrants had mounted since
the mid-nineteenth century. In addition to accusing Chinese immigrants
of racial inferiority and unfitness for American citizenship, opponents
claimed that they were also economically and morally corrupting American society with cheap labor and immoral practices, such as prostitution.
Immigration restriction was necessary for the "Caucasian race of California," as one anti-Chinese politician declared, and for European Americans to "preserve and maintain their homes, their business, and their
high social and moral position." In 1875, the anti-Chinese crusade in
California moved Congress to pass the Page Act, which banned the entry
of convicted criminals, Asian laborers brought involuntarily, and women
imported "for the purposes of prostitution," a stricture designed chiefly
to exclude Chinese women. Then, in May 1882, Congress suspended
the immigration of all Chinese laborers with the Chinese Exclusion Act,
making the Chinese the first immigrant group subject to admission restrictions on the basis of race. They became the first illegal immigrants.[30]

On the other side of the country, Atlantic Seaboard states also facilitated the formation of federal immigration policy. Since the colonial period,
East Coast states had regulated immigration through their own passenger
laws, which prohibited the landing of destitute foreigners unless shipmas-
ters prepaid certain amounts of money in the support of those passengers.
State-level control of pauper immigration developed into federal policy in
the early 1880s. In August 1882, Congress passed the Immigration Act,
denying admission to people who were not able to support themselves and
those, such as paupers, people with mental illnesses, or convicted criminals, who might otherwise threaten the security of the nation.

The category of excludable people expanded continuously after 1882.
In 1885, in response to American workers' complaints about cheap immigrant labor, Congress added foreign workers migrating under labor
contracts with American employers to the list of excludable people. Six
years later, the federal government included people who seemed likely
to become wards of the state, people with contagious diseases, and
polygamists, and made all groups of excludable people deportable. In
1903, those who would pose ideological threats to American republican
democracy, such as anarchists and socialists, also became the subject of
new immigration restrictions.

The idea of America as a melting pot, a still-common metaphor, was a way of arguing for the ethnic assimilation of all immigrants into a nebulous "American" identity at the turn of the twentieth century. A play of the same name premiered in 1908 to great acclaim. The former president Theodore Roosevelt told the playwright, "That's a great play, Mr. Zangwill, that's a great play." Cover of theater program for Israel Zangwill's play *The Melting Pot*, 1916. Wikimedia.

Many immigration critics were responding to the shifting demographics of American immigration. The center of immigrant-sending regions shifted from northern and western Europe to southern and eastern Europe and Asia. These "new immigrants" were poorer, spoke languages other than English, and were likely Catholic or Jewish. White Protestant Americans typically regarded them as inferior, and American immigration policy began to reflect more explicit prejudice than ever before. One restrictionist declared that these immigrants were "races with which the English-speaking people have never hitherto assimilated, and who are most alien to the great body of the people of the United States." The increased immigration of people from southern and eastern Europe, such as Italians, Jews, Slavs, and Greeks, led directly to calls for tighter restrictive measures. In 1907, the immigration of Japanese laborers was practically suspended when the American and Japanese governments reached the so-called Gentlemen's Agreement, according to which Japan would stop issuing passports to working-class emigrants. In its forty-two-volume report of 1911, the U.S. Immigration Commission highlighted the impossibility of incorporating these new immigrants into American

society. The report highlighted their supposed innate inferiority, asserting that they were the causes of rising social problems in America, such
as poverty, crime, prostitution, and political radicalism.[31]

The assault against immigrants' Catholicism provides an excellent
example of the challenges immigrant groups faced in the United States.
By 1900, Catholicism in the United States had grown dramatically in size
and diversity, from 1 percent of the population a century earlier to the
largest religious denomination in America (though still outnumbered by
Protestants as a whole). As a result, Catholics in America faced two intertwined challenges: one external, related to Protestant anti-Catholicism,
and the other internal, having to do with the challenges of assimilation.

Externally, the Church and its members remained an "outsider" religion in a nation that continued to see itself as culturally and religiously
Protestant. Torrents of anti-Catholic literature and scandalous rumors
maligned Catholics. Many Protestants doubted whether Catholics could
ever make loyal Americans because they supposedly owed primary allegiance to the pope.

Internally, Catholics in America faced the question every immigrant
group has had to answer: to what extent should they become more like
native-born Americans? This question was particularly acute, as Catholics encompassed a variety of languages and customs. Beginning in the
1830s, Catholic immigration to the United States had exploded with the
increasing arrival of Irish and German immigrants. Subsequent Catholic
arrivals from Italy, Poland, and other Eastern European countries chafed
at Irish dominance over the Church hierarchy. Mexican and Mexican
American Catholics, whether recent immigrants or incorporated into the
nation after the Mexican-American War, expressed similar frustrations.
Could all these different Catholics remain part of the same Church?

Catholic clergy approached this situation from a variety of perspectives. Some bishops advocated rapid assimilation into the English-speaking mainstream. These "Americanists" advocated an end to "ethnic
parishes"—the unofficial practice of permitting separate congregations
for Poles, Italians, Germans, and so on—in the belief that such isolation
only delayed immigrants' entry into the American mainstream. They anticipated that the Catholic Church could thrive in a nation that espoused
religious freedom, if only they assimilated. Meanwhile, however, more
conservative clergy cautioned against assimilation. While they conceded
that the United States had no official religion, they felt that Protestant
notions of the separation of church and state and of licentious individual liberty posed a threat to the Catholic faith. They further saw ethnic

parishes as an effective strategy protecting immigrant communities and worried that Protestants would use public schools to attack the Catholic faith. Eventually, the head of the Catholic Church, Pope Leo XIII, weighed in on the controversy. In 1899, he sent a special letter (an encyclical) to an archbishop in the United States. Leo reminded the Americanists that the Catholic Church was a unified global body and that American liberties did not give Catholics the freedom to alter church teachings. The Americanists denied any such intention, but the conservative clergy claimed that the pope had sided with them. Tension between Catholicism and American life, however, would continue well into the twentieth century.[32]

The American encounter with Catholicism—and Catholicism's encounter with America—testified to the tense relationship between native-born and foreign-born Americans, and to the larger ideas Americans used to situate themselves in a larger world, a world of empire and immigrants.

VII. Conclusion

While American imperialism flared most brightly for a relatively brief time at the turn of the century, new imperial patterns repeated old practices and lived on into the twentieth century. But suddenly the United States had embraced its cultural, economic, and religious influence in the world, along with a newfound military power, to exercise varying degrees of control over nations and peoples. Whether as formal subjects or unwilling partners on the receiving end of Roosevelt's "big stick," those who experienced U.S. expansionist policies confronted new American ambitions. At home, debates over immigration and imperialism drew attention to the interplay of international and domestic policy and the ways in which imperial actions, practices, and ideas affected and were affected by domestic questions. How Americans thought about the conflict in the Philippines, for example, was affected by how they approached immigration in their own cities. And at the turn of the century, those thoughts were very much on the minds of Americans.

VIII. Reference Material

This chapter was edited by Ellen Adams and Amy Kohout, with content contributions by Ellen Adams, Alvita Akiboh, Simon Balto, Jacob Betz, Tizoc Chavez, Morgan Deane, Dan Du, Hidetaka Hirota, Amy Kohout, Jose Juan Perez Melendez, Erik Moore, and Gregory Moore.

Recommended citation: Ellen Adams et al., "American Empire," Ellen Adams and Amy Kohout, eds., in *The American Yawp*, eds. Joseph Locke and Ben Wright (Stanford, CA: Stanford University Press, 2019).

NOTES TO CHAPTER 19

1. Tyler Dennett, *Americans in Eastern Asia: A Critical Study of the Policy of the United States with Reference to China, Japan and Korea in the 19th Century* (New York: Macmillan, 1922), 580.

2. Robert E. Hannigan, *The New World Power: American Foreign Policy, 1898–1917* (Philadelphia: University of Pennsylvania Press, 2002).

3. Jimmy M. Skaggs, *The Great Guano Rush: Entrepreneurs and American Overseas Expansion* (New York: Macmillan, 1994); Robert A. Wines, *Fertilizer in America: From Waste Recycling to Resource Exploitation* (Philadelphia: Temple University Press, 1985).

4. Elvi Whittaker, *The Mainland Haole: The White Experience in Hawai'i* (New York: Columbia University Press, 1986).

5. John Mason Hart, *Empire and Revolution: The Americans in Mexico Since the Civil War* (Berkeley: University of California Press, 2002), 271–307; Mark Benbow, *Leading Them to the Promised Land: Woodrow Wilson, Covenant Theology, and the Mexican Revolution, 1913–1915* (Kent, OH: Kent State University Press, 2010), 25–44; Lloyd C. Gardner, *Safe for Democracy: The Anglo-American Response to Revolution, 1913–1923* (New York: Oxford University Press, 1984).

6. Hart, *Empire and Revolution*, 326–333.

7. Mark Twain, *The Innocents Abroad, or The New Pilgrims' Progress* (Hartford, CT: American, 1869), 379.

8. Ussama Makdisi, *Artillery of Heaven American Missionaries and the Failed Conversion of the Middle East* (Ithaca, NY: Cornell University Press, 2008).

9. Lyman Abbott, *Inspiration for Daily Living: Selections from the Writings of Lyman Abbott* (Boston: Pilgrim Press, 1919), 175.

10. Albert J. Beveridge, *The Meaning of the Times: And Other Speeches* (Indianapolis: Bobbs-Merrill, 1908), 48.

11. Finley Peter Dunne, *Mr. Dooley in the Hearts of His Countrymen* (Boston: Small, Maynard, 1899), 6.

12. Susan K. Harris, *God's Arbiters: Americans and the Philippines, 1898–1902* (New York: Oxford University Press, 2011); Paul A. Kramer, *The Blood of Government: Race, Empire, the United States, and the Philippines* (Chapel Hill: University of North Carolina Press, 2006).

13. Harris, *God's Arbiters*; Kramer, *Blood of Government*.

14. John F. Bass, compiled in Marrion Wilcox, *Harper's History of the War in the Philippines* (New York: Harper, 1900), 162.

15. Harris, *God's Arbiters*; Kramer, *Blood of Government*.

16. William Henry Harbaugh, *The Life and Times of Theodore Roosevelt* (London: Oxford University Press, 1961); Morton Keller, *Theodore Roosevelt; A Profile* (New York: Hill and Wang, 1967).

17. R. A. Hart, *The Great White Fleet: Its Voyage Around the World, 1907–1909* (New York: Little, Brown, 1965).

18. Richard Collin, *Theodore Roosevelt's Caribbean: The Panama Canal, The Monroe Doctrine, and the Latin American Context* (Baton Rouge: LSU Press, 1990).

19. Ibid.

20. Emily S. Rosenberg, *Financial Missionaries to the World: The Politics and Culture of Dollar Diplomacy, 1900–1930* (Cambridge, MA: Harvard University Press, 1999), 3.

21. William Everett Kane, *Civil Strife in Latin America: A Legal History of U.S. Involvement* (Baltimore: Johns Hopkins University Press, 1972), 73.

22. Theodore Roosevelt to Elihu Root, May 20, 1904, in *The Letters of Theodore Roosevelt*, vol. 4, ed. Elting E. Morrison (Cambridge, MA: Harvard University Press, 1951), 801.

23. Hannigan, *New World Power.*

24. Theodore Roosevelt to William Bayard Hale, February 26, 1904, in Morrison, *Letters of Theodore Roosevelt*, vol. 4, 740.

25. Mona Domosh, *American Commodities in an Age of Empire* (New York: Routledge, 2006).

26. Kristin L. Hoganson, *Fighting for American Manhood: How Gender Politics Provoked the Spanish-American and Philippine-American Wars* (New Haven, CT: Yale University Press, 1998).

27. Domosh, *American Commodities.*

28. Matthew Frye Jacobson, *Barbarian Virtues: The United States Encounters Foreign Peoples at Home and Abroad, 1876–1917* (New York: Hill and Wang, 2000).

29. Massachusetts Board of State Charities, *Annual Report of the State Board of Charity of Massachusetts* (Boston: Wright, 1877), xlvii.

30. Jacobson, *Barbarian Virtues.*

31. Roger Daniels, *The Politics of Prejudice: The Anti-Japanese Movement in California and the Struggle for Japanese Exclusion* (Berkeley: University of California Press, 1999).

32. James M. O'Toole, *The Faithful: A History of Catholics in America* (Cambridge, MA: Harvard University Press, 2009).

RECOMMENDED READING

Bederman, Gail. *Manliness and Civilization: A Cultural History of Gender and Race in the United States, 1880–1917.* Chicago: University of Chicago Press, 1995.

Brooks, Charlotte. *Alien Neighbors, Foreign Friends: Asian Americans, Housing, and the Transformation of Urban California.* Chicago: University of Chicago Press, 2009.

Gabaccia, Donna. *Foreign Relations: American Immigration in Global Perspective.* Princeton, NJ: Princeton University Press, 2012.

Greene, Julie. *The Canal Builders: Making America's Empire at the Panama Canal.* New York: Penguin, 2009.

Guglielmo, Thomas A. *White on Arrival: Italians, Race, Color, and Power in Chicago, 1890–1945*. New York: Oxford University Press, 2004.

Harris, Susan K. *God's Arbiters: Americans and the Philippines, 1898–1902*. New York: Oxford University Press, 2011.

Higham, John. *Strangers in the Land: Patterns of American Nativism, 1860–1925*. New Brunswick, NJ: Rutgers University Press, 1988.

Hirota, Hidetaka. *Expelling the Poor: Atlantic Seaboard States and the Nineteenth-Century Origins of American Immigration Policy*. New York: Oxford University Press, 2016.

Hoganson, Kristin. *Consumers' Imperium: The Global Production of American Domesticity, 1865–1920*. Chapel Hill: University of North Carolina Press, 2007.

Hoganson, Kristin L. *Fighting for American Manhood: How Gender Politics Provoked the Spanish-American and Philippine-American Wars*. New Haven, CT: Yale University Press, 1998.

Jacobson, Matthew Frye. *Barbarian Virtues: The United States Encounters Foreign People at Home and Abroad, 1876–1917*. New York: Hill and Wang, 2001.

Jacobson, Matthew Frye. *Whiteness of a Different Color: European Immigrants and the Alchemy of Race*. Cambridge, MA: Harvard University Press, 1999.

Kaplan, Amy. *The Anarchy of Empire in the Making of U.S. Culture*. Cambridge, MA: Harvard University Press, 2002.

Kramer, Paul A. *The Blood of Government: Race, Empire, the United States, and the Philippines*. Chapel Hill: University of North Carolina Press, 2006.

Lafeber, Walter. *The New Empire: An Interpretation of American Expansion, 1860–1898*. Ithaca, NY: Cornell University Press, 1963.

Lears, T. J. Jackson. *Rebirth of a Nation: The Making of Modern America, 1877–1920*. New York: HarperCollins, 2009.

Linn, Brian McAllister. *The Philippine War, 1899–1902*. Lawrence: University Press of Kansas, 2000.

Love, Eric T. L. *Race over Empire: Racism and U.S. Imperialism, 1865–1900*. Chapel Hill: University of North Carolina Press, 2004.

Pascoe, Peggy. *What Comes Naturally: Miscegenation Law and the Making of Race in America*. New York: Oxford University Press, 2009.

Perez, Louis A., Jr. *The War of 1898: The United States and Cuba in History and Historiography*. New Haven, CT: Yale University Press, 2000.

Renda, Mary. *Taking Haiti: Military Occupation and the Culture of US Imperialism, 1915–40*. Chapel Hill: University of North Carolina Press, 2001.

Rosenberg, Emily S. *Spreading the American Dream: American Economic and Cultural Expansion, 1890–1945*. New York: Hill and Wang, 1982.

Silbey, David. *A War of Frontier and Empire: The Philippine-American War, 1899–1902*. New York: Hill and Wang, 2007.

Wexler, Laura. *Tender Violence: Domestic Visions in an Age of US Imperialism*. Chapel Hill: University of North Carolina Press, 2000.

Williams, William Appleman. *The Tragedy of American Diplomacy*, 50th Anniversary Edition. New York: Norton, 2009 [1959].

20

The Progressive Era

I. Introduction

"Never in the history of the world was society in so terrific flux as it is right now," Jack London wrote in *The Iron Heel*, his 1908 dystopian novel in which a corporate oligarchy comes to rule the United States. He wrote, "The swift changes in our industrial system are causing equally swift changes in our religious, political, and social structures. An unseen and fearful revolution is taking place in the fiber and structure of society. One can only dimly feel these things, but they are in the air, now, today."[1]

The many problems associated with the Gilded Age—the rise of unprecedented fortunes and unprecedented poverty, controversies over imperialism, urban squalor, a near-war between capital and labor, loosening social mores, unsanitary food production, the onrush of foreign

From an undated William Jennings Bryan campaign print, "Shall the People Rule?" Library of Congress.

immigration, environmental destruction, and the outbreak of political radicalism—confronted Americans. Terrible forces seemed out of control and the nation seemed imperiled. Farmers and workers had been waging political war against capitalists and political conservatives for decades, but then, slowly, toward the end of the nineteenth century a new generation of middle-class Americans interjected themselves into public life and advocated new reforms to tame the runaway world of the Gilded Age.

Widespread dissatisfaction with new trends in American society spurred the Progressive Era, named for the various progressive movements that attracted various constituencies around various reforms. Americans had many different ideas about how the country's development should be managed and whose interests required the greatest protection. Reformers sought to clean up politics; Black Americans continued their long struggle for civil rights; women demanded the vote with greater intensity while also demanding a more equal role in society at large; and workers demanded higher wages, safer workplaces, and the union recognition that would guarantee these rights. Whatever their goals, *reform* became the word of the age, and the sum of their efforts, whatever their ultimate impact or original intentions, gave the era its name.

II. Mobilizing for Reform

In 1911 the Triangle Shirtwaist Factory in Manhattan caught fire. The doors of the factory had been chained shut to prevent employees from taking unauthorized breaks (the managers who held the keys saved themselves, but left over two hundred women behind). A rickety fire ladder on the side of the building collapsed immediately. Women lined the rooftop and windows of the ten-story building and jumped, landing in a "mangled, bloody pulp." Life nets held by firemen tore at the impact of the falling bodies. Among the onlookers, "women were hysterical, scores fainted; men wept as, in paroxysms of frenzy, they hurled themselves against the police lines." By the time the fire burned itself out, 71 workers were injured and 146 had died.[2]

A year before, the Triangle workers had gone on strike demanding union recognition, higher wages, and better safety conditions. Remembering their workers' "chief value," the owners of the factory decided that a viable fire escape and unlocked doors were too expensive and called in the city police to break up the strike. After the 1911 fire, reporter Bill Shepherd reflected, "I looked upon the heap of dead bod-

Policemen place the bodies of workers who were burned alive in the 1911 Triangle Shirtwaist fire into coffins. Photographs like this made real the atrocities that could result from unsafe working conditions. March 25, 1911. Library of Congress.

ies and I remembered these girls were shirtwaist makers. I remembered their great strike last year in which the same girls had demanded more sanitary conditions and more safety precautions in the shops. These dead bodies were the answer."[3] Former Triangle worker and labor organizer Rose Schneiderman said, "This is not the first time girls have been burned alive in this city. Every week I must learn of the untimely death of one of my sister workers . . . the life of men and women is so cheap and property is so sacred! There are so many of us for one job, it matters little if 140-odd are burned to death."[4] After the fire, Triangle owners Max Blanck and Isaac Harris were brought up on manslaughter charges. They were acquitted after less than two hours of deliberation. The outcome continued a trend in the industrializing economy that saw workers' deaths answered with little punishment of the business owners responsible for such dangerous conditions. But as such tragedies mounted and working and living conditions worsened and inequality grew, it became increasingly difficult to develop justifications for this new modern order.

Events such as the Triangle Shirtwaist fire convinced many Americans of the need for reform, but the energies of activists were needed to spread a new commitment to political activism and government interference in the economy. Politicians, journalists, novelists, religious leaders, and activists all raised their voices to push Americans toward reform.

Reformers turned to books and mass-circulation magazines to publicize the plight of the nation's poor and the many corruptions endemic to the new industrial order. Journalists who exposed business practices, poverty, and corruption—labeled by Theodore Roosevelt as "muckrakers"—aroused public demands for reform. Magazines such as *McClure's* detailed political corruption and economic malfeasance. The muckrakers confirmed Americans' suspicions about runaway wealth and political corruption. Ray Stannard Baker, a journalist whose reports on U.S. Steel exposed the underbelly of the new corporate capitalism, wrote, "I think I can understand now why these exposure articles took such a hold upon the American people. It was because the country, for years, had been swept by the agitation of soap-box orators, prophets crying in the wilderness, and political campaigns based upon charges of corruption and privilege which everyone believed or suspected had some basis of truth, but which were largely unsubstantiated."[5]

Journalists shaped popular perceptions of Gilded Age injustice. In 1890, New York City journalist Jacob Riis published *How the Other Half Lives*, a scathing indictment of living and working conditions in the city's slums. Riis not only vividly described the squalor he saw, he documented it with photography, giving readers an unflinching view of urban poverty. Riis's book led to housing reform in New York and other cities and helped instill the idea that society bore at least some responsibility for alleviating poverty.[6] In 1906, Upton Sinclair published *The Jungle*, a novel dramatizing the experiences of a Lithuanian immigrant family who moved to Chicago to work in the stockyards. Although Sinclair intended the novel to reveal the brutal exploitation of labor in the meatpacking industry, and thus to build support for the socialist movement, its major impact was to lay bare the entire process of industrialized food production. The growing invisibility of slaughterhouses and livestock production for urban consumers had enabled unsanitary and unsafe conditions. "The slaughtering machine ran on, visitors or no visitors," wrote Sinclair, "like some horrible crime committed in a dungeon, all unseen and unheeded, buried out of sight and of memory."[7] Sinclair's exposé led to the passage of the Meat Inspection Act and Pure Food and Drug Act in 1906.

Jacob Riis, "Home of an Italian Ragpicker." c. 1888–1889. Wikimedia.

Of course, it was not only journalists who raised questions about American society. One of the most popular novels of the nineteenth century, Edward Bellamy's 1888 *Looking Backward,* was a national sensation. In it, a man falls asleep in Boston in 1887 and awakens in 2000 to find society radically altered. Poverty and disease and competition gave way as new industrial armies cooperated to build a utopia of social harmony and economic prosperity. Bellamy's vision of a reformed society enthralled readers, inspired hundreds of Bellamy clubs, and pushed many young readers onto the road to reform.[8] It led countless Americans to question the realities of American life in the nineteenth century:

> I am aware that you called yourselves free in the nineteenth century. The meaning of the word could not then, however, have been at all what it is at present, or you certainly would not have applied it to a society of which nearly every member was in a position of galling personal dependence upon others as to the very means of life, the poor upon the rich, or employed upon employer, women upon men, children upon parents.[9]

But Americans were urged to action not only by books and magazines but by preachers and theologians, too. Confronted by both the benefits and the ravages of industrialization, many Americans asked themselves, "What Would Jesus Do?" In 1896, Charles Sheldon, a Congregational minister in Topeka, Kansas, published *In His Steps: What Would Jesus Do?* The novel told the story of Henry Maxwell, a pastor in a small Midwestern town one day confronted by an unemployed migrant who criticized his congregation's lack of concern for the poor and downtrodden. Moved by the man's plight, Maxwell preached a series of sermons in which he asked his congregation: "Would it not be true, think you, that if every Christian in America did as Jesus would do, society itself, the business world, yes, the very political system under which our commercial and government activity is carried on, would be so changed that human suffering would be reduced to a minimum?"[10] Sheldon's novel became a best seller, not only because of its story but because the book's plot connected with a new movement transforming American religion: the social gospel.

The social gospel emerged within Protestant Christianity at the end of the nineteenth century. It emphasized the need for Christians to be concerned for the salvation of society, and not simply individual souls. Instead of just caring for family or fellow church members, social gospel advocates encouraged Christians to engage society; challenge social, political, and economic structures; and help those less fortunate than themselves. Responding to the developments of the industrial revolution in America and the increasing concentration of people in urban spaces, with its attendant social and economic problems, some social gospelers went so far as to advocate a form of Christian socialism, but all urged Americans to confront the sins of their society.

One of the most notable advocates of the social gospel was Walter Rauschenbusch. After graduating from Rochester Theological Seminary, in 1886 Rauschenbusch accepted the pastorate of a German Baptist church in the Hell's Kitchen section of New York City, where he confronted rampant crime and stark poverty, problems not adequately addressed by the political leaders of the city. Rauschenbusch joined with fellow reformers to elect a new mayoral candidate, but he also realized that a new theological framework had to reflect his interest in society and its problems. He revived Jesus's phrase, "the Kingdom of God," claiming that it encompassed every aspect of life and made every part of society a purview of the proper Christian. Like Charles Sheldon's fictional Rev.

Maxwell, Rauschenbusch believed that every Christian, whether they were a businessperson, a politician, or a stay-at-home parent, should ask themselves what they could do to enact the kingdom of God on Earth.[11]

> The social gospel is the old message of salvation, but enlarged and intensified. The individualistic gospel has taught us to see the sinfulness of every human heart and has inspired us with faith in the willingness and power of God to save every soul that comes to him. But it has not given us an adequate understanding of the sinfulness of the social order and its share in the sins of all individuals within it. It has not evoked faith in the will and power of God to redeem the permanent institutions of human society from their inherited guilt of oppression and extortion. Both our sense of sin and our faith in salvation have fallen short of the realities under its teaching. The social gospel seeks to bring men under repentance for their collective sins and to create a more sensitive and more modern conscience. It calls on us for the faith of the old prophets who believed in the salvation of nations.[12]

Glaring blind spots persisted within the proposals of most social gospel advocates. As men, they often ignored the plight of women, and thus most refused to support women's suffrage. Many were also silent on the plight of African Americans, Native Americans, and other oppressed minority groups. However, the writings of Rauschenbusch and other social gospel proponents had a profound influence on twentieth-century American life. Most immediately, they fueled progressive reform. But they also inspired future activists, including Martin Luther King Jr., who envisioned a "beloved community" that resembled Rauschenbusch's "Kingdom of God."

III. Women's Movements

Reform opened new possibilities for women's activism in American public life and gave new impetus to the long campaign for women's suffrage. Much energy for women's work came from female "clubs," social organizations devoted to various purposes. Some focused on intellectual development; others emphasized philanthropic activities. Increasingly, these organizations looked outward, to their communities and to the place of women in the larger political sphere.

Women's clubs flourished in the late nineteenth and early twentieth centuries. In the 1890s women formed national women's club federations. Particularly significant in campaigns for suffrage and women's rights were the General Federation of Women's Clubs (formed in New York City in 1890) and the National Association of Colored Women (or-

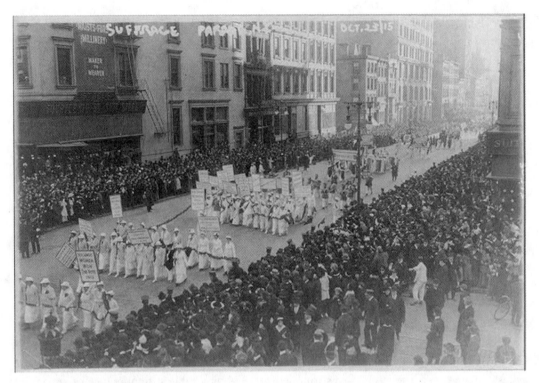

Suffragists campaigned tirelessly for the vote in the first two decades of the twentieth century, taking to the streets in public displays like this 1915 pre-election parade in New York City. During this one event, twenty thousand women defied the gender norms that tried to relegate them to the private sphere and deny them the vote. 1915. Wikimedia.

ganized in Washington, D.C., in 1896), both of which were dominated by upper-middle-class, educated, northern women. Few of these organizations were biracial, a legacy of the sometimes uneasy midnineteenth-century relationship between socially active African Americans and white women. Rising American prejudice led many white female activists to ban inclusion of their African American sisters. Black women produced vibrant organizations that could promise racial uplift and civil rights for all Black Americans as well as equal rights for all women. Black abolitionist Mary Jane Richardson Jones organized Black women in Chicago around settlement work, moral uplift, and suffrage. Josephine St. Pierre Ruffin, who had also worked for abolition and suffrage, worked with club women in Boston and organized, in 1895, the First National Conference of the Colored Women of America. The following year, Mary Church Terrell and other Black activists formed the National Association of Colored Women, later known as the National Association of Colored Women's Clubs. These leagues of service-oriented women's organizations provided powerful networks to organize and amplify Black women's efforts not only to secure suffrage but to challenge discrimination and uplift Black communities across the United States.[13]

Other women worked through churches and moral reform organizations to clean up American life. And still others worked as moral vigilantes. The fearsome Carrie A. Nation, an imposing woman who believed she worked God's will, won headlines for destroying saloons. In Wichita, Kansas, on December 27, 1900, Nation took a hatchet and broke bottles and bars at the luxurious Carey Hotel. Arrested and charged with causing $3,000 in damages, Nation spent a month in jail before the county dismissed the charges on account of "a delusion to such an extent as to be practically irresponsible." But Nation's "hatchetation" drew national attention. Describing herself as "a bulldog running along at the feet of Jesus, barking at what He doesn't like," she continued her assaults, and days later she smashed two more Wichita bars.[14]

Few women followed in Nation's footsteps, and many more worked within more reputable organizations. Nation, for instance, had founded a chapter of the Woman's Christian Temperance Union (WCTU), but the organization's leaders described her as "unwomanly and unchristian." The WCTU was founded in 1874 as a modest temperance organization devoted to combating the evils of drunkenness. But then, from 1879 to 1898, Frances Willard invigorated the organization by transforming it into a national political organization, embracing a "do everything" policy that adopted any and all reasonable reforms that would improve social welfare and advance women's rights. WCTU women worked to alleviate urban poverty, pursued prison reform, championed the eight-hour workday, pushed for child labor laws, advocated "home protection," and fought for numerous other progressive causes. Temperance, and then the full prohibition of alcohol, however, always loomed large.

Many American reformers associated alcohol with nearly every social ill. Alcohol was blamed for domestic abuse, poverty, crime, and disease. The 1912 Anti-Saloon League *Yearbook*, for instance, presented charts indicating comparable increases in alcohol consumption alongside rising divorce rates. The WCTU called alcohol a "home wrecker." More insidiously, perhaps, reformers also associated alcohol with cities and immigrants, necessarily maligning America's immigrants, Catholics, and working classes in their crusade against liquor. Still, reformers believed that the abolition of "strong drink" would bring about social progress, obviate the need for prisons and insane asylums, save women and children from domestic abuse, and usher in a more just, progressive society.

Powerful female activists emerged out of the club movement and temperance campaigns. Perhaps no American reformer matched Jane Addams in fame, energy, and innovation. Born in Cedarville, Illinois, in 1860, Addams lost her mother by age two and lived under the attentive care of her father. At seventeen, she left home to attend Rockford Female Seminary. An idealist, Addams sought the means to make the world a better place. She believed that well-educated women of means, such as herself, lacked practical strategies for engaging everyday reform. After four years at Rockford, Addams embarked on a multiyear "grand tour" of Europe. She found herself drawn to English settlement houses, a kind of prototype for social work in which philanthropists embedded themselves among communities and offered services to disadvantaged populations. After visiting London's Toynbee Hall in 1887, Addams returned to the United States and in 1889 founded Hull House in Chicago with her longtime confidant and companion Ellen Gates Starr.[15]

> The Settlement . . . is an experimental effort to aid in the solution of the social and industrial problems which are engendered by the modern conditions of life in a great city. It insists that these problems are not confined to any one portion of the city. It is an attempt to relieve, at the same time, the overaccumulation at one end of society and the destitution at the other. . . . It must be grounded in a philosophy whose foundation is on the solidarity of the human race, a philosophy which will not waver when the race happens to be represented by a drunken woman or an idiot boy.[16]

Hull House workers provided for their neighbors by running a nursery and a kindergarten, administering classes for parents and clubs for children, and organizing social and cultural events for the community. Reformer Florence Kelley, who stayed at Hull House from 1891 to 1899, convinced Addams to move into the realm of social reform.[17] Hull House began exposing conditions in local sweatshops and advocated for the organization of workers. She called the conditions caused by urban poverty and industrialization a "social crime." Hull House workers surveyed their community and produced statistics on poverty, disease, and living conditions. Addams began pressuring politicians. Together Kelley and Addams petitioned legislators to pass antisweatshop legislation that limited the hours of work for women and children to eight per day. Yet Addams was an upper-class white Protestant woman who, like many reformers, refused to embrace more radical policies. While Addams called labor organizing a "social obligation," she also warned the labor movement against the "constant temptation towards class warfare." Addams, like many reformers, favored cooperation between rich and poor and bosses and workers, whether cooperation was a realistic possibility or not.[18]

Addams became a kind of celebrity. In 1912, she became the first woman to give a nominating speech at a major party convention when she seconded the nomination of Theodore Roosevelt as the Progressive Party's candidate for president. Her campaigns for social reform and women's rights won headlines and her voice became ubiquitous in progressive politics.[19]

Addams's advocacy grew beyond domestic concerns. Beginning with her work in the Anti-Imperialist League during the Spanish-American War, Addams increasingly began to see militarism as a drain on resources better spent on social reform. In 1907 she wrote *Newer Ideals of Peace*, a book that would become for many a philosophical foundation of pacifism. Addams emerged as a prominent opponent of America's entry into World War I. She received the Nobel Peace Prize in 1931.[20]

It would be suffrage, ultimately, that would mark the full emergence of women in American public life. Generations of women—and, occasionally, men—had pushed for women's suffrage. Suffragists' hard work resulted in slow but encouraging steps forward during the last decades of the nineteenth century. Notable victories were won in the West, where suffragists mobilized large numbers of women and male politicians were open to experimental forms of governance. By 1911, six western states had passed suffrage amendments to their constitutions.

Women protested silently in front of the White House for over two years before passage of the Nineteenth Amendment. Here, women represent their alma maters as they picket the White House in support of women's suffrage. 1917. Library of Congress.

Women's suffrage was typically entwined with a wide range of reform efforts. Many suffragists argued that women's votes were necessary to clean up politics and combat social evils. By the 1890s, for example, the WCTU, then the largest women's organization in America, endorsed suffrage. An alliance of working-class and middle- and upper-class women organized the Women's Trade Union League (WTUL) in 1903 and campaigned for the vote alongside the National American Woman Suffrage Association, a leading suffrage organization composed largely of middle- and upper-class women. WTUL members viewed the vote as a way to further their economic interests and to foster a new sense of respect for working-class women. "What the woman who labors wants is the right to live, not simply exist," said Rose Schneiderman, a WTUL leader, during a 1912 speech. "The worker must have bread, but she must have roses, too."[21]

Many suffragists adopted a much crueler message. Some, even outside the South, argued that white women's votes were necessary to maintain white supremacy. Many white American women argued that enfranchising white upper- and middle-class women would counteract Black voters. These arguments even stretched into international politics. But whether the message advocated gender equality, class politics, or white supremacy, the suffrage campaign was winning.

The final push for women's suffrage came on the eve of World War I. Determined to win the vote, the National American Woman Suffrage Association developed a dual strategy that focused on the passage of state voting rights laws and on the ratification of an amendment to the U.S. Constitution. Meanwhile, a new, more militant, suffrage organization emerged on the scene. Led by Alice Paul, the National Woman's Party took to the streets to demand voting rights, organizing marches and protests that mobilized thousands of women. Beginning in January 1917, National Woman's Party members also began to picket the White House, an action that led to the arrest and imprisonment of over 150 women.[22]

In January 1918, President Woodrow Wilson declared his support for the women's suffrage amendment, and two years later women's suffrage became a reality. After the ratification of the Nineteenth Amendment, women from all walks of life mobilized to vote. They were driven by the promise of change but also in some cases by their anxieties about the future. Much had changed since their campaign began; the United States was now more industrial than not, increasingly more urban than rural. The activism and activities of these new urban denizens also gave rise to a new American culture.

IV. Targeting the Trusts

In one of the defining books of the Progressive Era, *The Promise of American Life*, Herbert Croly argued that because "the corrupt politician has usurped too much of the power which should be exercised by the people," the "millionaire and the trust have appropriated too many of the economic opportunities formerly enjoyed by the people." Croly and other reformers believed that wealth inequality eroded democracy and reformers had to win back for the people the power usurped by the moneyed trusts. But what exactly were these "trusts," and why did it suddenly seem so important to reform them?[22]

In the late nineteenth and early twentieth centuries, a trust was a monopoly or cartel associated with the large corporations of the Gilded and Progressive Eras who entered into agreements—legal or otherwise—or consolidations to exercise exclusive control over a specific product or industry under the control of a single entity. Certain types of monopolies, specifically for intellectual property like copyrights, patents, trademarks, and trade secrets, are protected under the Constitution "to promote the progress of science and useful arts," but for powerful entities to control entire national markets was something wholly new, and, for many Americans, wholly unsettling.

An illustration shows a "Standard Oil" storage tank as an octopus with tentacles wrapped around the steel, copper, and shipping industries, as well as a statehouse and the U.S. Capitol, and one tentacle reaching for the White House. The only building not yet within reach of the octopus is the White House—President Teddy Roosevelt had won a reputation as a trust buster. Udo Keppler, "Next!" 1904. Library of Congress.

The rapid industrialization, technological advancement, and urban growth of the 1870s and 1880s triggered major changes in the way businesses structured themselves. The Second Industrial Revolution, made possible by available natural resources, growth in the labor supply through immigration, increasing capital, new legal economic entities, novel production strategies, and a growing national market, was commonly asserted to be the natural product of the federal government's laissez faire, or "hands off," economic policy. An unregulated business climate, the argument went, allowed for the growth of major trusts, most notably Andrew Carnegie's Carnegie Steel (later consolidated with other producers as U.S. Steel) and John D. Rockefeller's Standard Oil Company. Each displayed the vertical and horizontal integration strategies common to the new trusts: Carnegie first used vertical integration by controlling every phase of business (raw materials, transportation, manufacturing, distribution), and Rockefeller adhered to horizontal integration by buying out competing refineries. Once dominant in a market, critics alleged, the trusts could artificially inflate prices, bully rivals, and bribe politicians.

Between 1897 and 1904, over four thousand companies were consolidated down into 257 corporate firms. As one historian wrote, "By 1904 a total of 318 trusts held 40% of US manufacturing assets and boasted a capitalization of $7 billion, seven times bigger than the US national debt."[24] With the twentieth century came the age of monopoly. Mergers and the aggressive business policies of wealthy men such as Carnegie and Rockefeller earned them the epithet *robber barons*. Their cutthroat stifling of economic competition, mistreatment of workers, and corruption of politics sparked an opposition that pushed for regulations to rein in the power of monopolies. The great corporations became a major target of reformers.

Big business, whether in meatpacking, railroads, telegraph lines, oil, or steel, posed new problems for the American legal system. Before the Civil War, most businesses operated in a single state. They might ship goods across state lines or to other countries, but they typically had offices and factories in just one state. Individual states naturally regulated industry and commerce. But extensive railroad routes crossed several state lines and new mass-producing corporations operated across the nation, raising questions about where the authority to regulate such practices rested. During the 1870s, many states passed laws to check the growing power of vast new corporations. In the Midwest, farmers formed a network of organizations that were part political pressure group, part social club, and part mutual aid society. Together they pushed for so-called Granger laws that regulated railroads and other new companies. Railroads and others opposed these regulations because they restrained profits and because of the difficulty of meeting the standards of each state's separate regulatory laws. In 1877, the U.S. Supreme Court upheld these laws in a series of rulings, finding in cases such as *Munn v. Illinois* and *Stone v. Wisconsin* that railroads and other companies of such size necessarily affected the public interest and could thus be regulated by individual states. In *Munn*, the court declared, "Property does become clothed with a public interest when used in a manner to make it of public consequence, and affect the community at large. When, therefore, one devoted his property to a use in which the public has an interest, he, in effect, grants to the public an interest in that use, and must submit to be controlled by the public for the common good, to the extent of the interest he has thus created."[25]

Later rulings, however, conceded that only the federal government could constitutionally regulate interstate commerce and the new national businesses operating it. And as more and more power and capital and market share flowed to the great corporations, the onus of regulation passed to the federal government. In 1887, Congress passed the Interstate Commerce Act, which established the Interstate Commerce Commission to stop discriminatory and predatory pricing practices. The Sherman Anti-Trust Act of 1890 aimed to limit anticompetitive practices, such as those institutionalized in cartels and monopolistic corporations. It stated that a "trust . . . or conspiracy, in restraint of trade or commerce . . . is declared to be illegal" and that those who "monopolize . . . any part of the trade or commerce . . . shall be deemed guilty."[26] The Sherman Anti-Trust Act declared that not all monopolies were illegal, only those that "unreasonably" stifled free trade. The courts seized on the law's vague language, however, and the act was turned against itself, manipulated and used, for instance, to limit the growing power of labor unions. Only in 1914, with the Clayton Anti-Trust Act, did Congress attempt to close loopholes in previous legislation.

Aggression against the trusts—and the progressive vogue for "trust busting"—took on new meaning under the presidency of Theodore Roosevelt, a reform-minded Republican who ascended to the presidency after the death of William McKinley in 1901. Roosevelt's youthful energy and confrontational politics captivated the nation.[27] Roosevelt was by no means antibusiness. Instead, he envisioned his presidency as a mediator between opposing forces, such as between labor unions and corporate executives. Despite his own wealthy background, Roosevelt pushed for antitrust legislation and regulations, arguing that the courts could not be relied on to break up the trusts. Roosevelt also used his own moral judgment to determine which monopolies he would pursue. Roosevelt believed that there were good and bad trusts, necessary monopolies and corrupt ones. Although his reputation as a trust buster was wildly exaggerated, he was the first major national politician to go after the trusts. "The great corporations which we have grown to speak of rather loosely as trusts," he said, "are the creatures of the State, and the State not only has the right to control them, but it is in duty bound to control them wherever the need of such control is shown."[28]

His first target was the Northern Securities Company, a "holding" trust in which several wealthy bankers, most famously J. P. Morgan, used to hold controlling shares in all the major railroad companies in the American Northwest. Holding trusts had emerged as a way to circumvent the Sherman Anti-Trust Act: by controlling the majority of shares, rather than the principal, Morgan and his collaborators tried to claim that it was not a monopoly. Roosevelt's administration sued and won in court, and in 1904 the Northern Securities Company was ordered to disband into separate competitive companies. Two years later, in 1906, Roosevelt signed the Hepburn Act, allowing the Interstate Commerce Commission to regulate best practices and set reasonable rates for the railroads.

Roosevelt was more interested in regulating corporations than breaking them apart. Besides, the courts were slow and unpredictable. However, his successor after 1908, William Howard Taft, firmly believed in court-oriented trust busting and during his four years in office more than doubled the number of monopoly breakups that occurred during Roosevelt's seven years in office. Taft notably went after U.S. Steel, the world's first billion-dollar corporation formed from the consolidation of nearly every major American steel producer.

Trust busting and the handling of monopolies dominated the election of 1912. When the Republican Party spurned Roosevelt's return to politics and renominated the incumbent Taft, Roosevelt left and formed his own coalition, the Progressive or "Bull Moose" Party. Whereas Taft took an all-encompassing view on the illegality of monopolies, Roosevelt adopted a New Nationalism program, which once again emphasized the regulation of already existing corporations or the expansion of federal power over the economy. In contrast, Woodrow Wilson, the Democratic Party nominee, emphasized in his New Freedom agenda neither trust busting nor federal regulation but rather small-business incentives so that individual companies could increase their competitive chances. Yet once he won the election, Wilson edged nearer to Roosevelt's position, signing the Clayton Anti-Trust Act of 1914. The Clayton Anti-Trust Act substantially enhanced the Sherman Act, specifically regulating mergers and price discrimination and protecting labor's access to collective bargaining and related strategies of picketing, boycotting, and protesting. Congress further created the Federal Trade Commission to enforce the Clayton Act, ensuring at least some measure of implementation.[29]

While the three presidents—Roosevelt, Taft, and Wilson—pushed the development and enforcement of antitrust law, their commitments were uneven, and trust busting itself manifested the political pressure put on politicians by the workers, farmers, and progressive writers who so strongly drew attention to the ramifications of trusts and corporate capital on the lives of everyday Americans.

V. Progressive Environmentalism

Photograph of the Hetch Hetchy Valley before damming, January 1908. Wikimedia.

The potential scope of environmental destruction wrought by industrial capitalism was unparalleled in human history. Professional bison hunting expeditions nearly eradicated an entire species, industrialized logging companies denuded whole forests, and chemical plants polluted an entire

region's water supply. As American development and industrialization marched westward, reformers embraced environmental protections.

Historians often cite preservation and conservation as two competing strategies that dueled for supremacy among environmental reformers during the Progressive Era. The tensions between these two approaches crystalized in the debate over a proposed dam in the Hetch Hetchy Valley in California. The fight revolved around the provision of water for San Francisco. Engineers identified the location where the Tuolumne River ran through Hetch Hetchy as an ideal site for a reservoir. The project had been suggested in the 1880s but picked up momentum in the early twentieth century. But the valley was located inside Yosemite National Park. (Yosemite was designated a national park in 1890, though the land had been set aside earlier in a grant approved by President Lincoln in 1864.) The debate over Hetch Hetchy revealed two distinct positions on the value of the valley and on the purpose of public lands.

John Muir, a naturalist, a writer, and founder of the Sierra Club, invoked the "God of the Mountains" in his defense of the valley in its supposedly pristine condition. Gifford Pinchot, arguably the father of American forestry and a key player in the federal management of national forests, meanwhile emphasized what he understood to be the purpose of conservation: "to take every part of the land and its resources and put it to that use in which it will serve the most people." Muir took a wider view of what the people needed, writing that "everybody needs beauty as well as bread."[30] These dueling arguments revealed the key differences in environmental thought: Muir, on the side of the preservationists, advocated setting aside pristine lands for their aesthetic and spiritual value, for those who could take his advice to "[get] in touch with the nerves of Mother Earth."[31] Pinchot, on the other hand, led the charge for conservation, a kind of environmental utilitarianism that emphasized the efficient

The photograph below, taken almost a century later, shows the obvious difference after damming, with the submergence of the valley floor under the reservoir waters. Photograph of the Hetch Hetchy Valley before damming, from the *Sierra Club Bulletin*, January 1908. Wikimedia; Daniel Mayer (photographer), May 2002.

use of available resources, through planning and control and "the prevention of waste."[32] In Hetch Hetchy, conservation won out. Congress approved the project in 1913. The dam was built and the valley flooded for the benefit of San Francisco residents.

While preservation was often articulated as an escape from an increasingly urbanized and industrialized way of life and as a welcome respite from the challenges of modernity (at least, for those who had the means to escape), the conservationists were more closely aligned with broader trends in American society. Although the "greatest good for the greatest number" was very nearly the catchphrase of conservation, conservationist policies most often benefited the nation's financial interests. For example, many states instituted game laws to regulate hunting and protect wildlife, but laws could be entirely unbalanced. In Pennsylvania, local game laws included requiring firearm permits for noncitizens, barred hunting on Sundays, and banned the shooting of songbirds. These laws disproportionately affected Italian immigrants, critics said, as Italians often hunted songbirds for subsistence, worked in mines for low wages every day but Sunday, and were too poor to purchase permits or to pay the fines levied against them when game wardens caught them breaking these new laws. Other laws, for example, offered up resources to businesses at costs prohibitive to all but the wealthiest companies and individuals, or with regulatory requirements that could be met only by companies with extensive resources.

But Progressive Era environmentalism addressed more than the management of American public lands. After all, reformers addressing issues facing the urban poor were also doing environmental work. Settlement house workers like Jane Addams and Florence Kelley focused on questions of health and sanitation, while activists concerned with working conditions, most notably Dr. Alice Hamilton, investigated both worksite hazards and occupational and bodily harm. The progressives' commitment to the provision of public services at the municipal level meant more coordination and oversight in matters of public health, waste management, and even playgrounds and city parks. Their work focused on the intersection of communities and their material environments, highlighting the urgency of urban environmental concerns.

While reform movements focused their attention on the urban poor, other efforts targeted rural communities. The Country Life movement, spearheaded by Liberty Hyde Bailey, sought to support agrarian families and encourage young people to stay in their communities and run family farms. Early-twentieth-century educational reforms included a commitment to environmentalism at the elementary level. Led by Bailey and Anna Botsford Comstock, the nature study movement took students outside to experience natural processes and to help them develop observational skills and an appreciation for the natural world.

Other examples highlight the interconnectedness of urban and rural communities in the late nineteenth and early twentieth centuries. The extinction of the North American passenger pigeon reveals the complexity of Progressive Era relationships between people and nature. Passenger pigeons were actively hunted, prepared at New York's finest restaurants and in the humblest of farm kitchens. Some hunted them for pay; others shot them in competitions at sporting clubs. And then they were gone, their ubiquity giving way only to nostalgia. Many Americans took notice at the great extinction of a species that had perhaps numbered in the billions and then was eradicated. Women in Audubon Society chapters organized against the fashion of wearing feathers—even whole birds—on ladies' hats. Upper- and middle-class women made up the lion's share of the membership of these societies. They used their social standing to fight for birds. Pressure created national wildlife refuges and key laws and regulations that included the Lacey Act of 1900, banning the shipment of species killed illegally across state lines. Examining how women mobilized contemporary notions of womanhood in the service of protecting birds reveals a tangle of cultural and economic processes. Such examples also reveal the range of ideas, policies, and practices wrapped up in figuring out what—and who—American nature should be for.

VI. Jim Crow and African American Life

America's tragic racial history was not erased by the Progressive Era. In fact, in all too many ways, reform removed African Americans ever farther from American public life. In the South, electoral politics remained a parade of electoral fraud, voter intimidation, and race-baiting. Democratic Party candidates stirred southern whites into frenzies with warnings of "negro domination" and of Black men violating white women. The region's culture of racial violence and the rise of lynching as a mass public spectacle accelerated. And as the remaining African American voters threatened the dominance of Democratic leadership in the South, southern Democrats turned to what many white southerners understood as a series of progressive electoral and social reforms—disenfranchisement and segregation. Just as reformers would clean up politics by taming city political machines, white southerners would "purify" the ballot box by restricting Black voting, and they would prevent racial strife by legislating the social separation of the races. The strongest supporters of such measures in the South were progressive Democrats and former Populists, both of whom saw in these reforms a way to eliminate the racial demagoguery that conservative Democratic party leaders had so effectively wielded. Leaders in both the North and South embraced and proclaimed the reunion of the sections on the basis of white supremacy. As the nation took up the "white man's burden" to uplift the world's racially inferior peoples, the North looked to the South as an example of how to manage nonwhite populations. The South had become the nation's racial vanguard.[33]

The question was how to accomplish disfranchisement. The Fifteenth Amendment clearly prohibited states from denying any citizen the right to vote on the basis of race. In 1890, a Mississippi state newspaper called on politicians to devise "some legal defensible substitute for the abhorrent and evil methods on which white supremacy lies."[34] The state's Democratic Party responded with a new state constitution designed to purge corruption at the ballot box through disenfranchisement. African Americans hoping to vote in Mississippi would have to jump through a series of hurdles designed with the explicit purpose of excluding them from political power. The state first established a poll tax, which required voters to pay for the privilege of voting. Second, it stripped suffrage from those convicted of petty crimes most common among the state's African Americans. Next, the state required voters to pass a literacy test. Local voting officials, who were themselves part of the local party machine, were responsible for judging whether voters were able to read and understand a section of the Constitution. In order to protect illiterate whites from exclusion, the so-called "understanding clause" allowed a voter to qualify if they could adequately explain the meaning of a section that was read to them. In practice these rules were systematically abused to the point where local election officials effectively wielded the power to permit and deny suffrage at will. The disenfranchisement laws effectively moved electoral conflict from the ballot box, where public attention was greatest, to the voting registrar, where supposedly color-blind laws allowed local party officials to deny the ballot without the appearance of fraud.[35]

Between 1895 and 1908, the rest of the states in the South approved new constitutions including these disenfranchisement tools. Six southern states also added a grandfather clause, which bestowed suffrage on anyone whose grandfather was eligible to vote in 1867. This ensured that whites who would have been otherwise excluded through mechanisms such as poll taxes or literacy tests would still be eligible, at least until grandfather clauses were struck down by the Supreme Court in 1915. Finally, each southern state adopted an all-white primary and excluded Black Americans from the Democratic primary, the only political contests that mattered across much of the South.[36]

For all the legal double-talk, the purpose of these laws was plain. James Kimble Vardaman, later governor of Mississippi, boasted that "there is no use to equivocate or lie about the matter. Mississippi's constitutional convention was held for no other purpose than to eliminate the nigger from politics; not the ignorant—but the nigger."[37] These technically color-blind tools did their work well. In 1900 Alabama had 121,159 literate Black men of voting age. Only 3,742 were registered to vote. Louisiana had 130,000 Black voters in the contentious election of 1896. Only 5,320 voted in 1900. Black people were clearly the target of these laws, but that did not prevent some whites from being disenfranchised as well. Louisiana dropped 80,000 white voters over the same period. Most politically engaged southern whites considered this a price worth paying to prevent the alleged fraud that plagued the region's elections.[38]

At the same time that the South's Democratic leaders were adopting the tools to disenfranchise the region's Black voters, these same legislatures were constructing a system of racial segregation even more pernicious. While it built on earlier practice, segregation was primarily a modern and urban system of enforcing racial subordination and deference. In rural areas, white and Black southerners negotiated the meaning of racial difference within the context of personal relationships of kinship and patronage. An African American who broke the local community's racial norms could expect swift personal sanction that often included violence. The crop lien and convict lease systems were the most important legal tools of racial control in the rural South. Maintaining white supremacy there did not require segregation. Maintaining white supremacy within the city, however, was a different matter altogether. As the region's railroad networks and cities expanded, so too did the anonymity and therefore freedom of southern Black people. Southern cities were becoming a center of Black middle-class life that was an implicit threat to racial hierarchies. White southerners created the system of segregation as a way to maintain white supremacy in restaurants, theaters, public restrooms, schools, water fountains, train cars, and hospitals. Segregation inscribed the superiority of whites and the deference of Black people into the very geography of public spaces.

As with disenfranchisement, segregation violated a plain reading of the Constitution—in this case the Fourteenth Amendment. Here the Supreme Court intervened, ruling in the *Civil Rights Cases* (1883) that the Fourteenth Amendment only prevented discrimination directly by states. It did not prevent discrimination by individuals, businesses, or other entities. Southern states exploited this interpretation with the first legal segregation of railroad cars in 1888. In a case that reached the Supreme Court in 1896, New Orleans resident Homer Plessy challenged the constitutionality of Louisiana's segregation of streetcars. The court ruled against Plessy and, in the process, established the legal principle of separate but equal. Racially segregated facilities were legal provided they were equivalent. In practice this was almost never the case. The court's majority defended its position with logic that reflected the racial assumptions of the day. "If one race be inferior to the other socially," the court explained, "the Constitution of the United States cannot put them upon the same plane." Justice John Harlan, the lone dissenter, countered, "Our Constitution is color-blind, and neither knows nor tolerates classes among citizens. In respect of civil rights, all citizens are equal before the law." Harlan went on to warn that the court's decision would "permit the seeds of race hatred to be planted under the sanction of law."[39] In their rush to fulfill Harlan's prophecy, southern whites codified and enforced the segregation of public spaces.

Segregation was built on a fiction—that there could be a white South socially and culturally distinct from African Americans. Its legal basis rested on the constitutional fallacy of "separate but equal." Southern whites erected a bulwark of white supremacy that would last for nearly sixty years. Segregation and disenfranchisement in the South rejected Black citizenship and relegated Black social and cultural life to segregated spaces. African Americans lived divided lives, acting the part whites demanded of them in public, while maintaining their own world apart from whites. This segregated world provided a measure of independence for the region's growing Black middle class, yet at the cost of poisoning the relationship between Black and white citizens. Segregation and disenfranchisement created entrenched structures of racism that completed the total rejection of the promises of Reconstruction.

And yet many Black Americans of the Progressive Era fought back. Just as activists such as Ida Wells worked against southern lynching,

Booker T. Washington and W. E. B. Du Bois vied for leadership among African American activists, resulting in years of intense rivalry and debated strategies for the uplifting of Black Americans.

Born into the world of bondage in Virginia in 1856, Booker Taliaferro Washington was subjected to the degradation and exploitation of slavery early in life. But Washington also developed an insatiable thirst to learn. Working against tremendous odds, Washington matriculated into Hampton University in Virginia and thereafter established a southern institution that would educate many Black Americans, the Tuskegee Institute, located in Alabama. Washington envisioned that Tuskegee's contribution to Black life would come through industrial education and vocational training. He believed that such skills would help African Americans accomplish economic independence while developing a sense of self-worth and pride of accomplishment, even while living within the putrid confines of Jim Crow. Washington poured his life into Tuskegee, and thereby connected with leading white philanthropic interests. Individuals such as Andrew Carnegie, for instance, financially assisted Washington and his educational ventures.

The strategies of Booker T. Washington and W. E. B. Du Bois differed, but their desire was the same: better lives for African Americans. Harris & Ewing, "WASHINGTON BOOKER T," between 1905 and 1915. Library of Congress.

Washington became a leading spokesperson for Black Americans at the turn of the twentieth century, particularly after Frederick Douglass's death in early 1895. Washington's famous "Atlanta Compromise" speech from that same year encouraged Black Americans to "cast your bucket down" to improve life's lot under segregation. In the same speech, delivered one year before the Supreme Court's *Plessy* v. *Ferguson* decision that legalized segregation under the "separate but equal" doctrine, Washington said to white Americans, "In all things that are purely social we can be as separate as the fingers, yet one as the hand in all things essential to mutual progress."[40] Washington was both praised as a race leader and pilloried as an accommodationist to America's unjust racial hierarchy; his public advocacy of a conciliatory posture toward white supremacy concealed the efforts to which he went to assist African Americans in the legal and economic quest for racial justice. In addition to founding Tuskegee, Washington also published a handful of influential books, including the autobiography *Up from Slavery* (1901). Like Du Bois, Washington was also active in Black journalism, working to fund and support Black newspaper publications, most of which sought to counter Du Bois's growing influence. Washington died in 1915, during World War I, of ill health in Tuskegee, Alabama.

Speaking decades later, Du Bois said Washington had, in his 1895 "Compromise" speech, "implicitly abandoned all political and social rights. . . . I never thought Washington was a bad man . . . I believed him to be sincere, though wrong." Du Bois would directly attack Washington in his classic 1903 *The Souls of Black Folk*, but at the turn of the century he could never escape the shadow of his longtime rival. "I admired much about him," Du Bois admitted. "Washington . . . died in 1915. A lot of people think I died at the same time."[41]

Du Bois's criticism reveals the politicized context of the Black freedom struggle and exposes the many positions available to Black activists. Born in Great Barrington, Massachusetts, in 1868, Du Bois entered the world as a free person of color three years after the Civil War ended. He was raised by a hardworking and independent mother; his New England childhood alerted him to the reality of race even as it invested the emerging thinker with an abiding faith in the power of education. Du Bois graduated at the top of his high school class and attended Fisk University. Du Bois's sojourn to the South in 1880s left a distinct impression that would guide his life's work to study what he called the "Negro problem," the systemic racial and economic discrimination that Du Bois prophetically pronounced would be *the* problem of the twentieth century. After Fisk,

Photograph of W. E. B. Du Bois taken in 1919. Library of Congress.

Du Bois's educational path trended back North. He attended Harvard, earned his second degree, crossed the Atlantic for graduate work in Germany, and circulated back to Harvard, and in 1895, he became the first Black American to receive a PhD there.

Du Bois became one of America's foremost intellectual leaders on questions of social justice by producing scholarship that underscored the humanity of African Americans. Du Bois's work as an intellectual, scholar, and college professor began during the Progressive Era, a time in American history marked by rapid social and cultural change as well as complex global political conflicts and developments. Du Bois addressed these domestic and international concerns not only in his classrooms at Wilberforce University in Ohio and Atlanta University in Georgia but also in a number of his early publications on the history of the transatlantic slave trade and Black life in urban Philadelphia. The most well-known of these early works included *The Souls of Black Folk* (1903) and *Darkwater* (1920). In these books, Du Bois combined incisive historical analysis with engaging literary drama to validate Black personhood *and* attack the inhumanity of white supremacy, particularly in the lead-up to and during World War I. In addition to publications and teaching, Du Bois set his sights on political organizing for civil rights, first with the Niagara Movement and later with its offspring, the NAACP. Du Bois's main work with the NAACP lasted from 1909 to 1934 as editor of *The Crisis*, one of America's leading Black publications. Du Bois attacked Washington and urged Black Americans to concede to nothing, to make no compromises and advocate for equal rights under the law. Throughout his early career, he pushed for civil rights legislation, launched legal challenges against discrimination, organized protests against injustice, and applied his capacity for clear research and sharp prose to expose the racial sins of Progressive Era America.

> We refuse to allow the impression to remain that the Negro-American assents to inferiority, is submissive under oppression and apologetic before insults. . . . Any discrimination based simply on race or color is barbarous, we care not how hallowed it be by custom, expediency or prejudice . . . discriminations based simply and solely on physical peculiarities, place of birth, color of skin, are relics of that unreasoning human savagery of which the world is and ought to be thoroughly ashamed. . . . Persistent manly agitation is the way to liberty.[42]

W. E. B. Du Bois and Booker T. Washington made a tremendous historical impact and left a notable historical legacy. They were reared under markedly different circumstances, and thus their early life experiences and even personal temperaments oriented both leaders' lives and outlooks in decidedly different ways. Du Bois's confrontational voice boldly targeted white supremacy. He believed in the power of social science to arrest the reach of white supremacy. Washington advocated incremental change for longer-term gain. He contended that economic self-sufficiency would pay off at a future date. Four years after Du Bois directly spoke out against Washington in the chapter "Of Mr. Booker T. Washington" in *Souls of Black Folk*, the two men shared the same lectern at Philadelphia Divinity School to address matters of race, history, and culture in the American South. Although their philosophies often differed, both men inspired others to demand that America live up to its democratic creed.

VII. Conclusion

Industrial capitalism unleashed powerful forces in American life. Along with wealth, technological innovation, and rising standards of living, a host of social problems unsettled many who turned to reform politics to set the world right again. The Progressive Era signaled that a turning point had been reached for many Americans who were suddenly willing to confront the age's problems with national political solutions. Reformers sought to bring order to chaos, to bring efficiency to inefficiency, and to bring justice to injustice. Causes varied, constituencies shifted, and the tangible effects of so much energy was difficult to measure, but the Progressive Era signaled a bursting of long-simmering tensions and introduced new patterns in the relationship between American society, American culture, and American politics.

VIII. Reference Material

This chapter was edited by Mary Anne Henderson, with content contributions by Andrew C. Baker, Peter Catapano, Blaine Hamilton, Mary Anne Henderson, Amanda Hughett, Amy Kohout, Maria Montalvo, Brent Ruswick, Philip Luke Sinitiere, Nora Slonimsky, Whitney Stewart, and Brandy Thomas Wells.

Recommended citation: Andrew C. Baker et al., "The Progressive Era," Mary Anne Henderson, ed., in *The American Yawp*, eds. Joseph Locke and Ben Wright (Stanford, CA: Stanford University Press, 2019).

NOTES TO CHAPTER 20

1. Jack London, *The Iron Heel* (New York: Macmillan, 1908), 104.

2. Philip Foner, *Women and the American Labor Movement: From Colonial Times to the Eve of World War I* (New York: Free Press, 1979).

3. Leon Stein, *The Triangle Fire* (Ithaca, NY: Syracuse University Press, 1962), 20.

4. Ibid., 144.

5. Ray Stannard Baker, *American Chronicle: The Autobiography of Ray Stannard Baker* (New York: Scribner, 1945), 183.

6. Jacob A. Riis, *How the Other Half Lives: Studies Among the Tenements of New York* (New York: Scribner, 1890).

7. Upton Sinclair, *The Jungle* (New York: Doubleday, 1906), 40.

8. Edward Bellamy, *Looking Backward: 2000–1887* (Boston: Ticknor, 1888).

9. Ibid., 368.

10. Charles M. Sheldon, *In His Steps: "What Would Jesus Do?"* (Chicago: Advance, 1896), 273.

11. Walter Rauschenbusch, *A Theology for the Social Gospel* (New York: Macmillan, 1917).

12. Ibid., 5.

13. See, for instance, Anne Firor Scott, "Most Invisible of All: Black Women's Voluntary Associations," *Journal of Southern History* 56 (January 1990): 3–22.

14. John Kobler, *Ardent Spirits: The Rise and Fall of Prohibition* (Boston: Da Capo Press, 1993), 147.

15. Toynbee Hall was the first settlement house. It was built in 1884 by Samuel Barnett as a place for Oxford students to live while at the same time working in the house's poor neighborhood. Daniel Rodgers, *Atlantic Crossings: Social Politics in a Progressive Age* (Cambridge, MA: Belknap Press, 1998), 64–65; Victoria Bissell Brown, *The Education of Jane Addams* (Philadelphia: University of Pennsylvania Press, 2004).

16. Jane Addams, *Twenty Years at Hull House* (New York: Macmillan, 1911), 125–126.

17. Allen Davis, *American Heroine: The Life and Legend of Jane Addams* (New York: Oxford University Press, 1979), 77.

18. Jane Addams, "The Settlement as a Factor in the Labor Movement," reprinted in *Hull-House Maps and Papers: A Presentation of Nationalities and Wages in a Congested District of Chicago Together with Comments and Essays on Problems Growing out of the Social Conditions* (Chicago: University of Illinois Press, 2007), 145, 149.

19. Kathryn Kish Sklar, "'Some of Us Who Deal with the Social Fabric': Jane Addams Blends Peace and Social Justice, 1907–1919," *Journal of the Gilded Age and Progressive Era* 2, no. 1 (January 2003).

20. Karen Manners Smith, "New Paths to Power: 1890–1920," in *No Small Courage: A History of Women in the United States*, ed. Nancy Cott (New York: Oxford University Press, 2000), 392.

21. Sarah Eisenstein, *Give Us Bread but Give Us Roses: Working Women's Consciousness in the United States, 1890 to the First World War* (New York: Routledge, 1983), 32.

22. Ellen Carol Dubois, *Women's Suffrage and Women's Rights* (New York: New York University Press, 1998).

23. Herbert Croly, *The Promise of American Life* (New York: Macmillan, 1911), 145.

24. Kevin P. Phillips, *Wealth and Democracy: A Political History of the American Rich* (New York: Broadway Books, 2003), 307.

25. *Munn v. Illinois*, 94 U.S. 113 (1877).

26. Interstate Commerce Act of 1887.

27. The writer Henry Adams said that he "showed the singular primitive quality that belongs to ultimate matter—the quality that medieval theology assigned to God—he was pure act." Henry Adams, *The Education of Henry Adams* (New York: Houghton Mifflin, 1918), 413.

28. Theodore Roosevelt, *Addresses and Presidential Messages of Theodore Roosevelt, 1902–1904*, 15.

29. The historiography on American progressive politics is vast. See, for instance, Michael McGerr, *A Fierce Discontent: The Rise and Fall of the Progressive Movement in America, 1870–1920* (New York: Free Press, 2003).

30. Roderick Nash, *Wilderness and the American Mind*, 4th ed. (New Haven, CT: Yale University Press, 2001), 167–168, 171, 165.

31. John Muir, *Our National Parks* (Boston: Houghton Mifflin, 1901).

32. Gifford Pinchot, *The Fight for Conservation* (New York: Doubleday Page, 1910), 44.

33. Michael Perman, *Struggle for Mastery: Disfranchisement in the South, 1888–1908* (Chapel Hill: University of North Carolina Press, 2001).

34. Edward Ayers, *The Promise of the New South* (New York: Oxford University Press, 1992), 147.

35. Ibid.

36. Ibid.

37. Neil R. McMillen, *Dark Journey: Black Mississippians in the Age of Jim Crow* (Champaign: University of Illinois Press, 1990), 43.

38. Perman, *Struggle for Mastery*, 147.

39. *Plessy v. Ferguson*, 163 U.S. 537 (1896).

40. Booker T. Washington, *Up from Slavery: An Autobiography* (New York: Doubleday, 1901), 221–222.

41. Kate A. Baldwin, *Beyond the Color Line and the Iron Curtain: Reading Encounters Between Black and Red* (Durham, NC: Duke University Press, 2002), 297 n. 28.

42. W. E. B. Du Bois, "Niagara's Declaration of Principles, 1905," Gilder Lehrman Center for the Study of Slavery, Resistance, and Abolition, https://glc .yale.edu/niagaras-declaration-principles-1905, accessed June 15, 2018.

RECOMMENDED READING

Ayers, Edward. *The Promise of the New South*. New York: Oxford University Press, 1992.

Bay, Mia. *To Tell the Truth Freely: The Life of Ida B. Wells*. New York: Hill and Wang, 2010.

Cott, Nancy. *The Grounding of Modern Feminism*. New Haven, CT: Yale University Press, 1987.

Dawley, Alan. *Struggles for Justice: Social Responsibility and the Liberal State*. Cambridge, MA: Harvard University Press, 1991.

Dubois, Ellen Carol. *Women's Suffrage and Women's Rights*. New York: New York University Press, 1998.

Filene, Peter. "An Obituary for 'The Progressive Movement,'" *American Quarterly* 22 (Spring 1970): 20–34.

Flanagan, Maureen. *America Reformed: Progressives and Progressivisms, 1890s–1920s*. New York: Oxford University Press, 2007.

Foley, Neil. *The White Scourge: Mexicans, Blacks, and Poor Whites in Texas Cotton Culture*. Berkeley: University of California Press, 1997.

Gilmore, Glenda E. *Gender and Jim Crow: Women and the Politics of White Supremacy in North Carolina, 1896–1920*. Chapel Hill: University of North Carolina Press, 1996.

Hale, Grace Elizabeth. *Making Whiteness: The Culture of Segregation in the South, 1890–1940*. New York: Oxford University Press, 1998.

Hicks, Cheryl. *Talk with You Like a Woman: African American Women, Justice, and Reform in New York, 1890–1935*. Chapel Hill: University of North Carolina Press, 2010.

Hofstadter, Richard. *The Age of Reform: From Bryan to F.D.R.* New York: Knopf, 1955.

Johnson, Kimberley. *Governing the American State: Congress and the New Federalism, 1877–1929.* Princeton, NJ: Princeton University Press, 2006.

Kessler-Harris, Alice. *In Pursuit of Equity: Women, Men, and the Quest for Economic Citizenship in 20th-Century America.* New York: Oxford University Press, 2001.

Kloppenberg, James T. *Uncertain Victory: Social Democracy and Progressivism in European and American Thought, 1870–1920.* New York: Oxford University Press, 1986.

Kolko, Gabriel. *The Triumph of Conservatism.* New York: Free Press, 1963.

Kousser, J. Morgan. *The Shaping of Southern Politics: Suffrage Restriction and the Establishment of the One-Party South, 1880–1910.* New Haven, CT: Yale University Press, 1974.

McGerr, Michael. *A Fierce Discontent: The Rise and Fall of the Progressive Movement in America, 1870–1920.* New York: Free Press, 2003.

Molina, Natalia. *Fit to Be Citizens?: Public Health and Race in Los Angeles, 1879–1939.* Berkeley: University of California Press, 2006.

Muncy, Robyn. *Creating a Female Dominion in American Reform, 1890–1935.* New York: Oxford University Press, 1991.

Rodgers, Daniel T. *Atlantic Crossings: Social Politics in a Progressive Age.* Cambridge, MA: Harvard University Press, 2000.

Sanders, Elizabeth. *The Roots of Reform: Farmers, Workers, and the American State, 1877–1917.* Chicago: University of Chicago Press, 1999.

Stromquist, Shelton. *Re-Inventing "The People": The Progressive Movement, the Class Problem, and the Origins of Modern Liberalism.* Champaign: University of Illinois Press, 2006.

White, Deborah. *Too Heavy a Load: In Defense of Themselves.* New York: Norton, 1999.

Wiebe, Robert. *The Search for Order, 1877–1920.* New York: Hill and Wang, 1967.

21

World War I and Its Aftermath

I. Introduction

World War I ("The Great War") toppled empires, created new nations, and sparked tensions that would explode across future years. On the battlefield, gruesome modern weaponry wrecked an entire generation of young men. The United States entered the conflict in 1917 and was never again the same. The war heralded to the world the United States' potential as a global military power, and, domestically, it advanced but then beat back American progressivism by unleashing vicious waves of repression. The war simultaneously stoked national pride and fueled disenchantments that burst Progressive Era hopes for the modern world. And it laid the groundwork for a global depression, a second world war, and an entire history of national, religious, and cultural conflict around the globe.

Striking steel mill workers holding bulletins in Chicago, Illinois, September 22, 1919. ExplorePAhistory .com.

II. Prelude to War

As the German empire rose in power and influence at the end of the nineteenth century, skilled diplomats maneuvered this disruption of traditional powers and influences into several decades of European peace. In Germany, however, a new ambitious monarch would overshadow years of tactful diplomacy. Wilhelm II rose to the German throne in 1888. He admired the British Empire of his grandmother, Queen Victoria, and envied the Royal Navy of Great Britain so much that he attempted to build a rival German navy and plant colonies around the globe. The British viewed the prospect of a German navy as a strategic threat, but, jealous of what he perceived as a lack of prestige in the world, Wilhelm II pressed Germany's case for access to colonies and symbols of status suitable for a world power. Wilhelm's maneuvers and Germany's rise spawned a new system of alliances as rival nations warily watched Germany's expansion.

In 1892, German posturing worried the leaders of Russia and France and prompted a defensive alliance to counter the existing triple threat between Germany, Austro-Hungary, and Italy. Britain's Queen Victoria remained unassociated with the alliances until a series of diplomatic crises and an emerging German naval threat led to British agreements with Tsar Nicholas II and French President Émile Loubet in the early twentieth century. (The alliance between Great Britain, France, and Russia became known as the Triple Entente.)

The other great threat to European peace was the Ottoman Empire, in Turkey. While the leaders of the Austro-Hungarian Empire showed little interest in colonies elsewhere, Turkish lands on its southern border appealed to their strategic goals. However, Austro-Hungarian expansion in Europe worried Tsar Nicholas II, who saw Russia as both the historic guarantor of the Slavic nations in the Balkans and the competitor for territories governed by the Ottoman Empire.

By 1914, the Austrian-Hungarian Empire had control of Bosnia and Herzegovina and viewed Slavic Serbia, a nation protected by Russia, as its next challenge. On June 28, 1914, after Serbian Gavrilo Princip assassinated the Austro-Hungarian heirs to the throne, Archduke Franz Ferdinand and his wife, Grand Duchess Sophie, vengeful nationalist leaders believed the time had arrived to eliminate the rebellious ethnic Serbian threat.[1]

On the other side of the Atlantic, the United States played an insignificant role in global diplomacy—it rarely forayed into internal European politics. The federal government did not participate in international diplomatic alliances but nevertheless championed and assisted with the expansion of the transatlantic economy. American businesses and consumers benefited from the trade generated as the result of the extended period of European peace.

Stated American attitudes toward international affairs followed the advice given by President George Washington in his 1796 Farewell Address, 120 years before America's entry into World War I. He had recommended that his fellow countrymen avoid "foreign alliances, attachments, and intrigues" and "those overgrown military establishments which, under any form of government, are inauspicious to liberty, and which are to be regarded as particularly hostile to republican liberty."[2]

A foreign policy of neutrality reflected America's inward-looking focus on the construction and management of its new powerful industrial economy (built in large part with foreign capital). The federal government possessed limited diplomatic tools with which to engage in international struggles for world power. America's small and increasingly antiquated military precluded forceful coercion and left American diplomats to persuade by reason, appeals to justice, or economic coercion. But in the 1880s, as Americans embarked upon empire, Congress authorized the construction of a modern navy. The army nevertheless remained small and underfunded compared to the armies of many industrializing nations.

After the turn of the century, the army and navy faced a great deal of organizational uncertainty. New technologies—airplanes, motor vehicles, submarines, modern artillery—stressed the capability of army and navy personnel to effectively procure and use them. The nation's army could police Native Americans in the West and garrison recent overseas acquisitions, but it could not sustain a full-blown conflict of any size. The Davis Act of 1908 and the National Defense Act of 1916 inaugurated the rise of the modern versions of the National Guard and military reserves. A system of state-administered units available for local emergencies that received conditional federal funding for training could be activated for use in international wars. The National Guard program encompassed individual units separated by state borders. The program supplied summer training for college students as a reserve officer corps. Federal and state governments now had a long-term strategic reserve of trained soldiers and sailors.[3]

Border troubles in Mexico served as an important field test for modern American military forces. Revolution and chaos threatened American

business interests in Mexico. Mexican reformer Francisco Madero challenged Porfirio Diaz's corrupt and unpopular conservative regime. He
was jailed, fled to San Antonio, and penned the Plan of San Luis Potosí,
paving the way for the Mexican Revolution and the rise of armed revolutionaries across the country.

In April 1914, President Woodrow Wilson ordered Marines to ac-
company a naval escort to Veracruz on the lower eastern coast of Mexico. After a brief battle, the Marines supervised the city government and
prevented shipments of German arms to Mexican leader Victoriano
Huerta until they departed in November 1914. The raid emphasized the
continued reliance on naval forces and the difficulty in modernizing the
military during a period of European imperial influence in the Caribbean and elsewhere. The threat of war in Europe enabled passage of the
Naval Act of 1916. President Wilson declared that the national goal was
to build the Navy as "incomparably, the greatest . . . in the world." And
yet Mexico still beckoned. The Wilson administration had withdrawn its
support of Diaz but watched warily as the revolution devolved into assassinations and deceit. In 1916, Pancho Villa, a popular revolutionary in
northern Mexico, raided Columbus, New Mexico, after being provoked
by American support for his rivals. His raiders killed seventeen Americans and burned down the town center before American soldiers forced
their retreat. In response, President Wilson commissioned Army general
John "Black Jack" Pershing to capture Villa and disperse his rebels. Motorized vehicles, reconnaissance aircraft, and the wireless telegraph aided
in the pursuit of Villa. Motorized vehicles in particular allowed General
Pershing to obtain supplies without relying on railroads controlled by the
Mexican government. The aircraft assigned to the campaign crashed or
were grounded by mechanical malfunctions, but they provided invalu-
able lessons in their worth and use in war. Wilson used the powers of
the new National Defense Act to mobilize over one hundred thousand
National Guardsmen across the country as a show of force in northern
Mexico.[4]

The conflict between the United States and Mexico might have escalated into full-scale war if the international crisis in Europe had not
overwhelmed the public's attention. After the outbreak of war in Europe
in 1914, President Wilson declared American neutrality. He insisted from
the start that the United States be neutral "in fact as well as in name," a
policy the majority of American people enthusiastically endorsed. It was
unclear, however, what "neutrality" meant in a world of close economic

connections. Ties to the British and French proved strong, and those nations obtained far more loans and supplies than the Germans. In October 1914, President Wilson approved commercial credit loans to the combatants, which made it increasingly difficult for the nation to claim impartiality as war spread through Europe. Trade and financial relations with the Allied nations ultimately drew the United States further into the conflict. In spite of mutually declared blockades between Germany, Great Britain, and France, munitions and other war suppliers in the United States witnessed a brisk and booming increase in business. The British naval blockades that often stopped or seized ships proved annoying and costly, but the unrestricted and surprise torpedo attacks from German submarines were deadly. In May 1915, Germans sank the RMS *Lusitania*. Over a hundred American lives were lost. The attack, coupled with other German attacks on American and British shipping, raised the ire of the public and stoked the desire for war.[5]

American diplomatic tradition avoided formal alliances, and the Army seemed inadequate for sustained overseas fighting. However, the United States outdistanced the nations of Europe in one important measure of world power: by 1914, the nation held the top position in the global industrial economy. The United States was producing slightly more than one third of the world's manufactured goods, roughly equal to the outputs of France, Great Britain, and Germany combined.

III. War Spreads Through Europe

After the assassination of Archduke Ferdinand and Grand Duchess Sophie, Austria secured the promise of aid from its German ally and issued a list of ten ultimatums to Serbia. On July 28, 1914, Austria declared war on Serbia for failure to meet all of the demands. Russia, determined to protect Serbia, began to mobilize its armed forces. On August 1, 1914, Germany declared war on Russia to protect Austria after warnings directed at Tsar Nicholas II failed to stop Russian preparations for war.

In spite of the central European focus of the initial crises, the first blow was struck against neutral Belgium in northwestern Europe. Germany planned to take advantage of sluggish Russian mobilization by focusing the German army on France. German military leaders recycled tactics developed earlier and activated the Schlieffen Plan, which moved German armies rapidly by rail to march through Belgium and into France. However, this violation of Belgian neutrality also ensured that Great Britain

A French assault on German positions in Champagne, France. 1917. National Archives.

entered the war against Germany. On August 4, 1914, Great Britain declared war on Germany for failing to respect Belgium as a neutral nation.

In 1915, the European war had developed into a series of bloody trench stalemates that continued through the following year. Offensives, largely carried out by British and French armies, achieved nothing but huge numbers of casualties. Peripheral campaigns against the Ottoman Empire in Turkey at Gallipoli, throughout the Middle East, and in various parts of Africa either were unsuccessful or had little bearing on the European contest for victory. The third year of the war, however, witnessed a coup for German military prospects: the regime of Tsar Nicholas II collapsed in Russia in March 1917. At about the same time, the Germans again pursued unrestricted submarine warfare to deprive the Allies of replenishment supplies from the United States.[6]

The Germans, realizing that submarine warfare could spark an American intervention, hoped the European war would be over before American soldiers could arrive in sufficient numbers to alter the balance of power. A German diplomat, Arthur Zimmermann, planned to complicate the potential American intervention. He offered support to the Mexican government via a desperate bid to regain Texas, New Mexico, and Arizona. Mexican national leaders declined the offer, but the revelation of the Zimmermann Telegram helped usher the United States into the war.

IV. America Enters the War

By the fall of 1916 and spring of 1917, President Wilson believed an imminent German victory would drastically and dangerously alter the balance of power in Europe. Submarine warfare and the Zimmermann Telegram, meanwhile, inflamed public opinion. Congress declared war on Germany on April 4, 1917. The nation entered a war three thousand miles away with a small and unprepared military. The United States was unprepared in nearly every respect for modern war. Considerable time elapsed before an effective army and navy could be assembled, trained, equipped, and deployed to the Western Front in Europe. The process of building the army and navy for the war proved to be different from previous conflicts. Unlike the largest European military powers of Germany, France, and Austro-Hungary, no tradition existed in the United States to maintain large standing armed forces or trained military reserves during peacetime. Moreover, there was no American counterpart to the European practice of rapidly equipping, training, and mobilizing reservists and conscripts.

The Boy Scouts of America charge up Fifth Avenue in New York City in a "Wake Up, America" parade in 1917 to support recruitment efforts. Nearly sixty thousand people attended the single parade. Wikimedia.

The United States historically relied solely on traditional volunteerism to fill the ranks of the armed forces. Notions of patriotic duty and adventure appealed to many young men who not only volunteered for wartime service but sought and paid for their own training at army camps before the war. American labor organizations favored voluntary service over conscription. Labor leader Samuel Gompers argued for volunteerism in letters to the congressional committees considering the question. "The organized labor movement," he wrote, "has always been fundamentally opposed to compulsion." Referring to American values as a role model for others, he continued, "It is the hope of organized labor to demonstrate that under voluntary conditions and institutions the Republic of the United States can mobilize its greatest strength, resources and efficiency."[7]

Despite fears of popular resistance, Congress quickly instituted a reasonably equitable and locally administered system to draft men for the military. On May 18, 1917, Congress approved the Selective Service Act, and President Wilson signed it a week later. The new legislation avoided the unpopular system of bonuses and substitutes used during the Civil War and was generally received without major objection by the American people.[8]

The conscription act initially required men from ages twenty-one to thirty to register for compulsory military service. Basic physical fitness was the primary requirement for service. The resulting tests offered the emerging fields of social science a range of data collection tools and new screening methods. The Army Medical Department examined the general condition of young American men selected for service from the population. The Surgeon General compiled his findings from draft records in the 1919 report, "Defects Found in Drafted Men," a snapshot of the 2.5 million men examined for military service. Of that group, 1,533,937 physical defects were recorded (often more than one per individual). More than 34 percent of those examined were rejected for service or later discharged for neurological, psychiatric, or mental deficiencies.[9]

To provide a basis for the neurological, psychiatric, and mental evaluations, the army used cognitive skills tests to determine intelligence. About 1.9 million men were tested on intelligence. Soldiers who could read took the Army Alpha test. Illiterates and non-English-speaking immigrants took the nonverbal equivalent, the Army Beta test, which relied on visual testing procedures. Robert M. Yerkes, president of the American Psychological Association and chairman of the Committee on the Psychological Examination of Recruits, developed and analyzed the tests. His data argued that the actual mental age of recruits was only about thirteen years. Among recent immigrants, he said, it was even lower. As a eugenicist, he interpreted the results as roughly equivalent to a mild level of retardation and as an indication of racial deterioration. Years later, experts agreed that the results misrepresented the levels of education for the recruits and revealed defects in the design of the tests.

The experience of service in the army expanded many individual social horizons as native-born and foreign-born soldiers served together. Immigrants had been welcomed into Union ranks during the Civil War, including large numbers of Irish and Germans who had joined and fought alongside native-born men. Some Germans in the Civil War fought in units where German was the main language. Between 1917 and 1918, the army accepted immigrants with some hesitancy because of the widespread public agitation against "hyphenated Americans." Others were segregated.

Prevailing racial attitudes among white Americans mandated the assignment of white and Black soldiers to different units. Despite racial discrimination, many Black American leaders, such as W. E. B. Du Bois, supported the war effort and sought a place at the front for Black soldiers. Black leaders viewed military service as an opportunity to demonstrate to white society the willingness and ability of Black men to assume all duties and responsibilities of citizens, including wartime sacrifice. If Black soldiers were drafted and fought and died on equal footing with white soldiers, then white Americans would see that they deserved full citizenship. The War Department, however, barred Black troops from

Propagandistic images increased patriotism in a public relatively detached from events taking place overseas. This photograph, showing two United States soldiers sprinting past the bodies of two German soldiers toward a bunker, showed Americans the heroism evinced by their men in uniform. Likely a staged image, taken after the fighting ended, it nonetheless played on the public's patriotism, telling them to step up and support the troops. "At close grips with the Hun, we bomb the corkshafer's, etc.," c. 1922?. Library of Congress.

combat and relegated Black soldiers to segregated service units where they worked as general laborers.

The army also often restricted the privileges of Black soldiers to ensure that the conditions they encountered in Europe did not lead them to question their place in American society. In France, however, the experiences of Black soldiers during training and periods of leave, coupled with their service, proved transformative. The U.S. government exercised significant social control over its overseas soldiers. To ensure that American "doughboys" did not succumb to European vices, several religious and progressive organizations created an extensive program designed to keep the men pure of heart, mind, and body. With assistance from the Young Men's Christian Association (YMCA) and other temperance organizations, the War Department put together a program of schools, sightseeing tours, and recreational facilities to provide wholesome and educational outlets. The soldiers welcomed most of the activities from these groups, but many still managed to find and enjoy the traditional recreations of soldiers at war.[10]

Women reacted to the war preparations by joining several military and civilian organizations. Their enrollment and actions in these organizations proved to be a pioneering effort for American women in war. Military leaders authorized the permanent gender transition of several occupations that gave women opportunities to don uniforms where none had existed before in history. Civilian wartime organizations, although chaired by male members of the business elite, boasted all-female volunteer workforces. Women performed the bulk of volunteer work during the war.[11]

The admittance of women brought considerable upheaval. The War and Navy Departments authorized the enlistment of women to fill positions in several established administrative occupations. The gendered transition of these jobs freed more men to join combat units. Army women served as telephone operators (Hello Girls) for the Signal Corps, navy women enlisted as yeomen (clerical workers), and the first groups of women joined the Marine Corps in July 1918. Approximately twenty-five thousand nurses served in the Army and Navy Nurse Corps for duty stateside and overseas, and about a hundred female physicians were contracted by the army. Neither the female nurses nor the doctors served as commissioned officers in the military. The army and navy chose to appoint them instead, which left the status of professional medical women hovering somewhere between the enlisted and officer ranks. As a result, many female nurses and doctors suffered various physical and mental abuses at the hands of their male coworkers with no system of redress in place.[12]

Millions of women also volunteered in civilian organizations such as the American Red Cross, the Young Men's and Women's Christian Associations (YMCA/YWCA), and the Salvation Army. Most women performed their volunteer duties in communal spaces owned by the leaders of the municipal chapters of these organizations. Women met at designated times to roll bandages, prepare and serve meals and snacks, package and ship supplies, and organize community fund-raisers. The variety of volunteer opportunities gave women the ability to appear in public spaces and promote charitable activities for the war effort. Female volunteers encouraged entire communities, including children, to get involved in war work. While most of these efforts focused on support for the home front, a small percentage of female volunteers served with the American Expeditionary Force in France.[13]

Jim Crow segregation in both the military and the civilian sector stood as a barrier for Black women who wanted to give their time to the war effort. The military prohibited Black women from serving as enlisted or appointed medical personnel. The only avenue for Black women to wear a military uniform existed with the armies of the allied nations. A few Black female doctors and nurses joined the French Foreign Legion to escape the racism in the American army. Black female volunteers faced the same discrimination in civilian wartime organizations. White leaders of the American Red Cross, YMCA/YWCA, and Salvation Army municipal chapters refused to admit Black women as equal participants. Black women were forced to charter auxiliary units as subsidiary divisions and were given little guidance on organizing volunteers. They turned instead to the community for support and recruited millions of women for auxiliaries that supported the nearly two hundred thousand Black soldiers and sailors serving in the military. While most female volunteers labored to care for Black families on the home front, three YMCA secretaries worked with the Black troops in France.[14]

V. On the Homefront

In the early years of the war, Americans were generally detached from the events in Europe. Progressive Era reform politics dominated the political landscape, and Americans remained most concerned with the shifting

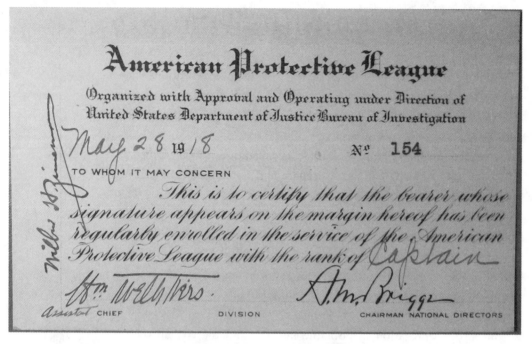

A membership card for the American Protective League, issued May 28, 1918. German immigrants in the United States aroused popular suspicions during World War I and the American Protective League (APL), a group of private citizens, worked directly with the U.S. government to identify suspected German sympathizers and to eradicate all antiwar and politically radical activities through surveillance, public shaming, and government raids. J. Edgar Hoover, the head of the Bureau of Investigation (later the Federal Bureau of Investigation, or FBI), used the APL to gather intelligence. Wikimedia.

role of government at home. However, the facts of the war could not be ignored by the public. The destruction taking place on European battle-fields and the ensuing casualty rates exposed the unprecedented brutality of modern warfare. Increasingly, a sense that the fate of the Western world lay in the victory or defeat of the Allies took hold in the United States.

President Wilson, a committed progressive, articulated a global vision of democracy even as he embraced neutrality. As war engulfed Europe, it seemed apparent that the United States' economic power would shape the outcome of the conflict regardless of any American military intervention. By 1916, American trade with the Allies tripled, while trade with the Central Powers shrank to less than 1 percent of previous levels.

The progression of the war in Europe generated fierce national debates about military preparedness. The Allies and the Central Powers had quickly raised and mobilized vast armies and navies. The United States still had a small military. When America entered the war, the mobilization of military resources and the cultivation of popular support consumed the country, generating enormous publicity and propaganda campaigns. President Wilson created the Committee on Public Information, known as the Creel Committee, headed by Progressive George Creel, to inspire patriotism and generate support for military adventures. Creel enlisted the help of Hollywood studios and other budding media outlets to cultivate a view of the war that pitted democracy against imperialism and framed America as a crusading nation rescuing Western civilization from medievalism and militarism. As war passions flared, challenges to the onrushing patriotic sentiment that America was making the world "safe for democracy" were considered disloyal. Wilson signed the Espionage Act in 1917 and the Sedition Act in 1918, stripping dissenters and protesters of their rights to publicly resist the war. Critics and protesters were imprisoned. Immigrants, labor unions, and political radicals became targets of government investigations and an ever more hostile public culture. Meanwhile, the government insisted that individual financial contributions made a discernible difference for the men on the Western Front. Americans lent their financial support to the war effort by purchasing war bonds or supporting the Liberty Loan Drive. Many Americans, however, sacrificed much more than money.[15]

VI. Before the Armistice

European powers struggled to adapt to the brutality of modern war. Until the spring of 1917, the Allies possessed few effective defensive measures against submarine attacks. German submarines sank more than a thousand ships by the time the United States entered the war. The rapid addition of American naval escorts to the British surface fleet and the establishment of a convoy system countered much of the effect of German submarines. Shipping and military losses declined rapidly, just as the American army arrived in Europe in large numbers. Although much of the equipment still needed to make the transatlantic passage, the physical presence of the army proved a fatal blow to German war plans.[16]

In July 1917, after one last disastrous offensive against the Germans, the Russian army disintegrated. The tsarist regime collapsed and in November 1917 Vladimir Lenin's Bolshevik party came to power. Russia soon surrendered to German demands and exited the war, freeing Germany to finally fight the one-front war it had desired since 1914. The German military quickly shifted hundreds of thousands of soldiers from the eastern theater in preparation for a new series of offensives planned for the following year in France.[17]

In March 1918, Germany launched the Kaiserschlacht (Spring Offensive), a series of five major attacks. By the middle of July 1918, each and every one had failed to break through the Western Front. On August 8, 1918, two million men of the American Expeditionary Forces joined British and French armies in a series of successful counteroffensives that pushed the disintegrating German lines back across France. German general Erich Ludendorff referred to the launch of the counteroffensive as the "black day of the German army." The German offensive gamble exhausted Germany's faltering military effort. Defeat was inevitable. Kaiser Wilhelm II abdicated at the request of the German military leaders and the new democratic government agreed to an armistice (cease-fire) on November 11, 1918. German military forces withdrew from France and Belgium and returned to a Germany teetering on the brink of chaos.[18]

By the end of the war, more than 4.7 million American men had served in all branches of the military: four million in the army, six hundred thousand in the navy, and about eighty thousand in the Marine Corps. The United States lost over one hundred thousand men (fifty-three thousand died in battle, and even more from disease). Their terrible sacrifice, however, paled before the Europeans'. After four years of brutal stalemate, France had suffered almost a million and a half military dead and Germany even more. Both nations lost about 4 percent of their population to the war. And death was not done.[19]

VII. The War and the Influenza Pandemic

Even as war raged on the Western Front, a new deadly threat loomed: influenza. In the spring of 1918, a strain of the flu virus appeared in the farm country of Haskell County, Kansas, and hit nearby Camp Funston, one of the largest army training camps in the nation. The virus spread like wildfire. The camp had brought disparate populations together, shuffled them between bases, sent them back to their homes across the nation, and, in consecutive waves, deployed them around the world. Between March and May 1918, fourteen of the largest American military training camps reported outbreaks of influenza. Some of the infected soldiers carried the virus on troop transports to France. By September 1918, influenza spread to all training camps in the United States. And then it mutated.[20]

The second wave of the virus, a mutated strain, was even deadlier than the first. It struck down those in the prime of their lives: a disproportionate amount of influenza victims were between ages eighteen and thirty-five. In Europe, influenza hit both sides of the Western Front. The

"Spanish Influenza," or the "Spanish Lady," misnamed due to accounts of the disease that first appeared in the uncensored newspapers of neutral Spain, resulted in the deaths of an estimated fifty million people world-wide. Reports from the Surgeon General of the Army revealed that while 227,000 American soldiers were hospitalized from wounds received in battle, almost half a million suffered from influenza. The worst part of the epidemic struck during the height of the Meuse-Argonne Offensive in the fall of 1918 and weakened the combat capabilities of the American and German armies. During the war, more soldiers died from influenza than combat. The pandemic continued to spread after the armistice be-fore finally fading in the early 1920s. No cure was ever found.[21]

VIII. The Fourteen Points and the League of Nations

As the flu virus wracked the world, Europe and America rejoiced at the end of hostilities. On December 4, 1918, President Wilson became the first American president to travel overseas during his term. He intended to shape the peace. The war brought an abrupt end to four great European imperial powers. The German, Russian, Austro-Hungarian, and Ottoman Empires evaporated, and the map of Europe was redrawn to accommo-date new independent nations. As part of the armistice, Allied forces fol-lowed the retreating Germans and occupied territories in the Rhineland to prevent Germany from reigniting war. As Germany disarmed, Wilson and the other Allied leaders gathered in France at Versailles for the Paris Peace Conference to dictate the terms of a settlement to the war. After months of deliberation, the Treaty of Versailles officially ended the war.

Earlier that year, on January 8, 1918, before a joint session of Congress, President Wilson offered an ambitious statement of war aims and peace terms known as the Fourteen Points. The plan not only dealt with territo-rial issues but offered principles on which a long-term peace could be built. But in January 1918, Germany still anticipated a favorable verdict on the battlefield and did not seriously consider accepting the terms of the Four-teen Points. The Allies were even more dismissive. French prime minister Georges Clemenceau remarked, "The good Lord only had ten [points]."[22]

President Wilson labored to realize his vision of the postwar world. The United States had entered the fray, Wilson proclaimed, "to make the world safe for democracy." At the center of the plan was a novel inter-national organization—the League of Nations—charged with keeping a worldwide peace by preventing the kind of destruction that tore across Europe and "affording mutual guarantees of political independence and territorial integrity to great and small states alike." This promise of collective security, that an attack on one sovereign member would be viewed as an attack on all, was a key component of the Fourteen Points.[23]

But the fight for peace was daunting. While President Wilson was celebrated in Europe and welcomed as the "God of Peace," his fellow statesmen were less enthusiastic about his plans for postwar Europe. America's closest allies had little interest in the League of Nations. Allied leaders sought to guarantee the future safety of their own nations. Unlike the United States, the Allies endured the horrors of the war firsthand. They refused to sacrifice further. The negotiations made clear that British prime minister David Lloyd-George was more interested in preserving Britain's imperial domain, while French prime minister Clemenceau sought a peace that recognized the Allies' victory and the Central Powers' culpability: he wanted reparations—severe financial penalties—and limits on Germany's future ability to wage war. The fight for the League of Nations was therefore largely on the shoulders of President Wilson. By June 1919, the final version of the treaty was signed and President Wilson was able to return home. The treaty was a compromise that included demands for German reparations, provisions for the League of Nations, and the promise of collective security. For President Wilson, it was an imperfect peace, but an imperfect peace was better than none at all.

The real fight for the League of Nations was on the American home front. Republican senator Henry Cabot Lodge of Massachusetts stood as the most prominent opponent of the League of Nations. As chair of the Senate Foreign Relations Committee and an influential Republican Party leader, he could block ratification of the treaty. Lodge attacked the treaty for potentially robbing the United States of its sovereignty. Never an isolationist, Lodge demanded instead that the country deal with its own problems in its own way, free from the collective security—and oversight—offered by the League of Nations. Unable to match Lodge's influence in the Senate, President Wilson took his case to the American people in the hopes that ordinary voters might be convinced that the only guarantee of future world peace was the League of Nations. During his grueling cross-country trip, however, President Wilson suffered an incapacitating stroke. His opponents had the upper hand.[24]

President Wilson's dream for the League of Nations died on the floor of the Senate. Lodge's opponents successfully blocked America's entry into the League of Nations, an organization conceived and championed by the American president. The League of Nations operated with fifty-eight sovereign members, but the United States refused to join, refused to lend it American power, and refused to provide it with the power needed to fulfill its purpose.[25]

IX. Aftermath of World War I

The war transformed the world. The Middle East, for instance, was drastically changed. For centuries the Ottoman Empire had shaped life in the region. Before the war, the Middle East had three main centers of power: the Ottoman Empire, Egypt, and Iran. President Wilson's call for self-determination appealed to many under the Ottoman Empire's rule. In the aftermath of the war, Wilson sent a commission to investigate the region to determine the conditions and aspirations of the populace. The King-Crane Commission found that most of the inhabitants favored an independent state free of European control. However, these wishes were largely ignored, and the lands of the former Ottoman Empire were divided into mandates through the Treaty of Sèvres at the San Remo Conference in 1920. The Ottoman Empire disintegrated into several nations, many created by European powers with little regard to ethnic realities. These Arab provinces were ruled by Britain and France, and the new nation of Turkey emerged from the former heartland of Anatolia. According to the League of Nations, mandates "were inhabited by peoples not yet able to stand by themselves under the strenuous conditions of the modern world." Though allegedly for the benefit of the people of the Middle East, the mandate system was essentially a reimagined form of nineteenth-century imperialism. France received Syria; Britain took control of Iraq, Palestine, and Transjordan (Jordan). The United States was asked to become a mandate power but declined. The geographical realignment of the Middle East also included the formation of two new nations: the Kingdom of Hejaz and Yemen. (The Kingdom of Hejaz was ruled by Sharif Hussein and only lasted until the 1920s, when it became part of Saudi Arabia.)[26]

The 1917 Russian Revolution, meanwhile enflamed American fears of communism. The fates of Nicola Sacco and Bartolomeo Vanzetti, two Italian-born anarchists who were convicted of robbery and murder in 1920 epitomized a sudden American Red Scare. Their arrest, trial, and execution, meanwhile, inspired many leftists and dissenting artists to express their sympathy with the accused, such as in Maxwell Anderson's *Gods of the Lightning* or Upton Sinclair's *Boston*. The Sacco-Vanzetti case demonstrated an exacerbated nervousness about immigrants and the potential spread of radical ideas, especially those related to international communism.[27]

When in March 1918 the Bolsheviks signed a separate peace treaty with Germany, the Allies planned to send troops to northern Russia and Siberia to prevent German influence and fight the Bolshevik Revolution. Wilson agreed, and, in a little-known foreign intervention, American troops remained in Russia as late as 1920. Although the Bolshevik rhetoric of self-determination followed many of the ideals of Wilson's Fourteen Points—Vladimir Lenin supported revolutions against imperial rule across the world—the American commitment to self-rule was hardly strong enough to overcome powerful strains of anticommunism.

At home, the United States grappled with harsh postwar realities. Racial tensions culminated in the Red Summer of 1919 when violence broke out in at least twenty-five cities, including Chicago and Washington, D.C. The riots originated from wartime racial tensions. Industrial war production and massive wartime service created vast labor shortages, and thousands of Black southerners traveled to the North and Midwest to escape the traps of southern poverty. But the so-called Great Migration sparked significant racial conflict as white northerners and returning veterans fought to reclaim their jobs and their neighborhoods from new Black migrants.[28]

With America still at war in World War I, President Wilson sent American troops to Siberia during the Russian civil war to oppose the Bolsheviks. This August 1918 photograph shows American soldiers in Vladivostok parading before the building occupied by the staff of the Czecho-Slovaks. To the left, Japanese marines stand to attention as the American troops march. Wikimedia.

Many Black Americans, who had fled the Jim Crow South and traveled halfway around the world to fight for the United States, would not so easily accept postwar racism. The overseas experience of Black Americans and their return triggered a dramatic change in Black communities. W. E. B. Du Bois wrote boldly of returning soldiers: "We return. We return from fighting. We return fighting. Make way for Democracy!"[29] But white Americans desired a return to the status quo, a world that did not include social, political, or economic equality for Black people.

In 1919, America suffered through the "Red Summer." Riots erupted across the country from April until October. The massive bloodshed included thousands of injuries, hundreds of deaths, and vast destruction of private and public property across the nation. The Chicago Riot, from July 27 to August 3, 1919, considered the summer's worst, sparked a week of mob violence, murder, and arson. Race riots had rocked the nation before, but the Red Summer was something new. Recently empowered Black Americans actively defended their families and homes from hostile white rioters, often with militant force. This behavior galvanized many in Black communities, but it also shocked white Americans who alternatively interpreted Black resistance as a desire for total revolution or as a new positive step in the path toward Black civil rights. In the riots' aftermath, James Weldon Johnson wrote, "Can't they understand that the more Negroes they outrage, the more determined the whole race becomes to secure the full rights and privileges of freemen?" Those six hot months in 1919 forever altered American society and roused and terrified those that experienced the sudden and devastating outbreaks of violence.[30]

X. Conclusion

World War I decimated millions and profoundly altered the course of world history. Postwar instabilities led directly toward a global depression and a second world war. The war sparked the Bolshevik Revolution, which led to the Soviet Union and later the Cold War. It created Middle Eastern nations and aggravated ethnic tensions that the United States could never overcome. And the United States had fought on the European mainland as a major power. America's place in the world was never the same. By whipping up nationalist passions, American attitudes toward radicalism, dissent, and immigration were poisoned. Postwar disillusionment shattered Americans' hopes for the progress of the modern world. The war came and went, leaving in its place the bloody wreckage of an old world through which the United States traveled to a new and uncertain future.

XI. Reference Material

This chapter was edited by Paula Fortier, with content contributions by Tizoc Chavez, Zachary W. Dresser, Blake Earle, Morgan Deane, Paula Fortier, Larry A. Grant, Mariah Hepworth, Jun Suk Hyun, and Leah Richier.

Recommended citation: Tizoc Chavez et al., "World War I and Its Aftermath," Paula Fortier, ed., in *The American Yawp*, eds. Joseph Locke and Ben Wright (Stanford, CA: Stanford University Press, 2019).

NOTES TO CHAPTER 21

1. David Stevenson, *The First World War and International Politics* (London: Oxford University Press, 1988); David Stevenson, *Cataclysm: The First World War as Political Tragedy* (New York: Basic Books, 2004).

2. George Washington, Farewell Address, *Annals of Congress*, 4th Congress, 2869–2870.

3. Paul Koistinen, *Mobilizing for Modern War: The Political Economy of American Warfare, 1865–1919* (Lawrence: University Press of Kansas, 1997).

4. John S. D. Eisenhower, *Intervention! The United States and the Mexican Revolution, 1913–1917* (New York: Norton, 1995); Friedrich Katz, *The Secret War in Mexico: Europe, the United States, and the Mexican Revolution* (Chicago: University of Chicago Press, 1981).

5. Arthur S. Link, *Wilson: The Struggle for Neutrality, 1914–1915* (Princeton, NJ: Princeton University Press, 1960).

6. Michael S. Neiberg, *Fighting the Great War: A Global History* (Cambridge, MA: Harvard University Press, 2005).

7. American Federation of Labor, *Report of the Proceedings of the Annual Convention* (Washington, DC: Law Reporter, 1917), 112.

8. Christopher Capozzola, *Uncle Sam Wants You: World War I and the Making of the Modern American Citizen* (New York: Oxford University Press, 2010).

9. Albert Gallitin Love, *Defects Found in Drafted Men* (Washington, DC: U.S. Government Printing Office, 1920), 73.

10. Alan Dawley, *Changing the World: American Progressives in War and Revolution* (Princeton, NJ: Princeton University Press, 2005).

11. Susan Zeiger, *In Uncle Sam's Service: Women Workers with the American Expeditionary Force, 1917–1919* (Philadelphia: University of Pennsylvania Press, 2004), 2–4.

12. Lettie Gavin, *American Women in World War I: They Also Served* (Boulder: University Press of Colorado, 1997); Kimberly Jensen, *Mobilizing Minerva: American Women in the First World War* (Chicago: University of Illinois Press, 2008), 170–172.

13. Gavin, *American Women*, 129–240.

14. Nikki Brown, *Private Politics and Public Voices: Black Women's Activism from World War I to the New Deal* (Bloomington: Indiana University Press, 2006), 66–107.

15. David Kennedy, *Over Here: The First World War and American Society* (New York: Oxford University Press, 1980).

16. Neiberg, *Fighting the Great War.*

17. Ibid.

18. Ibid.

19. Ibid.

20. Nancy K. Bristow, *American Pandemic: The Lost Worlds of the 1918 Influenza Epidemic* (New York: Oxford University Press, 2012); Alfred W. Crosby, *America's Forgotten Pandemic: The Influenza of 1918* (Cambridge, UK: Cambridge University Press, 2003).

21. Bristow, *American Pandemic;* Crosby, *America's Forgotten Pandemic.*

22. Dawley, *Changing the World.*

23. Thomas J. Knock, *To End All Wars: Woodrow Wilson and the Quest for a New World Order* (New York: Oxford University Press, 1992).

24. John Milton Cooper, *Breaking the Heart of the World: Woodrow Wilson and the Fight for the League of Nations* (Cambridge, UK: Cambridge University Press, 2001).

25. Ibid.

26. David Fromkin, *A Peace to End All Peace: The Fall of the Ottoman Empire and the Creation of the Modern Middle East* (New York: Holt, 1989).

27. Moshik Temkin, *The Sacco-Vanzetti Affair: America on Trial* (New Haven, CT: Yale University Press, 2009).

28. Isabel Wilkerson, *The Warmth of Other Suns: The Epic Story of America's Great Migration* (New York: Vintage Books, 2011).

29. W. E. B. Du Bois, "Returning Soldiers," *The Crisis* (May 1919): 14.

30. William Tuttle, *Race Riot: Chicago in the Red Summer of 1919* (Champaign: University of Illinois Press, 1970); Cameron McWhirter, *Red Summer: The Summer of 1919 and the Awakening of Black America* (New York: Holt, 2011).

RECOMMENDED READING

Capozzola, Christopher. *Uncle Sam Wants You: World War I and the Making of the Modern American Citizen.* New York: Oxford University Press, 2010.

Coffman, Edward M. *The War to End All Wars: The American Military Experience in World War I.* New York: Oxford University Press, 1968.

Cooper, John Milton. *Breaking the Heart of the World: Woodrow Wilson and the Fight for the League of Nations.* New York: Cambridge University Press, 2001.

Dawley, Alan. *Changing the World: American Progressives in War and Revolution.* Princeton, NJ: Princeton University Press, 2003.

Doenecke, Justus D. *Nothing Less than War: A New History of America's Entry into World War I.* Lexington: University Press of Kentucky, 2011.

Freeberg, Ernest. *Democracy's Prisoners: Eugene V. Debs, the Great War, and the Right to Dissent.* Cambridge, MA: Harvard University Press, 2008.

Fussell, Paul. *The Great War and Modern Memory*. New York: Oxford University Press, 1975.

Gerwarth, Robert, and Erez Manela, eds. *Empires at War: 1911–1923*. New York: Oxford University Press, 2015.

Greenwald, Maurine W. *Women, War, and Work: The Impact of World War I on Women Workers in the United States*. Westport, CT: Greenwood, 1980.

Hahn, Steven. *A Nation Under Our Feet: Black Political Struggles in the Rural South from Slavery to the Great Migration*. Cambridge, MA: Harvard University Press, 2003.

Hawley, Ellis. *The Great War and the Search for Modern Order*. New York: St. Martin's Press, 1979.

Jensen, Kimberly. *Mobilizing Minerva: American Women in the First World War*. Champaign: University of Illinois Press, 2009.

Keene, Jennifer. *Doughboys, The Great War, and the Remaking of America*. Baltimore: Johns Hopkins University Press, 2001.

Kennedy, David. *Over Here: The First World War and American Society*. New York: Oxford University Press, 1980.

Knock, Thomas J. *To End All Wars: Woodrow Wilson and the Quest for a New World Order*. New York: Oxford University Press, 1992.

MacMillan, Margaret. *The War That Ended Peace: The Road to 1914*. New York: Random House, 2014.

Manela, Erez. *The Wilsonian Movement: Self-Determination and the International Origins of Anticolonial Nationalism*. New York: Oxford University Press, 2007.

Montgomery, David. *The Fall of the House of Labor: The Workplace, the State, and American Labor Activism, 1865–1925*. Cambridge, UK: Cambridge University Press, 1988.

Murphy, Paul. *World War I and the Origins of Civil Liberties in the United States*. New York: Norton, 1979.

Neiberg, Michael S. *The Path to War: How the First World War Created Modern America*. New York: Oxford University Press, 2016.

Rosenberg, Emily. *Financial Missionaries to the World: The Politics and Culture of Dollar Diplomacy, 1900–1930*. Durham, NC: Duke University Press, 2003.

Smith, Tony. *Why Wilson Matters: The Origin of American Liberal Internationalism and Its Crisis Today*. Princeton, NJ: Princeton University Press, 2017.

Tuttle, William. *Race Riot: Chicago in the Red Summer of 1919*. Champaign: University of Illinois Press, 1970.

Wilkerson, Isabel. *The Warmth of Other Sons: The Epic Story of America's Great Migration*. New York: Vintage Books, 2010.

Williams, Chad L. *Torchbearers of Democracy: African American Soldiers in the World War I Era*. Chapel Hill: University of North Carolina Press, 2010.

22

The New Era

I. Introduction

On a sunny day in early March 1921, Warren G. Harding took the oath to become the twenty-ninth president of the United States. He had won a landslide election by promising a "return to normalcy." "Our supreme task is the resumption of our onward, normal way," he declared in his inaugural address. Two months later, he said, "America's present need is not heroics, but healing; not nostrums, but normalcy; not revolution, but restoration." The nation still reeled from the shock of World War I, the explosion of racial violence and political repression in 1919, and, a lingering "Red Scare" sparked by the Bolshevik Revolution in Russia.

More than 115,000 American soldiers had lost their lives in barely a year of fighting in Europe. Then, between 1918 and 1920, nearly seven hundred thousand Americans died in a flu epidemic that hit nearly 20 percent of the American population. Waves of labor strikes, meanwhile,

"Women competing in low hurdle race, Washington, D.C.," c. 1920s. Library of Congress.

hit soon after the war. Radicals bellowed. Anarchists and others sent more than thirty bombs through the mail on May 1, 1919. After wartime controls fell, the economy tanked and national unemployment hit 20 percent. Farmers' bankruptcy rates, already egregious, now skyrocketed. Harding could hardly deliver the peace that he promised, but his message nevertheless resonated among a populace wracked by instability.

The 1920s, of course, would be anything but "normal." The decade so reshaped American life that it came to be called by many names: the New Era, the Jazz Age, the Age of the Flapper, the Prosperity Decade, and, most commonly, the Roaring Twenties. The mass production and consumption of automobiles, household appliances, film, and radio fueled a new economy and new standards of living. New mass entertainment introduced talking films and jazz while sexual and social restraints loosened. But at the same time, many Americans turned their back on political and economic reform, denounced America's shifting demographics, stifled immigration, retreated toward "old-time religion," and revived the Ku Klux Klan with millions of new members. On the other hand, many Americans fought harder than ever for equal rights and cultural observers noted the appearance of "the New Woman" and "the New Negro." Old immigrant communities that had predated new immigration quotas, meanwhile, clung to their cultures and their native faiths. The 1920s were a decade of conflict and tension. But whatever it was, it was not "normalcy."

II. Republican White House, 1921–1933

To deliver on his promises of stability and prosperity, Harding signed legislation to restore a high protective tariff and dismantled the last wartime controls over industry. Meanwhile, the vestiges of America's involvement in World War I and its propaganda and suspicions of anything less than "100 percent American" pushed Congress to address fears of immigration and foreign populations. A sour postwar economy led elites to raise the specter of the Russian Revolution and sideline not just the various American socialist and anarchist organizations but nearly all union activism. During the 1920s, the labor movement suffered a sharp decline in memberships. Workers lost not only bargaining power but also the support of courts, politicians, and, in large measure, the American public.[1]

Harding's presidency would go down in history as among the most corrupt. Many of Harding's cabinet appointees, however, were individuals of true stature that answered to various American constituencies. For instance, Henry C. Wallace, the vocal editor of *Wallace's Farmer* and a well-known proponent of scientific farming, was made secretary of agriculture. Herbert Hoover, the popular head and administrator of the wartime Food Administration and a self-made millionaire, was made secretary of commerce. To satisfy business interests, the conservative businessman Andrew Mellon became secretary of the treasury. Mostly, however, it was the appointing of friends and close supporters, dubbed "the Ohio gang," that led to trouble.[2]

Harding's administration suffered a tremendous setback when several officials conspired to lease government land in Wyoming to oil companies in exchange for cash. Known as the Teapot Dome scandal (named after the nearby rock formation that resembled a teapot), interior secretary Albert Fall and navy secretary Edwin Denby both resigned, and Fall was convicted and sent to jail. Harding took vacation in the summer of 1923 so that he could think deeply on how to deal "with my God-damned friends"—it was his friends, and not his enemies, that kept him up walking the halls at nights. But then, in August 1923, Harding died suddenly of a heart attack and Vice President Calvin Coolidge ascended to the highest office in the land.[3]

The son of a shopkeeper, Coolidge climbed the Republican ranks from city councilman to governor of Massachusetts. As president, Coolidge sought to remove the stain of scandal but otherwise continued Harding's economic approach, refusing to take actions in defense of workers or consumers against American business. "The chief business of the American people," the new president stated, "is business." One observer called Coolidge's policy "active inactivity," but Coolidge was not afraid of supporting business interests and wealthy Americans by lowering taxes or maintaining high tariff rates. Congress, for instance, had already begun to reduce taxes on the wealthy from wartime levels of 66 percent to 20 percent, which Coolidge championed.[4]

While Coolidge supported business, other Americans continued their activism. The 1920s, for instance, represented a time of great activism among American women, who had won the vote with the passage of the Nineteenth Amendment in 1920. Female voters, like their male counterparts, pursued many interests. Concerned about squalor, poverty, and domestic violence, women had already lent their efforts to prohibition, which went into effect under the Eighteenth Amendment in January 1920. After that point, alcohol could no longer be manufactured or sold.

During the 1920s, the National Women's Party fought for the rights of women beyond that of secured suffrage, which they had through the Nineteenth Amendment in 1920. They organized private events, like the
tea party pictured here, and public campaigning, such as the introduction of the Equal Rights Amendment
to Congress, as they continued the struggle for equality. Library of Congress.

Other reformers urged government action to ameliorate high mortality rates among infants and children, provide federal aid for education,
and ensure peace and disarmament. Some activists advocated protective
legislation for women and children, while Alice Paul and the National
Woman's Party called for the elimination of all legal distinctions "on
account of sex" through the proposed Equal Rights Amendment (ERA),
which was introduced but defeated in Congress.[5]

National politics in the 1920s were dominated by the Republican
Party, which held not only the presidency but both houses of Congress
as well. Coolidge decided not to seek a second term in 1928. A man of
few words, "Silent Cal" publicized his decision by handing a scrap of
paper to a reporter that simply read: "I do not choose to run for president in 1928." That year's race became a contest between the Democratic
governor of New York, Al Smith, whose Catholic faith and immigrant
background aroused nativist suspicions and whose connections to Tammany Hall and anti-Prohibition politics offended reformers, and the Republican candidate, Herbert Hoover, whose all-American, Midwestern,
Protestant background and managerial prowess during World War I en-
deared him to American voters.[6] Hoover focused on economic growth
and prosperity. He had served as secretary of commerce under Harding

and Coolidge and claimed credit for the sustained growth seen during the 1920s. "We in America to-day are nearer to the final triumph over poverty than ever before in the history of any land," he said when he launched his 1928 presidential campaign. "Given a chance to go forward with the policies of the last eight years, and we shall soon with the help of God be in sight of the day when poverty will be banished from this nation."[7] Despite Hoover's claims—which, after the onset of the Great Depression the following year, would seem farcical—much of the election centered on Smith's religion and his opposition to Prohibition. Many Protestant ministers preached against Smith and warned that he would be enthralled to the pope. Hoover won in a landslide. While Smith won handily in the nation's largest cities, portending future political trends, he lost most of the rest of the country. Even several solidly Democratic southern states pulled the lever for a Republican for the first time since Reconstruction.[8]

III. Culture of Consumption

"Change is in the very air Americans breathe, and consumer changes are the very bricks out of which we are building our new kind of civilization," announced marketing expert and home economist Christine Frederick in her influential 1929 monograph, *Selling Mrs. Consumer*. The book, which was based on one of the earliest surveys of American buying habits, advised manufacturers and advertisers how to capture the purchasing power of women, who, according to Frederick, accounted for 90 percent of household expenditures. Aside from granting advertisers insight into the psychology of the "average" consumer, Frederick's text captured the tremendous social and economic transformations that had been wrought over the course of her lifetime.[9]

Indeed, the America of Frederick's birth looked very different from the one she confronted in 1929. The consumer change she studied had resulted from the industrial expansion of the late nineteenth and early twentieth centuries. With the discovery of new energy sources and manufacturing technologies, industrial output flooded the market with a range of consumer products such as ready-to-wear clothing, convenience foods, and home appliances. By the end of the nineteenth century, output had risen so dramatically that many contemporaries feared supply had outpaced demand and that the nation would soon face the devastating financial consequences of overproduction. American businessmen attempted to avoid this catastrophe by developing new merchandising and marketing strategies that transformed distribution and stimulated a new culture of consumer desire.[10]

The department store stood at the center of this early consumer revolution. By the 1880s, several large dry-goods houses blossomed into modern retail department stores. These emporiums concentrated a broad array of goods under a single roof, allowing customers to purchase shirtwaists and gloves alongside toy trains and washbasins. To attract customers, department stores relied on more than variety. They also employed innovations in service (such as access to restaurants, writing rooms, and babysitting) and spectacle (such as elaborately decorated store windows, fashion shows, and interior merchandise displays). Marshall Field & Co. was among the most successful of these ventures. Located on State Street in Chicago, the company pioneered many of these strategies, including establishing a tearoom that provided refreshment to the well-heeled female shoppers who composed the store's clientele. Reflecting on the success of Field's marketing techniques, Thomas W. Goodspeed, an early trustee of the University of Chicago, wrote, "Perhaps the most notable of Mr. Field's innovations was that he made a store in which it was a joy to buy."[11]

The joy of buying infected a growing number of Americans in the early twentieth century as the rise of mail-order catalogs, mass-circulation magazines, and national branding further stoked consumer desire. The automobile industry also fostered the new culture of consumption by promoting the use of credit. By 1927, more than 60 percent of American

In the 1920s, Americans across the country bought magazines like *Photoplay* in order to get more information about the stars of their new favorite entertainment media: the movies. Advertisers took advantage of this broad audience to promote a wide range of consumer goods and services to both men and women. Archive.org.

automobiles were sold on credit, and installment purchasing was made available for nearly every other large consumer purchase. Spurred by access to easy credit, consumer expenditures for household appliances, for example, grew by more than 120 percent between 1919 and 1929. Henry Ford's assembly line, which advanced production strategies practiced within countless industries, brought automobiles within the reach of middle-income Americans and further drove the spirit of consumerism. By 1925, Ford's factories were turning out a Model-T every ten seconds. The number of registered cars ballooned from just over nine million in 1920 to nearly twenty-seven million by the decade's end. Americans owned more cars than Great Britain, Germany, France, and Italy combined. In the late 1920s, 80 percent of the world's cars drove on American roads.

IV. Culture of Escape

As transformative as steam and iron had been in the previous century, gasoline and electricity—embodied most dramatically for many Americans in automobiles, film, and radio—propelled not only consumption but also the famed popular culture in the 1920s. "We wish to escape," wrote Edgar Burroughs, author of the Tarzan series, ". . . the restrictions of manmade laws, and the inhibitions that society has placed upon us." Burroughs authored a new Tarzan story nearly every year from 1914 until 1939. "We would each like to be Tarzan," he said. "At least I would; I admit it." Like many Americans in the 1920s, Burroughs sought to challenge and escape the constraints of a society that seemed more industrialized with each passing day.[12]

Just like Burroughs, Americans escaped with great speed. Whether through the automobile, Hollywood's latest films, jazz records produced on Tin Pan Alley, or the hours spent listening to radio broadcasts of Jack Dempsey's prizefights, the public wrapped itself in popular culture. One observer estimated that Americans belted out the silly musical hit "Yes, We Have No Bananas" more than "The Star Spangled Banner" and all the hymns in all the hymnals combined.[13]

As the automobile became more popular and more reliable, more people traveled more frequently and attempted greater distances. Women increasingly drove themselves to their own activities as well as those of their children. Vacationing Americans sped to Florida to escape northern winters. Young men and women fled the supervision of courtship, exchanging the staid parlor couch for sexual exploration in the backseat

Side view of a Ford sedan with four passengers and a woman getting in on the driver's side, c. 1923. Library of Congress.

of a sedan. In order to serve and capture the growing number of drivers, Americans erected gas stations, diners, motels, and billboards along the roadside. Automobiles themselves became objects of entertainment: nearly one hundred thousand people gathered to watch drivers compete for the $50,000 prize of the Indianapolis 500.

Meanwhile, the United States dominated the global film industry. By 1930, as moviemaking became more expensive, a handful of film companies took control of the industry. Immigrants, mostly of Jewish heritage from central and Eastern Europe, originally "invented Hollywood" because most turn-of-the-century middle- and upper-class Americans viewed cinema as lower-class entertainment. After their parents emigrated from Poland in 1876, Harry, Albert, Sam, and Jack Warner (who were, according to family lore, given the name when an Ellis Island official could not understand their surname) founded Warner Bros. In 1918, Universal, Paramount, Columbia, and Metro-Goldwyn-Mayer (MGM) were all founded by or led by Jewish executives. Aware of their social status as outsiders, these immigrants (or sons of immigrants) purposefully produced films that portrayed American values of opportunity, democracy, and freedom.

Not content with distributing thirty-minute films in nickelodeons, film moguls produced longer, higher-quality films and showed them in palatial theaters that attracted those who had previously shunned the film industry. But as filmmakers captured the middle and upper classes, they maintained working-class moviegoers by blending traditional and

Mary Pickford's film personas led the glamorous and lavish lifestyle that female moviegoers of the 1920s desired so much. Mary Pickford. 1920. Library of Congress.

modern values. Cecil B. DeMille's 1923 epic *The Ten Commandments* depicted orgiastic revelry, for instance, while still managing to celebrate a biblical story. But what good was a silver screen in a dingy theater? Moguls and entrepreneurs soon constructed picture palaces. Samuel Rothafel's Roxy Theater in New York held more than six thousand patrons who could be escorted by a uniformed usher past gardens and statues to their cushioned seat. In order to show *The Jazz Singer* (1927), the first movie with synchronized words and pictures, the Warners spent half a million to equip two theaters. "Sound is a passing fancy," one MGM producer told his wife, but Warner Bros.' assets, which increased from just $5,000,000 in 1925 to $230,000,000 in 1930, tell a different story.[14]

Americans fell in love with the movies. Whether it was the surroundings, the sound, or the production budgets, weekly movie attendance skyrocketed from sixteen million in 1912 to forty million in the early 1920s. Hungarian immigrant William Fox, founder of Fox Film Corporation, declared that "the motion picture is a distinctly American institution" because "the rich rub elbows with the poor" in movie theaters. With no seating restriction, the one-price admission was accessible for nearly all Americans (African Americans, however, were either excluded or segregated). Women represented more than 60 percent of moviegoers, packing theaters to see Mary Pickford, nicknamed "America's Sweetheart," who was earning one million dollars a year by 1920 through a combination of film and endorsements contracts. Pickford and other female stars popularized the "flapper," a woman who favored short skirts, makeup, and cigarettes.

As Americans went to the movies more and more, at home they had the radio. Italian scientist Guglielmo Marconi transmitted the first transatlantic wireless (radio) message in 1901, but radios in the home did not become available until around 1920, when they boomed across the country. Around half of American homes contained a radio by 1930. Radio stations brought entertainment directly into the living room through the sale of advertisements and sponsorships, from *The Maxwell House Hour* to the *Lucky Strike Orchestra*. Soap companies sponsored daytime dramas so frequently that an entire genre—"soap operas"—was born, providing housewives with audio adventures that stood in stark contrast to common chores. Though radio stations were often under the control of corporations like the National Broadcasting Company (NBC) or the Columbia Broadcasting System (CBS), radio programs were less constrained by traditional boundaries in order to capture as wide an audience as possible, spreading popular culture on a national level.

Radio exposed Americans to a broad array of music. Jazz, a uniquely American musical style popularized by the African-American community in New Orleans, spread primarily through radio stations and records. The *New York Times* had ridiculed jazz as "savage" because of its racial heritage, but the music represented cultural independence to others. As Harlem-based musician William Dixon put it, "It did seem, to a little boy, that . . . white people really owned everything. But that wasn't entirely true. They didn't own the music that I played." The fast-paced and spontaneity-laced tunes invited the listener to dance along. "When a good orchestra plays a 'rag,'" dance instructor Vernon Castle recalled, "one has simply got to move." Jazz became a national sensation, played and heard by both white and Black Americans. Jewish Lithuanian-born singer Al Jolson—whose biography inspired *The Jazz Singer* and who played the film's titular character—became the most popular singer in America.[15]

The 1920s also witnessed the maturation of professional sports. Play-by-play radio broadcasts of major collegiate and professional sporting events marked a new era for sports, despite the institutionalization of racial segregation in most. Suddenly, Jack Dempsey's left crosses and right uppercuts could almost be felt in homes across the United States. Dempsey, who held the heavyweight championship for most of the decade, drew million-dollar gates and inaugurated "Dempseymania" in newspapers across the country. Red Grange, who carried the football with a similar recklessness, helped popularize professional football, which was then in the shadow of the college game. Grange left the University of Illinois before graduating to join the Chicago Bears in 1925. "There had never been such evidence of public interest since our professional league began," recalled Bears owner George Halas of Grange's arrival.[16]

Perhaps no sports figure left a bigger mark than did Babe Ruth. Born George Herman Ruth, the "Sultan of Swat" grew up in an orphanage in Baltimore's slums. Ruth's emergence onto the national scene was much needed, as the baseball world had been rocked by the so-called Black Sox Scandal in which eight players allegedly agreed to throw the 1919 World Series. Ruth hit fifty-four home runs in 1920, which was more than any other team combined. Baseball writers called Ruth a superman, and more Americans could recognize Ruth than they could then-president Warren G. Harding.

After an era of destruction and doubt brought about by World War I, Americans craved heroes who seemed to defy convention and break boundaries. Dempsey, Grange, and Ruth dominated their respective sports, but only Charles Lindbergh conquered the sky. On May 21, 1927, Lindbergh concluded the first ever nonstop solo flight from New York to Paris. Armed with only a few sandwiches, some bottles of water, paper maps, and a flashlight, Lindbergh successfully navigated over the Atlantic Ocean in thirty-three hours. Some historians have dubbed Lindbergh the "hero of the decade," not only for his transatlantic journey but because he helped to restore the faith of many Americans in individual effort and technological advancement. In a world so recently devastated by machine guns, submarines, and chemical weapons, Lindbergh's flight demonstrated that technology could inspire and accomplish great things. *Outlook Magazine* called Lindbergh "the heir of all that we like to think is best in America."[17]

The decade's popular culture seemed to revolve around escape. Coney Island in New York marked new amusements for young and old. Americans drove their sedans to massive theaters to enjoy major motion pictures. Radio towers broadcasted the bold new sound of jazz, the adventures of soap operas, and the feats of amazing athletes. Dempsey

Babe Ruth's incredible talent accelerated the popularity of baseball, cementing it as America's pastime. Ruth's propensity to shatter records made him a national hero. Library of Congress.

and Grange seemed bigger, stronger, and faster than any who dared to challenge them. Babe Ruth smashed home runs out of ball parks across the country. And Lindbergh escaped the earth's gravity and crossed an entire ocean. Neither Dempsey nor Ruth nor Lindbergh made Americans forget the horrors of World War I and the chaos that followed, but they made it seem as if the future would be that much brighter.

V. "The New Woman"

The rising emphasis on spending and accumulation nurtured a national ethos of materialism and individual pleasure. These impulses were embodied in the figure of the flapper, whose bobbed hair, short skirts, makeup, cigarettes, and carefree spirit captured the attention of American novelists such as F. Scott Fitzgerald and Sinclair Lewis. Rejecting the old Victorian values of desexualized modesty and self-restraint, young "flappers" seized opportunities for the public coed pleasures offered by new commercial leisure institutions, such as dance halls, cabarets, and nickelodeons, not to mention the illicit blind tigers and speakeasies spawned by Prohibition. So doing, young American women had helped

This "new breed" of women—known as the flapper—went against the gender proscriptions of the era, bobbing their hair, wearing short dresses, listening to jazz, and flouting social and sexual norms. While liberating in many ways, these behaviors also reinforced stereotypes of female carelessness and obsessive consumerism that would continue throughout the twentieth century. Library of Congress.

usher in a new morality that permitted women greater independence, freedom of movement, and access to the delights of urban living. In the words of psychologist G. Stanley Hall, "She was out to see the world and, incidentally, be seen of it."

Such sentiments were repeated in an oft-cited advertisement in a 1930 edition of the *Chicago Tribune*: "Today's woman gets what she wants. The vote. Slim sheaths of silk to replace voluminous petticoats. Glassware in sapphire blue or glowing amber. The right to a career. Soap to match her bathroom's color scheme." As with so much else in the 1920s, however, sex and gender were in many ways a study in contradictions. It was the decade of the "New Woman," and one in which only 10 percent of married women—although nearly half of unmarried women—worked outside the home.[18] It was a decade in which new technologies decreased time requirements for household chores, and one in which standards of cleanliness and order in the home rose to often impossible standards. It was a decade in which women finally could exercise their right to vote, and one in which the often thinly bound women's coalitions that had won that victory splintered into various causes. Finally, it was a decade in which images such as the "flapper" gave women new modes of representing femininity, and one in which such representations were often inaccessible to women of certain races, ages, and socioeconomic classes.

Women undoubtedly gained much in the 1920s. There was a profound and keenly felt cultural shift that, for many women, meant increased opportunity to work outside the home. The number of professional women, for example, significantly rose in the decade. But limits still existed, even for professional women. Occupations such as law and medicine remained overwhelmingly male: most female professionals were in feminized professions such as teaching and nursing. And even within these fields, it was difficult for women to rise to leadership positions.

Further, it is crucial not to overgeneralize the experience of all women based on the experiences of a much-commented-upon subset of the population. A woman's race, class, ethnicity, and marital status all had an impact on both the likelihood that she worked outside the home and the types of opportunities that were available to her. While there were exceptions, for many minority women, work outside the home was not a cultural statement but rather a financial necessity (or both), and physically demanding, low-paying domestic service work continued to be the most common job type. Young, working-class white women were joining the workforce more frequently, too, but often in order to help support their struggling mothers and fathers.

For young, middle-class, white women—those most likely to fit the image of the carefree flapper—the most common workplace was the office. These predominantly single women increasingly became clerks, jobs that had been primarily male earlier in the century. But here, too, there was a clear ceiling. While entry-level clerk jobs became increasingly feminized, jobs at a higher, more lucrative level remained dominated by men. Further, rather than changing the culture of the workplace, the entrance of women into lower-level jobs primarily changed the coding of the jobs themselves. Such positions simply became "women's work."

Finally, as these same women grew older and married, social changes became even subtler. Married women were, for the most part, expected to remain in the domestic sphere. And while new patterns of consumption gave them more power and, arguably, more autonomy, new household technologies and philosophies of marriage and child-rearing increased expectations, further tying these women to the home—a paradox that becomes clear in advertisements such as the one in the *Chicago Tribune*.

Of course, the number of women in the workplace cannot exclusively measure changes in sex and gender norms. Attitudes towards sex, for example, continued to change in the 1920s as well, a process that had begun decades before. This, too, had significantly different impacts on different social groups. But for many women—particularly young, college-educated white women—an attempt to rebel against what they saw as a repressive Victorian notion of sexuality led to an increase in premarital sexual activity strong enough that it became, in the words of one historian, "almost a matter of conformity."[19]

Meanwhile, especially in urban centers such as New York, the gay community flourished. While gay males had to contend with the increased policing of their daily lives, especially later in the decade, they generally lived more openly in such cities than they would be able to for many · decades following World War II.[20] At the same time, for many lesbians in the decade, the increased sexualization of women brought new scrutiny to same-sex female relationships previously dismissed as harmless.[21]

Ultimately, the most enduring symbol of the changing notions of gender in the 1920s remains the flapper. And indeed, that image was a "new" available representation of womanhood in the 1920s. But it is just that:

The frivolity, decadence, and obliviousness of the 1920s was embodied in the image of the flapper, the stereotyped carefree and indulgent woman of the Roaring Twenties depicted in Russell Patterson's drawing. Library of Congress.

a representation of womanhood of the 1920s. There were many women in the decade of differing races, classes, ethnicities, and experiences, just as there were many men with different experiences. For some women, the 1920s were a time of reorganization, new representations, and new opportunities. For others, it was a decade of confusion, contradiction, new pressures, and struggles new and old.

VI. "The New Negro"

The iniquities of Jim Crow segregation, the barbarities of America's lynching epidemic, and the depravities of 1919's Red Summer weighed heavily upon Black Americans as they entered the 1920s. The injustices and the violence continued. In Tulsa, Oklahoma, Black Americans had built up the Greenwood District with commerce and prosperity. Booker T. Washington called it the "Black Wall Street." On the evening of May 31, 1921, spurred by a false claim of sexual assault levied against a young Black man—nineteen-year-old Dick Rowland had likely either tripped over a young white elevator operator's foot or tripped and brushed a woman's shoulder with his hand—a white mob mobilized, armed themselves, and destroyed the prosperous neighborhood. Over thirty square blocks were ruined. Mobs burned more than 1,000 homes and killed as many as several hundred Black Tulsans. Survivors recalled the mob using heavy machine guns, and others reported planes circling overhead, firing rifles and dropping firebombs. When order was finally restored the next day, the bodies of the victims were buried in mass graves. Thousands of survivors were left homeless.

The relentlessness of racial violence awoke a new generation of Black Americans to new alternatives. The Great Migration had pulled enormous numbers of Black southerners northward, and, just as cultural limits loosened across the nation, the 1920s represented a period of self-reflection among African Americans, especially those in northern cities. New York City was a popular destination of Black Americans during the Great Migration. The city's Black population grew 257 percent, from 91,709 in 1910 to 327,706 by 1930 (the white population grew only 20 percent).[22] Moreover, by 1930, some 98,620 foreign-born Black people had migrated to the United States. Nearly half made their home in Manhattan's Harlem district.[23]

Harlem originally lay between Fifth Avenue and Eighth Avenue and 130th Street to 145th Street. By 1930, the district had expanded to 155th Street and was home to 164,000 people, mostly African Americans. Continuous relocation to "the greatest Negro City in the world" exacerbated problems with crime, health, housing, and unemployment.[24] Nevertheless, it brought together a mass of Black people energized by race pride, military service in World War I, the urban environment, and, for many, ideas of Pan-Africanism or Garveyism (discussed shortly). James Weldon Johnson called Harlem "the Culture Capital."[25] The area's cultural ferment produced the Harlem Renaissance and fostered what was then termed the New Negro Movement.

Alain Locke did not coin the term *New Negro*, but he did much to popularize it. In the 1925 book *The New Negro*, Locke proclaimed that the generation of subservience was no more—"we are achieving something like a spiritual emancipation." Bringing together writings by men and women, young and old, Black and white, Locke produced an anthology that was *of* African Americans, rather than only *about* them. The book joined many others. Popular Harlem Renaissance writers published some twenty-six novels, ten volumes of poetry, and countless short stories between 1922 and 1935.[26] Alongside the well-known Langston Hughes and Claude McKay, female writers like Jessie Redmon Fauset and Zora Neale Hurston published nearly one third of these novels. While themes varied, the literature frequently explored and countered pervading stereotypes and forms of American racial prejudice.

The Harlem Renaissance was manifested in theater, art, and music. For the first time, Broadway presented Black actors in serious roles. The 1924 production *Dixie to Broadway* was the first all-Black show with mainstream showings.[27] In art, Meta Vaux Warrick Fuller, Aaron Douglas, and Palmer Hayden showcased Black cultural heritage and captured the population's current experience. In music, jazz rocketed in popularity. Eager to hear "real jazz," whites journeyed to Harlem's Cotton Club and Smalls. Next to Greenwich Village, Harlem's nightclubs and speakeasies (venues where alcohol was publicly consumed) presented a place where sexual freedom and gay life thrived. Unfortunately, while headliners like Duke Ellington were hired to entertain at Harlem's venues, the surrounding Black community was usually excluded. Furthermore, Black performers were often restricted from restroom use and relegated to service door entry. As the Renaissance faded to a close, several Harlem Renaissance artists went on to produce important works indicating that this movement was but one component in African American's long history of cultural and intellectual achievements.[28]

The explosion of African American self-expression found multiple outlets in politics. In the 1910s and 1920s, perhaps no one so attracted disaffected Black activists as Marcus Garvey. Garvey was a Jamaican publisher and labor organizer who arrived in New York City in 1916. Within just a few years of his arrival, he built the largest Black nationalist organization in the world, the Universal Negro Improvement Association (UNIA).[29] Inspired by Pan-Africanism and Booker T. Washington's model of industrial education, and critical of what he saw as Du Bois's elitist strategies in service of Black elites, Garvey sought to promote racial pride, encourage Black economic independence, and root out racial oppression in Africa and the Diaspora.[30]

Headquartered in Harlem, the UNIA published a newspaper, *Negro World*, and organized elaborate parades in which members, known as Garveyites, dressed in ornate, militaristic regalia and marched down city streets. The organization criticized the slow pace of the judicial focus of the NAACP as well as its acceptance of memberships and funds from whites. "For the Negro to depend on the ballot and his industrial progress alone," Garvey opined, "will be hopeless as it does not help him when he is lynched, burned, jim-crowed, and segregated." In 1919, the

Garveyism, criticized as too radical, nevertheless formed a substantial following and was a major stimulus for later Black nationalistic movements. Photograph of Marcus Garvey, August 5, 1924. Library of Congress.

UNIA announced plans to develop a shipping company called the Black Star Line as part of a plan that pushed for Black Americans to reject the political system and to "return to Africa" instead. Most of the investments came in the form of shares purchased by UNIA members, many of whom heard Garvey give rousing speeches across the country about the importance of establishing commercial ventures between African Americans, Afro-Caribbeans, and Africans.[31]

Garvey's detractors disparaged these public displays and poorly managed business ventures, and they criticized Garvey for peddling empty gestures in place of measures that addressed the material concerns of African Americans. NAACP leaders depicted Garvey's plan as one that simply said, "Give up! Surrender! The struggle is useless." Enflamed by his aggressive attacks on other Black activists and his radical ideas of racial independence, many African American and Afro-Caribbean leaders worked with government officials and launched the "Garvey Must Go" campaign, which culminated in his 1922 indictment and 1925 imprisonment and subsequent deportation for "using the mails for fraudulent purposes." The UNIA never recovered its popularity or financial support, even after Garvey's pardon in 1927, but his movement made a lasting impact on Black consciousness in the United States and abroad. He inspired the likes of Malcolm X, whose parents were Garveyites, and Kwame Nkrumah, the first president of Ghana. Garvey's message, perhaps best captured by his rallying cry, "Up, you mighty race," resonated with African Americans who found in Garveyism a dignity not granted them in their everyday lives. In that sense, it was all too typical of the Harlem Renaissance.[32]

VII. Culture War

For all of its cultural ferment, however, the 1920s were also a difficult time for radicals and immigrants and anything "modern." Fear of foreign radicals led to the executions of Nicola Sacco and Bartolomeo Vanzetti, two Italian anarchists, in 1927. In May 1920, the two had been arrested for robbery and murder connected with an incident at a Massachusetts factory. Their guilty verdicts were appealed for years as the evidence surrounding their convictions was slim. For instance, while one eyewitness claimed that Vanzetti drove the getaway car, accounts of others described a different person altogether. Nevertheless, despite worldwide lobbying by radicals and a respectable movement among middle-class Italian organizations in the United States, the two men were executed on August 23, 1927. Vanzetti conceivably provided the most succinct reason for his death, saying, "This is what I say . . . . I am suffering because I am a radical and indeed I am a radical; I have suffered because I was an Italian, and indeed I am an Italian."[33]

Many Americans expressed anxieties about the changes that had remade the United States and, seeking scapegoats, many middle-class white Americans pointed to Eastern European and Latin American immigrants (Asian immigration had already been almost completely prohibited), African Americans who now pushed harder for civil rights, and, after migrating out of the American South to northern cities as a part of the Great Migration, the mass exodus that carried nearly half a million Black southerners out of the South between 1910 and 1920. Protestants, meanwhile, continued to denounce the Roman Catholic Church and charged that American Catholics gave their allegiance to the pope and not to their country.

In 1921, Congress passed the Emergency Immigration Act as a stopgap immigration measure and then, three years later, permanently established country-of-origin quotas through the National Origins Act. The number of immigrants annually admitted to the United States from each nation was restricted to 2 percent of the population who had come from that country and resided in the United States in 1890. (By pushing back three decades, past the recent waves of "new" immigrants from southern and Eastern Europe, Latin America, and Asia, the law made it extremely difficult for immigrants outside northern Europe to legally enter the United States.) The act also explicitly excluded all Asians, although, to satisfy southern and western growers, it temporarily omitted restrictions on Mexican immigrants. The Sacco and Vanzetti trial and sweeping immigration restrictions pointed to a rampant nativism. A great number of Americans worried about a burgeoning America that did not resemble the one of times past. Many writers perceived that the country was now riven by a culture war.

VIII. Fundamentalist Christianity

In addition to alarms over immigration and the growing presence of Catholicism and Judaism, a new core of Christian fundamentalists were very much concerned about relaxed sexual mores and increased social freedoms, especially as found in city centers. Although never a centralized group, most fundamentalists lashed out against what they saw as a sagging public morality, a world in which Protestantism seemed challenged by Catholicism, women exercised ever greater sexual freedoms, public amusements encouraged selfish and empty pleasures, and critics mocked Prohibition through bootlegging and speakeasies.

Christian Fundamentalism arose most directly from a doctrinal dispute among Protestant leaders. Liberal theologians sought to intertwine religion with science and secular culture. These Modernists, influenced by the biblical scholarship of nineteenth-century German academics, argued that Christian doctrines about the miraculous might be best understood metaphorically. The Church, they said, needed to adapt itself to the world. According to the Baptist pastor Harry Emerson Fosdick, the "coming of Christ" might occur "slowly . . . but surely, [as] His will and principles [are] worked out by God's grace in human life and institutions."[34] The social gospel, which encouraged Christians to build the Kingdom of God on earth by working against social and economic inequality, was very much tied to liberal theology.

During the 1910s, funding from oil barons Lyman and Milton Stewart enabled the evangelist A. C. Dixon to commission some ninety essays to combat religious liberalism. The collection, known as *The Fundamentals*, became the foundational documents of Christian fundamentalism, from which the movement's name is drawn. Contributors agreed that Christian faith rested on literal truths, that Jesus, for instance, would physically return to earth at the end of time to redeem the righteous and damn the wicked. Some of the essays put forth that human endeavor would not build the Kingdom of God, while others covered such subjects as the virgin birth and biblical inerrancy. American fundamentalists spanned Protestant denominations and borrowed from diverse philosophies and theologies, most notably the holiness movement, the larger revivalism of the nineteenth century, and new dispensationalist theology (in which history proceeded, and would end, through "dispensations" by God). They did, however, all agree that modernism was the enemy and the Bible was the inerrant word of God. It was a fluid movement often without clear boundaries, but it featured many prominent clergymen, including the well-established and extremely vocal John Roach Straton (New York), J. Frank Norris (Texas), and William Bell Riley (Minnesota).[35]

On March 21, 1925, in a tiny courtroom in Dayton, Tennessee, fundamentalists gathered to tackle the issues of creation and evolution. A young biology teacher, John T. Scopes, was being tried for teaching his students evolutionary theory in violation of the Butler Act, a state law preventing evolutionary theory or any theory that denied "the Divine Creation of man as taught in the Bible" from being taught in publicly funded Tennessee classrooms. Seeing the act as a threat to personal liberty, the American Civil Liberties Union (ACLU) immediately sought a volunteer for a "test" case, hoping that the conviction and subsequent ap-

During the Scopes trial, Clarence Darrow (right) savaged the idea of a literal interpretation of the Bible. "Dudley Field Malone, Dr. John R. Neal, and Clarence Darrow in Chicago, Illinois." The Clarence Darrow Digital Collection, University of Minnesota.

peals would lead to a day in the Supreme Court, testing the constitutionality of the law. It was then that Scopes, a part-time teacher and coach, stepped up and voluntarily admitted to teaching evolution (Scopes's violation of the law was never in question). Thus the stage was set for the pivotal courtroom showdown—"the trial of the century"—between the champions and opponents of evolution that marked a key moment in an enduring American "culture war."[36]

The case became a public spectacle. Clarence Darrow, an agnostic attorney and a keen liberal mind from Chicago, volunteered to aid the defense and came up against William Jennings Bryan. Bryan, the "Great Commoner," was the three-time presidential candidate who in his younger days had led the political crusade against corporate greed. He had done so then with a firm belief in the righteousness of his cause, and now he defended biblical literalism in similar terms. The theory of evolution, Bryan said, with its emphasis on the survival of the fittest, "would eliminate love and carry man back to a struggle of tooth and claw."[37]

Newspapermen and spectators flooded the small town of Dayton. Across the nation, Americans tuned their radios to the national broadcasts of a trial that dealt with questions of religious liberty, academic freedom, parental rights, and the moral responsibility of education. For six days in July, the men and women of America were captivated as Bryan presented his argument on the morally corrupting influence of evolutionary theory (and pointed out that Darrow made a similar argument about the corruptive potential of education during his defense of the famed killers Nathan Leopold and Richard Loeb a year before). Darrow eloquently fought for academic freedom.[38]

At the request of the defense, Bryan took the stand as an "expert witness" on the Bible. At his age, he was no match for Darrow's famous skills as a trial lawyer and his answers came across as blundering and incoherent, particularly as he was not in fact a literal believer in *all* of the Genesis account (believing—as many anti-evolutionists did—that the meaning of the word *day* in the book of Genesis could be taken as allegory) and only hesitantly admitted as much, not wishing to alienate his fundamentalist followers. Additionally, Darrow posed a series of unanswerable questions: Was the "great fish" that swallowed the prophet Jonah created for that specific purpose? What precisely happened astronomically when God made the sun stand still? Bryan, of course, could cite only his faith in miracles. Tied into logical contradictions, Bryan's testimony was a public relations disaster, although his statements were expunged from the record the next day and no further experts were allowed—Scopes's guilt being established, the jury delivered a guilty verdict in minutes. The case was later thrown out on a technicality. But few cared about the verdict. Darrow had, in many ways, at least to his defenders, already won: the fundamentalists seemed to have taken a beating in the national limelight. Journalist and satirist H. L. Mencken characterized the "circus in Tennessee" as an embarrassment for fundamentalism, and modernists remembered the "Monkey Trial" as a smashing victory. If fundamentalists retreated from the public sphere, they did not disappear entirely. Instead, they went local, built a vibrant subculture, and emerged many decades later stronger than ever.[39]

IX. Rebirth of the Ku Klux Klan (KKK)

Suspicions of immigrants, Catholics, and modernists contributed to a string of reactionary organizations. None so captured the imaginations of the country as the reborn Ku Klux Klan (KKK), a white supremacist organization that expanded beyond its Reconstruction Era anti-Black politics to now claim to protect American values and the American way of life from Black people, feminists (and other radicals), immigrants, Catholics, Jews, atheists, bootleggers, and a host of other imagined moral enemies.

Two events in 1915 are widely credited with inspiring the rebirth of the Klan: the lynching of Leo Frank and the release of *The Birth of a Nation*, a popular and groundbreaking film that valorized the Reconstruction Era Klan as a protector of feminine virtue and white racial purity. Taking advantage of this sudden surge of popularity, Colonel William

This photo by popular news photographers Underwood and Underwood shows a gathering of a reported three hundred Ku Klux Klansmen just outside Washington, D.C., to initiate a new group of men into their order. The proximity of the photographer to his subjects for one of the Klan's notorious nighttime rituals suggests that this was yet another of the Klan's numerous publicity stunts. Underwood and Underwood, "Klan assembles short distance from U.S. Capitol," c. 1920s. Library of Congress.

Joseph Simmons organized what is often called the "second" Ku Klux Klan in Georgia in late 1915. This new Klan, modeled after other fraternal organizations with elaborate rituals and a hierarchy, remained largely confined to Georgia and Alabama until 1920, when Simmons began a professional recruiting effort that resulted in individual chapters being formed across the country and membership rising to an estimated five million.[40]

Partly in response to the migration of Black southerners to northern cities during World War I, the KKK expanded above the Mason-Dixon Line. Membership soared in Philadelphia, Detroit, Chicago, and Portland, while Klan-endorsed mayoral candidates won in Indianapolis, Denver, and Atlanta.[41] The Klan often recruited through fraternal organizations such as the Freemasons and through various Protestant churches. In many areas, local Klansmen visited churches of which they approved and bestowed a gift of money on the presiding minister, often during services. The Klan also enticed people to join through large picnics, parades, rallies, and ceremonies. The Klan established a women's auxiliary in 1923 headquartered in Little Rock, Arkansas. The Women of the Ku Klux Klan mirrored the KKK in practice and ideology and soon had chapters in all forty-eight states, often attracting women who were already part of the Prohibition movement, the defense of which was a centerpiece of Klan activism.[42]

Contrary to its perception of as a primarily southern and lower-class phenomenon, the second Klan had a national reach composed largely of middle-class people. Sociologist Rory McVeigh surveyed the KKK newspaper *Imperial Night-Hawk* for the years 1923 and 1924, at the organization's peak, and found the largest number of Klan-related activities to have occurred in Texas, Pennsylvania, Indiana, Illinois, and Georgia. The Klan was even present in Canada, where it was a powerful force within Saskatchewan's Conservative Party. In many states and localities, the Klan dominated politics to such a level that one could not be elected without the support of the KKK. For example, in 1924, the Klan supported William Lee Cazort for governor of Arkansas, leading his opponent in the Democratic Party primary, Thomas Terral, to seek honorary membership through a Louisiana klavern so as not to be tagged as the anti-Klan candidate. In 1922, Texans elected Earle B. Mayfield, an avowed Klansman who ran openly as that year's "klandidate," to the U.S. Senate. At its peak the Klan claimed between four and five million members.[43]

Despite the breadth of its political activism, the Klan is today remembered largely as a violent vigilante group—and not without reason. Members of the Klan and affiliated organizations often carried out acts of lynching and "nightriding"—the physical harassment of bootleggers, union activists, civil rights workers, or any others deemed "immoral" (such as suspected adulterers) under the cover of darkness or while wearing their hoods and robes. In fact, Klan violence was extensive enough in Oklahoma that Governor John C. Walton placed the entire state under martial law in 1923. Witnesses testifying before the military court disclosed accounts of Klan violence ranging from the flogging of clandestine brewers to the disfiguring of a prominent Black Tulsan for registering African Americans to vote. In Houston, Texas, the Klan maintained an extensive system of surveillance that included tapping telephone lines and putting spies in the local post office in order to root out "undesirables." A mob organized and led by Klan members in Aiken, South Carolina, lynched Bertha Lowman and her two brothers in 1926, but no one was ever prosecuted: the sheriff, deputies, city attorney, and state representative all belonged to the Klan.[44]

The Klan dwindled in the face of scandal and diminished energy over the last years of the 1920s. By 1930, the Klan only had about thirty thousand members and it was largely spent as a national force, only to appear again as a much diminished force during the civil rights movement in the 1950s and 1960s.

X. Conclusion

In his inauguration speech in 1929, Herbert Hoover told Americans that the Republican Party had brought prosperity. Even ignoring stubbornly high rates of poverty and unparalleled levels of inequality, he could not see the weaknesses behind the decade's economy. Even as the new culture of consumption promoted new freedoms, it also promoted new insecurities. An economy built on credit exposed the nation to tremendous risk. Flailing European economies, high tariffs, wealth inequality, a construction bubble, and an ever-more flooded consumer market loomed dangerously until the Roaring Twenties ground to a halt. In a moment the nation's glitz and glamour seemed to give way to decay and despair. For farmers, racial minorities, unionized workers, and other populations that did not share in 1920s prosperity, the veneer of a Jazz Age and a booming economy had always been a fiction. But for them, as for millions of Americans, the end of an era was close. The Great Depression loomed.

XI. Reference Material

This chapter was edited by Brandy Thomas Wells, with content contributions by Micah Childress, Mari Crabtree, Maggie Flamingo, Guy Lancaster, Emily Remus, Colin Reynolds, Kristopher Shields, and Brandy Thomas Wells.

Recommended citation: Micah Childress et al., "The New Era," Brandy Thomas Wells, ed., in *The American Yawp*, eds. Joseph Locke and Ben Wright (Stanford, CA: Stanford University Press, 2019).

NOTES TO CHAPTER 22

1. David Montgomery, *The Fall of the House of Labor: The Workplace, the State, and American Labor Activism, 1865–1925* (New York: Cambridge University Press, 1988).

2. William E. Leuchtenburg, *The Perils of Prosperity, 1914–1932* (Chicago: University of Chicago Press, 1993).

3. Robert K. Murray, *The Harding Era: Warren G. Harding and His Administration* (Minneapolis: University of Minnesota Press, 1969.

4. Leuchtenburg, *Perils of Prosperity*.

5. Nancy Cott, *The Grounding of Modern Feminism* (New Haven, CT: Yale University Press, 1987).

6. Allan J. Lichtman, *Prejudice and the Old Politics: The Presidential Election of 1928* (Chapel Hill: University of North Carolina Press, 1979).

7. "Hoover Accepts the Republican Nomination," *Sacramento Bee*, August 11, 1928.

8. Allan J. Lichtman, *Prejudice and the Old Politics: The Presidential Election of 1928* (Chapel Hill: University of North Carolina Press, 1979).

9. Christine Frederick, *Selling Mrs. Consumer*, (New York: Business Bourse, 1929), 29.

10. T. J. Jackson Lears, "From Salvation to Self-Realization: Advertising and the Therapeutic Roots of the Consumer Culture, 1880–1930," in *The Culture of Consumption: Critical Essays in American History, 1880–1980*, ed. Richard Wightman Fox and T. J. Jackson Lears (New York: Pantheon Books, 1983), 1–38.

11. Thomas W. Goodspeed, "Marshall Field," *University of Chicago Magazine, Vol. III* (Chicago: University of Chicago Press, 1922), 48.

12. LeRoy Ashby, *With Amusement for All: A History of American Popular Culture Since 1830* (Lexington: University Press of Kentucky, 2006), 177.

13. Ibid., 183.

14. Ibid., 216.

15. Ibid., 210.

16. Ibid., 181.

17. John W. Ward, "The Meaning of Lindbergh's Flight," in *Studies in American Culture: Dominant Ideas and Images*, ed. Joseph J. Kwiat and Mary C. Turpie (Minneapolis: University of Minnesota Press, 1960), 33.

18. See Lynn Dumenil, *The Modern Temper: American Culture and Society in the 1920s* (New York: Hill and Wang, 1995), 113.

19. Cott, *Grounding of Modern Feminism*, 150.

20. George Chauncey, *Gay New York: Gender, Urban Culture, and the Makings of the Gay Male World, 1890–1940* (New York: Basic Books, 1994).

21. Cott, *Grounding of Modern Feminism*, 160.

22. Mark R. Schneider, *"We Return Fighting": The Civil Rights Movement in the Jazz Age* (Boston: Northeastern University Press, 2002), 21.

23. Philip Kasinitz, *Caribbean New York: Black Immigrants and the Politics of Race* (Ithaca, NY: Cornell University Press, 1992), 25.

24. James Weldon Johnson, "Harlem: The Culture Capital," in *The New Negro: An Interpretation*, ed. Alain Locke (New York: Albert and Charles Boni, 1925), 301.

25. Ibid.

26. Joan Marter, ed., *The Grove Encyclopedia of American Art, Volume 1* (Oxford, UK: Oxford University Press, 2011), 448.

27. James F. Wilson, *Bulldaggers, Pansies, and Chocolate Babies: Performance, Race, and Sexuality in the Harlem Renaissance* (Ann Arbor: University of Michigan Press, 2010), 116.

28. Cary D. Wintz and Paul Finkelman, *Encyclopedia of the Harlem Renaissance*, Vol. 2 (New York: Routledge, 2004), 910–911.

29. For Garvey, see Colin Grant, *Negro with a Hat: The Rise and Fall of Marcus Garvey* (New York: Oxford University Press, 2008); Judith Stein, *The World of Marcus Garvey: Race and Class in Modern Society* (Baton Rouge: LSU Press, 1986); and Ula Yvette Taylor, *The Veiled Garvey: The Life and Times of Amy Jacques Garvey* (Chapel Hill: University of North Carolina Press, 2002).

30. Winston James, *Holding Aloft the Banner of Ethiopia: Caribbean Radicalism in Early Twentieth-Century America* (London: Verso, 1998).

31. Grant, *Negro with a Hat*; Stein, *World of Marcus Garvey*; Taylor, *Veiled Garvey*.

32. Grant, *Negro with a Hat*; Stein, *World of Marcus Garvey*; Taylor, *Veiled Garvey*.

33. Nicola Sacco and Bartolomeo Vanzetti, *The Letters of Sacco and Vanzetti* (New York: Viking, 1928), 272.

34. Harry Emerson Fosdick, "Shall the Fundamentalists Win?" *Christian Work* 102 (June 10, 1922): 716–722.

35. George Marsden, *Fundamentalism and American Culture* (New York: Oxford University Press, 1980).

36. Edward J. Larson, *Summer for the Gods: The Scopes Trial and America's Continuing Debate over Science and Religion* (Cambridge, MA: Harvard University Press, 1997).

37. Leslie H. Allen, ed., *Bryan and Darrow at Dayton: The Record and Documents of the "Bible-Evolution" Trial* (New York: Arthur Lee, 1925).

38. Larson, *Summer for the Gods*.

39. Ibid.

40. Nancy MacLean, *Behind the Mask of Chivalry: The Making of the Second Ku Klux Klan* (New York: Oxford University Press, 1994).

41. Kenneth T. Jackson, *The Ku Klux Klan in the City, 1915–1930* (New York: Oxford University Press, 1967).

42. MacLean, *Behind the Mask of Chivalry*.

43. George Brown Tindall, *The Emergence of the New South: 1913–1945* (Baton Rouge: LSU Press, 1967).

44. MacLean, *Behind the Mask of Chivalry*; Wyn Craig Wade, *The Fiery Cross: The Ku Klux Klan in America* (New York: Oxford University Press, 1998).

RECOMMENDED READING

Allen, Frederick Lewis. *Only Yesterday: An Informal History of the 1920s*. New York: Harper and Row, 1931.

Baldwin, Davarian. *Chicago's New Negroes: Modernity, the Great Migration, and Black Urban Life*. Chapel Hill: University of North Carolina Press, 2007.

Blee, Kathleen M. *Women of the Klan: Racism and Gender in the 1920s*. Berkeley: University of California Press, 1991.

Chauncey, George. *Gay New York: Gender, Urban Culture, and the Making of the Gay Male World, 1890–1940*. New York: Basic Books, 1995.

Cohen, Lizabeth. *Making a New Deal: Industrial Workers in Chicago, 1919–1939*. New York: Cambridge University Press, 1990.

Douglas, Ann. *Terrible Honesty: Mongrel Manhattan in the 1920s*. New York: Farrar, Straus and Giroux, 1995.

Dumenil, Lynn. *The Modern Temper: American Culture and Society in the 1920s*. New York: Hill and Wang, 1995.

Fox, Richard Wightman, and T. J. Jackson Lears, eds. *The Culture of Consumption: Critical Essays in American History, 1880–1980.* New York: Pantheon Books, 1983.

Gage, Beverly. *The Day Wall Street Exploded: A Story of America in Its First Age of Terror.* New York: Oxford University Press, 2009.

Grant, Colin. *Negro with a Hat: The Rise and Fall of Marcus Garvey.* New York: Oxford University Press, 2008.

Hall, Jacquelyn. *Like a Family: The Making of a Southern Cotton Mill World.* Chapel Hill: University of North Carolina Press, 1987.

Heap, Chad. *Slumming: Sexual and Racial Encounters in American Nightlife, 1885–1940.* Chicago: University of Chicago Press, 2010.

Hernández, Kelly Lytle. *Migra! A History of the U.S. Border Patrol.* New York: University of California Press, 2010.

Huggins, Nathan. *Harlem Renaissance.* New York: Oxford University Press, 1971.

Larson, Edward. *Summer for the Gods: The Scopes Trial and America's Continuing Debate over Science and Religion.* Cambridge, MA: Harvard University Press, 1997.

MacLean, Nancy. *Behind the Mask of Chivalry: The Making of the Second Ku Klux Klan.* New York: Oxford University Press, 1994.

Marsden, George M. *Fundamentalism and American Culture: The Shaping of Twentieth-Century Evangelicalism: 1870–1925.* New York: Oxford University Press, 1980.

McGirr, Lisa. *The War on Alcohol: Prohibition and the Rise of the American State.* New York: Norton, 2016.

Montgomery, David. *The Fall of the House of Labor: The Workplace, the State, and American Labor Activism, 1865–1925.* New York: Cambridge University Press, 1988.

Ngai, Mae M., *Impossible Subjects: Illegal Aliens and the Making of Modern America.* Princeton, NJ: Princeton University Press, 2004.

Okrent, Daniel. *Last Call: The Rise and Fall of Prohibition.* New York: Scribner, 2010.

Sanchez, George. *Becoming Mexican American: Ethnicity, Culture, and Identity in Chicano Los Angeles, 1900–1945.* New York: Oxford University Press, 1993.

Tindall, George Brown. *The Emergence of the New South, 1913–1945.* Baton Rouge: LSU Press, 1967.

Weinrib, Laura. *The Taming of Free Speech: America's Civil Liberties Compromise.* Cambridge, MA: Harvard University Press, 2016.

Wilkerson, Isabel. *The Warmth of Other Sons: The Epic Story of America's Great Migration.* New York: Vintage Books, 2010.

23

The Great Depression

I. Introduction

Hard times had hit the United States before, but never had an economic crisis lasted so long or inflicted as much harm as the slump that followed the 1929 crash. After nearly a decade of supposed prosperity, the economy crashed to a halt. People suddenly stopped borrowing and buying. Industries built on debt-fueled purchases sold fewer goods. Retailers lowered prices, and when that did not attract enough buyers to turn profits, they laid off workers to lower labor costs. With so many people out of work and without income, shops sold even less, dropped their prices lower still, and then shed still more workers, creating a vicious downward cycle.

Four years after the crash, the Great Depression reached its lowest point: nearly one in four Americans who wanted a job could not find one and, of those who could, more than half had to settle for part-time

In this famous 1936 photograph by Dorothea Lange, a destitute, thirty-two-year-old mother of seven captures the agonies of the Great Depression. Library of Congress.

work. Farmers could not make enough money from their crops to make harvesting worthwhile. Food rotted in the fields of a starving nation.

The needy drew down whatever savings they had, turned to their families, and sought out charities for public assistance. Soon they all were depleted. Unemployed workers and cash-strapped farmers defaulted on their debts, including mortgages. Already over-extended banks, deprived of income, took savings accounts down with them when they closed. Fear-stricken observers went to their own banks and demanded their deposits. Banks that otherwise might have endured the crisis fell prey to panic and shut down as well.

With so little being bought and sold, and so little lent and spent, with even bankers unable to lay their hands on money, the nation's economy ground nearly to a halt. None of the remedies adopted by the president or Congress succeeded—not higher tariffs, nor restriction of immigration, nor sticking to sound money, nor expressions of confidence in the resilience of the American people. Whatever good these measures achieved, it was not enough.

In the 1932 presidential election, the incumbent president, Herbert Hoover, a Republican, promised that he would stand firm against those who, he said, would destroy the U.S. Constitution to restore the economy. Chief among these supposedly dangerous experimenters was the Democratic presidential nominee, New York governor Franklin D. Roosevelt, who began his campaign by pledging a New Deal for the American people.

The voters chose Roosevelt in a landslide, inaugurating a rapid and enduring transformation in the U.S. government. Even though the New Deal never achieved as much as its proponents hoped or its opponents feared, it did more than any other peacetime program to change how Americans saw their country.

II. The Origins of the Great Depression

On Thursday, October 24, 1929, stock market prices suddenly plummeted. Ten billion dollars in investments (roughly equivalent to about $100 billion today) disappeared in a matter of hours. Panicked selling set in, stock values sank to sudden lows, and stunned investors crowded the New York Stock Exchange demanding answers. Leading bankers met privately at the offices of J. P. Morgan and raised millions in personal and institutional contributions to halt the slide. They marched across the street and ceremoniously bought stocks at inflated prices. The mar-

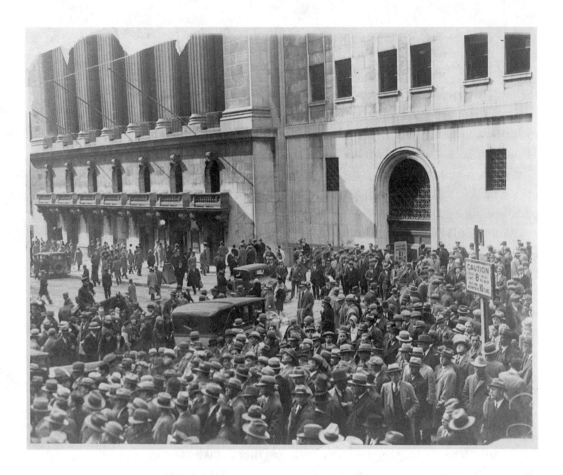

Crowds of people gather outside the New York Stock Exchange following the crash of 1929. Library of Congress.

ket temporarily stabilized but fears spread over the weekend and the following week frightened investors dumped their portfolios to avoid further losses. On October 29, Black Tuesday, the stock market began its long precipitous fall. Stock values evaporated. Shares of U.S. Steel dropped from $262 to $22. General Motors stock fell from $73 a share to $8. Four fifths of J. D. Rockefeller's fortune—the greatest in American history—vanished.

Although the crash stunned the nation, it exposed the deeper, underlying problems with the American economy in the 1920s. The stock market's popularity grew throughout the decade, but only 2.5 percent of Americans had brokerage accounts; the overwhelming majority of Americans had no direct personal stake in Wall Street. The stock market's collapse, no matter how dramatic, did not by itself depress the American economy. Instead, the crash exposed a great number of factors that, when combined with the financial panic, sank the American economy into the greatest of all economic crises. Rising inequality, declining demand, rural

collapse, overextended investors, and the bursting of speculative bubbles all conspired to plunge the nation into the Great Depression.

Despite resistance by Progressives, the vast gap between rich and poor accelerated throughout the early twentieth century. In the aggregate, Americans were better off in 1929 than in 1920. Per capita income had risen 10 percent for all Americans, but 75 percent for the nation's wealthiest citizens.[1] The return of conservative politics in the 1920s reinforced federal fiscal policies that exacerbated the divide: low corporate and personal taxes, easy credit, and depressed interest rates overwhelmingly favored wealthy investors who, flush with cash, spent their money on luxury goods and speculative investments in the rapidly rising stock market.

The pro-business policies of the 1920s were designed for an American economy built on the production and consumption of durable goods. Yet by the late 1920s, much of the market was saturated. The boom of automobile manufacturing, the great driver of the American economy in the 1920s, slowed as fewer and fewer Americans with the means to purchase a car had not already done so. More and more, the well-to-do had no need for the new automobiles, radios, and other consumer goods that fueled gross domestic product (GDP) growth in the 1920s. When

While a manufacturing innovation, Henry Ford's assembly line produced so many cars that it flooded the automobile market in the 1920s. Wikimedia.

products failed to sell, inventories piled up, manufacturers scaled back production, and companies fired workers, stripping potential consumers of cash, blunting demand for consumer goods, and replicating the downward economic cycle. The situation was only compounded by increased automation and rising efficiency in American factories. Despite impressive overall growth throughout the 1920s, unemployment hovered around 7 percent throughout the decade, suppressing purchasing power for a great swath of potential consumers.[2]

For American farmers, meanwhile, hard times began long before the markets crashed. In 1920 and 1921, after several years of larger-than-average profits, farm prices in the South and West continued their long decline, plummeting as production climbed and domestic and international demand for cotton, foodstuffs, and other agricultural products stalled. Widespread soil exhaustion on western farms only compounded the problem. Farmers found themselves unable to make payments on loans taken out during the good years, and banks in agricultural areas tightened credit in response. By 1929, farm families were overextended, in no shape to make up for declining consumption, and in a precarious economic position even before the Depression wrecked the global economy.[3]

Despite serious foundational problems in the industrial and agricultural economy, most Americans in 1929 and 1930 still believed the economy would bounce back. In 1930, amid one of the Depression's many false hopes, President Herbert Hoover reassured an audience that "the depression is over."[4] But the president was not simply guilty of false optimism. Hoover made many mistakes. During his 1928 election campaign, Hoover promoted higher tariffs as a means for encouraging domestic consumption and protecting American farmers from foreign competition. Spurred by the ongoing agricultural depression, Hoover signed into law the highest tariff in American history, the Smoot-Hawley Tariff of 1930, just as global markets began to crumble. Other countries responded in kind, tariff walls rose across the globe, and international trade ground to a halt. Between 1929 and 1932, international trade dropped from $36 billion to only $12 billion. American exports fell by 78 percent. Combined with overproduction and declining domestic consumption, the tariff exacerbated the world's economic collapse.[5]

But beyond structural flaws, speculative bubbles, and destructive protectionism, the final contributing element of the Great Depression was a quintessentially human one: panic. The frantic reaction to the market's fall aggravated the economy's other many failings. More economic policies backfired. The Federal Reserve overcorrected in their response to speculation by raising interest rates and tightening credit. Across the country, banks denied loans and called in debts. Their patrons, afraid that reactionary policies meant further financial trouble, rushed to withdraw money before institutions could close their doors, ensuring their fate. Such bank runs were not uncommon in the 1920s, but in 1930, with the economy worsening and panic from the crash accelerating, 1,352 banks failed. In 1932, nearly 2,300 banks collapsed, taking personal deposits, savings, and credit with them.[6]

The Great Depression was the confluence of many problems, most of which had begun during a time of unprecedented economic growth. Fiscal policies of the Republican "business presidents" undoubtedly widened the gap between rich and poor and fostered a standoff over international trade, but such policies were widely popular and, for much of the decade, widely seen as a source of the decade's explosive growth. With fortunes to be won and standards of living to maintain, few Americans had the foresight or wherewithal to repudiate an age of easy credit, rampant consumerism, and wild speculation. Instead, as the Depression worked its way across the United States, Americans hoped to weather the economic storm as best they could, hoping for some relief, from ever-mounting economic collapse that was strangling so many lives.

III. Herbert Hoover and the Politics of the Depression

As the Depression spread, public blame settled on President Herbert Hoover and the conservative politics of the Republican Party. In 1928, having won the presidency in a landslide, Hoover had no reason to believe that his presidency would be any different than that of his predecessor, Calvin Coolidge, whose time in office was marked by relative government inaction, seemingly rampant prosperity, and high approval ratings.[7]

Hoover entered office on a wave of popular support, but by October 1929 the economic collapse had overwhelmed his presidency. Like all too many Americans, Hoover and his advisors assumed—or perhaps simply hoped—that the sharp financial and economic decline was a temporary downturn, another "bust" of the inevitable boom-bust cycles that stretched back through America's commercial history. "Any lack of confidence in the economic future and the basic strength of business in the United States is simply foolish," he said in November.[8] And yet the crisis

Unemployed men queued outside a depression soup kitchen opened in Chicago by Al Capone. February 1931. Wikimedia.

grew. Unemployment commenced a slow, sickening rise. New car registrations dropped by almost a quarter within a few months.[9] Consumer spending on durable goods dropped by a fifth in 1930.[10]

When suffering Americans looked to Hoover for help, Hoover could only answer with volunteerism. He *asked* business leaders to promise to maintain investments and employment and *encouraged* state and local charities to assist those in need. Hoover established the President's Organization for Unemployment Relief, or POUR, to help organize the efforts of private agencies. While POUR urged charitable giving, charitable relief organizations were overwhelmed by the growing needs of the many-multiplying unemployed, underfed, and unhoused Americans. By mid-1932, for instance, a quarter of all of New York's private charities closed: they had simply run out of money. In Atlanta, solvent relief charities could provide only $1.30 per week to needy families. The size and scope of the Depression overpowered the radically insufficient capacity of private volunteer organizations to mediate the crisis.[11]

Although Hoover is sometimes categorized as a "business president" in line with his Republican predecessors, he also embraced a kind of business progressivism, a system of voluntary action called *associationalism* that assumed Americans could maintain a web of voluntary cooperative organizations dedicated to providing economic assistance and services to those in need. Businesses, the thinking went, would willingly limit harmful practice for the greater economic good. To Hoover, direct government aid would discourage a healthy work ethic while associationalism would encourage the self-control and self-initiative that fueled economic growth. But when the Depression exposed the incapacity of such strategies to produce an economic recovery, Hoover proved insufficiently flexible to recognize the limits of his ideology.[12] "We cannot legislate ourselves out of a world economic depression," he told Congress in 1931.[13]

Hoover resisted direct action. As the crisis deepened, even bankers and businessmen and the president's own advisors and appointees all pleaded with him to use the government's power to fight the Depression. But his conservative ideology wouldn't allow him to. He believed in limited government as a matter of principle. Senator Robert Wagner of New York said in 1931 that the president's policy was "to do nothing and when the pressure becomes irresistible to do as little as possible."[14] By 1932, with the economy long since stagnant and a reelection campaign looming, Hoover, hoping to stimulate American industry, created the Reconstruction Finance Corporation (RFC) to provide emergency loans to banks, building-and-loan societies, railroads, and other private industries. It was radical in its use of direct government aid and out of character for the normally laissez-faire Hoover, but it also bypassed needy Americans to bolster industrial and financial interests. New York congressman Fiorello La Guardia, who later served as mayor of New York City, captured public sentiment when he denounced the RFC as a "millionaire's dole."[15]

IV. The Lived Experience of the Great Depression

In 1934 a woman from Humboldt County, California, wrote to First Lady Eleanor Roosevelt seeking a job for her husband, a surveyor, who had been out of work for nearly two years. The pair had survived on the meager income she received from working at the county courthouse. "My salary could keep us going," she explained, "but—I am to have a baby." The family needed temporary help, and, she explained, "after that I can go back to work and we can work out our own salvation. But to have this baby come to a home full of worry and despair, with no money for the things it needs, is not fair. It needs and deserves a happy start in life."[16]

As the United States slid ever deeper into the Great Depression, such tragic scenes played out time and time again. Individuals, families, and communities faced the painful, frightening, and often bewildering collapse of the economic institutions on which they depended. The more fortunate were spared the worst effects, and a few even profited from it, but by the end of 1932, the crisis had become so deep and so widespread that most Americans had suffered directly. Markets crashed through no fault of their own. Workers were plunged into poverty because of impersonal forces for which they shared no responsibility.

With rampant unemployment and declining wages, Americans slashed expenses. The fortunate could survive by simply deferring vacations and regular consumer purchases. Middle- and working-class Americans might rely on disappearing credit at neighborhood stores, default on utility bills, or skip meals. Those who could borrowed from relatives or took in boarders in homes or "doubled up" in tenements.

But such resources couldn't withstand the unending relentlessness of the economic crisis. As one New York City official explained in 1932,

> When the breadwinner is out of a job he usually exhausts his savings if he has any. . . . He borrows from his friends and from his relatives until they can stand the burden no longer. He gets credit from the corner grocery store and the butcher shop, and the landlord forgoes collecting the rent until interest and taxes have to be paid and something has to be done.
>
> All of these resources are finally exhausted over a period of time, and it becomes necessary for these people, who have never before been in want, to go on assistance.[17]

But public assistance and private charities were quickly exhausted by the scope of the crisis. As one Detroit city official put it in 1932,

> Many essential public services have been reduced beyond the minimum point absolutely essential to the health and safety of the city. . . . The salaries of city employees have been twice reduced . . . and hundreds of faithful employees . . . have been furloughed. Thus has the city borrowed from its own future welfare to keep its unemployed on the barest subsistence levels. . . . A wage work plan which had supported 11,000 families collapsed last month because the city was unable to find funds to pay these unemployed—men who wished to earn their own support. For

the coming year, Detroit can see no possibility of preventing widespread hunger and slow starvation through its own unaided resources.[18]

These most desperate Americans, the chronically unemployed, encamped on public or marginal lands in "Hoovervilles," spontaneous shantytowns that dotted America's cities, depending on breadlines and street-corner peddling. One doctor recalled that "every day . . . someone would faint on a streetcar. They'd bring him in, and they wouldn't ask any questions. . . . They knew what it was. Hunger."[19]

"A man is not a man without work," one of the jobless told an interviewer.[20] The ideal of the "male breadwinner" was always a fiction for poor Americans, and, during the crisis, women and young children entered the labor force, as they always had. But, in such a labor crisis, many employers, subscribing to traditional notions of male breadwinning, were less likely to hire married women and more likely to dismiss those they already employed.[21] As one politician remarked at the time, the woman worker was "the first orphan in the storm."[22]

American suppositions about family structure meant that women suffered disproportionately from the Depression. Since the start of the

A Hooverville in Seattle, Washington, between 1932 and 1937. Washington State Archives.

twentieth century, single women had become an increasing share of the workforce, but married women, Americans were likely to believe, took a job because they wanted to and not because they needed it. Once the Depression came, employers were therefore less likely to hire married women and more likely to dismiss those they already employed.[23] Women on their own and without regular work suffered a greater threat of sexual violence than their male counterparts; accounts of such women suggest they depended on each other for protection.[24]

The Great Depression was particularly tough for nonwhite Americans. "The Negro was born in depression," one Black pensioner told interviewer Studs Terkel. "It didn't mean too much to him. The Great American Depression . . . only became official when it hit the white man."[25] Black workers were generally the last hired when businesses expanded production and the first fired when businesses experienced downturns.

As a National Urban League study found, "So general is this practice that one is warranted in suspecting that it has been adopted as a method of relieving unemployment of whites without regard to the consequences upon Negroes."[26] In 1932, with the national unemployment average hovering around 25 percent, Black unemployment reached as high as 50 percent, while even Black workers who kept their jobs saw their already low wages cut dramatically.[27]

V. Migration and the Great Depression

On the Great Plains, environmental catastrophe deepened America's longstanding agricultural crisis and magnified the tragedy of the Depression. Beginning in 1932, severe droughts hit from Texas to the Dakotas and lasted until at least 1936. The droughts compounded years of agricultural mismanagement. To grow their crops, Plains farmers had plowed up natural ground cover that had taken ages to form over the surface of the dry Plains states. Relatively wet decades had protected them, but, during the early 1930s, without rain, the exposed fertile topsoil turned to dust, and without sod or windbreaks such as trees, rolling winds churned the dust into massive storms that blotted out the sky, choked settlers and livestock, and rained dirt not only across the region but as far east as Washington, D.C., New England, and ships on the Atlantic Ocean. The Dust Bowl, as the region became known, exposed all-too-late the need for conservation. The region's farmers, already hit by years of foreclosures and declining commodity prices, were decimated.[28] For many in

This iconic 1936 photograph by Dorothea Lange of a destitute, thirty-two-year-old mother of seven made real the suffering of millions during the Great Depression. Library of Congress.

Texas, Oklahoma, Kansas, and Arkansas who were "baked out, blown out, and broke," their only hope was to travel west to California, whose rains still brought bountiful harvests and—potentially—jobs for farm-workers. It was an exodus. Oklahoma lost 440,000 people, or a full 18.4 percent of its 1930 population, to outmigration.[29]

Dorothea Lange's *Migrant Mother* became one of the most enduring images of the Dust Bowl and the ensuing westward exodus. Lange, a photographer for the Farm Security Administration, captured the image at a migrant farmworker camp in Nipomo, California, in 1936. In the photograph a young mother stares out with a worried, weary expression. She was a migrant, having left her home in Oklahoma to follow the crops to the Golden State. She took part in what many in the mid-1930s were beginning to recognize as a vast migration of families out of the southwestern Plains states. In the image she cradles an infant and supports two older children, who cling to her. Lange's photo encapsulated the nation's struggle. The subject of the photograph seemed used to hard work but down on her luck, and uncertain about what the future might hold.

The Okies, as such westward migrants were disparagingly called by their new neighbors, were the most visible group who were on the move during the Depression, lured by news and rumors of jobs in far-flung regions of the country. Men from all over the country, some abandoning families, hitched rides, hopped freight cars, or otherwise made their way around the country. By 1932, sociologists were estimating that millions of men were on the roads and rails traveling the country.[30] Popular magazines and newspapers were filled with stories of homeless boys and the veterans-turned-migrants of the Bonus Army commandeering boxcars. Popular culture, such as William Wellman's 1933 film, *Wild Boys of the Road,* and, most famously, John Steinbeck's *The Grapes of Wrath*, published in 1939 and turned into a hit movie a year later, captured the Depression's dislocated populations.

These years witnessed the first significant reversal in the flow of people between rural and urban areas. Thousands of city dwellers fled the jobless cities and moved to the country looking for work. As relief efforts floundered, many state and local officials threw up barriers to migration, making it difficult for newcomers to receive relief or find work. Some state legislatures made it a crime to bring poor migrants into the state and allowed local officials to deport migrants to neighboring states. In

During her assignment as a photographer for the Works Progress Administration (WPA), Dorothea Lange documented the movement of migrant families forced from their homes by drought and economic depression. This family, captured by Lange in 1938, was in the process of traveling 124 miles by foot, across Oklahoma, because the father was ill and therefore unable to receive relief or WPA work. Library of Congress.

the winter of 1935–1936, California, Florida, and Colorado established "border blockades" to block poor migrants from their states and reduce competition with local residents for jobs. A billboard outside Tulsa, Oklahoma, informed potential migrants that there were "NO JOBS in California" and warned them to "KEEP OUT."[31]

Sympathy for migrants, however, accelerated late in the Depression with the publication of John Steinbeck's *The Grapes of Wrath*. The Joad family's struggles drew attention to the plight of Depression-era migrants and, just a month after the nationwide release of the film version, Congress created the Select Committee to Investigate the Interstate Migration of Destitute Citizens. Starting in 1940, the committee held widely publicized hearings. But it was too late. Within a year of its founding, defense industries were already gearing up in the wake of the outbreak of World War II, and the "problem" of migration suddenly became a *lack* of migrants needed to fill war industries. Such relief was nowhere to be found in the 1930s.

Americans meanwhile feared foreign workers willing to work for even lower wages. The *Saturday Evening Post* warned that foreign immigrants, who were "compelled to accept employment on any terms and conditions offered," would exacerbate the economic crisis.[32] On September 8, 1930, the Hoover administration issued a press release on the administration of immigration laws "under existing conditions of unemployment." Hoover instructed consular officers to scrutinize carefully the visa applications of those "likely to become public charges" and suggested that this might include denying visas to most, if not all, alien laborers and artisans. The crisis itself had stifled foreign immigration, but such restrictive and exclusionary actions in the first years of the Depression intensified its effects. The number of European visas issued fell roughly 60 percent while deportations dramatically increased. Between 1930 and 1932, fifty-four thousand people were deported. An additional forty-four thousand deportable aliens left "voluntarily."[33]

Exclusionary measures hit Mexican immigrants particularly hard. The State Department made a concerted effort to reduce immigration from Mexico as early as 1929, and Hoover's executive actions arrived the following year. Officials in the Southwest led a coordinated effort to push out Mexican immigrants. In Los Angeles, the Citizens Committee on Coordination of Unemployment Relief began working closely with federal officials in early 1931 to conduct deportation raids, while the Los Angeles County Department of Charities began a simultaneous drive to repatriate Mexicans and Mexican Americans on relief, negotiating a charity rate with the railroads to return Mexicans "voluntarily" to their mother country. According to the federal census, from 1930 to 1940 the Mexican-born population living in Arizona, California, New Mexico, and Texas fell from 616,998 to 377,433. Franklin Roosevelt did not indulge anti-immigrant sentiment as willingly as Hoover had. Under the New Deal, the Immigration and Naturalization Service halted some of the Hoover administration's most divisive practices, but with jobs suddenly scarce, hostile attitudes intensified, and official policies less than welcoming, immigration plummeted and deportations rose. Over the course of the Depression, more people left the United States than entered it.[34]

VI. The Bonus Army

Shacks, put up by the Bonus Army on the Anacostia flats, Washington, D.C., burning after the battle with the military. The Capitol in the background. 1932. Wikimedia.

In the summer of 1932, more than fifteen-thousand unemployed veterans and their families converged on Washington, D.C., to petition for a bill authorizing immediate payment of cash bonuses to veterans of World War I that were originally scheduled to be paid out in 1945. Given the economic hardships facing the country, the bonus came to

symbolize government relief for the most deserving recipients. The veterans in D.C. erected a tent city across the Potomac River in Anacostia Flats, a "Hooverville" in the spirit of the camps of homeless and unemployed Americans then appearing in American cities. Calling themselves the Bonus Expeditionary Force, or the Bonus Army, they drilled and marched and demonstrated for their bonuses. "While there were billions for bankers, there was nothing for the poor," they complained.

Concerned with what immediate payment would do to the federal budget, Hoover opposed the bill, which was eventually voted down by the Senate. While most of the "Bonus Army" left Washington in defeat, many stayed to press their case. Hoover called the remaining veterans "insurrectionists" and ordered them to leave. When thousands failed to heed the vacation order, General Douglas MacArthur, accompanied by local police, infantry, cavalry, tanks, and a machine gun squadron, stormed the tent city and routed the Bonus Army. Troops chased down men and women, tear-gassed children, and torched the shantytown.[35] Two marchers were shot and killed and a baby was killed by tear gas.

The national media reported on the raid, newsreels showed footage, and Americans recoiled at Hoover's insensitivity toward suffering Americans. His overall unwillingness to address widespread economic problems and his repeated platitudes about returning prosperity condemned his presidency. Hoover, of course, was not responsible for the Depression, not personally. But neither he nor his advisors conceived of the enormity of the crisis, a crisis his conservative ideology could neither accommodate nor address. Americans had so far found little relief from Washington. But they were still looking for it.

VII. Franklin Delano Roosevelt and the "First" New Deal

The early years of the Depression were catastrophic. The crisis, far from relenting, deepened each year. Unemployment peaked at 25 percent in 1932. With no end in sight, and with private firms crippled and charities overwhelmed by the crisis, Americans looked to their government as the last barrier against starvation, hopelessness, and perpetual poverty.

Few presidential elections in modern American history have been more consequential than that of 1932. The United States was struggling through the third year of the Depression, and exasperated voters overthrew Hoover in a landslide to elect the Democratic governor of New York, Franklin Delano Roosevelt. Roosevelt came from a privileged

Posters like this 1936 production showing the extent of the Federal Art Project were used to prove the value of the WPA—and, by extension, the entire New Deal—to the American people. Wikimedia.

background in New York's Hudson River Valley (his distant cousin, Theodore Roosevelt, became president while Franklin was at Harvard, and he embarked on a slow but steady ascent through state and national politics. In 1913, he was appointed assistant secretary of the navy, a position he held during the defense emergency of World War I. In the course of his rise, in the summer of 1921, Roosevelt suffered a sudden bout of lower-body pain and paralysis. He was diagnosed with polio. The disease left him a paraplegic, but, encouraged and assisted by his wife, Eleanor, Roosevelt sought therapeutic treatment and maintained sufficient political connections to reenter politics. In 1928, Roosevelt won election as governor of New York. He oversaw the rise of the Depression and drew from the tradition of American progressivism to address the economic crisis. He explained to the state assembly in 1931, the crisis demanded a government response "not as a matter of charity, but as a matter of social duty." As governor he established the Temporary Emergency Relief Administration (TERA), supplying public works jobs at the prevailing wage and in-kind aid—food, shelter, and clothes—to those unable to afford it. Soon the TERA was providing work and relief to ten percent of the state's families.[36] Roosevelt relied on like-minded advisors. Frances Perkins, for example, the commissioner of the state's labor department, successfully advocated pioneering legislation that enhanced workplace safety and reduced the use of child labor in factories. Perkins later accompanied Roosevelt to Washington and served as the nation's first female secretary of labor.[37]

On July 1, 1932, Roosevelt, the newly designated presidential nominee of the Democratic Party, delivered the first and one of the most famous on-site acceptance speeches in American presidential history. Building to a conclusion, he said, "I pledge you, I pledge myself, to a new deal for the American people." Newspaper editors seized on the phrase "new deal," and it entered the American political lexicon as shorthand for Roosevelt's program to address the Great Depression.[38]

Roosevelt proposed jobs programs, public works projects, higher wages, shorter hours, old-age pensions, unemployment insurance, farm subsidies, banking regulations, and lower tariffs. Hoover warned that such a program represented "the total abandonment of every principle upon which this government and the American system is founded." He warned that it reeked of European communism, and that "the so called new deals would destroy the very foundations of the American system of life."[39]

Americans didn't buy it. Roosevelt crushed Hoover in November. He won more counties than any previous candidate in American history. He spent the months between his election and inauguration—the Twentieth Amendment, ratified in 1933, would subsequently move the inauguration from March 4 to January 20—traveling, planning, and assembling a team of advisors, the famous Brain Trust of academics and experts, to help him formulate a plan of attack. On March 4, 1933, in his first inaugural address, Roosevelt famously declared, "This great Nation will endure as it has endured, will revive and will prosper. So, first of all, let me assert my firm belief that the only thing we have to fear is fear itself—nameless, unreasoning, unjustified terror which paralyzes needed efforts to convert retreat into advance."[40]

Roosevelt's reassuring words would have rung hollow if he had not taken swift action against the economic crisis. In his first days in office, Roosevelt and his advisors prepared, submitted, and secured congressional enactment of numerous laws designed to arrest the worst of the Great Depression. His administration threw the federal government headlong into the fight against the Depression.

Roosevelt immediately looked to stabilize the collapsing banking system. Two out of every five banks open in 1929 had been shuttered, and some Federal Reserve banks were on the verge of insolvency.[41] Roosevelt declared a national "bank holiday" closing American banks and set to work pushing the Emergency Banking Act swiftly through Congress. On March 12, the night before select banks reopened under stricter federal guidelines, Roosevelt appeared on the radio in the first of his Fireside Chats. The addresses, which the president continued delivering through four terms, were informal, even personal. Roosevelt used his airtime to explain New Deal legislation, to encourage confidence in government action, and to mobilize the American people's support. In the first chat, Roosevelt described the new banking safeguards and asked the public to place their trust and their savings in banks. Americans responded and deposits outpaced withdrawals across the country. The act was a major success. In June, Congress passed the Glass-Steagall Banking Act, which instituted a federal deposit insurance system through the Federal Deposit Insurance Corporation (FDIC) and barred the mixing of commercial and investment banking.[42]

Stabilizing the banks was only a first step. In the remainder of his First Hundred Days, Roosevelt and his congressional allies focused especially on relief for suffering Americans.[43] Congress debated, amended, and passed what Roosevelt proposed. As one historian noted, the president "directed the entire operation like a seasoned field general."[44] And despite some questions over the constitutionality of many of his actions, Americans and their congressional representatives conceded that the crisis demanded swift and immediate action. The Civilian Conservation Corps (CCC) employed young men on conservation and reforestation projects; the Federal Emergency Relief Administration (FERA) provided direct cash assistance to state relief agencies struggling to care for the unemployed;[45] the Tennessee Valley Authority (TVA) built a series of hydroelectric dams along the Tennessee River as part of a comprehensive program to economically develop a chronically depressed region;[46] and several agencies helped home and farm owners refinance their mortgages. And Roosevelt wasn't done.

The heart of Roosevelt's early recovery program consisted of two massive efforts to stabilize and coordinate the American economy: the Agricultural Adjustment Administration (AAA) and the National Recovery Administration (NRA). The AAA, created in May 1933, aimed to raise the prices of agricultural commodities (and hence farmers' income) by offering cash incentives to voluntarily limit farm production (decreasing supply, thereby raising prices).[47] The National Industrial Recovery Act (NIRA), which created the NRA in June 1933, suspended antitrust laws to allow businesses to establish "codes" that would coordinate prices, regulate production levels, and establish conditions of employment to curtail "cutthroat competition." In exchange for these exemptions, businesses agreed to provide reasonable wages and hours, end child labor, and allow workers the right to unionize. Participating businesses earned the right to display a placard with the NRA's Blue Eagle, showing their cooperation in the effort to combat the Great Depression.[48]

The programs of the First Hundred Days stabilized the American economy and ushered in a robust though imperfect recovery. GDP climbed once more, but even as output increased, unemployment remained stubbornly high. Though the unemployment rate dipped from its high in 1933, when Roosevelt was inaugurated, vast numbers remained out of work. If the economy could not put people back to work, the New Deal would try. The Civil Works Administration (CWA) and, later, the Works Progress Administration (WPA) put unemployed men and women to work on projects designed and proposed by local governments. The Public Works Administration (PWA) provided grants-in-aid to local governments for large infrastructure projects, such as bridges, tunnels, schoolhouses, libraries, and America's first federal public housing projects. Together, they provided not only tangible projects of immense public good but employment for millions. The New Deal was reshaping much of the nation.[49]

VIII. The New Deal in the South

The impact of initial New Deal legislation was readily apparent in the South, a region of perpetual poverty especially plagued by the Depression. In 1929 the average per capita income in the American Southeast was $365, the lowest in the nation. Southern farmers averaged $183 per year at a time when farmers on the West Coast made more than four times that.[50] Moreover, they were trapped into the production of cotton and corn, crops that depleted the soil and returned ever-diminishing profits. Despite the ceaseless efforts of civic boosters, what little industry the South had remained low-wage, low-skilled, and primarily extractive. Southern workers made significantly less than their national counterparts: 75 percent of nonsouthern textile workers, 60 percent of iron

The accusation of rape brought against the so-called Scottsboro Boys, pictured with their attorney in 1932, generated controversy across the country. Wikipedia.

and steel workers, and a paltry 45 percent of lumber workers. At the time of the crash, southerners were already underpaid, underfed, and undereducated.[51]

Major New Deal programs were designed with the South in mind. FDR hoped that by drastically decreasing the amount of land devoted to cotton, the AAA would arrest its long-plummeting price decline. Farmers plowed up existing crops and left fields fallow, and the market price did rise. But in an agricultural world of landowners and landless farmworkers (such as tenants and sharecroppers), the benefits of the AAA bypassed the southerners who needed them most. The government relied on landowners and local organizations to distribute money fairly to those most affected by production limits, but many owners simply kicked tenants and croppers off their land, kept the subsidy checks for keeping those acres fallow, and reinvested the profits in mechanical farming equipment that further suppressed the demand for labor. Instead of making farming profitable again, the AAA pushed landless southern farmworkers off the land.[52]

But Roosevelt's assault on southern poverty took many forms. Southern industrial practices attracted much attention. The NRA encouraged higher wages and better conditions. It began to suppress the rampant use of child labor in southern mills and, for the first time, provided federal protection for unionized workers all across the country. Those gains were eventually solidified in the 1938 Fair Labor Standards Act, which set a national minimum wage of $0.25/hour (eventually rising to $0.40/hour). The minimum wage disproportionately affected low-paid southern workers and brought southern wages within the reach of northern wages.[53]

The president's support for unionization further impacted the South. Southern industrialists had proven themselves ardent foes of unionization, particularly in the infamous southern textile mills. In 1934, when workers at textile mills across the southern Piedmont struck over low wages and long hours, owners turned to local and state authorities to quash workers' groups, even as they recruited thousands of strikebreakers from the many displaced farmers swelling industrial centers looking for work. But in 1935 the National Labor Relations Act, also known as the Wagner Act, guaranteed the rights of most workers to unionize and bargain collectively. And so unionized workers, backed by the support of the federal government and determined to enforce the reforms of the New Deal, pushed for higher wages, shorter hours, and better conditions. With growing success, union members came to see Roosevelt as a protector of workers' rights. Or, as one union leader put it, an "agent of God."[54]

Perhaps the most successful New Deal program in the South was the TVA, an ambitious program to use hydroelectric power, agricultural and industrial reform, flood control, economic development, education, and healthcare to radically remake the impoverished watershed region of the Tennessee River. Though the area of focus was limited, Roosevelt's TVA sought to "make a different type of citizen" out of the area's penniless residents.[55] The TVA built a series of hydroelectric dams to control flooding and distribute electricity to the otherwise nonelectrified areas at government-subsidized rates. Agents of the TVA met with residents and offered training and general education classes to improve agricultural practices and exploit new job opportunities. The TVA encapsulates Roosevelt's vision for uplifting the South and integrating it into the larger national economy.[56]

Roosevelt initially courted conservative southern Democrats to ensure the legislative success of the New Deal, all but guaranteeing that the racial and economic inequalities of the region remained intact, but by the end of his second term, he had won the support of enough non-southern voters that he felt confident confronting some of the region's most glaring inequalities. Nowhere was this more apparent than in his endorsement of a report, formulated by a group of progressive southern New Dealers, titled "A Report on Economic Conditions in the South." The pamphlet denounced the hardships wrought by the southern economy—in his introductory letter to the report, Roosevelt called the region "the Nation's No. 1 economic problem"—and blasted reactionary southern anti–New Dealers. He suggested that the New Deal could save the South and thereby spur a nationwide recovery. The report was among the first broadsides in Roosevelt's coming reelection campaign that addressed the inequalities that continued to mark southern and national life.[57]

IX. Voices of Protest

Despite the unprecedented actions taken in his first year in office, Roosevelt's initial relief programs could often be quite conservative. He had usually been careful to work within the bounds of presidential authority and congressional cooperation. And, unlike Europe, where several nations had turned toward state-run economies, and even fascism and socialism, Roosevelt's New Deal demonstrated a clear reluctance to radically tinker with the nation's foundational economic and social

Huey Long was an indomitable force who campaigned tirelessly for the common man during the Great Depression. He demanded that all Americans "Share the Wealth." Wikimedia.

structures. Many high-profile critics attacked Roosevelt for not going far enough, and, beginning in 1934, Roosevelt and his advisors were forced to respond.

Senator Huey Long, a flamboyant Democrat from Louisiana, was perhaps the most important "voice of protest." Long's populist rhetoric appealed to those who saw deeply rooted but easily addressed injustice in the nation's economic system. Long proposed a Share Our Wealth program in which the federal government would confiscate the assets of the extremely wealthy and redistribute them to the less well-off through guaranteed minimum incomes. "How many men ever went to a barbecue and would let one man take off the table what's intended for nine-tenths of the people to eat?" he asked. Over twenty-seven thousand Share the Wealth clubs sprang up across the nation as Long traveled the country explaining his program to crowds of impoverished and unemployed Americans. Long envisioned the movement as a stepping-stone to the presidency, but his crusade ended in late 1935 when he was assassinated on the floor of the Louisiana state capitol. Even in death, however, Long convinced Roosevelt to more stridently attack the Depression and American inequality.

But Huey Long was not alone in his critique of Roosevelt. Francis Townsend, a former doctor and public health official from California, promoted a plan for old-age pensions which, he argued, would provide economic security for the elderly (who disproportionately suffered poverty) and encourage recovery by allowing older workers to retire from the workforce. Reverend Charles Coughlin, meanwhile, a priest and radio personality from the suburbs of Detroit, Michigan, gained a following by making vitriolic, anti-Semitic attacks on Roosevelt for cooperating with banks and financiers and proposing a new system of "social justice" through a more state-driven economy instead. Like Long, both Townsend and Coughlin built substantial public followings.

If many Americans urged Roosevelt to go further in addressing the economic crisis, the president faced even greater opposition from conservative politicians and business leaders. By late 1934, complaints increased from business-friendly Republicans about Roosevelt's willingness to regulate industry and use federal spending for public works and employment programs. In the South, Democrats who had originally supported the president grew more hostile toward programs that challenged the region's political, economic, and social status quo. Yet the greatest opposition came from the Supreme Court, filled with conservative appointments made during the long years of Republican presidents.

By early 1935 the Court was reviewing programs of the New Deal. On May 27, a day Roosevelt's supporters called Black Monday, the justices struck down one of the president's signature reforms: in a case revolving around poultry processing, the Court unanimously declared the NRA unconstitutional. In early 1936, the AAA fell.[58]

X. The "Second" New Deal (1935–1936)

The New Deal enjoyed broad popularity. Democrats gained seats in the 1934 midterm elections, securing massive majorities in both the House and Senate. Bolstered by these gains, facing reelection in 1936 and confronting rising opposition from both the left and the right, Roosevelt rededicated himself to bold programs and more aggressive approaches, a set of legislation often termed the Second New Deal. It included a nearly five-billion-dollar appropriation that in 1935 established the Works

Unionization was met with fierce opposition from owners and managers, particularly in the manufacturing belt of the Midwest. In this 1937 image, strikers guard the entrance to a Flint, Michigan, manufacturing plant. Library of Congress.

Progress Administration (WPA), a permanent version of the CWA, which would ultimately employ millions of Americans on public works projects. It would employ "the maximum number of persons in the shortest time possible," Roosevelt said.[59] Americans employed by the WPA paved more than half a million miles of roads, constructed thousands of bridges, built schools and post offices, and even painted murals and recorded oral histories. Not only did the program build much of America's physical infrastructure, it came closer than any New Deal program to providing the federal jobs guarantee Roosevelt had promised in 1932. Also in 1935, hoping to reconstitute some of the protections afforded workers in the now-defunct NRA, Roosevelt worked with Congress to pass the National Labor Relations Act (known as the Wagner Act for its chief sponsor, New York senator Robert Wagner), offering federal legal protection, for the first time, for workers to organize unions.

The labor protections extended by Roosevelt's New Deal were revolutionary. In northern industrial cities, workers responded to worsening conditions by banding together and demanding support for workers' rights. In 1935, the head of the United Mine Workers, John L. Lewis, took the lead in forming a new national workers' organization, the Congress of Industrial Organizations (CIO), breaking with the more conservative, craft-oriented AFL. The CIO won a major victory in 1937 when affiliated members in the United Automobile Workers (UAW) struck for recognition and better pay and hours at a General Motors (GM) plant in Flint, Michigan. Launching a "sit-down" strike, the workers remained in the building until management agreed to negotiate. GM recognized the UAW and granted a pay increase. GM's recognition gave the UAW new legitimacy, and unionization spread rapidly across the auto industry. Across the country, unions and workers took advantage of the New Deal's protections to organize and win major concessions from employers. Three years after the NLRA, Congress passed the Fair Labor Standards Act, creating the modern minimum wage.

The Second New Deal also oversaw the restoration of a highly progressive federal income tax, mandated new reporting requirements for publicly traded companies, refinanced long-term home mortgages for struggling homeowners, and attempted rural reconstruction projects to bring farm incomes in line with urban ones.[60] Perhaps the signature piece of Roosevelt's Second New Deal, however, was the Social Security Act. It provided for old-age pensions, unemployment insurance, and economic aid, based on means, to assist both the elderly and dependent children. The president was careful to mitigate some of the criticism from what was, at the time, in the American context, a revolutionary concept. He specifically insisted that social security be financed from payroll, not the federal government; "No dole," Roosevelt said repeatedly, "mustn't have a dole."[61] He thereby helped separate social security from the stigma of being an undeserved "welfare" entitlement. While such a strategy saved the program from suspicions, social security became the centerpiece of the modern American social welfare state. It was the culmination of a long progressive push for government-sponsored social welfare, an answer to the calls of Roosevelt's opponents on the Left for reform, a response to the intractable poverty among America's neediest groups, and a recognition that the government would now assume some responsibility for the economic well-being of its citizens. Nevertheless, the Act excluded large swaths of the American population. Its pension program excluded domestic workers and farm workers, for instance, a policy that disproportionately affected African Americans. Roosevelt recognized that Social Security's programs would need expansion and improvement. "This law," he said, "represents a cornerstone in a structure which is being built but is by no means complete."[62]

XI. Equal Rights and the New Deal

Black Americans faced discrimination everywhere but suffered especially severe legal inequality in the Jim Crow South. In 1931, for instance, a group of nine young men riding the rails between Chattanooga and Memphis, Tennessee, were pulled from the train near Scottsboro, Alabama, and charged with assaulting two white women. Despite clear evidence that the assault had not occurred, and despite one of the women later recanting, the young men endured a series of sham trials in which all but one were sentenced to death. Only the communist-oriented International Labor Defense (ILD) came to the aid of the "Scottsboro Boys," who soon became a national symbol of continuing racial prejudice in America and a rallying point for civil rights–minded Americans. In appeals, the ILD successfully challenged the boys' sentencing, and the death sentences were either commuted or reversed, although the last of the accused did not receive parole until 1946.[63]

Despite a concerted effort to appoint Black advisors to some New Deal programs, Franklin Roosevelt did little to specifically address the particular difficulties Black communities faced. To do so openly would provoke southern Democrats and put his New Deal coalition——the uneasy alliance of national liberals, urban laborers, farm workers, and southern whites—at risk. Roosevelt not only rejected such proposals as abolishing the poll tax and declaring lynching a federal crime, he refused to specifically target African American needs in any of his larger relief and reform packages. As he explained to the national secretary of the NAACP, "I just can't take that risk."[64]

In fact, many of the programs of the New Deal had made hard times more difficult. When the codes of the NRA set new pay scales, they usually took into account regional differentiation and historical data. In the South, where African Americans had long suffered unequal pay, the new codes simply perpetuated that inequality. The codes also exempted those involved in farm work and domestic labor, the occupations of a majority of southern Black men and women. The AAA was equally problematic as owners displaced Black tenants and sharecroppers, many of whom were forced to return to their farms as low-paid day labor or to migrate to cities looking for wage work.[65]

Perhaps the most notorious failure of the New Deal to aid African Americans came with the passage of the Social Security Act. Southern politicians chafed at the prospect of African Americans benefiting from federally sponsored social welfare, afraid that economic security would allow Black southerners to escape the cycle of poverty that kept them tied to the land as cheap, exploitable farm laborers. The *Jackson* (Mississippi) *Daily News* callously warned that "The average Mississippian can't imagine himself chipping in to pay pensions for able-bodied Negroes to sit around in idleness . . . while cotton and corn crops are crying for workers." Roosevelt agreed to remove domestic workers and farm laborers from the provisions of the bill, excluding many African Americans, already laboring under the strictures of legal racial discrimination, from the benefits of an expanding economic safety net.[66]

Women, too, failed to receive the full benefits of New Deal programs. On one hand, Roosevelt included women in key positions within his administration, including the first female cabinet secretary, Frances Perkins, and a prominently placed African American advisor in the National Youth Administration, Mary McLeod Bethune. First Lady Eleanor Roosevelt was a key advisor to the president and became a major voice for economic and racial justice. But many New Deal programs were built on the assumption that men would serve as breadwinners and women as mothers, homemakers, and consumers. New Deal programs aimed to help both but usually by forcing such gendered assumptions, making it difficult for women to attain economic autonomy. New Deal social welfare programs tended to funnel women into means-tested, state-administered relief programs while reserving entitlement benefits for male workers, creating a kind of two-tiered social welfare state. And so, despite great advances, the New Deal failed to challenge core inequalities that continued to mark life in the United States.[67]

XII. The End of the New Deal (1937–1939)

By 1936, Roosevelt and his New Deal won record popularity. In November, Roosevelt annihilated his Republican challenger, Governor Alf Landon of Kansas, who lost in every state save Maine and Vermont. The Great Depression had certainly not ended, but it appeared to be retreating, and Roosevelt, now safely reelected, appeared ready to take advantage of both his popularity and the improving economic climate to press for even more dramatic changes. But conservative barriers continued to limit the power of his popular support. The Supreme Court, for instance, continued to gut many of his programs.

In 1937, concerned that the Court might overthrow social security in an upcoming case, Roosevelt called for legislation allowing him to expand the Court by appointing a new, younger justice for every sitting member over age seventy. Roosevelt argued that the measure would speed up the Court's ability to handle a growing backlog of cases; however, his "court-packing scheme," as opponents termed it, was clearly designed to allow the president to appoint up to six friendly, pro–New Deal justices to drown the influence of old-time conservatives on the Court. Roosevelt's "scheme" riled opposition and did not become law, but the chastened Court thereafter upheld social security and other pieces of New Deal legislation. Moreover, Roosevelt was slowly able to appoint more amenable justices as conservatives died or retired. Still, the court-packing scheme damaged the Roosevelt administration and emboldened New Deal opponents.[68]

Compounding his problems, Roosevelt and his advisors made a costly economic misstep. Believing the United States had turned a corner, Roosevelt cut spending in 1937. The American economy plunged nearly to the depths of 1932–1933. Roosevelt reversed course and, adopting the approach popularized by the English economist John Maynard Keynes, hoped that countercyclical, compensatory spending would pull the country out of the recession, even at the expense of a growing budget deficit. It was perhaps too late. The Roosevelt Recession of 1937 became fodder for critics. Combined with the court-packing scheme, the recession allowed for significant gains by a conservative coalition of southern Democrats and Midwestern Republicans in the 1938 midterm elections. By 1939, Roosevelt struggled to build congressional support for new reforms, let alone maintain existing agencies. Moreover, the growing threat of war in Europe stole the public's attention and increasingly dominated Roosevelt's interests. The New Deal slowly receded into the background, outshined by war.[69]

XIII. The Legacy of the New Deal

By the end of the 1930s, Roosevelt and his Democratic Congresses had presided over a transformation of the American government and a realignment in American party politics. Before World War I, the American national state, though powerful, had been a "government out of sight." After the New Deal, Americans came to see the federal government as a potential ally in their daily struggles, whether finding work, securing a decent wage, getting a fair price for agricultural products, or organizing a union. Voter turnout in presidential elections jumped in 1932 and again in 1936, with most of these newly mobilized voters forming a durable piece of the Democratic Party that would remain loyal well into the 1960s. Even as affluence returned with the American intervention in World War II, memories of the Depression continued to shape the outlook of two generations of Americans.[70] Survivors of the Great Depression, one man would recall in the late 1960s, "are still riding with the ghost—the ghost of those days when things came hard."[71]

Historians debate when the New Deal ended. Some identify the Fair Labor Standards Act of 1938 as the last major New Deal measure. Others see wartime measures such as price and rent control and the G.I. Bill (which afforded New Deal–style social benefits to veterans) as species of New Deal legislation. Still others conceive of a "New Deal order," a constellation of "ideas, public policies, and political alliances," which, though changing, guided American politics from Roosevelt's Hundred Days forward to Lyndon Johnson's Great Society—and perhaps even beyond. Indeed, the New Deal's legacy still remains, and its battle lines still shape American politics.

XIV. Reference Material

This chapter was edited by Matthew Downs and Eric Rauchway, with content contributed by Dana Cochran, Matthew Downs, Benjamin Helwege, Elisa Minoff, Eric Rauchway, Caitlin Verboon, and Mason Williams.

Recommended citation: Dana Cochran et al., "The Great Depression," Matthew Downs, ed., in *The American Yawp*, eds. Joseph Locke and Ben Wright (Stanford, CA: Stanford University Press, 2019).

NOTES TO CHAPTER 23

1. George Donelson Moss, *The Rise of Modern America: A History of the American People, 1890–1945* (New York: Prentice-Hall, 1995), 185–186.

2. Ibid., 186.

3. Robert S. McElvaine, *The Great Depression: America, 1921–1940* (New York: Random House, 1984), 36.

4. John Steele Gordon, *An Empire of Wealth: The Epic History of American Economic Power* (New York: HarperCollins, 2004), 320.

5. Moss, *Rise of Modern America*, 186–187.

6. David M. Kennedy, *Freedom from Fear: The American People in Depression and War, 1929–1945* (New York: Oxford University Press, 1999), 65, 68.

7. Richard Norton Smith, *An Uncommon Man: The Triumph of Herbert Hoover* (New York: Simon and Schuster, 1987).

8. Herbert Hoover, "The President's News Conference of November 15, 1929," *Public Papers of the Presidents of the United States: Herbert Hoover, 1929* (Washington, DC: Government Printing Office, 1974), 280.

9. Christina D. Romer, "The Great Crash and the Onset of the Great Depression," *Quarterly Journal of Economics* 105, no. 3 (1990): 606.

10. Peter Fearon, *Origins and Nature of the Great Slump, 1929–1932* (Atlantic Highlands, NJ: Humanities Press, 1979), 34.

11. Ibid.

12. Kennedy, *Freedom from Fear*, 70–103.

13. William E. Leuchtenburg, *The American President from Teddy Roosevelt to Bill Clinton* (New York: Oxford University Press, 2015), 135.

14. "Wagner Puts Party in Progressive Role," *New York Times*, May 15, 1931, 2.

15. Ibid., 76.

16. Mrs. M. H. A. to Eleanor Roosevelt, June 14, 1934, in Robert S. McElvaine, ed., *Down and Out in the Great Depression: Letters from the Forgotten Man* (Chapel Hill: University of North Carolina Press, 1983), 54–55.

17. Lester V. Chandler, *America's Greatest Depression, 1929–1941* (New York: Harper & Row, 1970), 41.

18. Chandler, *America's Greatest Depression*, 44.

19. Studs Terkel, *Hard Times: An Oral History of the Great Depression* (New York: New Press, 2000), 20–21.

20. Mirra Komarovsky, *The Unemployed Man and His Family* (New York: Arno Press, 1971), 133.

21. Claudia Dale Goldin, *Understanding the Gender Gap: An Economic History of American Women* (New York: Oxford University Press, 1990), 34.

22. William H. Chafe, *The Paradox of Change: American Women in the 20th Century* (New York: Oxford University Press, 1991), 71.

23. Claudia Dale Goldin, *Understanding the Gender Gap: An Economic History of American Women* (New York: Oxford University Press, 1990), 34.

24. William H. Chafe, *The Paradox of Change: American Women in the 20th Century* (New York: Oxford University Press, 1991), 71.

25. Studs Terkel, *Hard Times: An Oral History of the Great Depression* (New York: Pantheon Books, 1970): 81–82.

26. William A. Sundstrom, "Last Hired, First Fired? Unemployment and Urban Black Workers During the Great Depression," *Journal of American History* 65, no. 1 (1978): 70–71.

27. Anthony J. Badger, *The New Deal: The Depression Years, 1933–1940* (New York: Hill and Wang, 1989), 15–23.

28. Robert S. McElvaine, ed., *Encyclopedia of the Great Depression* (New York: Macmillan, 2004), 320.

29. Donald Worster, *Dust Bowl: The Southern Plains in the 1930s* (New York: Oxford University Press, 1979), 48.

30. James R. McGovern, *And a Time For Hope: Americans in the Great Depression*, (Westport, CT: Praeger, 2000), 10.

31. James N. Gregory, *American Exodus: The Dust Bowl Migration and Okie Culture in California* (New York: Oxford University Press, 1989), 22.

32. Cybelle Fox, *Three Worlds of Relief* (Princeton, NJ: Princeton University Press, 2012), 126.

33. Ibid., 127.

34. Aristide Zolberg, *A Nation by Design: Immigration Policy in the Fashioning of America* (New York: Sage, 2006), 269.

35. Ibid., 92.

36. Eric Rauchway, *Why the New Deal Matters* (New Haven: Yale University Press, 2021), 144–146.

37. Biographies of Roosevelt include Kenneth C. Davis, *FDR: The Beckoning of Destiny: 1882–1928* (New York: Rand, 1972); and Jean Edward Smith, *FDR* (New York: Random House, 2007).

38. Outstanding general treatments of the New Deal include Arthur M. Schlesinger Jr., *The Age of Roosevelt*, 3 vols. (Boston: Houghton Mifflin, 1956–1960); William E. Leuchtenburg, *Franklin D. Roosevelt and the New Deal* (New York: Harper and Row, 1963); Anthony J. Badger, *The New Deal: The Depression Years, 1933–1940* (New York: Hill and Wang), 1989; and Kennedy, *Freedom from Fear*. On Roosevelt, see especially James MacGregor Burns, *Roosevelt: The Lion and the Fox* (New York: Harcourt, Brace, 1956); Frank B. Friedel, *Franklin D. Roosevelt*, 4 vols. (Boston: Little, Brown, 1952–1973); Patrick J. Maney, *The Roosevelt Presence: A Biography of Franklin D. Roosevelt* (New York: Twayne, 1992); and Alan Brinkley, *Franklin Delano Roosevelt* (New York: Oxford University Press, 2010).

39. Eric Rauchway, "The New Deal Was on the Ballot in 1932," *Modern American History* 2, no. 2 (2019): 202–203.

40. Franklin D. Roosevelt: "Inaugural Address," March 4, 1933. http://www.presidency.ucsb.edu/ws/?pid=14473.

41. Eric Rauchway, *Winter War: Hoover, Roosevelt, and the First Clash over the New Deal* (New York: Basic Books, 2018), 140.

42. Michael E. Parrish, *Securities Regulation and the New Deal* (New Haven, CT: Yale University Press, 1970).

43. See especially Anthony J. Badger, *FDR: The First Hundred Days* (New York: Hill and Wang, 2008).

44. Leuchtenburg, *Franklin D. Roosevelt and the New Deal*.

45. Neil Maher, *Nature's New Deal: The Civilian Conservation Corps and the Roots of the American Environmental Movement* (New York: Oxford University Press, 2008).

46. Thomas K. McCraw, *TVA and the Power Fight, 1933–1939* (Philadelphia: Lippincott, 1971).

47. Ellis W. Hawley, *The New Deal and the Problem of Monopoly: A Study in Economic Ambivalence* (Princeton, NJ: Princeton University Press, 1969); Gavin Wright, *Old South, New South: Revolutions in the Southern Economy Since the Civil War* (Baton Rouge: LSU Press, 1986), 217.

48. Theodore Saloutos, *The American Farmer and the New Deal* (Ames: Iowa State University Press, 1982).

49. Bonnie Fox Schwartz, *The Civil Works Administration, 1933–1934: The Business of Emergency Employment in the New Deal* (Princeton, NJ: Princeton University Press, 1984); Edwin Amenta, *Bold Relief: Institutional Politics and the Origins of Modern American Social Policy* (Princeton, NJ: Princeton University Press, 1998); Jason Scott Smith, *Building New Deal Liberalism: The Political Economy of Public Works, 1933–1956* (New York: Cambridge University Press, 2006); Mason B. Williams, *City of Ambition: FDR, La Guardia, and the Making of Modern New York* (New York: Norton, 2013).

50. Howard Odum, *Southern Regions of the United States* (Chapel Hill: University of North Carolina Press, 1936), quoted in David L. Carlton and Peter Coclanis, eds., *Confronting Southern Poverty in the Great Depression: The Report on Economic Conditions of the South with Related Documents* (Boston: Bedford St. Martin's, 1996), 118–119.

51. Wright, *Old South, New South*, 217.

52. Ibid., 227–228.

53. Ibid., 216–220.

54. William Leuchtenburg, *The White House Looks South: Franklin D. Roosevelt, Harry S. Truman, Lyndon B. Johnson* (Baton Rouge: LSU Press, 2005), 74.

55. "Press Conference #160," November 23, 1934, 214, in *Roosevelt, Complete Presidential Press Conferences of Franklin D. Roosevelt, Volumes 3–4, 1934* (New York: Da Capo Press, 1972).

56. McCraw, *TVA and the Power Fight*.

57. Carlton and Coclanis, *Confronting Southern Poverty*, 42.

58. William E. Leuchtenburg, *The Supreme Court Reborn: The Constitutional Revolution in the Age of Roosevelt* (New York: Oxford University Press, 1995); Theda Skocpol and Kenneth Finegold, *State and Party in America's New Deal* (Madison: University of Wisconsin Press, 1995); Colin Gordon, *New Deals: Business, Labor, and Politics in America, 1920–1935* (New York: Cambridge University Press, 1994).

59. Alexander J. Field, *A Great Leap Forward: 1930s Depression and U.S. Economic Growth* (New Haven: Yale University Press, 2011), 40.

60. Mark H. Leff, *The Limits of Symbolic Reform: The New Deal and Taxation, 1933–1939* (New York: Cambridge University Press, 1984); Kenneth T. Jackson, *Crabgrass Frontier: The Suburbanization of the United States* (New York: Oxford University Press, 1985); Sarah T. Phillips, *This Land, This Nation: Conservation, Rural America, and the New Deal* (New York: Cambridge University Press, 2007).

61. Kennedy, *Freedom from Fear*, 267.

62. Gareth Davies and Martha Derthick, "Race and Social Welfare Policy: The Social Security Act of 1935," *Political Science Quarterly* 112, no. 2 (Summer 1997): 217–235.

63. Dan T. Carter, *Scottsboro: A Tragedy of the American South* (Baton Rouge: LSU Press, 1969).

64. Kennedy, *Freedom from Fear*, 201.

65. Ira Katznelson, *When Affirmative Action Was White: An Untold History of Racial Inequality in Twentieth-Century America* (New York: Norton, 2005).

66. George Brown Tindall, *The Emergence of the New South, 1913–1945* (Baton Rouge: LSU Press, 1967), 491.

67. Alice Kessler-Harris, *In Pursuit of Equity: Women, Men, and the Quest for Economic Citizenship in 20th Century America* (New York: Oxford University Press, 2001); Linda Gordon, *Pitied but Not Entitled: Single Mothers and the History of Welfare, 1890–1935* (New York: Free Press, 1994).

68. William E. Leuchtenburg, "The Origins of Franklin D. Roosevelt's 'Court-Packing' Plan," *The Supreme Court Review* (1966): 347–400.

69. Alan Brinkley, *The End of Reform: New Deal Liberalism in Recession and War* (New York: Knopf, 1995).

70. Cohen, *Making a New Deal*; Kristi Andersen, *The Creation of a Democratic Majority, 1928–1936* (Chicago: University of Chicago Press, 1979); Caroline Bird, *The Invisible Scar* (New York: McKay, 1966).

71. Quoted in Terkel, *Hard Times*, 34.

RECOMMENDED READING

Balderrama, Francisco E., and Raymond Rodríguez. *Decade of Betrayal: Mexican Repatriation in the 1930s*, rev. ed. Albuquerque: University of New Mexico Press, 2006.

Brinkley, Alan. *The End of Reform: New Deal Liberalism in Recession and War.* New York: Knopf, 1995.

———. *Voices of Protest: Huey Long, Father Coughlin, and the Great Depression.* New York: Knopf, 1982.

Cohen, Lizabeth. *Making a New Deal: Industrial Workers in Chicago, 1919–1939.* New York: Cambridge University Press, 1990.

Cowie, Jefferson, and Nick Salvatore. "The Long Exception: Rethinking the Place of the New Deal in American History." *International Labor and Working-Class History* 74 (Fall 2008): 1–32.

Dickstein, Morris. *Dancing in the Dark: A Cultural History of the Great Depression.* New York: Norton, 2009.

Fraser, Steve, and Gary Gerstle, eds. *The Rise and Fall of the New Deal Order, 1930–1980*. Princeton, NJ: Princeton University Press, 1989.

Gilmore, Glenda E. *Defying Dixie: The Radical Roots of Civil Rights, 1919–1950*. New York: Norton, 2009.

Gordon, Colin. *New Deals: Business, Labor, and Politics in America 1920–1935*. New York: Cambridge University Press, 1994.

Gordon, Linda. *Dorothea Lange: A Life Beyond Limits*. New York: Norton, 2009.

Gordon, Linda. *Pitied but Not Entitled: Single Mothers and the History of Welfare 1890–1935*. New York: Free Press, 1994.

Greene, Alison Collis. *No Depression in Heaven: The Great Depression, the New Deal, and the Transformation of Religion in the Delta*. New York: Oxford University Press, 2015.

Katznelson, Ira. *Fear Itself: The New Deal and the Origins of Our Time*. New York: Norton, 2013.

Kelly, Robin D. G. *Hammer and Hoe: Alabama Communists During the Great Depression*. Chapel Hill: University of North Carolina Press, 1990.

Kennedy, David. *Freedom from Fear: America in Depression and War, 1929–1945*. New York: Oxford University Press, 1999.

Kessler-Harris, Alice. *In Pursuit of Equity: Women, Men, and the Quest for Economic Citizenship in 20th-Century America*. New York: Oxford University Press, 2003.

Leach, William. *Land of Desire: Merchants, Power, and the Rise of a New American Culture*. New York: Pantheon Books, 1993.

Leuchtenburg, William. *Franklin Roosevelt and the New Deal, 1932–1940*. New York: Harper and Row, 1963.

Pells, Richard. *Radical Visions and American Dreams: Culture and Social Thought in the Depression Years*. New York: Harper and Row, 1973.

Phillips, Kimberly L. *Alabama North: African-American Migrants, Community and Working-Class Activism in Cleveland, 1915–1945*. Champaign: University of Illinois Press, 1999.

Phillips–Fein, Kim. *Invisible Hands: The Businessmen's Crusade Against the New Deal*. New York: Norton, 2010

Sitkoff, Harvard. *A New Deal for Blacks: The Emergence of Civil Rights as a National Issue*. New York: Oxford University Press, 1978.

Sullivan, Patricia. *Days of Hope: Race and Democracy in the New Deal Era*. Chapel Hill: University of North Carolina Press, 1996.

Tani, Karen. *States of Dependency: Welfare, Rights, and American Governance, 1935–1972*. Cambridge, UK: Cambridge University Press, 2016.

Wright, Gavin. *Old South, New South: Revolutions in the Southern Economy Since the Civil War*. Baton Rouge: LSU Press, 1986.

24

World War II

I. Introduction

The 1930s and 1940s were trying times. A global economic crisis gave way to a global war that became the deadliest and most destructive in human history. Perhaps eighty million individuals lost their lives during World War II. The war saw industrialized genocide and nearly threatened the eradication of an entire people. It also unleashed the most fearsome technology ever used in war. And when it ended, the United States found itself alone as the world's greatest superpower. Armed with the world's greatest economy, it looked forward to the fruits of a prosperous consumers' economy. But the war raised as many questions as it would settle and unleashed new social forces at home and abroad that confronted generations of Americans to come.

American soldiers recover the dead on Omaha Beach in 1944. Library of Congress.

II. The Origins of the Pacific War

Although the United States joined the war in 1941, two years after Europe exploded into conflict in 1939, the path to the Japanese bombing of Pearl Harbor, the surprise attack that threw the United States headlong into war, began much earlier. For the Empire of Japan, the war had begun a decade before Pearl Harbor.

On September 18, 1931, a small explosion tore up railroad tracks controlled by the Japanese-owned South Manchuria Railway near the city of Shenyang (Mukden) in the Chinese province of Manchuria. The railway company condemned the bombing as the work of anti-Japanese Chinese dissidents. Evidence, though, suggests that the initial explosion was neither an act of Chinese anti-Japanese sentiment nor an accident but an elaborate ruse planned by the Japanese to provide a basis for invasion. In response, the privately operated Japanese Guandong (Kwangtung) army began shelling the Shenyang garrison the next day, and the garrison fell before nightfall. Hungry for Chinese territory and witnessing the weakness and disorganization of Chinese forces, but under the pretense of protecting Japanese citizens and investments, the Japanese Imperial Army ordered a full-scale invasion of Manchuria. The invasion was swift. Without a centralized Chinese army, the Japanese quickly defeated isolated Chinese warlords and by the end of February 1932, all of Manchuria was firmly under Japanese control. Japan established the nation of Manchukuo out of the former province of Manchuria.[1]

This seemingly small skirmish—known by the Chinese as the September 18 Incident and the Japanese as the Manchurian Incident—sparked a war that would last thirteen years and claim the lives of over thirty-five million people. Comprehending Japanese motivations for attacking China and the grueling stalemate of the ensuing war are crucial for understanding Japan's seemingly unprovoked attack on Pearl Harbor, Hawaii, on December 7, 1941, and, therefore, for understanding the involvement of the United States in World War II as well.

Despite their rapid advance into Manchuria, the Japanese put off the invasion of China for nearly three years. Japan occupied a precarious domestic and international position after the September 18 Incident. At home, Japan was riven by political factionalism due to its stagnating economy. Leaders were torn as to whether to address modernization and lack of natural resources through unilateral expansion (the conquest of resource-rich areas such as Manchuria to export raw materials to domestic Japanese industrial bases such as Hiroshima and Nagasaki) or international cooperation (a philosophy of pan-Asianism in an anti-Western coalition that would push the colonial powers out of Asia). Ultimately, after a series of political crises and assassinations inflamed tensions, pro-war elements within the Japanese military triumphed over the more moderate civilian government. Japan committed itself to aggressive military expansion.

Chinese leaders Chiang Kai-shek and Zhang Xueliang appealed to the League of Nations for assistance against Japan. The United States supported the Chinese protest, proclaiming the Stimson Doctrine in January 1932, which refused to recognize any state established as a result of Japanese aggression. Meanwhile, the League of Nations sent Englishman Victor Bulwer-Lytton to investigate the September 18 Incident. After a six-month investigation, Bulwer-Lytton found the Japanese guilty of inciting the September 18 incident and demanded the return of Manchuria to China. The Japanese withdrew from the League of Nations in March 1933.

Japan isolated itself from the world. Its diplomatic isolation empowered radical military leaders who could point to Japanese military success in Manchuria and compare it to the diplomatic failures of the civilian government. The military took over Japanese policy. And in the military's eyes, the conquest of China would not only provide for Japan's industrial needs, it would secure Japanese supremacy in East Asia.

The Japanese launched a full-scale invasion of China. It assaulted the Marco Polo Bridge on July 7, 1937, and routed the forces of the Chinese National Revolutionary Army led by Chiang Kai-shek. The broken Chinese army gave up Beiping (Beijing) to the Japanese on August 8, Shanghai on November 26, and the capital, Nanjing (Nanking), on December 13. Between 250,000 and 300,000 people were killed, and tens of thousands of women were raped, when the Japanese besieged and then sacked Nanjing. The Western press labeled it the Rape of Nanjing. To halt the invading enemy, Chiang Kai-shek adopted a scorched-earth strategy of "trading space for time." His Nationalist government retreated inland, burning villages and destroying dams, and established a new capital at the Yangtze River port of Chongqing (Chungking). Although the Nationalists' scorched-earth policy hurt the Japanese military effort, it alienated scores of dislocated Chinese civilians and became a potent propaganda tool of the emerging Chinese Communist Party (CCP).[2]

Americans read about the brutal fighting in China, but the United States lacked both the will and the military power to oppose the Japanese invasion. After the gut-wrenching carnage of World War I, many

Americans retreated toward isolationism by opposing any involvement in the conflagrations burning in Europe and Asia. And even if Americans wished to intervene, their military was lacking. The Japanese army was a technologically advanced force consisting of 4,100,000 men and 900,000 Chinese collaborators—and that was in China alone. The Japanese military was armed with modern rifles, artillery, armor, and aircraft. By 1940, the Japanese navy was the third-largest and among the most technologically advanced in the world.

Still, Chinese Nationalists lobbied Washington for aid. Chiang Kai-shek's wife, Soong May-ling—known to the American public as Madame Chiang—led the effort. Born into a wealthy Chinese merchant family in 1898, Madame Chiang spent much of her childhood in the United States and graduated from Wellesley College in 1917 with a major in English literature. In contrast to her gruff husband, Madame Chiang was charming and able to use her knowledge of American culture and values to garner support for her husband and his government. But while the United States denounced Japanese aggression, it took no action during the 1930s.

As Chinese Nationalists fought for survival, the Communist Party was busy collecting people and supplies in the northwestern Shaanxi Province. China had been at war with itself when the Japanese came. Nationalists battled a stubborn communist insurgency. In 1935 the Nationalists threw the communists out of the fertile Chinese coast, but an ambitious young commander named Mao Zedong recognized the power of the Chinese peasant population. In Shaanxi, Mao recruited from the local peasantry, building his force from a meager seven thousand survivors at the end of the Long March in 1935 to a robust 1.2 million members by the end of the war.

Although Japan had conquered much of the country, the Nationalists regrouped and the communists rearmed. An uneasy truce paused the country's civil war and refocused efforts on the invaders. The Chinese could not dislodge the Japanese, but they could stall their advance. The war mired in stalemate.

III. The Origins of the European War

Across the globe in Europe, the continent's major powers were still struggling with the aftereffects of World War I when the global economic crisis spiraled much of the continent into chaos. Germany's Weimar Republic collapsed with the economy, and out of the ashes emerged Adolf Hitler's

National Socialists—the Nazis. Championing German racial supremacy, fascist government, and military expansionism, Hitler rose to power
and, after aborted attempts to take power in Germany, became chancel-
lor in 1933 and the Nazis conquered German institutions. Democratic
traditions were smashed. Leftist groups were purged. Hitler repudiated
the punitive damages and strict military limitations of the Treaty of Versailles. He rebuilt the German military and navy. He reoccupied regions
lost during the war and remilitarized the Rhineland, along the border
with France. When the Spanish Civil War broke out in 1936, Hitler and
Benito Mussolini—the fascist Italian leader who had risen to power in
the 1920s—intervened for the Spanish fascists, toppling the communist
Spanish Republican Party. Britain and France stood by warily and began
to rebuild their militaries, anxious in the face of a renewed Germany but
still unwilling to draw Europe into another bloody war.[3]

In his autobiographical manifesto, *Mein Kampf*, Hitler advocated for
the unification of Europe's German peoples under one nation and that

The massive Nuremberg rallies, such as this
one in 1935, instilled a fierce loyalty to (or
fearful silence about) Hitler and the National
Socialist Party in Germany. Wikimedia.

nation's need for *Lebensraum*, or living space, particularly in Eastern Europe, to supply Germans with the land and resources needed for future prosperity. The *Untermenschen* (lesser humans) would have to go. Once in power, Hitler worked toward the twin goals of unification and expansion.

In 1938, Germany annexed Austria and set its sights on the Sudetenland, a large, ethnically German area of Czechoslovakia. Britain and France, alarmed but still anxious to avoid war, agreed—without Czechoslovakia's input—that Germany could annex the region in return for a promise to stop all future German aggression. They thought that Hitler could be appeased, but it became clear that his ambitions would continue pushing German expansion. In March 1939, Hitler took the rest of Czechoslovakia and began to make demands on Poland. Britain and France promised war. And war came.

Hitler signed a secret agreement—the Molotov-Ribbentrop Pact—with the Soviet Union that coordinated the splitting of Poland between the two powers and promised nonaggression thereafter. The European war began when the German Wehrmacht invaded Poland on September 1, 1939. Britain and France declared war two days later and mobilized their armies. Britain and France hoped that the Poles could hold out for three to four months, enough time for the Allies to intervene. Poland fell in three weeks. The German army, anxious to avoid the rigid, grinding war of attrition that took so many millions in the stalemate of World War I, built their new modern army for speed and maneuverability. German doctrine emphasized the use of tanks, planes, and motorized infantry (infantry that used trucks for transportation instead of marching) to concentrate forces, smash front lines, and wreak havoc behind the enemy's defenses. It was called *Blitzkrieg*, or lightning war.

After the fall of Poland, France and its British allies braced for an inevitable German attack. Throughout the winter of 1939–1940, however, fighting was mostly confined to smaller fronts in Norway. Belligerents called it the *Sitzkrieg* (sitting war). But in May 1940, Hitler launched his attack into Western Europe. Mirroring the German's Schlieffen Plan of 1914 in the previous war, Germany attacked through the Netherlands and Belgium to avoid the prepared French defenses along the French-German border. Poland had fallen in three weeks; France lasted only a few weeks more. By June, Hitler was posing for photographs in front of the Eiffel Tower. Germany split France in half. Germany occupied and governed the north, and the south would be ruled under a puppet government in Vichy.

With France under heel, Hitler turned to Britain. Operation Sea Lion—the planned German invasion of the British Isles—required air superiority over the English Channel. From June until October the German Luftwaffe fought the Royal Air Force (RAF) for control of the skies. Despite having fewer planes, British pilots won the so-called Battle of Britain, saving the islands from immediate invasion and prompting the new prime minister, Winston Churchill, to declare, "Never before in the field of human conflict has so much been owed by so many to so few."

If Britain was safe from invasion, it was not immune from additional air attacks. Stymied in the Battle of Britain, Hitler began the Blitz—a bombing campaign against cities and civilians. Hoping to crush the British will to fight, the Luftwaffe bombed the cities of London, Liverpool, and Manchester every night from September to the following May.

The German bombing of London left thousands homeless, hurt, or dead. This child, holding a stuffed toy, sits in the rubble as adults ponder their fate in the background. 1945. Library of Congress.

Children were sent far into the countryside to live with strangers to shield them from the bombings. Remaining residents took refuge in shelters and subway tunnels, emerging each morning to put out fires and bury the dead. The Blitz ended in June 1941, when Hitler, confident that Britain was temporarily out of the fight, launched Operation Barbarossa—the invasion of the Soviet Union.

Hoping to capture agricultural lands, seize oil fields, and break the military threat of Stalin's Soviet Union, Hitler broke the two powers' 1939 nonaggression pact and, on June 22, invaded the Soviet Union. It was the largest land invasion in history. France and Poland had fallen in weeks, and German officials hoped to break Russia before the winter. And initially, the *Blitzkrieg* worked. The German military quickly conquered enormous swaths of land and netted hundreds of thousands of prisoners. But Russia was too big and the Soviets were willing to sacrifice millions to stop the fascist advance. After recovering from the initial shock of the German invasion, Stalin moved his factories east of the Urals, out of range of the Luftwaffe. He ordered his retreating army to adopt a "scorched earth" policy, to move east and destroy food, rails, and shelters to stymie the advancing German army. The German army slogged forward. It split into three pieces and stood at the gates of Moscow, Stalingrad, and Leningrad, but supply lines now stretched thousands of miles, Soviet infrastructure had been destroyed, partisans harried German lines, and the brutal Russian winter arrived. Germany had won massive gains but the winter found Germany exhausted and overextended. In the north, the German army starved Leningrad to death during an interminable siege; in the south, at Stalingrad, the two armies bled themselves to death in the destroyed city; and, in the center, on the outskirts of Moscow, in sight of the capital city, the German army faltered and fell back. It was the Soviet Union that broke Hitler's army. Twenty-five million Soviet soldiers and civilians died during the Great Patriotic War, and roughly 80 percent of all German casualties during the war came on the Eastern Front. The German army and its various conscripts suffered 850,000 casualties at the Battle of Stalingrad alone.[4]

IV. The United States and the European War

While Hitler marched across Europe, the Japanese continued their war in the Pacific. In 1939 the United States dissolved its trade treaties with Japan and the following year cut off supplies of war materials by embargoing oil, steel, rubber, and other vital goods. It was hoped that economic pressure would shut down the Japanese war machine. Instead, Japan's resource-starved military launched invasions across the Pacific to sustain its war effort. The Japanese called their new empire the Greater East Asia Co-Prosperity Sphere and, with the cry of "Asia for the Asians," made war against European powers and independent nations throughout the region. Diplomatic relations between Japan and the United States collapsed. The United States demanded that Japan withdraw from China; Japan considered the oil embargo a de facto declaration of war.[5]

Japanese military planners, believing that American intervention was inevitable, planned a coordinated Pacific offensive to neutralize the United States and other European powers and provide time for Japan to complete its conquests and fortify its positions. On the morning of December 7, 1941, the Japanese launched a surprise attack on the American naval base at Pearl Harbor, Hawaii. Japanese military planners hoped to destroy enough battleships and aircraft carriers to cripple American naval power for years. Twenty-four hundred Americans were killed in the attack.

American isolationism fell at Pearl Harbor. Japan also assaulted Hong Kong, the Philippines, and American holdings throughout the Pacific, but it was the attack on Hawaii that threw the United States into a global conflict. Franklin Roosevelt called December 7 "a date which will live in infamy" and called for a declaration of war, which Congress answered within hours. Within a week of Pearl Harbor the United States had declared war on the entire Axis, turning two previously separate conflicts into a true world war.

The American war began slowly. Britain had stood alone militarily in Europe, but American supplies had bolstered their resistance. Hitler unleashed his U-boat "wolf packs" into the Atlantic Ocean with orders to sink anything carrying aid to Britain, but Britain's and the United States' superior tactics and technology won them the Battle of the Atlantic. British code breakers cracked Germany's radio codes and the surge of intelligence, dubbed Ultra, coupled with massive naval convoys escorted by destroyers armed with sonar and depth charges, gave the advantage to the Allies and by 1942, Hitler's Kriegsmarine was losing ships faster than they could be built.[6]

In North Africa in 1942, British victory at El Alamein began pushing the Germans back. In November, the first American combat troops

This pair of U.S. military recruiting posters demonstrates the way that two branches of the military—the Marines and the Women's Army Corps—borrowed techniques from professional advertisers to "sell" a romantic vision of war to Americans. One shows Marines at war in a lush jungle, reminding viewers that the war was taking place in exotic lands; the other depicted women taking on new jobs as a patriotic duty. Bradshaw Crandall, *Are You a Girl with a Star-Spangled Heart?* Recruiting Publicity Bureau, U.S. Women's Army Corps Recruiting Poster (1943); Unknown, *Let's Go Get 'Em.* Beck Engraving Co. (1942). Library of Congress.

entered the European war, landing in French Morocco and pushing the Germans east while the British pushed west.[7] By 1943, the Allies had pushed Axis forces out of Africa. In January President Roosevelt and Prime Minister Churchill met at Casablanca to discuss the next step of the European war. Churchill convinced Roosevelt to chase the Axis up Italy, into the "soft underbelly" of Europe. Afterward, Roosevelt announced to the press that the Allies would accept nothing less than unconditional surrender.

Meanwhile, the Army Air Force (AAF) sent hundreds (and eventually thousands) of bombers to England in preparation for a massive strategic bombing campaign against Germany. The plan was to bomb Germany around the clock. American bombers hit German ball-bearing factories, rail yards, oil fields, and manufacturing centers during the day, while the British RAF carpet-bombed German cities at night. Flying in forma-

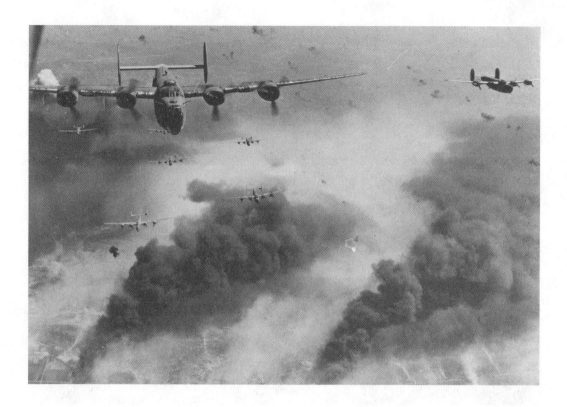

tion, they initially flew unescorted, since many believed that bombers equipped with defensive firepower flew too high and too fast to be attacked. However, advanced German technology allowed fighters to easily shoot down the lumbering bombers. On some disastrous missions, the Germans shot down almost 50 percent of American aircraft. However, the advent and implementation of a long-range escort fighter let the bombers hit their targets more accurately while fighters confronted opposing German aircraft.

In the wake of the Soviets' victory at Stalingrad, the Big Three (Roosevelt, Churchill, and Stalin) met in Tehran in November 1943. Dismissing Africa and Italy as a sideshow, Stalin demanded that Britain and the United States invade France to relieve pressure on the Eastern Front. Churchill was hesitant, but Roosevelt was eager. The invasion was tentatively scheduled for 1944.

Back in Italy, the "soft underbelly" turned out to be much tougher than Churchill had imagined. Italy's narrow, mountainous terrain gave the defending Axis the advantage. Movement up the peninsula was slow, and in some places conditions returned to the trenchlike warfare of World War I. Americans attempted to land troops behind them at Anzio on the western coast of Italy, but, surrounded, they suffered heavy

In 1943, Allied forces began bombing railroad and oil targets in Bucharest, part of the wider policy of bombing expeditions meant to incapacitate German transportation. Bucharest was considered the number one oil target in Europe. Photograph, August 1, 1943. Wikimedia.

Bombings throughout Europe caused complete devastation in some areas, leveling beautiful ancient cities like Cologne, Germany. Cologne experienced an astonishing 262 separate air raids by Allied forces, leaving the city in ruins, as in the photograph above. Amazingly, the Cologne Cathedral stood nearly undamaged even after being hit numerous times, while the area around it crumbled. Photograph, April 24, 1945. Wikimedia.

casualties. Still, the Allies pushed up the peninsula, Mussolini's government revolted, and a new Italian government quickly made peace.

On the day the American army entered Rome, American, British and Canadian forces launched Operation Overlord, the long-awaited invasion of France. D-Day, as it became popularly known, was the largest amphibious assault in history. American general Dwight Eisenhower was uncertain enough of the attack's chances that the night before the invasion he wrote two speeches: one for success and one for failure. The Allied landings at Normandy were successful, and although progress across France was much slower than hoped for, Paris was liberated roughly two months later. Allied bombing expeditions meanwhile continued to level German cities and industrial capacity. Perhaps four hundred thousand German civilians were killed by allied bombing.[8]

The Nazis were crumbling on both fronts. Hitler tried but failed to turn the war in his favor in the west. The Battle of the Bulge failed to drive the Allies back to the English Channel, but the delay cost the Allies the winter. The invasion of Germany would have to wait, while the Soviet Union continued its relentless push westward, ravaging German populations in retribution for German war crimes.[9]

German counterattacks in the east failed to dislodge the Soviet advance, destroying any last chance Germany might have had to regain the initiative. 1945 dawned with the end of European war in sight. The Big Three met again at Yalta in the Soviet Union, where they reaffirmed the demand for Hitler's unconditional surrender and began to plan for postwar Europe.

The Soviet Union reached Germany in January, and the Americans crossed the Rhine in March. In late April American and Soviet troops met at the Elbe while the Soviets pushed relentlessly by Stalin to reach Berlin first and took the capital city in May, days after Hitler and his high command had died by suicide in a city bunker. Germany was conquered. The European war was over. Allied leaders met again, this time at Potsdam, Germany, where it was decided that Germany would be divided into pieces according to current Allied occupation, with Berlin likewise divided, pending future elections. Stalin also agreed to join the fight against Japan in approximately three months.[10]

V. The United States and the Japanese War

As Americans celebrated V-E (Victory in Europe) Day, they redirected their full attention to the still-raging Pacific War. As in Europe, the war in the Pacific started slowly. After Pearl Harbor, the American-controlled Philippine archipelago fell to Japan. After running out of ammunition and supplies, the garrison of American and Filipino soldiers surrendered. The prisoners were marched eighty miles to their prisoner-of-war camp without food, water, or rest. Ten thousand died on the Bataan Death March.[11]

But as Americans mobilized their armed forces, the tide turned. In the summer of 1942, American naval victories at the Battle of the Coral Sea and the aircraft carrier duel at the Battle of Midway crippled Japan's Pacific naval operations. To dislodge Japan's hold over the Pacific, the U.S. military began island hopping: attacking island after island, bypassing the strongest but seizing those capable of holding airfields to continue pushing Japan out of the region. Combat was vicious. At Guadalcanal American soldiers saw Japanese soldiers launch suicidal charges rather than surrender. Many Japanese soldiers refused to be taken prisoner or to take prisoners themselves. Such tactics, coupled with American racial prejudice, turned the Pacific Theater into a more brutal and barbarous conflict than the European Theater.[12]

Japanese defenders fought tenaciously. Few battles were as one-sided as the Battle of the Philippine Sea, or what the Americans called the Japanese counterattack, the Great Marianas Turkey Shoot. Japanese soldiers bled the Americans in their advance across the Pacific. At Iwo Jima, an eight-square-mile island of volcanic rock, seventeen thousand Japanese soldiers held the island against seventy thousand Marines for over a month. At the cost of nearly their entire force, they inflicted almost thirty thousand casualties before the island was lost.

By February 1945, American bombers were in range of the mainland. Bombers hit Japan's industrial facilities but suffered high casualties. To spare bomber crews from dangerous daylight raids, and to achieve maximum effect against Japan's wooden cities, many American bombers dropped incendiary weapons that created massive firestorms and wreaked havoc on Japanese cities. Over sixty Japanese cities were firebombed. American fire bombs killed one hundred thousand civilians in Tokyo in March 1945.

In June 1945, after eighty days of fighting and tens of thousands of casualties, the Americans captured the island of Okinawa. The mainland of Japan was open before them. It was a viable base from which to launch a full invasion of the Japanese homeland and end the war.

Estimates varied, but given the tenacity of Japanese soldiers fighting on islands far from their home, some officials estimated that an invasion of the Japanese mainland could cost half a million American casualties and perhaps millions of Japanese civilians. Historians debate the many motivations that ultimately drove the Americans to use atomic weapons against Japan, and many American officials criticized the decision, but these would be the numbers later cited by government leaders and military officials to justify their use.[13]

Early in the war, fearing that the Germans might develop an atomic bomb, the U.S. government launched the Manhattan Project, a hugely expensive, ambitious program to harness atomic energy and create a single weapon capable of leveling entire cities. The Americans successfully exploded the world's first nuclear device, Trinity, in New Mexico in July 1945. (Physicist J. Robert Oppenheimer, the director of the Los Alamos Laboratory, where the bomb was designed, later recalled that the event reminded him of Hindu scripture: "Now I am become death,

the destroyer of worlds.") Two more bombs—Fat Man and Little Boy—
were built and detonated over two Japanese cities in August. Hiroshima
was hit on August 6. Over one hundred thousand civilians were killed.
Nagasaki followed on August 9. Perhaps eighty thousand civilians were
killed.

Emperor Hirohito announced the surrender of Japan on August 15.
On September 2, aboard the battleship USS *Missouri*, delegates from the
Japanese government formally signed their surrender. World War II was
finally over.

VI. Soldiers' Experiences

Almost eighteen million men served in World War II. Volunteers rushed to
join the military after Pearl Harbor, but the majority—over ten million—
were drafted into service. Volunteers could express their preference for
assignment, and many preempted the draft by volunteering. Regardless,
recruits judged I-A, "fit for service," were moved into basic training,
where soldiers were developed physically and trained in the basic use of
weapons and military equipment. Soldiers were indoctrinated into the
chain of command and introduced to military life. After basic, soldiers
moved on to more specialized training. For example, combat infantrymen
received additional weapons and tactical training, and radio operators
learned transmission codes and the operation of field radios. Afterward,
an individual's experience varied depending on what service he entered
and to what theater he was assigned.[14]

Soldiers and Marines bore the brunt of on-the-ground combat. After
transportation to the front by trains, ships, and trucks, they could expect to march carrying packs weighing anywhere from twenty to fifty
pounds containing rations, ammunition, bandages, tools, clothing, and
miscellaneous personal items in addition to their weapons. Sailors, once
deployed, spent months at sea operating their assigned vessels. Larger
ships, particularly aircraft carriers, were veritable floating cities. In most,
sailors lived and worked in cramped conditions, often sleeping in bunks
stacked in rooms housing dozens of sailors. Senior officers received small
rooms of their own. Sixty thousand American sailors lost their lives in
the war.

During World War II, the Air Force was still a branch of the U.S.
Army and soldiers served in ground and air crews. World War II saw
the institutionalization of massive bombing campaigns against cities
and industrial production. Large bombers like the B-17 Flying Fortress

required pilots, navigators, bombardiers, radio operators, and four dedicated machine gunners. Airmen on bombing raids left from bases in England or Italy or from Pacific islands and endured hours of flight before approaching enemy territory. At high altitude, and without pressurized cabins, crews used oxygen tanks to breathe and on-board temperatures plummeted. Once in enemy airspace, crews confronted enemy fighters and anti-aircraft flak from the ground. While fighter pilots flew as escorts, the Air Corps suffered heavy casualties. Tens of thousands of airmen lost their lives.

On the ground, conditions varied. Soldiers in Europe endured freezing winters, impenetrable French hedgerows, Italian mountain ranges, and dense forests. Germans fought with a Western mentality familiar to Americans. Soldiers in the Pacific endured heat and humidity, monsoons, jungles, and tropical diseases. And they confronted an unfamiliar foe. Americans, for instance, could understand surrender as prudent; many Japanese soldiers saw it as cowardice. What Americans saw as a fanatical waste of life, the Japanese saw as brave and honorable. Moreover, American soldiers and American military leadership brought their historical anti-Asian prejudices to bear against the Japanese. Atrocities flourished in the Pacific at a level unmatched in Europe.

VII. The Wartime Economy

Economies win wars no less than militaries. The war converted American factories to wartime production, reawakened Americans' economic might, armed Allied belligerents and the American armed forces, effectively pulled America out of the Great Depression, and ushered in an era of unparalleled economic prosperity.[15]

Roosevelt's New Deal had ameliorated the worst of the Depression, but the economy still limped its way forward into the 1930s. But then Europe fell into war, and, despite its isolationism, Americans were glad to sell the Allies arms and supplies. And then Pearl Harbor changed everything. The United States drafted the economy into war service. The "sleeping giant" mobilized its unrivaled economic capacity to wage worldwide war. Governmental entities such as the War Production Board and the Office of War Mobilization and Reconversion managed economic production for the war effort and economic output exploded. An economy that was unable to provide work for a quarter of the workforce less than a decade earlier now struggled to fill vacant positions.

Government spending during the four years of war *doubled* all federal spending in all of American history up to that point. The budget deficit soared, but, just as Depression-era economists had counseled, the government's massive intervention annihilated unemployment and propelled growth. The economy that came out of the war looked nothing like the one that had begun it.

Military production came at the expense of the civilian consumer economy. Appliance and automobile manufacturers converted their plants to produce weapons and vehicles. Consumer choice was foreclosed. Every American received rationing cards and, legally, goods such as gasoline, coffee, meat, cheese, butter, processed food, firewood, and sugar could not be purchased without them. The housing industry was shut down, and the cities became overcrowded.

But the wartime economy boomed. The Roosevelt administration urged citizens to save their earnings or buy war bonds to prevent inflation. Bond drives were held nationally and headlined by Hollywood

As in World War I, citizens were urged to buy war bonds to support the effort overseas. Rallies, such as this 1943 event, appealed to Americans' sense of patriotism. Wikimedia.

celebrities. Such drives were hugely successful. They not only funded much of the war effort, they helped tame inflation as well. So too did tax rates. The federal government raised income taxes and boosted the top marginal tax rate to 94 percent.

With the economy booming and twenty million American workers placed into military service, unemployment virtually disappeared. More and more African Americans continued to leave the agrarian South for the industrial North. And as more and more men joined the military, and more and more positions went unfilled, women joined the workforce en masse. Other American producers looked outside the United States, southward, to Mexico, to fill its labor force. Between 1942 and 1964, the United States contracted thousands of Mexican nationals to work in American agriculture and railroads in the Bracero Program. Jointly administered by the State Department, the Department of Labor, and the Department of Justice, the binational agreement secured five million contracts across twenty-four states.[16]

With factory work proliferating across the country and agricultural labor experiencing severe labor shortages, the presidents of Mexico and the United States signed an agreement in July 1942 to bring the first group of legally contracted workers to California. Discriminatory policies toward people of Mexican descent prevented bracero contracts in Texas until 1947. The Bracero Program survived the war, enshrined in law until the 1960s, when the United States liberalized its immigration laws. Though braceros suffered exploitative labor conditions, for the men who participated the program was a mixed blessing. Interviews with ex-braceros captured the complexity. "They would call us pigs . . . they didn't have to treat us that way," one said of his employers, while another said, "For me it was a blessing, the United States was a blessing . . . it is a nation I fell in love with because of the excess work and good pay."[17] After the exodus of Mexican migrants during the Depression, the program helped reestablish Mexican migration, institutionalized migrant farm work across much of the country, and further planted a Mexican presence in the southern and western United States.

VIII. Women and World War II

President Franklin D. Roosevelt and his administration had encouraged all able-bodied American women to help the war effort. He considered the role of women in the war critical for American victory, and the public expected women to assume various functions to free men for active military service. While most women opted to remain at home or volunteer with charitable organizations, many went to work or donned a military uniform.

World War II brought unprecedented labor opportunities for American women. Industrial labor, an occupational sphere dominated by men, shifted in part to women for the duration of wartime mobilization. Women applied for jobs in converted munitions factories. The iconic illustrated image of Rosie the Riveter, a muscular woman dressed in coveralls with her hair in a kerchief and inscribed with the phrase *We Can Do It!*, came to stand for female factory labor during the war. But women also worked in various auxiliary positions for the government. Although such jobs were often traditionally gendered female, over a million administrative jobs at the local, state, and national levels were transferred from men to women for the duration of the war.[18]

For women who elected not to work, many volunteer opportunities presented themselves. The American Red Cross, the largest charitable organization in the nation, encouraged women to volunteer with local city

With so many American workers deployed overseas and so many new positions created by war production, women entered the work force in massive numbers. Wikimedia Commons.

chapters. Millions of women organized community social events for families, packed and shipped almost half a million tons of medical supplies overseas, and prepared twenty-seven million care packages of nonperishable items for American and other Allied prisoners of war. The American Red Cross further required all female volunteers to certify as nurse's aides, providing an extra benefit and work opportunity for hospital staffs that suffered severe personnel losses. Other charity organizations, such as church and synagogue affiliates, benevolent associations, and social club auxiliaries, gave women further outlets for volunteer work.

Military service was another option for women who wanted to join the war effort. Over 350,000 women served in several all-female units of the military branches. The Army and Navy Nurse Corps Reserves, the Women's Army Auxiliary Corps, the Navy's Women Accepted for Volunteer Emergency Service, the Coast Guard's SPARs (named for the Coast Guard motto, *Semper Paratus*, "Always Ready"), and Marine Corps units gave women the opportunity to serve as either commissioned officers or enlisted members at military bases at home and abroad. The Nurse Corps Reserves alone commissioned 105,000 army and navy nurses recruited by the American Red Cross. Military nurses worked at base hospitals, mobile medical units, and onboard hospital "mercy" ships.[19]

Jim Crow segregation in both the civilian and military sectors remained a problem for Black women who wanted to join the war effort. Even after President Roosevelt signed Executive Order 8802 in 1941, supervisors who hired Black women still often relegated them to the most menial tasks on factory floors. Segregation was further upheld in factory lunchrooms, and many Black women were forced to work at night to keep them separate from whites. In the military, only the Women's Army Auxiliary Corps and the Nurse Corps Reserves accepted Black women for active service, and the army set a limited quota of 10 percent of total end strength for Black female officers and enlisted women and segregated Black units on active duty. The American Red Cross, meanwhile, recruited only four hundred Black nurses for the Army and Navy Nurse Corps Reserves, and Black Army and Navy nurses worked in segregated military hospitals on bases stateside and overseas.

And for all of the postwar celebration of Rosie the Riveter, after the war ended the men returned and most women voluntarily left the workforce or lost their jobs. Meanwhile, former military women faced a litany of obstacles in obtaining veteran's benefits during their transition to civilian life. The nation that beckoned the call for assistance to millions of women during the four-year crisis hardly stood ready to accommodate their postwar needs and demands.

IX. Race and World War II

World War II affected nearly every aspect of life in the United States, and America's racial relationships were not immune. African Americans, Mexicans and Mexican Americans, Jews, and Japanese Americans were profoundly impacted.

In early 1941, months before the Japanese attack on Pearl Harbor, A. Philip Randolph, president of the Brotherhood of Sleeping Car Porters, the largest Black trade union in the nation, made headlines by threatening President Roosevelt with a march on Washington, D.C. In this "crisis of democracy," Randolph said, many defense contractors still refused to hire Black workers and the armed forces remained segregated. In exchange for Randolph calling off the march, Roosevelt issued Executive Order 8802, the Fair Employment Practice in Defense Industries Act, banning racial and religious discrimination in defense industries and establishing the Fair Employment Practices Committee (FEPC) to monitor defense industry hiring practices. While the armed forces remained segregated throughout the war, and the FEPC had limited influence, the order showed that the federal government could stand against discrimination. The Black workforce in defense industries rose from 3 percent in 1942 to 9 percent in 1945.[20]

More than one million African Americans fought in the war. Most Back servicemen served in segregated, noncombat units led by white officers. Some gains were made, however. The number of Black officers increased from five in 1940 to over seven thousand in 1945. The all-Black pilot squadrons, known as the Tuskegee Airmen, completed more than 1,500 missions, escorted heavy bombers into Germany, and earned several hundred merits and medals. Many bomber crews specifically requested the Red Tail Angels as escorts. And near the end of the war, the army and navy began integrating some of their units and facilities, before the U.S. government finally ordered the full integration of its armed forces in 1948.[21]

While Black Americans served in the armed forces (though they were segregated), on the home front they became riveters and welders, rationed food and gasoline, and bought victory bonds. But many Black Americans saw the war as an opportunity not only to serve their country

The Tuskegee Airmen stand at attention in 1941 as Major James A. Ellison returns the salute of Mac Ross, one of the first graduates of the Tuskegee cadets. The photograph captures the pride and poise of the Tuskegee Airmen, who continued the tradition of African Americans' military service despite widespread racial discrimination and inequality at home. Wikimedia.

but to improve it. The *Pittsburgh Courier*, a leading Black newspaper, spearheaded the Double V campaign. It called on African Americans to fight two wars: the war against Nazism and fascism abroad and the war against racial inequality at home. To achieve victory, to achieve "real democracy," the *Courier* encouraged its readers to enlist in the armed forces, volunteer on the home front, and fight against racial segregation and discrimination.[22]

During the war, membership in the NAACP jumped tenfold, from fifty thousand to five hundred thousand. The Congress of Racial Equality (CORE) was formed in 1942 and spearheaded the method of nonviolent direct action to achieve desegregation. Between 1940 and 1950, some 1.5 million Black southerners, the largest number of any decade since the beginning of the Great Migration, also indirectly demonstrated their opposition to racism and violence by migrating out of the Jim Crow South to the North. But transitions were not easy. Racial tensions erupted in 1943 in a series of riots in cities such as Mobile, Beaumont, and Harlem. The bloodiest race riot occurred in Detroit and resulted in the death of twenty-five Black and nine white Americans. Still, the war ignited in African Americans an urgency for equality that they would carry with them into the subsequent years.[23]

Many Americans had to navigate American prejudice, and America's entry into the war left foreign nationals from the belligerent nations in a precarious position. The Federal Bureau of Investigation (FBI) targeted many on suspicions of disloyalty for detainment, hearings, and possible internment under the Alien Enemy Act. Those who received an order for internment were sent to government camps secured by barbed wire and armed guards. Such internments were supposed to be for cause. Then, on February 19, 1942, President Roosevelt signed Executive Order 9066, authorizing the removal of any persons from designated "exclusion zones"—which ultimately covered nearly a third of the country—at the discretion of military commanders. Thirty thousand Japanese Americans fought for the United States in World War II, but wartime anti-Japanese sentiment built on historical prejudices, and under the order, people of Japanese descent, both immigrants and American citizens, were detained and placed under the custody of the War Relocation Authority, the civil agency that supervised their relocation to internment camps. They lost their homes and jobs. Over ten thousand German nationals and a smaller number of Italian nationals were interned at various times in the United States during World War II, but American policies disproportionately targeted Japanese-descended populations, and individuals did not receive personalized reviews prior to their internment. This policy of mass exclusion and detention affected over 110,000 Japanese and Japanese-descended individuals. Seventy thousand were American citizens.[24]

In its 1982 report, *Personal Justice Denied*, the congressionally appointed Commission on Wartime Relocation and Internment of Civilians concluded that "the broad historical causes" shaping the relocation program were "race prejudice, war hysteria, and a failure of political leadership."[25] Although the exclusion orders were found to have been constitutionally permissible under the vagaries of national security, they were later judged, even by the military and judicial leaders of the time, to have been a grave injustice against people of Japanese descent. In 1988, President Reagan signed a law that formally apologized for internment and provided reparations to surviving internees.

But if actions taken during war would later prove repugnant, so too could inaction. As the Allies pushed into Germany and Poland, they uncovered the full extent of Hitler's genocidal atrocities. The Allies liberated massive camp systems set up for the imprisonment, forced labor, and extermination of all those deemed racially, ideologically, or biologically "unfit" by Nazi Germany. But the Holocaust—the systematic murder of eleven million civilians, including six million Jews—had been under way for years. How did America respond?

Initially, American officials expressed little official concern for Nazi persecutions. At the first signs of trouble in the 1930s, the State Department and most U.S. embassies did relatively little to aid European Jews. Roosevelt publicly spoke out against the persecution and even withdrew the U.S. ambassador to Germany after Kristallnacht. He pushed for the 1938 Evian Conference in France, in which international leaders discussed the Jewish refugee problem and worked to expand Jewish immigration quotas by tens of thousands of people per year. But the conference came to nothing, and the United States turned away countless Jewish refugees who requested asylum in the United States.

This photograph, originally from Jürgen Stroop's May 1943 report to Heinrich Himmler, circulated throughout Europe and America as an image of the Nazi Party's brutality. The original German caption read: "Forcibly pulled out of dugouts." Wikimedia Commons.

In 1939, the German ship *St. Louis* carried over nine hundred Jewish refugees. They could not find a country that would take them. The passengers could not receive visas under the U.S. quota system. A State Department wire to one passenger read that all must "await their turns on the waiting list and qualify for and obtain immigration visas before they may be admissible into the United States." The ship cabled the president for special privilege, but the president said nothing. The ship was forced to return to Europe. Hundreds of the *St. Louis*'s passengers would perish in the Holocaust.

Anti-Semitism still permeated the United States. Even if Roosevelt wanted to do more—it's difficult to trace his own thoughts and personal views—he judged the political price for increasing immigration quotas as too high. In 1938 and 1939, the U.S. Congress debated the Wagner-Rogers Bill, an act to allow twenty thousand German-Jewish children into the United States. First lady Eleanor Roosevelt endorsed the measure, but the president remained publicly silent. The bill was opposed by roughly two thirds of the American public and was defeated. Historians speculate that Roosevelt, anxious to protect the New Deal and his rearmament programs, was unwilling to expend political capital to protect foreign groups that the American public had little interest in protecting.[26]

Knowledge of the full extent of the Holocaust was slow in coming. When the war began, American officials, including Roosevelt, doubted initial reports of industrial death camps. But even when they conceded their existence, officials pointed to their genuinely limited options. The most plausible response for the U.S. military was to bomb either the camps or the railroads leading to them, but those options were rejected by military and civilian officials who argued that it would do little to stop the deportations, would distract from the war effort, and could cause casualties among concentration camp prisoners. Whether bombing would have saved lives remains a hotly debated question.[27]

Late in the war, secretary of the treasury Henry Morgenthau, himself born into a wealthy New York Jewish family, pushed through major changes in American policy. In 1944, he formed the War Refugees Board (WRB) and became a passionate advocate for Jewish refugees. The WRB saved perhaps two hundred thousand Jews and twenty thousand others. Morgenthau also convinced Roosevelt to issue a public statement condemning the Nazi's persecution. But it was already 1944, and such policies were far too little, far too late.[28]

X. Toward a Postwar World

Americans celebrated the end of the war. At home and abroad, the United States looked to create a postwar order that would guarantee global peace and domestic prosperity. Although the alliance of convenience with Stalin's Soviet Union would collapse, Americans nevertheless looked for the means to ensure postwar stability and economic security for returning veterans.

The inability of the League of Nations to stop German, Italian, and Japanese aggressions caused many to question whether any global organization or agreements could ever ensure world peace. This included Franklin Roosevelt, who, as Woodrow Wilson's undersecretary of the navy, witnessed the rejection of this idea by both the American people and the Senate. In 1941, Roosevelt believed that postwar security could be maintained by an informal agreement between what he termed the Four Policemen—the United States, Britain, the Soviet Union, and China—instead of a rejuvenated League of Nations. But others, including secretary of state Cordell Hull and British prime minister Winston Churchill, disagreed and convinced Roosevelt to push for a new global organization. As the war ran its course, Roosevelt came around to the idea. And so did the American public. Pollster George Gallup noted a "profound change" in American attitudes. The United States had rejected membership in the League of Nations after World War I, and in 1937 only a third of Americans polled supported such an idea. But as war broke out in Europe, half of Americans did. America's entry into the war bolstered support, and, by 1945, with the war closing, 81 percent of Americans favored the idea.[29]

Whatever his support, Roosevelt had long shown enthusiasm for the ideas later enshrined in the United Nations (UN) charter. In January 1941, he announced his Four Freedoms—freedom of speech, of worship, from want, and from fear—that all of the world's citizens should enjoy. That same year he signed the Atlantic Charter with Churchill, which reinforced those ideas and added the right of self-determination and promised some sort of postwar economic and political cooperation. Roosevelt first used the term *united nations* to describe the Allied powers, not the subsequent postwar organization. But the name stuck. At Tehran in 1943, Roosevelt and Churchill convinced Stalin to send a Soviet delegation to a conference at Dumbarton Oaks, in the Georgetown neighborhood of Washington, D.C., in August 1944, where they agreed on the basic structure of the new organization. It would have a Security Council—the original Four Policemen, plus France—which would consult on how best to keep the peace and when to deploy the military power of the assembled nations. According to one historian, the organization demonstrated an understanding that "only the Great Powers, working together, could provide real security." But the plan was a kind of hybrid between Roosevelt's policemen idea and a global organization of equal representation. There would also be a General Assembly, made up of all nations; an International Court of Justice; and a council for economic and social matters. Dumbarton Oaks was a mixed success—the Soviets especially expressed concern over how the Security Council would work—but the powers agreed to meet again in San Francisco between April and June 1945 for further negotiations. There, on June 26, 1945, fifty nations signed the UN charter.[30]

Anticipating victory in World War II, leaders not only looked to the postwar global order, they looked to the fate of returning American servicemen. American politicians and interest groups sought to avoid another economic depression—the economy had tanked after World War I—by gradually easing returning veterans back into the civilian economy. The brainchild of Henry Colmery, the former head of the American Legion, the G.I. Bill won support from progressives and conservatives alike. Passed in 1944, the G.I. Bill was a multifaceted, multibillion-dollar entitlement program that rewarded honorably discharged veterans with numerous benefits.[31]

Faced with the prospect of over fifteen million members of the armed services (including approximately 350,000 women) suddenly returning to civilian life, the G.I. Bill offered a bevy of inducements to slow their influx into the civilian workforce as well as reward their service with public benefits. The legislation offered a year's worth of unemployment benefits for veterans unable to secure work. About half of American veterans (eight million) received $4 billion in unemployment benefits over the life of the bill. The G.I. Bill also made postsecondary education a reality for many. The Veterans Administration (VA) paid the lion's share of educational expenses, including tuition, fees, supplies, and even stipends for living expenses. The G.I. Bill sparked a boom in higher education. Enrollments at accredited colleges, universities, and technical and professional schools spiked, rising from 1.5 million in 1940 to 3.6 million in 1960. The VA disbursed over $14 billon in educational aid in just over a decade. Furthermore, the bill encouraged home ownership. Roughly 40 percent of Americans owned homes in 1945, but that figure climbed to 60 percent a decade after the close of the war. Because the bill did away with down payment requirements, veterans could obtain home loans for as little as $1 down. Close to four million veterans purchased homes through the G.I. Bill, sparking a construction bonanza that fueled postwar growth. In addition, the VA also helped nearly two hundred thousand veterans secure farms and offered thousands more guaranteed financing for small businesses.[32]

Not all Americans, however, benefited equally from the G.I. Bill. Indirectly, since the military limited the number of female personnel, men qualified for the bill's benefits in far higher numbers. Colleges also limited the number of female applicants to guarantee space for male veterans. African Americans, too, faced discrimination. Segregation forced Black veterans into overcrowded "historically Black colleges" that had to turn away close to twenty thousand applicants. Meanwhile, residential segregation limited Black home ownership in various neighborhoods, denying Black homeowners the equity and investment that would come with home ownership. There were other limits and other disadvantaged groups. Veterans accused of homosexuality, for instance, were similarly unable to claim GI benefits.[33]

The effects of the G.I. Bill were significant and long-lasting. It helped sustain the great postwar economic boom and, even if many could not attain it, it nevertheless established the hallmarks of American middle class life.

XI. Conclusion

The United States entered the war in a crippling economic depression and exited at the beginning of an unparalleled economic boom. The war had been won, the United States was stronger than ever, and Americans looked forward to a prosperous future. And yet new problems loomed. Stalin's Soviet Union and the proliferation of nuclear weapons would disrupt postwar dreams of global harmony. Meanwhile, Americans who had fought a war for global democracy would find that very democracy eradicated around the world in reestablished colonial regimes and at home in segregation and injustice. The war had unleashed powerful forces that would reshape the United States at home and abroad.

XII. Reference Material

This chapter was edited by Joseph Locke, with content contributions by Mary Beth Chopas, Andrew David, Ashton Ellett, Paula Fortier, Joseph Locke, Jennifer Mandel, Valerie Martinez, Ryan Menath, Chris Thomas.

Recommended citation: Mary Beth Chopas et al., "World War II," Joseph Locke, ed., in *The American Yawp*, eds. Joseph Locke and Ben Wright (Stanford, CA: Stanford University Press, 2019).

NOTES TO CHAPTER 24

1. For the second Sino-Japanese War, see, for instance, Michael A. Barnhart, *Japan Prepares for Total War: The Search for Economic Security, 1919–1941* (Ithaca, NY: Cornell University Press, 1987); Dick Wilson, *When Tigers Fight: The Story of the Sino-Japanese War, 1937–1945* (New York: Viking, 1982); and Mark Peattie, Edward Drea, and Hans van de Ven, eds., *The Battle for China: Essays on the Military History of the Sino-Japanese War of 1937–1945* (Palo Alto, CA: Stanford University Press, 2011).

2. See Joshua A. Fogel, *The Nanjing Massacre in History and Historiography* (Berkeley: University of California Press, 2000).

3. On the origins of World War II in Europe, see, for instance, P. M. H. Bell, *The Origins of the Second World War in Europe* (New York: Routledge, 1986).

4. Antony Beevor, *Stalingrad: The Fateful Siege, 1942–1943* (New York: Penguin, 1999); Omer Bartov, *The Eastern Front, 1941–45: German Troops and the Barbarization of Warfare* (New York: Palgrave Macmillan, 1986); Catherine Merridale, *Ivan's War: Life and Death in the Red Army, 1939–1945* (New York: Picador, 2006).

5. Herbert Feis, *The Road to Pearl Harbor: The Coming of the War Between the United States and Japan* (Princeton, NJ: Princeton University Press, 1950).

6. For the United States on the European front, see, for instance, John Keegan, *The Second World War* (New York: Viking, 1990); and Gerhard L. Weinberg, *A World at Arms: A Global History of World War II* (New York: Cambridge University Press, 2005).

7. Rick Atkinson, *An Army at Dawn: The War in North Africa, 1942–1943* (New York: Holt, 2002).

8. Max Hastings, *Overlord: D-Day and the Battle for Normandy* (New York: Simon and Schuster, 1985).

9. Richard Overy, *Why the Allies Won* (New York: Norton, 1997).

10. Christopher Duffy, *Red Storm on the Reich: The Soviet March on Germany, 1945* (New York: Da Capo Press, 1993).

11. For the Pacific War, see, for instance, Ronald Spector, *Eagle Against the Sun: The American War with Japan* (New York: Vintage Books, 1985); Keegan, *Second World War*; John Costello, *The Pacific War: 1941–1945* (New York: Harper, 2009); and John W. Dower, *War Without Mercy: Race and Power in the Pacific War* (New York: Pantheon Books, 1986).

12. Dower, *War Without Mercy*.

13. Michael J. Hogan, *Hiroshima in History and Memory* (New York: Cambridge University Press, 1996); Gar Alperovitz, *The Decision to Use the Atomic Bomb* (New York: Vintage Books, 1996).

14. Works on the experiences of World War II soldiers are seemingly endless and include popular histories such as Stephen E. Ambrose's *Citizen Soldiers* (New

York: Simon and Schuster, 1997) and memoirs such as Eugene Sledge's *With the Old Breed: At Peleliu and Okinawa* (New York: Presidio Press, 1981).

15. See, for instance, Michael Adams, *The Best War Ever: America and World War II* (Baltimore: Johns Hopkins University Press, 1994); Mark Harrison, ed., *The Economics of World War II: Six Great Powers in International Comparison* (Cambridge, UK: Cambridge University Press, 1998); and Kennedy, *Freedom from Fear.*

16. Deborah Cohen, *Braceros: Migrant Citizens and Transnational Subjects in the Postwar United States and Mexico* (Chapel Hill: University of North Carolina Press, 2011).

17. Interview with Rogelio Valdez Robles by Valerie Martinez and Lydia Valdez, transcribed by Nancy Valerio, September 21, 2008; interview with Alvaro Hernández by Myrna Parra-Mantilla, February 5, 2003, Interview No. 33, Institute of Oral History, University of Texas at El Paso.

18. Alecea Standlee, "Shifting Spheres: Gender, Labor, and the Construction of National Identity in U.S. Propaganda During the Second World War," *Minerva Journal of Women and War* 4 (Spring 2010): 43–62.

19. Major Jeanne Holm, USAF (Ret.), *Women in the Military: An Unfinished Revolution* (Novato, CA: Presidio Press, 1982), 21–109; Portia Kernodle, *The Red Cross Nurse in Action, 1882–1948* (New York: Harper), 406–453.

20. William P. Jones, *The March on Washington: Jobs, Freedom, and the Forgotten History of Civil Rights* (New York: Norton, 2013).

21. Stephen Tuck, *Fog of War: The Second World War and the Civil Rights Movement* (New York: Oxford University Press, 2012); Daniel Kryder, *Divided Arsenal: Race and the American State During World War II* (New York: Cambridge University Press, 2000).

22. Andrew Buni, *Robert L. Vann of the Pittsburgh Courier: Politics and Black Journalism* (Pittsburgh, PA: University of Pittsburgh Press, 1974).

23. Dominic J. Capeci Jr. and Martha Wilkerson, *Layered Violence: The Detroit Rioters of 1943* (Jackson: University Press of Mississippi, 1991).

24. Greg Robinson, *By Order of the President: FDR and the Internment of Japanese Americans* (Cambridge, MA: Harvard University Press, 2001).

25. Commission on Wartime Relocation and Internment of Civilians, *Personal Justice Denied: Report of the Commission on Wartime Relocation and Internment of Civilians* (Washington, DC: U.S. Government Printing Office, 1982), 18.

26. Richard Breitman and Allan J. Lichtman, *FDR and the Jews* (Cambridge, MA: Belknap Press, 2013), 149.

27. Peter Novick, *The Holocaust in American Life* (New York: Houghton Mifflin, 1999).

28. David Mayers, *Dissenting Voices in America's Rise to Power* (Cambridge, UK: Cambridge University Press, 2007), 274.

29. Fraser J. Harbutt, *Yalta 1945: Europe and America at the Crossroads of Peace* (Cambridge, UK: Cambridge University Press, 2010), 258; Mark Mazower, *Governing the World: The History of a Modern Idea* (New York: Penguin, 2012, 208.

30. Paul Kennedy, *The Parliament of Man: The Past, Present, and Future of the United Nations* (New York: Random House, 2006).

31. Kathleen Frydl, *The G.I. Bill* (New York: Cambridge University Press, 2009); Suzanne Mettler, *Soldiers to Citizens: The G.I. Bill and the Making of the Greatest Generation* (New York: Oxford University Press, 2005).

32. Kathleen Frydl, *G.I. Bill*; Mettler, *Soldiers to Citizens.*

33. Lizabeth Cohen, *A Consumer's Republic: The Politics of Mass Consumption in Postwar America* (New York: Knopf, 2003).

RECOMMENDED READING

Adams, Michael. *The Best War Ever: America and World War II.* Baltimore: Johns Hopkins University Press, 1994.

Anderson, Karen. *Wartime Women: Sex Roles, Family Relations, and the Status of Women During WWII.* Westport, CT: Greenwood, 1981.

Black, Gregory D. *Hollywood Goes to War: How Politics, Profit and Propaganda Shaped World War II Movies.* New York: Free Press, 1987.

Blum, John Morton. *V Was for Victory: Politics and American Culture During World War II.* New York: Marine Books, 1976.

Borgwardt, Elizabeth. *A New Deal for the World: America's Vision for Human Rights.* Cambridge, MA: Harvard University Press, 2005.

Daniels, Roger. *Prisoners Without Trial: Japanese Americans in World War II.* New York: Hill and Wang, 1993.

Dower, John. *War without Mercy: Race and Power in the Pacific War.* New York: Pantheon, 1993.

Honey, Maureen. *Creating Rosie the Riveter: Class, Gender, and Propaganda During World War II.* Amherst: University of Massachusetts Press, 1984.

Hooks, Gregory Michael. *Forging the Military-Industrial Complex: World War II's Battle of the Potomac.* Champaign: University of Illinois Press, 1991.

Kaminski, Theresa. *Angels of the Underground: The American Women Who Resisted the Japanese in the Philippines in World War II.* New York: Oxford University Press, 2015.

Keegan, John. *The Second World War.* New York: Viking, 1990.

Kennedy, David. *Freedom from Fear: America in Depression and War, 1929–1945.* New York: Oxford University Press, 1999.

Leonard, Kevin Allen. *The Battle for Los Angeles: Racial Ideology and World War II.* Albuquerque: University of New Mexico Press, 2006.

Lichtenstein, Nelson. *Labor's War at Home: The CIO in World War II.* New York: Cambridge University Press, 1982.

Malloy, Sean L. *Atomic Tragedy: Henry L. Stimson and the Decision to Use the Bomb.* Ithaca, NY: Cornell University Press, 2008.

Meyer, Leisa D. *Creating G.I. Jane: The Regulation of Sexuality and Sexual Behavior in the Women's Army Corps During WWII.* New York: Columbia University Press, 1992.

Murray, Alice Yang. *Historical Memories of the Japanese American Internment and the Struggle for Redress.* Palo Alto, CA: Stanford University Press, 2007.

O'Neill, William L. *A Democracy at War: America's Fight at Home and Abroad in World War II*. Cambridge, MA: Harvard University Press, 1995.

Rhodes, Richard. *The Making of the Atomic Bomb*. New York: Simon and Schuster, 1988.

Russell, Jan Jarboe. *The Train to Crystal City: FDR's Secret Prisoner Exchange Program and America's Only Family Internment Camp During World War II*. New York: Scribner, 2015.

Schulman, Bruce J. *From Cotton Belt to Sunbelt: Federal Policy, Economic Development, and the Transformation of the South, 1938–1980*. New York: Oxford University Press, 1991.

Sparrow, James T. *Warfare State: World War II Americans and the Age of Big Government*. New York: Oxford University Press, 2011.

Spector, Ronald H. *Eagle Against the Sun: The American War with Japan*. New York: Random House, 1985

Takaki, Ronald T. *Double Victory: A Multicultural History of America in World War II*. New York: Little, Brown, 2000.

Wynn, Neil A. *The African American Experience During World War II*. New York: Rowman and Littlefield, 2010.

25

The Cold War

I. Introduction

Relations between the United States and the Soviet Union—erstwhile allies—soured soon after World War II. On February 22, 1946, less than a year after the end of the war, the chargé d'affaires of the U.S. embassy in Moscow, George Kennan, sent a famously lengthy telegram—literally referred to as the Long Telegram—to the State Department denouncing the Soviet Union. "World communism is like a malignant parasite which feeds only on diseased tissue," he wrote, and "the steady advance of uneasy Russian nationalism . . . in [the] new guise of international Marxism . . . is more dangerous and insidious than ever before."[1] There could be no cooperation between the United States and the Soviet Union, Kennan wrote. Instead, the Soviets had to be "contained." Less than two weeks later, on March 5, former British prime minister Winston Churchill visited President Harry Truman in his home state of Missouri and declared

Test of the tactical nuclear weapon "Small Boy" at the Nevada Test Site, July 14, 1962. National Nuclear Security Administration, #760-5-NTS.

that Europe had been cut in half, divided by an "iron curtain" that had "descended across the Continent."[2] Aggressive anti-Soviet sentiment seized the American government and soon the American people.[3]

The Cold War was a global political and ideological struggle between capitalist and communist countries, particularly between the two surviving superpowers of the postwar world: the United States and the Union of Soviet Socialist Republics (USSR). "Cold" because it was never a "hot," direct shooting war between the United States and the Soviet Union, the generations-long, multifaceted rivalry nevertheless bent the world to its whims. Tensions ran highest, perhaps, during the first Cold War, which lasted from the mid-1940s through the mid-1960s, after which followed a period of relaxed tensions and increased communication and cooperation, known by the French term *détente*, until the second Cold War interceded from roughly 1979 until the collapse of the Berlin Wall in 1989 and the dissolution of the Soviet Union in 1991. The Cold War reshaped the world and the generations of Americans that lived under its shadow.

II. Political, Economic, and Military Dimensions

The Cold War grew out of a failure to achieve a durable settlement among leaders from the Big Three Allies—the United States, Britain, and the Soviet Union—as they met at Yalta in Russian Crimea and at Potsdam in occupied Germany to shape the postwar order. The Germans had pillaged their way across Eastern Europe, and the Soviets had pillaged their way back. Millions of lives were lost. Stalin considered the newly conquered territory part of a Soviet sphere of influence. With Germany's defeat imminent, the Allies set terms for unconditional surrender. At the same time, deliberation began over reparations, tribunals, and the nature of an occupation regime that would initially be divided into American, British, French, and Soviet zones. Suspicion and mistrust were already mounting. The political landscape was altered drastically by Franklin Roosevelt's sudden death in April 1945, just days before the inaugural meeting of the UN. Although Roosevelt was skeptical of Stalin, he always held out hope that the Soviets could be brought into the "Free World." Truman, like Churchill, had no such illusions. He committed the United States to a hard-line, anti-Soviet approach.[4]

At the Potsdam Conference, held on the outskirts of Berlin from mid-July to early August, the Allies debated the fate of Soviet-occupied Poland. Toward the end of the meeting, the American delegation received word that Manhattan Project scientists had successfully tested an atomic bomb. On July 24, when Truman told Stalin about this "new weapon of unusual destructive force," the Soviet leader simply nodded his acknowledgment and said that he hoped the Americans would make "good use" of it.[5]

The Cold War had long roots. The World War II alliance of convenience was not enough to erase decades of mutual suspicions. The Bolshevik Revolution had overthrown the Russian tsarists during World War I. Bolshevik leader Vladimir Lenin urged an immediate worldwide peace that would pave the way for world socialism just as Woodrow Wilson brought the United States into the war with promises of global democracy and free trade. The United States had intervened militarily against the Red Army during the Russian Civil War, and when the Soviet Union was founded in 1922 the United States refused to recognize it. The two powers were brought together only by their common enemy, and without that common enemy, there was little hope for cooperation.[6]

On the eve of American involvement in World War II, on August 14, 1941, Roosevelt and Churchill had issued a joint declaration of goals for postwar peace, known as the Atlantic Charter. An adaptation of Wilson's Fourteen Points, the Atlantic Charter established the creation of the United Nations. The Soviet Union was among the fifty charter UN member-states and was given one of five seats—alongside the United States, Britain, France, and China—on the select Security Council. The Atlantic Charter also set in motion the planning for a reorganized global economy. The July 1944 UN Financial and Monetary Conference, more popularly known as the Bretton Woods Conference, created the International Monetary Fund (IMF) and the forerunner of the World Bank, the International Bank for Reconstruction and Development (IBRD). The Bretton Woods system was bolstered in 1947 with the addition of the General Agreement on Tariffs and Trade (GATT), forerunner of the World Trade Organization (WTO). The Soviets rejected it all.

Many officials on both sides knew that the Soviet-American relationship would dissolve into renewed hostility at the end of the war, and events proved them right. In 1946 alone, the Soviet Union refused to cede parts of occupied Iran, a Soviet defector betrayed a Soviet spy who had worked on the Manhattan Project, and the United States refused Soviet calls to dismantle its nuclear arsenal. In a 1947 article for *Foreign Affairs*—written under the pseudonym "Mr. X"—George Kennan warned that Americans should "continue to regard the Soviet Union as a rival, not a partner," since Stalin harbored "no real faith in the possibility of a permanent happy coexistence of the Socialist and capitalist worlds." He urged U.S. leaders to pursue "a policy of firm containment, designed to confront the Russians."[7]

Truman, on March 12, 1947, announced $400 million in aid to Greece and Turkey, where "terrorist activities . . . led by Communists" jeopardized "democratic" governance. With Britain "reducing or liquidating its commitments in several parts of the world, including Greece," it fell on the United States, Truman said, "to support free peoples . . . resisting attempted subjugation by . . . outside pressures."[8] The so-called Truman Doctrine became a cornerstone of the American policy of containment designed to stop Soviet expansion anywhere in the world.[9]

In the harsh winter of 1946–1947, famine loomed in much of continental Europe. Blizzards and freezing cold halted coal production. Factories closed. Unemployment spiked. Amid these conditions, the communist parties of France and Italy gained nearly a third of the seats in their respective parliaments. American officials worried that Europe's impoverished masses were increasingly vulnerable to Soviet propaganda. The situation remained dire through the spring, when secretary of state General George Marshall gave an address at Harvard University on June 5, 1947, suggesting that "the United States should do whatever it is able to do to assist in the return of normal economic health to the world, without which there can be no political stability and no assured peace."[10] Although Marshall had stipulated to potential critics that his proposal was "not directed against any country, but against hunger, poverty . . . and chaos," Stalin clearly understood this as an assault against communism in Europe. He saw it as a "Trojan Horse" designed to lure Germany and other countries into the capitalist web.[11]

The European Recovery Program (ERP), popularly known as the Marshall Plan, pumped enormous sums of capital into Western Europe. From 1948 to 1952 the United States invested $13 billion toward reconstruction while simultaneously loosening trade barriers. To avoid the postwar chaos that had followed in the wake of World War I, the Marshall Plan was designed to rebuild Western Europe, open markets, and win European support for capitalist democracies. The Soviets countered with their rival Molotov Plan, a symbolic pledge of aid to Eastern Europe. Polish leader Józef Cyrankiewicz was rewarded with a five-year, $450 million trade agreement from Russia for boycotting the Marshall Plan. Stalin was jealous of Eastern Europe. When Czechoslovakia received $200 million in American assistance, Stalin summoned Czech foreign minister Jan Masaryk to Moscow. Masaryk later recounted that he "went to Moscow as the foreign minister of an independent sovereign state" but "returned as a lackey of the Soviet Government." Stalin exercised ever tighter control over Soviet "satellite" countries in central and Eastern Europe.[12]

The situation in Germany meanwhile deteriorated. Berlin had been divided into communist and capitalist zones. In June 1948, when U.S., British, and French officials introduced a new currency, the Soviet Union initiated a ground blockade, cutting off rail and road access to West Berlin (landlocked within the Soviet occupation zone) to gain control over the entire city. The United States organized and coordinated a massive airlift that flew essential supplies into the beleaguered city for eleven months, until the Soviets lifted the blockade on May 12, 1949. Germany was officially broken in half. On May 23, the western half of the country was formally renamed the Federal Republic of Germany (FRG) and the eastern

The Berlin Blockade and resultant Allied airlift was one of the first major crises of the Cold War. Here, a U.S. Navy Douglas R4D and a U.S. Air Force C-47 aircraft unload at Tempelhof Airport in 1948 or 1949. Wikimedia.

Soviet zone became the German Democratic Republic (GDR) later that fall. Berlin, which lay squarely within the GDR, was divided into two sections (and, from August 1961 until November 1989, famously separated by physical walls).[13]

In the summer of 1949, American officials launched the North Atlantic Treaty Organization (NATO), a mutual defense pact in which the United States and Canada were joined by England, France, Belgium, Luxembourg, the Netherlands, Italy, Portugal, Norway, Denmark, and Iceland. The Soviet Union would formalize its own collective defensive agreement in 1955, the Warsaw Pact, which included Albania, Romania, Bulgaria, Hungary, Czechoslovakia, Poland, and East Germany.

Liberal journalist Walter Lippmann was largely responsible for popularizing the term *Cold War* in his book *The Cold War: A Study in U.S. Foreign Policy*, published in 1947. Lippmann envisioned a prolonged stalemate between the United States and the USSR, a war of words and ideas in which direct shots would not necessarily be fired between the two. Lippmann agreed that the Soviet Union would only be "prevented from expanding" if it were "confronted with . . . American power," but he felt "that the strategical conception and plan" recommended by Mr. X (George Kennan) was "fundamentally unsound," as it would require having "the money and the military power always available in sufficient amounts to apply 'counter-force' at constantly shifting points all over the world." Lippmann cautioned against making far-flung, open-ended commitments, favoring instead a more limited engagement that focused on halting the influence of communism in the "heart" of Europe; he believed that if the Soviet system were successfully restrained on the continent, it could otherwise be left alone to collapse under the weight of its own imperfections.[14]

A new chapter in the Cold War began on October 1, 1949, when the CCP, led by Mao Zedong, declared victory against Kuomintang nationalists led by the Western-backed Chiang Kai-shek. The Kuomintang retreated to the island of Taiwan and the CCP took over the mainland under the red flag of the People's Republic of China (PRC). Coming so soon after the Soviet Union's successful test of an atomic bomb, on August 29, the "loss of China," the world's most populous country, contributed to a sense of panic among American foreign policy makers, whose attention began to shift from Europe to Asia. After Dean Acheson became secretary of state in 1949, Kennan was replaced in the State Department by former investment banker Paul Nitze, whose first task was to help compose, as Acheson later described in his memoir, a document

designed to "bludgeon the mass mind of 'top government'" into approving a "substantial increase" in military expenditures.[15]

"National Security Memorandum 68: United States Objectives and Programs for National Security," a national defense memo known as NSC-68, achieved its goal. Issued in April 1950, the nearly sixty-page classified memo warned of "increasingly terrifying weapons of mass destruction," which served to remind "every individual" of "the ever-present possibility of annihilation." It said that leaders of the USSR and its "international communist movement" sought only "to retain and solidify their absolute power." As the central "bulwark of opposition to Soviet expansion," America had become "the principal enemy" that "must be subverted or destroyed by one means or another." NSC-68 urged a "rapid build-up of political, economic, and military strength" in order to "roll back the Kremlin's drive for world domination." Such a massive commitment of resources, amounting to more than a threefold increase in the annual defense budget, was necessary because the USSR, "unlike previous aspirants to hegemony," was "animated by a new fanatic faith," seeking "to impose its absolute authority over the rest of the world."[16] Both Kennan and Lippmann were among a minority in the foreign policy establishment who argued to no avail that such a "militarization of containment" was tragically wrongheaded.[17]

On June 25, 1950, as U.S. officials were considering the merits of NSC-68's proposals, including "the intensification of . . . operations by

Global communism was shaped by the relationship between the two largest communist nations—the Soviet Union and the People's Republic of China. Despite persistent tensions between the two, this 1950 Chinese stamp depicts Joseph Stalin shaking hands with Mao Zedong. Wikimedia.

covert means in the fields of economic . . . political and psychological warfare" designed to foment "unrest and revolt in . . . [Soviet] satellite countries," fighting erupted in Korea between communists in the north and American-backed anti-communists in the south.[18]

After Japan surrendered in September 1945, a U.S.-Soviet joint occupation had paved the way for the division of Korea. In November 1947, the UN passed a resolution that a united government in Korea should be created, but the Soviet Union refused to cooperate. Only the south held elections. The Republic of Korea (ROK), South Korea, was created three months after the election. A month later, communists in the north established the Democratic People's Republic of Korea (DPRK). Both claimed to stand for a unified Korean peninsula. The UN recognized the ROK, but incessant armed conflict broke out between North and South.[19]

In the spring of 1950, Stalin hesitantly endorsed North Korean leader Kim Il Sung's plan to liberate the South by force, a plan heavily influenced by Mao's recent victory in China. While he did not desire a military confrontation with the United States, Stalin thought correctly that he could encourage his Chinese comrades to support North Korea if the war turned against the DPRK. The North Koreans launched a successful surprise attack and Seoul, the capital of South Korea, fell to the communists on June 28. The UN passed resolutions demanding that North Korea cease hostilities and withdraw its armed forces to the thirty-eighth parallel and calling on member states to provide the ROK military assistance to repulse the northern attack.

That July, UN forces mobilized under American general Douglas MacArthur. Troops landed at Inchon, a port city about thirty miles from Seoul, and took the city on September 28. They moved on North Korea. On October 1, ROK/UN forces crossed the thirty-eighth parallel, and on October 26 they reached the Yalu River, the traditional Korea-China border. They were met by three hundred thousand Chinese troops who broke the advance and rolled up the offensive. On November 30, ROK/UN forces began a fevered retreat. They returned across the thirty-eighth parallel and abandoned Seoul on January 4, 1951. The United Nations forces regrouped, but the war entered into a stalemate. General MacArthur, growing impatient and wanting to eliminate the communist threats, requested authorization to use nuclear weapons against North Korea and China. Denied, MacArthur publicly denounced Truman. Truman, unwilling to threaten World War III and refusing to tolerate MacArthur's public insubordination, dismissed the general in April. On June 23, 1951, the Soviet ambassador to the UN suggested a cease-

With the stated policy of "containing" communism at home and abroad, the U.S. pressured the United Nations to support the South Koreans and deployed American troops to the Korean Peninsula. Though in the annals of American history, the Korean War caused over thirty thousand American deaths and one hundred thousand wounded, leaving an indelible mark on those who served. Wikimedia.

fire, which the U.S. immediately accepted. Peace talks continued for two years.

General Dwight Eisenhower defeated Illinois Governor Adlai Stevenson in the 1952 presidential election, and Stalin died in March 1953. The DPRK warmed to peace, and an armistice agreement was signed on July 27, 1953. More than thirty thousand Americans had died in the war. Millions of Korean soldiers and civilians lost their lives.[20]

Coming so soon after World War II and ending without clear victory, Korea became for many Americans a "forgotten war." Decades later, though, the nation's other major intervention in Asia would be anything but forgotten. The Vietnam War had deep roots in the Cold War world. Vietnam had been colonized by France and seized by Japan during World War II. The nationalist leader Ho Chi Minh had been backed by the United States during his anti-Japanese insurgency and, following

Japan's surrender in 1945, Viet Minh nationalists, quoting the American Declaration of Independence, created the independent Democratic Republic of Vietnam (DRV). Yet France moved to reassert authority over its former colony in Indochina, and the United States sacrificed Vietnamese self-determination for France's colonial imperatives. Ho Chi Minh turned to the Soviet Union for assistance in waging war against the French colonizers in a protracted war.

After French troops were defeated at the Battle of Dien Bien Phu in May 1954, U.S. officials helped broker a temporary settlement that partitioned Vietnam in two, with a Soviet/Chinese-backed state in the north and an American-backed state in the south. To stifle communist expansion southward, the United States would send arms, offer military advisors, prop up corrupt politicians, stop elections, and, eventually, send over five hundred thousand troops, of whom nearly sixty thousand would be lost before the communists finally reunified the country.

III. The Arms Buildup, the Space Race, and Technological Advancement

The world was never the same after the United States leveled Hiroshima and Nagasaki in August 1945 with atomic bombs. Not only had perhaps 180,000 civilians been killed, the nature of warfare was forever changed. The Soviets accelerated their nuclear research, expedited in no small part by "atom spies" such as Klaus Fuchs, who had stolen nuclear secrets from the Americans' secret Manhattan Project. Soviet scientists successfully tested an atomic bomb on August 29, 1949, years before American officials had estimated they would. This unexpectedly quick Russian success not only caught the United States off guard but alarmed the Western world and propelled a nuclear arms race between the United States and the USSR.

The United States detonated the first thermonuclear weapon, or hydrogen bomb (using fusion explosions of theoretically limitless power) on November 1, 1952. The blast measured over ten megatons and generated an inferno five miles wide with a mushroom cloud twenty-five miles high and a hundred miles across. The irradiated debris—fallout—from the blast circled the earth, occasioning international alarm about the effects of nuclear testing on human health and the environment. It only hastened the arms race, with each side developing increasingly advanced warheads and delivery systems. The USSR successfully tested a hydrogen bomb in

In response to the Soviet Union's test of a pseudo–hydrogen bomb in 1953, the United States began Castle Bravo—the first U.S. test of a dry-fuel hydrogen bomb. Detonated on March 1, 1954, it was the most powerful nuclear device ever tested by the United States. But the effects were more gruesome than expected, causing nuclear fallout and radiation poisoning in nearby Pacific islands. Wikimedia.

1953, and soon thereafter Eisenhower announced a policy of "massive retaliation." The United States would henceforth respond to threats or acts of aggression with perhaps its entire nuclear might. Both sides, then, would theoretically be deterred from starting a war, through the logic of mutually assured destruction (MAD). J. Robert Oppenheimer, director of Los Alamos nuclear laboratory that developed the first nuclear bomb, likened the state of "nuclear deterrence" between the United States and the USSR to "two scorpions in a bottle, each capable of killing the other," but only by risking their own lives.[21]

Fears of nuclear war produced a veritable atomic culture. Films such as *Godzilla*, *On the Beach*, *Fail-Safe*, and *Dr. Strangelove or: How I Learned to Stop Worrying and Love the Bomb* plumbed the depths of American anxieties with plots featuring radioactive monsters, nuclear accidents, and doomsday scenarios. Antinuclear protests in the United

States and abroad warned against the perils of nuclear testing and high-lighted the likelihood that a thermonuclear war would unleash a global environmental catastrophe. Yet at the same time, peaceful nuclear tech-nologies, such as fission- and fusion-based energy, seemed to herald a utopia of power that would be clean, safe, and "too cheap to meter." In 1953, Eisenhower proclaimed at the UN that the United States would share the knowledge and means for other countries to use atomic power. Henceforth, "the miraculous inventiveness of man shall not be dedicated to his death, but consecrated to his life." The "Atoms for Peace" speech brought about the establishment of the International Atomic Energy Agency (IAEA), along with worldwide investment in this new economic sector.[22]

As Germany fell at the close of World War II, the United States and the Soviet Union each sought to acquire elements of the Nazi's V-2 super-weapon program. A devastating rocket that had terrorized England, the V-2 was capable of delivering its explosive payload up to a distance of nearly six hundred miles, and both nations sought to capture the scien-tists, designs, and manufacturing equipment to make it work. A former top German rocket scientist, Wernher von Braun, became the leader of the American space program; the Soviet Union's program was secretly managed by former prisoner Sergei Korolev. After the end of the war, American and Soviet rocket engineering teams worked to adapt German technology in order to create an intercontinental ballistic missile (ICBM). The Soviets achieved success first. They even used the same launch vehi-cle on October 4, 1957, to send Sputnik 1, the world's first human-made satellite, into orbit. It was a decisive Soviet propaganda victory.[23]

In response, the U.S. government rushed to perfect its own ICBM technology and launch its own satellites and astronauts into space. In 1958, the National Aeronautics and Space Administration (NASA) was created as a successor to the National Advisory Committee for Aeronau-tics (NACA). Initial American attempts to launch a satellite into orbit using the Vanguard rocket suffered spectacular failures, heightening fears of Soviet domination in space. While the American space program floun-dered, on September 13, 1959, the Soviet Union's Luna 2 capsule became the first human-made object to touch the moon. The "race for survival," as it was called by the *New York Times*, reached a new level.[24] The So-viet Union successfully launched a pair of dogs (Belka and Strelka) into orbit and returned them to Earth while the American Mercury program languished behind schedule. Despite countless failures and one massive accident that killed nearly one hundred Soviet military and rocket engineers, Russian cosmonaut Yuri Gagarin was launched into orbit on April 12, 1961. American astronaut Alan Shepard accomplished a suborbital flight in the Freedom 7 capsule on May 5. The United States had lagged behind, and John Kennedy would use America's losses in the "space race" to bolster funding for a moon landing.

While outer space captivated the world's imagination, the Cold War still captured its anxieties. The ever-escalating arms race continued to foster panic. In the early 1950s, the Federal Civil Defense Administration (FCDA) began preparing citizens for the worst. Schoolchildren were instructed, via a film featuring Bert the Turtle, to "duck and cover" beneath their desks in the event of a thermonuclear war.[25]

Although it took a backseat to space travel and nuclear weapons, the advent of modern computing was yet another major Cold War scientific innovation, the effects of which were only just beginning to be understood. In 1958, following the humiliation of the Sputnik launches, Eisenhower authorized the creation of an Advanced Research Projects Agency (ARPA) housed within the Department of Defense (later changed to DARPA). As a secretive military research and development operation, ARPA was tasked with funding and otherwise overseeing the production of sensitive new technologies. Soon, in cooperation with university-based computer engineers, ARPA would develop the world's first system of "network packing switches," and computer networks would begin connecting to one another.

IV. The Cold War Red Scare, McCarthyism, and Liberal Anticommunism

Joseph McCarthy burst onto the national scene during a speech in Wheeling, West Virginia, on February 9, 1950. Waving a sheet of paper in the air, he proclaimed: "I have here in my hand a list of 205 . . . names that were made known to the Secretary of State as being members of the Communist party and who nevertheless are still working and shaping [U.S.] policy." Since the Wisconsin Republican had no actual list, when pressed, the number changed to fifty-seven, then, later, eighty-one. Finally, he promised to disclose the name of just one communist, the nation's "top Soviet agent." The shifting numbers brought ridicule, but it didn't matter: McCarthy's claims won him fame and fueled the ongoing "red scare."[26]

Joseph McCarthy, Republican senator from Wisconsin, fueled fears during the early 1950s that communism was rampant and growing. This intensified Cold War tensions felt by every segment of society, from government officials to ordinary American citizens. Photograph of Senator Joseph R. McCarthy, March 14, 1950. National Archives and Records Administration, http://research.archives.gov/description/6802721.

McCarthyism was only a symptom of a massive and widespread anticommunist hysteria that engulfed Cold War America. Popular fears, for instance, had long since shot through the federal government. Only two years after World War II, President Truman, facing growing anticommunist excitement and with a tough election on the horizon, gave in to pressure in March 1947 and issued his "loyalty order," Executive Order 9835, establishing loyalty reviews for federal employees. The FBI conducted closer examinations of all potential "security risks" among Foreign Service officers. In Congress, the House Un-American Activities Committee (HUAC) and the Senate Permanent Subcommittee on Investigations (SPSI) held hearings on communist influence in American society. Between 1949 and 1954, congressional committees conducted over one hundred investigations into subversive activities. Antisubversion committees emerged in over a dozen state legislatures, and review procedures

The environment of fear and panic instigated by McCarthyism led to the arrest of many innocent people. Still, some Americans accused of supplying top-secret information to the Soviets were, in fact, spies. Julius and Ethel Rosenberg were convicted of espionage and executed in 1953 for delivering information about the atomic bomb to the Soviets. Library of Congress.

proliferated in public schools and universities across the country. At the University of California, for example, thirty-one professors were dismissed in 1950 for refusing to sign a loyalty oath. The Internal Security Act, or McCarran Act, passed by Congress in September 1950, mandated all "communist organizations" to register with the government, gave the government greater powers to investigate sedition, and made it possible to prevent suspected individuals from gaining or keeping their citizenship.[27]

Anticommunist policies reflected national fears of a surging global communism. Within a ten-month span beginning in 1949, for instance, the USSR developed a nuclear bomb, China fell to communism, and over three hundred thousand American soldiers were deployed to fight a land war in Korea. Newspapers, meanwhile, were filled with headlines alleging Soviet espionage.

During the war, Julius Rosenberg worked briefly at the U.S. Army Signal Corps Laboratory in New Jersey, where he had access to classified information. He and his wife, Ethel, who had both been members of the Communist Party of the USA (CPUSA) in the 1930s, were accused of passing secret bomb-related documents to Soviet officials and were indicted in August 1950 on charges of giving nuclear secrets to the Russians. After a trial in March 1951, they were found guilty and executed on June 19, 1953.[28]

Alger Hiss, the highest-ranking government official linked to Soviet espionage, was another prize for conservatives. Hiss was a prominent official in the U.S. State Department and served as secretary-general of the UN Charter Conference in San Francisco from April to June 1945 before leaving the State Department in 1946. A young congressman and member of HUAC, Richard Nixon, made waves by accusing Hiss of espionage. On August 3, 1948, Whittaker Chambers testified before HUAC that he and Hiss had worked together as part of the secret "communist underground" in Washington, D.C., during the 1930s. Hiss, who always maintained his innocence, stood trial twice. After a hung jury in July 1949, he was convicted on two counts of perjury (the statute of limitations for espionage having expired). Later evidence suggested their guilt. At the time, their convictions fueled an anticommunist frenzy. Some began seeing communists everywhere.[29]

Alger Hiss and the Rosenbergs offered anticommunists such as Joseph McCarthy the evidence they needed to allege a vast Soviet conspiracy to infiltrate and subvert the U.S. government and justify the smearing of all left-liberals, even those who were resolutely anticommunist. Not long after his February 1950 speech in Wheeling, McCarthy's sensational charges became a source of growing controversy. Forced to respond, President Truman arranged a partisan congressional investigation designed to discredit McCarthy. The Tydings Committee held hearings from early March through July 1950 and issued a final report admonishing McCarthy for perpetrating a "fraud and a hoax" on the American public. American progressives saw McCarthy's crusade as nothing less than a political witch hunt. In June 1950, *The Nation* magazine editor Freda Kirchwey characterized "McCarthyism" as "the means by which a handful of men, disguised as hunters of subversion, cynically subvert the instruments of justice . . . in order to help their own political fortunes."[30] Truman's liberal supporters, and leftists like Kirchwey, hoped in vain that McCarthy and the new "ism" that bore his name would blow over quickly.

There had, of course, been a communist presence in the United States. The CPUSA was formed in the aftermath of the 1917 Russian Revolution when the Bolsheviks created a Communist International (the Comintern) and invited socialists from around the world to join. During its first two years of existence, the CPUSA functioned in secret, hidden from a surge of antiradical and anti-immigrant hysteria, investigations, deportations, and raids at the end of World War I. The CPUSA began its public life in 1921, after the panic subsided, but communism remained on the margins of American life until the 1930s, when leftists and liberals began to see the Soviet Union as a symbol of hope amid the Great Depression. Then many communists joined the Popular Front, an effort to make communism mainstream by adapting it to American history and American culture. During the Popular Front era, communists were integrated into mainstream political institutions through alliances with progressives in the Democratic Party. The CPUSA enjoyed most of its influence and popularity among workers in unions linked to the newly formed CIO. Communists also became strong opponents of Jim Crow segregation and developed a presence in both the NAACP and the ACLU. The CPUSA, moreover, established "front" groups, such as the League of American Writers, in which intellectuals participated without even knowing of its ties to the Comintern. But even at the height of the global economic crisis, communism never attracted many Americans. Even at the peak of its membership, the CPUSA had just eighty thousand national "card-carrying" members. From the mid-1930s through the mid-1940s, the party exercised most of its power indirectly, through coalitions with liberals and reformers. When news broke of Hitler's and Stalin's 1939 nonaggression pact, many fled the party, feeling betrayed. A bloc of left-liberal anticommunists, meanwhile, purged remaining communists in their ranks, and the Popular Front collapsed.[31]

Lacking the legal grounds to abolish the CPUSA, officials instead sought to expose and contain CPUSA influence. Following a series of predecessor committees, HUAC was established in 1938, then reorganized after the war and given the explicit task of investigating communism. By the time the Communist Control Act was passed in August 1954, effectively criminalizing party membership, the CPUSA had long ceased to have meaningful influence. Anticommunists were driven to eliminate remaining CPUSA influence from progressive institutions, including the NAACP and the CIO. The Taft-Hartley Act (1947) gave union officials the initiative to purge communists from the labor movement. A kind of Cold War liberalism took hold. In January 1947, anticommunist liberals formed Americans for Democratic Action (ADA), whose founding members included labor leader Walter Reuther and NAACP chairman Walter White, as well as historian Arthur Schlesinger Jr., theologian Reinhold Niebuhr, and former first lady Eleanor Roosevelt. Working to help Truman defeat former vice president Henry Wallace's Popular Front–backed campaign in 1948, the ADA combined social and economic reforms with staunch anticommunism.[32]

The domestic Cold War was bipartisan, fueled by a consensus drawn from a left-liberal and conservative anticommunist alliance that included politicians and policy makers, journalists and scientists, business and civic/religious leaders, and educators and entertainers. Led by its imperious director, J. Edgar Hoover, the FBI took an active role in the domestic battle against communism. Hoover's FBI helped incite panic by assisting the creation of blatantly propagandistic films and television shows, including *The Red Menace* (1949), *My Son John* (1951), and *I Led Three Lives* (1953–1956). Such alarmist depictions of espionage and treason in a "free world" imperiled by communism heightened the 1950s culture of fear. In the fall of 1947, HUAC entered the fray with highly publicized hearings of Hollywood. Film mogul Walt Disney and actor Ronald Reagan, among others, testified to aid investigators' attempts to expose communist influence in the entertainment industry. A group of writers, directors, and producers who refused to answer questions were held in contempt of Congress. This Hollywood Ten created the precedent for a blacklist in which hundreds of film artists were barred from industry work for the next decade.

HUAC made repeated visits to Hollywood during the 1950s, and their interrogation of celebrities often began with the same intimidating refrain: "Are you now, or have you ever been, a member of the Communist Party?" Many witnesses cooperated, and "named names," naming anyone they knew who had ever been associated with communist-related groups or organizations. In 1956, Black entertainer and activist Paul Robeson chided his HUAC inquisitors, claiming that they had put him on trial not for his politics but because he had spent his life "fighting for the rights" of his people. "You are the un-Americans," he told them, "and you ought to be ashamed of yourselves."[33] As Robeson and other victims of McCarthyism learned firsthand, this "second red scare," in the glow of nuclear annihilation and global totalitarianism, fueled an intolerant and skeptical political world, what Cold War liberal Arthur Schlesinger, in his *The Vital Center* (1949), called an "age of anxiety."[34]

Anticommunist ideology valorized overt patriotism, religious conviction, and faith in capitalism. Those who shunned such "American values" were open to attack. If communism was a plague spreading across Europe and Asia, anticommunist hyperbole infected cities, towns, and suburbs throughout the country. The playwright Arthur Miller's popular

Many accused of communist sentiments refused to denounce friends and acquaintances. One of the most well-known Americans of the time, African American actor and singer Paul Robeson was unwilling to sign an affidavit confirming he was not a communist and, as a result, his U.S. passport was revoked. During the Cold War, he was condemned by the press and neither his music nor films could be purchased in the United States. Wikimedia.

1953 play *The Crucible* compared the red scare to the Salem Witch Trials. Miller wrote, "In America any man who is not reactionary in his views is open to the charge of alliance with the Red hell. Political opposition, thereby, is given an inhumane overlay which then justifies the abrogation of all normally applied customs of civilized intercourse. A political policy is equated with moral right, and opposition to it with diabolical malevolence. Once such an equation is effectively made, society becomes a congerie of plots and counterplots, and the main role of government changes from that of the arbiter to that of the scourge of God."[35]

Rallying against communism, American society urged conformity. "Deviant" behavior became dangerous. Having entered the workforce en masse as part of a collective effort in World War II, middle-class women were told to return to housekeeping responsibilities. Having fought and died abroad for American democracy, Black soldiers were told to return home and acquiesce to the American racial order. Homosexuality, already stigmatized, became dangerous. Personal secrets were seen as a liability that exposed one to blackmail. The same paranoid mind-set that fueled the second red scare also ignited the Cold War "lavender scare" against gay Americans.[36]

American religion, meanwhile, was fixated on what McCarthy, in his 1950 Wheeling speech, called an "all-out battle between communistic atheism and Christianity." Cold warriors in the United States routinely referred to a fundamental incompatibility between "godless communism" and God-fearing Americanism. Religious conservatives championed the idea of the traditional nuclear, God-fearing family as a bulwark against the spread of atheistic totalitarianism. As Baptist minister Billy Graham sermonized in 1950, communism aimed to "destroy the American home and cause . . . moral deterioration," leaving the country exposed to communist infiltration.[37]

In an atmosphere in which ideas of national belonging and citizenship were so closely linked to religious commitment, Americans during the early Cold War years attended church, professed a belief in a supreme being, and stressed the importance of religion in their lives at higher rates than in any time in American history. Americans sought to differentiate themselves from godless communists through public displays of religiosity. Politicians infused government with religious symbols. The Pledge of Allegiance was altered to include the words *one nation, under God* in 1954. *In God We Trust* was adopted as the official national motto in 1956. In popular culture, one of the most popular films of the decade, *The Ten Commandments* (1956), retold the biblical Exodus story as a Cold War parable, echoing (incidentally) NSC-68's characterization of the Soviet Union as a "slave state." Monuments of the Ten Commandments went up at courthouses and city halls across the country.

While the link between American nationalism and religion grew much closer during the Cold War, many Americans began to believe that just believing in almost any religion was better than being an atheist. Gone was the overt anti-Catholic and anti-Semitic language of Protestants in the past. Now, leaders spoke of a common Judeo-Christian heritage. In December 1952, a month before his inauguration, Dwight Eisenhower said that "our form of government makes no sense unless it is founded in a deeply-felt religious faith, and I don't care what it is."[38]

Joseph McCarthy, an Irish Catholic, made common cause with prominent religious anticommunists, including southern evangelist Billy James Hargis of *Christian Crusade*, a popular radio and television ministry that peaked in the 1950s and 1960s. Cold War religion in America also crossed the political divide. During the 1952 campaign, Eisenhower spoke of U.S. foreign policy as "a war of light against darkness, freedom against slavery, Godliness against atheism."[39] His Democratic opponent, former Illinois governor Adlai Stevenson, said that America was engaged in a battle with the "Anti-Christ." While Billy Graham became a spiritual advisor to Eisenhower as well as other Republican and Democratic presidents, the same was true of the liberal Protestant Reinhold Niebuhr, perhaps the nation's most important theologian when he appeared on the cover of *Life* in March 1948.

Though publicly rebuked by the Tydings Committee, McCarthy soldiered on. In June 1951, on the floor of Congress, McCarthy charged that then secretary of defense (and former secretary of state) General George Marshall had fallen prey to "a conspiracy on a scale so immense as to dwarf any previous such venture in the history of man." He claimed that Marshall, a war hero, had helped to "diminish the United States in world affairs," enabling the United States to "finally fall victim to Soviet intrigue . . . and Russian military might." The speech caused an uproar. During the 1952 campaign, Eisenhower, who was in all things moderate and politically cautious, refused to publicly denounce McCarthy. "I will not . . . get into the gutter with that guy," he wrote privately. McCarthy campaigned for Eisenhower, who won a stunning victory.[40]

So did the Republicans, who regained Congress. McCarthy became chairman of the Senate Permanent Subcommittee on Investigations (SPSI). He turned his newfound power against the government's overseas broadcast division, the Voice of America (VOA). McCarthy's investigation in February–March 1953 resulted in several resignations or transfers. McCarthy's mudslinging had become increasingly unrestrained. Soon he went after the U.S. Army. After forcing the Army to again disprove theories of a Soviet spy ring at Fort Monmouth in New Jersey, McCarthy publicly berated officers suspected of promoting leftists. McCarthy's badgering of witnesses created cover for critics to publicly denounce his abrasive fearmongering.

On March 9, CBS anchor Edward R. Murrow, a respected journalist, told his television audience that McCarthy's actions had "caused alarm and dismay amongst . . . allies abroad, and given considerable comfort to our enemies." Yet, Murrow explained, "he didn't create this situation of fear; he merely exploited it—and rather successfully. Cassius was right. 'The fault, dear Brutus, is not in our stars, but in ourselves.'"[41]

Twenty million people saw the Army-McCarthy hearings unfold over thirty-six days in 1954. The army's head counsel, Joseph Welch, captured much of the mood of the country when he defended a fellow lawyer from McCarthy's public smears, saying, "Let us not assassinate this lad further, Senator. You've done enough. Have you no sense of decency, sir? At long last, have you left no sense of decency?" In September, a senate subcommittee recommended that McCarthy be censured. On December 2, 1954, his colleagues voted 67–22 to "condemn" his actions. Humiliated, McCarthy faded into irrelevance and alcoholism and died in May 1957 at age 48.[42]

By the late 1950s, the worst of the second red scare was over. Stalin's death, followed by the Korean War armistice, opened new space—and hope—for the easing of Cold War tensions. Détente and the upheavals of the late 1960s were on the horizon. But McCarthyism outlasted McCarthy and the 1950s. The tactics he perfected continued to be practiced long after his death. "Red-baiting," the act of smearing a political opponent by linking them to communism or some other demonized ideology, persevered. But McCarthy had hardly been alone.

Congressman Richard Nixon, for instance, used his place on HUAC and his public role in the campaign against Alger Hiss to catapult himself into the White House alongside Eisenhower and later into the presidency. Ronald Reagan bolstered the fame he had won in Hollywood with his testimony before Congress and his anticommunist work for major American corporations such as General Electric. He too would use anticommunism to enter public life and chart a course to the presidency. In 1958, radical anticommunists founded the John Birch Society, attacking liberals and civil rights activists such as Martin Luther King Jr. as communists. Although joined by Cold War liberals, the weight of anticommunism was used as part of an assault against the New Deal and its defenders. Even those liberals, such as historian Arthur Schlesinger, who had fought against communism found themselves smeared by the red scare. The leftist American tradition was in tatters, destroyed by anticommunist hysteria. Movements for social justice, from civil rights to gay rights to feminism, were all suppressed under Cold War conformity.

V. Decolonization and the Global Reach of the American Century

In an influential 1941 *Life* magazine editorial titled "The American Century," publishing magnate Henry Luce outlined his "vision of America as the principal guarantor of freedom of the seas" and "the dynamic leader of world trade." In his embrace of an American-led international system, the conservative Luce was joined by liberals including historian

Arthur Schlesinger, who in his 1949 Cold War tome *The Vital Center* proclaimed that a "world destiny" had been "thrust" upon the United States, with perhaps no other nation becoming "a more reluctant great power." Emerging from the war as the world's preeminent military and economic force, the United States was perhaps destined to compete with the Soviet Union for influence in the Third World, where a power vacuum had been created by the demise of European imperialism. As France and Britain in particular struggled in vain to control colonies in Asia, the Middle East, and North Africa, the United States assumed responsibility for maintaining order and producing a kind of "pax-Americana." Little of the postwar world, however, would be so peaceful.[43]

Based on the logic of militarized containment established by NSC-68 and American Cold War strategy, interventions in Korea and Vietnam were seen as appropriate American responses to the ascent of communism in China. Unless Soviet power in Asia was halted, Chinese influence

The Cuban revolution seemed to confirm the fears of many Americans that the spread of communism could not be stopped. In this photograph, Castro and fellow revolutionary Che Guevara march in a memorial for those killed in the explosion of a ship unloading munitions in Havana in March 1960. The U.S. government had been active in undermining Castro's regime, and although there was no evidence in this instance, Castro publicly blamed the United States for the explosion. Wikimedia.

would ripple across the continent, and one country after another would fall to communism. Easily transposed onto any region of the world, the Domino Theory became a standard basis for the justification of U.S. interventions abroad. Cuba was seen as a communist beachhead that imperiled Latin America, the Caribbean, and perhaps eventually the United States. Like Ho Chi Minh, Cuban leader Fidel Castro was a revolutionary nationalist whose career as a communist began in earnest after he was rebuffed by the United States, and American interventions targeted nations that never espoused official communist positions. Many interventions in Asia, Latin America, and elsewhere were driven by factors that were shaped by but also transcended anticommunist ideology.

Instead of the United States dismantling its military after World War II, as it had after every major conflict, the Cold War facilitated a new permanent defense establishment. Federal investments in national defense affected the entire country. Different regions housed various sectors of what sociologist C. Wright Mills, in 1956, called the "permanent war economy." The aerospace industry was concentrated in areas like Southern California and Long Island, New York; Massachusetts was home to several universities that received major defense contracts; the Midwest became home base for intercontinental ballistic missiles pointed at the Soviet Union; many of the largest defense companies and military installations were concentrated in the South, so much so that in 1956 author William Faulkner, who was born in Mississippi, remarked, "Our economy is the Federal Government."[44]

A radical critic of U.S. policy, Mills was one of the first thinkers to question the effects of massive defense spending, which, he said, corrupted the ruling class, or "power elite," who now had the potential to take the country into war for the sake of corporate profits. Yet perhaps the most famous critique of the entrenched war economy came from an unlikely source. During his farewell address to the nation in January 1961, President Eisenhower cautioned Americans against the "unwarranted influence" of a "permanent armaments industry of vast proportions" that could threaten "liberties" and "democratic processes." While the "conjunction of an immense military establishment and a large arms industry" was a fairly recent development, this "military-industrial complex" had cultivated a "total influence," which was "economic, political, even spiritual . . . felt in every city . . . Statehouse . . . [and] office of the Federal government." There was, he said, great danger in failing to "comprehend its grave implications."[45]

In Eisenhower's formulation, the "military-industrial complex" referred specifically to domestic connections between arms manufacturers, members of Congress, and the Department of Defense. Yet the new alliance between corporations, politicians, and the military was dependent on having an actual conflict to wage, without which there could be no ultimate financial gain. To critics, military-industrial partnerships at home were now linked to U.S. interests abroad. Suddenly American foreign policy had to secure foreign markets and protect favorable terms for American trade all across the globe. Seen in such a way, the Cold War was just a by-product of America's new role as the remaining Western superpower. Regardless, the postwar rise of U.S. power correlated with what many historians describe as a "national security consensus" that has dominated American policy since World War II. And so the United States was now more intimately involved in world affairs than ever before.

Ideological conflicts and independence movements erupted across the postwar world. More than eighty countries achieved independence, primarily from European control. As it took center stage in the realm of global affairs, the United States played a complicated and often contradictory role in this process of "decolonization." The sweeping scope of post-1945 U.S. military expansion was unique in the country's history. Critics believed that the advent of a "standing army," so feared by many of the founding fathers, set a disturbing precedent. But in the postwar world, American leaders eagerly set about maintaining a new permanent military juggernaut and creating viable international institutions.

But what of independence movements around the world? Roosevelt had spoken for many in his remark to British prime minister Winston Churchill, in 1941, that it was hard to imagine "fight[ing] a war against fascist slavery, and at the same time not work to free people all over the world from a backward colonial policy."[46] American postwar foreign policy leaders therefore struggled to balance support for decolonization against the reality that national independence movements often posed a threat to America's global interests.

American strategy became consumed with thwarting Russian power and the concomitant global spread of communism. Foreign policy officials increasingly opposed all insurgencies or independence movements that could in any way be linked to international communism. The Soviet Union, too, was attempting to sway the world. Stalin and his successors pushed an agenda that included not only the creation of Soviet client states in Eastern and Central Europe, but also a tendency to support leftwing liberation movements everywhere, particularly when they espoused anti-American sentiment. As a result, the United States and the Union of Soviet Socialist Republics (USSR) engaged in numerous proxy wars in the Third World.

American planners felt that successful decolonization could demonstrate the superiority of democracy and capitalism against competing Soviet models. Their goal was in essence to develop an informal system of world power based as much as possible on consent (hegemony) rather than coercion (empire). But European powers still defended colonization and American officials feared that anticolonial resistance would breed revolution and push nationalists into the Soviet sphere. And when faced with such movements, American policy dictated alliances with colonial regimes, alienating nationalist leaders in Asia and Africa.

The architects of American power needed to sway the citizens of decolonizing nations toward the United States. In 1948, Congress passed the Smith-Mundt Act to "promote a better understanding of the United States in other countries." The legislation established cultural exchanges

The Soviet Union took advantage of racial tensions in the United States to create anti-American propaganda. This 1930 Soviet poster shows a Black American being lynched from the Statue of Liberty, while the text below asserts the links between racism and Christianity. Wikimedia.

with various nations, including even the USSR, in order to showcase American values through American artists and entertainers. The Soviets did the same, through what they called an international peace offensive, which by most accounts was more successful than the American campaign. Although U.S. officials made strides through the initiation of various overt and covert programs, they still perceived that they were lagging behind the Soviet Union in the "war for hearts and minds." But as unrest festered in much of the Third World, American officials faced difficult choices.[47]

As Black Americans fought for justice at home, prominent American Black radicals, including Malcolm X, Paul Robeson, and the aging W. E. B. Du Bois, joined in solidarity with the global anticolonial movement, arguing that the United States had inherited the racist European imperial tradition. Supporters of the Soviet Union made their own effort to win over countries, claiming that Marxist-Leninist doctrine offered a road map for their liberation from colonial bondage. Moreover, Kremlin propaganda pointed to injustices of the American South as an example of American hypocrisy: how could the United States claim to fight for global freedom when it refused to guarantee freedoms for its own citizenry? In such ways the Cold War connected the Black freedom struggle, the Third World, and the global Cold War.

VI. Conclusion

In June 1987, American president Ronald Reagan stood at the Berlin Wall and demanded that Soviet premier Mikhail Gorbachev "Tear down this wall!" Less than three years later, amid civil unrest in November 1989, East German authorities announced that their citizens were free to travel to and from West Berlin. The concrete curtain would be lifted and East Berlin would be opened to the world. Within months, the Berlin Wall was reduced to rubble by jubilant crowds anticipating the reunification of their city and their nation, which took place on October 3, 1990. By July 1991 the Warsaw Pact had crumbled, and on December 25 of that year, the Soviet Union was officially dissolved. Hungary, Poland, Czechoslovakia, and the Baltic States (Latvia, Estonia, and Lithuania) were freed from Russian domination.

Partisans fought to claim responsibility for the breakup of the Soviet Union and the ending of the Cold War. Whether it was the triumphalist rhetoric and militaristic pressure of conservatives or the internal fracturing of ossified bureaucracies and work of Russian reformers that shaped the ending of the Cold War is a question of later decades. Questions about the Cold War's end must pause before appreciations of the Cold War's impact at home and abroad. Whether measured by the tens of millions killed in Cold War–related conflicts, in the reshaping of American politics and culture, or in the transformation of America's role in the world, the Cold War pushed American history upon a new path, one that it has yet to yield.

VII. Reference Material

This chapter was edited by Ari Cushner, with content contributions by Michael Brenes, Ari Cushner, Michael Franczak, Joseph Haker, Jonathan Hunt, Jun Suk Hyun, Zack Jacobson, Micki Kaufman, Lucie Kyrova, Celeste Day Moore, Joseph Parrott, Colin Reynolds, and Tanya Roth.

Recommended citation: Michael Brenes et al., "The Cold War," Ari Cushner, ed., in *The American Yawp*, eds. Joseph Locke and Ben Wright (Stanford, CA: Stanford University Press, 2019).

NOTES TO CHAPTER 25

1. Kennan to Secretary of State, February 22, 1946, in *Foreign Relations of the United States 1946*, Vol. 6 (Washington, DC: U.S. Government Printing Office, 1969), 696–709, 708, 700.

2. Martin McCauley, *Origins of the Cold War 1941–1949: Revised 3rd Edition* (New York: Routledge, 2013), 141.

3. For Kennan, see especially John Lewis Gaddis, *George F. Kennan: An American Life* (New York: Penguin, 2011); John Lukacs, ed., *George F. Kennan and the Origins of Containment, 1944–1946: The Kennan-Lukacs Correspondence* (Columbia: University of Missouri Press, 1997).

4. Harbutt, *Yalta 1945*.

5. Herbert Feis, *Between War and Peace: The Potsdam Conference* (Princeton, NJ: Princeton University Press, 1960).

6. For overviews of the Cold War, see especially John Lewis Gaddis, *Strategies of Containment: A Critical Appraisal of Postwar American National Security Policy* (New York: Oxford University Press, 1982); John Lewis Gaddis, *The Cold War: A New History* (New York: Penguin, 2005); Melvyn P. Leffler, *For the Soul of Mankind: The United States, the Soviet Union, and the Cold War* (New York: Hill and Wang, 2007); and Frederick Logevall, *America's Cold War: The Politics of Insecurity* (Cambridge, MA: Harvard University Press, 2009).

7. George Kennan, "The Sources of Soviet Conduct," *Foreign Affairs* (July 1947), 566–582.

8. Joyce P. Kaufman, *A Concise History of U.S. Foreign Policy* (Lanham, MD: Rowman and Littlefield, 2010), 86.

9. Denise M. Bostdorff, *Proclaiming the Truman Doctrine: The Cold War Call to Arms* (College Station: Texas A&M University Press, 1998).

10. Michael Beschloss, *Our Documents: 100 Milestone Documents from the National Archives* (New York: Oxford University Press, 2006), 199.

11. Charles L. Mee, *The Marshall Plan: The Launching of the Pax Americana* (New York: Simon and Schuster, 1984).

12. Melvyn P. Leffler and Odd Arne Westad, eds., *The Cambridge History of the Cold War: Volume 1, Origins* (Cambridge, MA: Cambridge University Press, 2010), 189.

13. Daniel F. Harrington, *Berlin on the Brink: The Blockade, the Airlift, and the Early Cold War* (Lexington: University of Kentucky Press, 2012).

14. Walter Lippman, *The Cold War: A Study in U.S. Foreign Policy* (New York: Harper, 1947), 10, 15.

15. James Chace, *Acheson: The Secretary of State Who Created the American World* (New York: Simon and Schuster, 2008), 441.

16. Quotes from Curt Cardwell, *NSC 68 and the Political Economy of the Early Cold War* (Cambridge, MA: Cambridge University Press, 2011), 10–12.

17. Gaddis, *Strategies of Containment.*

18. Gregory Mitrovich, *Undermining the Kremlin: America's Strategy to Subvert the Soviet Bloc, 1947–1956* (Ithaca, NY: Cornell University Press, 2000), 182.

19. For the Korean War, see especially Bruce Cumings, *The Origins of the Korean War*, 2 vols. (Princeton, NJ: Princeton University Press, 1981, 1990); William W. Stueck, *The Korean War: An International History* (Princeton, NJ: Princeton University Press, 1995).

20. Elizabeth Stanley, *Paths to Peace: Domestic Coalition Shifts, War Termination and the Korean War* (Stanford, CA: Stanford University Press, 2009), 208.

21. J. Robert Oppenheimer, "Atomic Weapons and American Policy," *Foreign Affairs* (July 1953): 529.

22. Andrew J. Dunar, *America in the Fifties* (Ithaca, NY: Syracuse University Press, 2006), 134.

23. Deborah Cadbury, *Space Race: The Epic Battle Between America and the Soviet Union for Dominance of Space* (New York: HarperCollins, 2006).

24. Tom Wolfe, *The Right Stuff* (New York: Farrar, Straus and Giroux), 115.

25. Kenneth D. Rose, *One Nation Underground: The Fallout Shelter in American Culture* (New York: New York University Press, 2004), 128.

26. David M. Oshinsky, *A Conspiracy So Immense: The World of Joe McCarthy* (New York: Oxford University Press, 2005), 109.

27. Ibid., 171–174.

28. Ibid., 102–103, 172, 335.

29. Ibid., 98–100, 123–125.

30. Sara Alpern, *Freda Kirchwey: A Woman of the Nation* (Cambridge, MA: Harvard University Press, 1987), 203.

31. Ellen Schrecker, *Many Are the Crimes: McCarthyism in America* (Princeton, NJ: Princeton University Press, 1999).

32. On anticommunist liberals and the decline of American communism, see especially Schrecker, *Many Are the Crimes.*

33. Paul Robeson, *Paul Robeson Speaks: Writings, Speeches, and Interviews, a Centennial Celebration,* ed. Philip Foner (New York: Citadel Press, 1978), 421, 433.

34. Arthur Schlesinger Jr., *The Vital Center: The Politics of Freedom* (Boston: Houghton Mifflin, 1949), 1.

35. Arthur Miller, *The Crucible* (New York: Penguin, 2003), 30.

36. Robert D. Dean, *Imperial Brotherhood: Gender and the Making of Cold War Foreign Policy* (Amherst: University of Massachusetts Press, 2003).

37. William G. McLoughlin, *Revivals, Awakenings, and Reform* (Chicago: University of Chicago Press, 2013), 189.

38. Quoted in Gastón Espinosa, *Religion and the American Presidency: George Washington to George W. Bush with Commentary and Primary Sources* (New York: Columbia University Press, 2009), 298.

39. Peter Gries, *The Politics of American Foreign Policy: How Ideology Divides Liberals and Conservatives over Foreign Affairs* (Stanford, CA: Stanford University Press, 2014), 215.

40. Oshinsky, *Conspiracy So Immense,* 272.

41. Ibid., 399.

42. Ibid., 475.

43. Henry R. Luce, "The American Century," *Life* (February 17, 1941), 61–65.

44. Bruce J. Schulman, *From Cotton Belt to Sunbelt: Federal Policy, Economic Development, and the Transformation of the South, 1938–1980* (Durham, NC: Duke University Press, 1994), 135.

45. Dwight D. Eisenhower, *Public Papers of the Presidents, Dwight D. Eisenhower,* 1960, 1035–1040.

46. Fredrick Logevall, *Embers of War: The Fall of an Empire and the Making of America's Vietnam* (New York: Random House, 2012), 48.

47. Frank Ninkovich, *The Diplomacy of Ideas: U.S. Foreign Policy and Cultural Relations, 1938–1950* (New York: Cambridge University Press, 1981).

RECOMMENDED READING

Borstelmann, Thomas. *The Cold War and the Color Line: American Race Relations in the Global Arena.* Cambridge, MA: Harvard University Press, 2001.

Boyer, Paul. *By the Bomb's Early Light: American Thought and Culture at the Dawn of the Atomic Age.* New York: Pantheon Books, 1985.

Brown, Kate. *Plutopia: Nuclear Families, Atomic Cities, and the Great Soviet and American Plutonium Disasters.* New York: Oxford University Press, 2013.

Carlton, Don E. *Red Scare! Right-Wing Hysteria, Fifties Fanaticism, and Their Legacy in Texas.* Austin: Texas Monthly Press, 1985.

Dean, Robert. *Imperial Brotherhood: Gender and the Making of Cold War Foreign Policy.* Amherst: University of Massachusetts Press, 2003.

Dudziak, Mary. *Cold War Civil Rights: Race and the Image of American Democracy.* Princeton, NJ: Princeton University Press, 2000.

Gaddis, John L. *The Cold War: A New History.* New York: Penguin, 2005.

———. *Strategies of Containment: A Critical Appraisal of Postwar American National Security Policy.* New York: Oxford University Press, 2005.

———. *The United States and the Origins of the Cold War.* New York: Columbia University Press, 2000.

Kolko, Gabriel. *Confronting the Third World: United States Foreign Policy 1945–1980.* New York: Pantheon Books, 1988.

Krenn, Michael L. *Fall-Out Shelters for the Human Spirit: American Art and the Cold War.* Chapel Hill: University of North Carolina Press, 2005.

Lafeber, Walter. *America, Russia, and the Cold War, 1945–1966.* New York: Wiley, 1967.

Leffler, Melvyn P. *For the Soul of Mankind: The United States, the Soviet Union, and the Cold War.* New York: Hill and Wang, 2008.

Linn, Brian McAllister. *Elvis's Army: Cold War GIs and the Atomic Battlefield.* Cambridge, MA: Harvard University Press, 2016.

May, Elaine Tyler. *Homeward Bound: American Families in the Cold War Era.* New York: Basic Books, 1988.

Oshinsky, David M. *A Conspiracy So Immense: The World of Joe McCarthy.* New York: Oxford University Press, 2005.

Patterson, James T. *Grand Expectations: The United States, 1945–1974.* New York: Oxford University Press, 1996.

Powers, Richard Gid. *Not Without Honor: The History of American Anticommunism.* New York: Free Press, 1995.

Rhodes, Richard. *Arsenals of Folly: The Making of the Nuclear Arms Race.* New York: Knopf, 2007.

Saunders, Frances Stonor. *The Cultural Cold War: The CIA and the World of Arts and Letters.* New York: New Press, 1999.

Schrecker, Ellen. *Many Are the Crimes: McCarthyism in America.* New York: Little, Brown, 1998.

Schulman, Bruce J. *From Cotton Belt to Sunbelt: Federal Policy, Economic Development, and the Transformation of the South, 1938–1980.* New York: Oxford University Press, 1991.

Von Eschen, Penny. *Satchmo Blows Up the World: Jazz Ambassadors Play the Cold War.* Cambridge, MA: Harvard University Press, 2004.

Westad, Odd Arne. *The Global Cold War: Third World Interventions and the Making of Our Times.* New York: Cambridge University Press, 2005.

Whitfield, Stephen. *The Culture of the Cold War.* Baltimore: Johns Hopkins University Press, 1991.

26

The Affluent Society

I. Introduction

In 1958, Harvard economist and public intellectual John Kenneth Galbraith published *The Affluent Society*. Galbraith's celebrated book examined America's new post–World War II consumer economy and political culture. While noting the unparalleled riches of American economic growth, it criticized the underlying structures of an economy dedicated only to increasing production and the consumption of goods. Galbraith argued that the U.S. economy, based on an almost hedonistic consumption of luxury products, would inevitably lead to economic inequality as private-sector interests enriched themselves at the expense of the American public. Galbraith warned that an economy where "wants are increasingly created by the process by which they are satisfied" was unsound, unsustainable, and, ultimately, immoral. "The Affluent Society," he said, was anything but.[1]

Little Rock schools closed rather than allow integration. This 1958 photograph shows an African American high school girl watching school lessons on television. Library of Congress.

While economists and scholars debate the merits of Galbraith's warnings and predictions, his analysis was so insightful that the title of his book has come to serve as a ready label for postwar American society. In the two decades after the end of World War II, the American economy witnessed massive and sustained growth that reshaped American culture through the abundance of consumer goods. Standards of living—across all income levels—climbed to unparalleled heights and economic inequality plummeted.[2]

And yet, as Galbraith noted, the Affluent Society had fundamental flaws. The new consumer economy that lifted millions of Americans into its burgeoning middle class also reproduced existing inequalities. Women struggled to claim equal rights as full participants in American society. The poor struggled to win access to good schools, good healthcare, and good jobs. The same suburbs that gave middle-class Americans new space left cities withering in spirals of poverty and crime and caused irreversible ecological disruptions. The Jim Crow South tenaciously defended segregation, and Black Americans and other minorities suffered discrimination all across the country.

The contradictions of the Affluent Society defined the decade: unrivaled prosperity alongside persistent poverty, life-changing technological innovation alongside social and environmental destruction, expanded opportunity alongside entrenched discrimination, and new, liberating lifestyles alongside a stifling conformity.

Levittown in the early 1950s. Flickr / Creative Commons.

II. The Rise of the Suburbs

The seeds of a suburban nation were planted in New Deal government programs. At the height of the Great Depression, in 1932, some 250,000 households lost their property to foreclosure. A year later, half of all U.S. mortgages were in default. The foreclosure rate stood at more than one thousand per day. In response, FDR's New Deal created the Home Owners' Loan Corporation (HOLC), which began purchasing and refinancing existing mortgages at risk of default. The HOLC introduced the amortized mortgage, allowing borrowers to pay back interest and principal regularly over fifteen years instead of the then standard five-year mortgage that carried large balloon payments at the end of the contract. The HOLC eventually owned nearly one of every five mortgages in America. Though homeowners paid more for their homes under this new system, home ownership was opened to the multitudes who could now gain residential stability, lower monthly mortgage payments, and accrue wealth as property values rose over time.[3]

Additionally, the Federal Housing Administration (FHA), another New Deal organization, increased access to home ownership by insuring mortgages and protecting lenders from financial loss in the event of a default. Lenders, however, had to agree to offer low rates and terms of up to twenty or thirty years. Even more consumers could afford homes. Though only slightly more than a third of homes had an FHA-backed mortgage by 1964, FHA loans had a ripple effect, with private lenders granting more and more home loans even to non-FHA-backed borrowers. Government programs and subsidies like the HOLC and the FHA fueled the growth of home ownership and the rise of the suburbs.

Government spending during World War II pushed the United States out of the Depression and into an economic boom that would be sustained after the war by continued government spending. Government expenditures provided loans to veterans, subsidized corporate research and development, and built the interstate highway system. In the decades after World War II, business boomed, unionization peaked, wages rose, and sustained growth buoyed a new consumer economy. The Servicemen's Readjustment Act (popularly known as the G.I. Bill), passed in 1944, offered low-interest home loans, a stipend to attend college, loans to start a business, and unemployment benefits.

The rapid growth of home ownership and the rise of suburban communities helped drive the postwar economic boom. Builders created sprawling neighborhoods of single-family homes on the outskirts of

American cities. William Levitt built the first Levittown, the prototypical suburban community, in 1946 in Long Island, New York. Purchasing large acreage, subdividing lots, and contracting crews to build countless homes at economies of scale, Levitt offered affordable suburban housing to veterans and their families. Levitt became the prophet of the new suburbs, and his model of large-scale suburban development was duplicated by developers across the country. The country's suburban share of the population rose from 19.5 percent in 1940 to 30.7 percent by 1960. Home ownership rates rose from 44 percent in 1940 to almost 62 percent in 1960. Between 1940 and 1950, suburban communities with more than ten thousand people grew 22.1 percent, and planned communities grew at an astonishing rate of 126.1 percent.[4] As historian Lizabeth Cohen notes, these new suburbs "mushroomed in territorial size and the populations they harbored."[5] Between 1950 and 1970, America's suburban population nearly doubled to seventy-four million. Eighty-three percent of all population growth occurred in suburban places.[6]

The postwar construction boom fed into countless industries. As manufacturers converted from war materials back to consumer goods, and as the suburbs developed, appliance and automobile sales rose dramatically. Flush with rising wages and wartime savings, homeowners also used newly created installment plans to buy new consumer goods at once instead of saving for years to make major purchases. Credit cards, first issued in 1950, further increased access to credit. No longer stymied by the Depression or wartime restrictions, consumers bought countless washers, dryers, refrigerators, freezers, and, suddenly, televisions. The percentage of Americans that owned at least one television increased from 12 percent in 1950 to more than 87 percent in 1960. This new suburban economy also led to increased demand for automobiles. The percentage of American families owning cars increased from 54 percent in 1948 to 74 percent in 1959. Motor fuel consumption rose from some twenty-two million gallons in 1945 to around fifty-nine million gallons in 1958.[7]

On the surface, the postwar economic boom turned America into a land of abundance. For advantaged buyers, loans had never been easier to obtain, consumer goods had never been more accessible, single-family homes had never been so cheap, and well-paying jobs had never been more abundant. "If you had a college diploma, a dark suit, and anything between the ears," a businessman later recalled, "it was like an escalator; you just stood there and you moved up."[8] But the escalator did not serve everyone. Beneath aggregate numbers, racial disparity, sexual discrimination, and economic inequality persevered, undermining many of the assumptions of an Affluent Society.

In 1939 real estate appraisers arrived in sunny Pasadena, California. Armed with elaborate questionnaires to evaluate the city's building conditions, the appraisers were well versed in the policies of the HOLC. In one neighborhood, most structures were rated in "fair" repair, and appraisers noted a lack of "construction hazards or flood threats." However, they concluded that the area "is detrimentally affected by 10 owner occupant Negro families." While "the Negroes are said to be of the better class," the appraisers concluded, "it seems inevitable that ownership and property values will drift to lower levels."[9]

Wealth created by the booming economy filtered through social structures with built-in privileges and prejudices. Just when many middle- and working-class white American families began their journey of upward mobility by moving to the suburbs with the help of government programs such as the FHA and the G.I. Bill, many African Americans and other racial minorities found themselves systematically shut out.

A look at the relationship between federal organizations such as the HOLC, the FHA, and private banks, lenders, and real estate agents tells the story of standardized policies that produced a segregated housing

Black communities in cities such as Detroit, Chicago, Brooklyn, and Atlanta (mapped here) experienced redlining, the process by which banks and other organizations demarcated minority neighborhoods on a map with a red line. Doing so made visible the areas they believed were unfit for their services, directly denying Black residents loans, but also, indirectly, housing, groceries, and other necessities of modern life. National Archives.

market. At the core of HOLC appraisal techniques, which reflected the existing practices of private real estate agents, was the pernicious insistence that mixed-race and minority-dominated neighborhoods were credit risks. In partnership with local lenders and real estate agents, the HOLC created Residential Security Maps to identify high- and low-risk lending areas. People familiar with the local real estate market filled out uniform surveys on each neighborhood. Relying on this information, the HOLC assigned every neighborhood a letter grade from A to D and a corresponding color code. The least secure, highest-risk neighborhoods for loans received a D grade and the color red. Banks limited loans in such "redlined" areas.[10]

Phrases like *subversive racial elements* and *racial hazards* pervade the redlined-area description files of surveyors and HOLC officials. Los Angeles's Echo Park neighborhood, for instance, had concentrations of Japanese and African Americans and a "sprinkling of Russians and Mexicans." The HOLC security map and survey noted that the neighborhood's "adverse racial influences which are noticeably increasing inevitably presage lower values, rentals and a rapid decrease in residential desirability."[11]

While the HOLC was a fairly short-lived New Deal agency, the influence of its security maps lived on in the FHA and Veterans Administration

1938 Brooklyn redlining map. National Archives.

(VA), the latter of which dispensed G.I. Bill–backed mortgages. Both of these government organizations, which reinforced the standards followed by private lenders, refused to back bank mortgages in "redlined" neighborhoods. On the one hand, FHA- and VA-backed loans were an enormous boon to those who qualified for them. Millions of Americans received mortgages that they otherwise would not have qualified for. But FHA-backed mortgages were not available to all. Racial minorities could not get loans for property improvements in their own neighborhoods and were denied mortgages to purchase property in other areas for fear that their presence would extend the red line into a new community. Levittown, the poster child of the new suburban America, only allowed whites to purchase homes. Thus, FHA policies and private developers increased home ownership and stability for white Americans while simultaneously creating and enforcing racial segregation.

The exclusionary structures of the postwar economy prompted protest from African Americans and other minorities who were excluded. Fair housing, equal employment, consumer access, and educational opportunity, for instance, all emerged as priorities of a brewing civil rights movement. In 1948, the U.S. Supreme Court sided with African American plaintiffs and, in *Shelley v. Kraemer*, declared racially restrictive neighborhood housing covenants—property deed restrictions barring sales to racial minorities—legally unenforceable. Discrimination and segregation continued, however, and activists would continue to push for fair housing practices.

During the 1950s and early 1960s many Americans retreated to the suburbs to enjoy the new consumer economy and search for some normalcy and security after the instability of depression and war. But many could not. It was both the limits and opportunities of housing, then, that shaped the contours of postwar American society. Moreover, the postwar suburban boom not only exacerbated racial and class inequalities, it precipitated a major environmental crisis.

The introduction of mass-production techniques in housing wrought ecological destruction. Developers sought cheaper land ever farther way from urban cores, wreaking havoc on particularly sensitive areas such as wetlands, hills, and floodplains. "A territory roughly the size of Rhode Island," historian Adam Rome wrote, "was bulldozed for urban development" every year.[12] Innovative construction strategies, government incentives, high consumer demand, and low energy prices all pushed builders away from more sustainable, energy-conserving building projects. Typical postwar tract houses were difficult to cool in the summer and heat in the

School desegregation was a tense experience for all involved, but none more so than the African American students who integrated white schools. The Little Rock Nine were the first to do so in Arkansas. Their escorts, the 101st Airborne Division of the U.S. Army, protected students who took that first step in 1957. Wikimedia.

winter. Many were equipped with malfunctioning septic tanks that polluted local groundwater. Such destructiveness did not go unnoticed. By the time Rachel Carson published *Silent Spring*, a forceful denunciation of the excessive use of pesticides such as DDT in agricultural and domestic settings, in 1962, many Americans were already primed to receive her message. Stories of kitchen faucets spouting detergent foams and children playing in effluents brought the point home: comfort and convenience did not have to come at such cost. And yet most of the Americans who joined the early environmentalist crusades of the 1950s and 1960s rarely questioned the foundations of the suburban ideal. Americans increasingly relied upon automobiles and idealized the single-family home, blunting any major push to shift prevailing patterns of land and energy use.[13]

III. Race and Education

Older battles over racial exclusion also confronted postwar American society. One long-simmering struggle targeted segregated schooling. In 1896, the Supreme Court declared the principle of "separate but equal" constitu-

The NAACP was a key organization in the fight to end legalized racial discrimination. In this 1956 photograph, NAACP leaders, including Thurgood Marshall, who would become the first African American Supreme Court Justice, hold a poster decrying racial bias in Mississippi in 1956. Library of Congress.

tional. Segregated schooling, however, was rarely "equal": in practice, Black Americans, particularly in the South, received fewer funds, attended inadequate facilities, and studied with substandard materials. African Americans' battle against educational inequality stretched across half a century before the Supreme Court again took up the merits of "separate but equal."

On May 17, 1954, after two years of argument, re-argument, and deliberation, Chief Justice Earl Warren announced the Supreme Court's decision on segregated schooling in *Brown v. Board of Education* (1954). The court found by a unanimous 9–0 vote that racial segregation violated the Equal Protection Clause of the Fourteenth Amendment. The court's decision declared, "Separate educational facilities are inherently unequal." "Separate but equal" was made unconstitutional.[14]

Decades of African American–led litigation, local agitation against racial inequality, and liberal Supreme Court justices made *Brown* possible. In the early 1930s, the NAACP began a concerted effort to erode the legal underpinnings of segregation in the American South. Legal, or de jure, segregation subjected racial minorities to discriminatory laws and policies. Law and custom in the South hardened anti-Black restrictions. But through a series of carefully chosen and contested court cases concerning education, disfranchisement, and jury selection, NAACP lawyers such as Charles Hamilton Houston, Robert L. Clark, and future Supreme Court Justice Thurgood Marshall undermined Jim Crow's constitutional underpinnings. These attorneys initially sought to demonstrate that states systematically failed to provide African American students "equal" resources and facilities, and thus failed to live up to *Plessy*. By the late 1940s activists began to more forcefully challenge the assumptions that "separate" was constitutional at all.

Though remembered as just one lawsuit, *Brown v. Board of Education* consolidated five separate cases that had originated in the southeastern United States: *Briggs v. Elliott* (South Carolina), *Davis v. County School Board of Prince Edward County* (Virginia), *Beulah v. Belton* (Delaware), *Bolling v. Sharpe* (Washington, D.C.), and *Brown v. Board of Education* (Kansas). Working with local activists already involved in desegregation fights, the NAACP purposely chose cases with a diverse set of local backgrounds to show that segregation was not just an issue in the Deep South, and that a sweeping judgment on the fundamental constitutionality of *Plessy* was needed.

Briggs v. Elliott, the first case accepted by the NAACP, illustrated the plight of segregated Black schools. *Briggs* originated in rural Clarendon County, South Carolina, where taxpayers in 1950 spent $179 to educate each white student and $43 for each Black student. The district's twelve white schools were cumulatively worth $673,850; the value of its sixty-one Black schools (mostly dilapidated, overcrowded shacks) was $194,575.[15] While *Briggs* underscored the South's failure to follow *Plessy*, the *Brown* suit focused less on material disparities between Black and white schools (which were significantly less than in places like Clarendon County) and more on the social and spiritual degradation that accompanied legal segregation. This case cut to the basic question of whether "separate" was itself inherently unequal. The NAACP said the two notions were incompatible. As one witness before the U.S. District Court of Kansas said, "The entire colored race is craving light, and the only way to reach the light is to start [Black and white] children together in their infancy and they come up together."[16]

To make its case, the NAACP marshaled historical and social scientific evidence. The Court found the historical evidence inconclusive and

In 1959, photographer John Bledsoe captured this image of the crowd on the steps of the Arkansas state capitol building protesting the federally mandated integration of Little Rock's Central High School. This image shows how worries about desegregation were bound up with other concerns, such as the reach of communism and government power. Library of Congress.

drew their ruling more heavily from the NAACP's argument that segregation psychologically damaged Black children. To make this argument, association lawyers relied on social scientific evidence, such as the famous doll experiments of Kenneth and Mamie Clark. The Clarks demonstrated that while young white girls would naturally choose to play with white dolls, young Black girls would, too. The Clarks argued that Black children's aesthetic and moral preference for white dolls demonstrated the pernicious effects and self-loathing produced by segregation.

Identifying and denouncing injustice, though, is different from rectifying it. Though *Brown* repudiated *Plessy*, the Court's orders did not extend to segregation in places other than public schools and, even then, to preserve a unanimous decision for such an historically important case, the justices set aside the divisive yet essential question of enforcement. Their infamously ambiguous order in 1955 (what came to be known as *Brown II*) that school districts desegregate "with all deliberate speed" was so vague and ineffectual that it left the actual business of desegregation in the hands of those who opposed it.

In most of the South, as well as the rest of the country, school integration did not occur on a wide scale until well after *Brown*. Only in the 1964 Civil Rights Act did the federal government finally implement some enforcement of the *Brown* decision by threatening to withhold funding from recalcitrant school districts, but even then southern districts found loopholes. Court decisions such as *Green v. New Kent County* (1968) and *Alexander v. Holmes* (1969) finally closed some of those loopholes, such as "freedom of choice" plans, to compel some measure of actual integration.

When *Brown* finally was enforced in the South, the quantitative impact was staggering. In 1968, fourteen years after *Brown*, some 80 percent of school-age Black southerners remained in schools that were 90 to 100 percent nonwhite. By 1972, though, just 25 percent were in such schools, and 55 percent remained in schools with a simple nonwhite minority. By many measures, the public schools of the South became, ironically, the most integrated in the nation.[17]

As a landmark moment in American history, *Brown*'s significance perhaps lies less in immediate tangible changes—which were slow, partial, and inseparable from a much longer chain of events—than in the idealism it expressed and the momentum it created. The nation's highest court had attacked one of the fundamental supports of Jim Crow segregation and offered constitutional cover for the creation of one of the greatest social movements in American history.

IV. Civil Rights in an Affluent Society

Education was but one aspect of the nation's Jim Crow machinery. African Americans had been fighting against a variety of racist policies, cultures, and beliefs in all aspects of American life. And while the struggle for Black inclusion had few victories before World War II, the war and the Double V campaign for victory against fascism abroad and racism at home, as well as the postwar economic boom, led to rising expectations for many African Americans. When persistent racism and racial segregation undercut the promise of economic and social mobility, African Americans began mobilizing on an unprecedented scale against the various discriminatory social and legal structures.

While many of the civil rights movement's most memorable and important moments, such as the sit-ins, the Freedom Rides, and especially the March on Washington, occurred in the 1960s, the 1950s were a significant decade in the sometimes tragic, sometimes triumphant march of civil rights in the United States. In 1953, years before Rosa Parks's iconic confrontation on a Montgomery city bus, an African American woman named Sarah Keys publicly challenged segregated public transportation.

Keys, then serving in the Women's Army Corps, traveled from her Army base in New Jersey back to North Carolina to visit her family. When the bus stopped in North Carolina, the driver asked her to give up her seat for a white customer. Her refusal to do so landed her in jail in 1953 and led to a landmark 1955 decision, *Sarah Keys v. Carolina Coach Company*, in which the Interstate Commerce Commission ruled that "separate but equal" violated the Interstate Commerce Clause of the U.S. Constitution. Poorly enforced, it nevertheless gave legal coverage for the Freedom Riders years later and motivated further assaults against Jim Crow.

But if some events encouraged civil rights workers with the promise of progress, others were so savage they convinced activists that they could do nothing but resist. In the summer of 1955, two white men in Mississippi kidnapped and brutally murdered fourteen-year-old Emmett Till. Till, visiting from Chicago and perhaps unfamiliar with the "etiquette" of Jim Crow, allegedly whistled at a white woman named Carolyn Bryant. Her husband, Roy Bryant, and another man, J. W. Milam, abducted Till from his relatives' home, beat him, mutilated him, shot him, and threw his body in the Tallahatchie River. Emmett's mother held an open-casket funeral so that Till's disfigured body could make national

This segregated drinking fountain was located on the grounds of the Halifax County courthouse in North Carolina. Photograph, April 1938. Wikimedia.

news. The men were brought to trial. The evidence was damning, but an all-white jury found the two not guilty. Mere months after the decision, the two boasted of their crime, in all of its brutal detail, in *Look* magazine. "They ain't gonna go to school with my kids," Milam said. They wanted "to make an example of [Till]—just so everybody can know how me and my folks stand."[18] The Till case became an indelible memory for the young Black men and women soon to propel the civil rights movement forward.

On December 1, 1955, four months after Till's death and six days after the *Keys v. Carolina Coach Company* decision, Rosa Parks refused to surrender her seat on a Montgomery city bus and was arrested. Montgomery's public transportation system had longstanding rules requiring African American passengers to sit in the back of the bus and to give up their seats to white passengers if the buses filled. Parks was not the first to protest the policy by staying seated, but she was the first around whom Montgomery activists rallied.

Activists sprang into action. Joanne Robinson, who as head of the Women's Political Council had long fought against the city's segregated busing, worked long into the night with a colleague and two students from Alabama State College to mimeograph over fifty thousand handbills calling for an immediate boycott. Montgomery's Black community responded, and local ministers and civil rights workers formed the Montgomery Improvement Association (MIA) to coordinate an organized, sustained boycott of the city's buses. The Montgomery Bus Boycott lasted from December 1955 until December 20, 1956, when the Supreme Court ordered their integration. The boycott not only crushed segregation in Montgomery's public transportation, it energized the entire civil rights movement and established the leadership of the MIA's president, a recently arrived, twenty-six-year-old Baptist minister named Martin Luther King Jr.

Motivated by the success of the Montgomery boycott, King and other Black leaders looked to continue the fight. In 1957, King, fellow ministers such as Ralph Abernathy and Fred Shuttlesworth, and key staffers such as Ella Baker and Septima Clark helped create and run the Southern Christian Leadership Conference (SCLC) to coordinate civil rights groups across the South in their efforts to organize and sustain boycotts, protests, and other assaults against Jim Crow discrimination.

As pressure built, Congress passed the Civil Rights Act of 1957, the first such measure passed since Reconstruction. The act was compromised away nearly to nothing, although it did achieve some gains, such as creating the Department of Justice's Civil Rights Commission, which was charged with investigating claims of racial discrimination. And yet, despite its weakness, the act signaled that pressure was finally mounting on Americans to confront the legacy of discrimination.

Despite successes at both the local and national level, the civil rights movement faced bitter opposition. Those opposed to the movement often used violent tactics to scare and intimidate African Americans and subvert legal rulings and court orders. For example, a year into the Montgomery bus boycott, angry white southerners bombed four African American churches as well as the homes of King and fellow civil rights leader E. D. Nixon. Though King, Nixon, and the MIA persevered in the face of such violence, it was only a taste of things to come. Such unremitting hostility and violence left the outcome of the burgeoning civil rights movement in doubt. Despite its successes, civil rights activists looked back on the 1950s as a decade of mixed results and incomplete accomplishments. While the bus boycott, Supreme Court rulings, and other civil rights activities signaled progress, church bombings, death threats, and stubborn legislators demonstrated the distance that still needed to be traveled.

As shown in this 1958 advertisement for a "Westinghouse with Cold Injector," a midcentury marketing frenzy targeted female consumers by touting technological innovations designed to make housework easier. Westinghouse.

V. Gender and Culture in the Affluent Society

America's consumer economy reshaped how Americans experienced culture and shaped their identities. The Affluent Society gave Americans new

You can shop at noon, serve the same afternoon

No more feeling and fumbling and waiting for things to get cold— not with a Westinghouse! Actual tests prove the Cold Injector recovers cold 4 times faster— floods the whole interior with quick chill. Here are the other ways the Westinghouse lives up to your dreams: ten Store-and-Serve units in a FROST-FREE refrigerator— separate home freezer that holds 190 lbs.—magnetic door—new styling. Yet Westinghouse refrigerators start as low as $199.95 less trade. See them for yourself—soon!

YOU CAN BE SURE...IF IT'S

Westinghouse

Westinghouse Electric Corp., Columbus, Ohio

experiences, new outlets, and new ways to understand and interact with one another.

"The American household is on the threshold of a revolution," the *New York Times* declared in August 1948. "The reason is television."[19] Television was presented to the American public at the New York World's Fair in 1939, but commercialization of the new medium in the United States lagged during the war years. In 1947, though, regular full-scale broadcasting became available to the public. Television was instantly popular, so much so that by early 1948 *Newsweek* reported that it was "catching on like a case of high-toned scarlet fever."[20] Indeed, between 1948 and 1955 close to two thirds of the nation's households purchased a television set. By the end of the 1950s, 90 percent of American families had one and the average viewer was tuning in for almost five hours a day.[21]

The technological ability to transmit images via radio waves gave birth to television. Television borrowed radio's organizational structure, too. The big radio broadcasting companies—NBC, CBS, and the American Broadcasting Corporation (ABC)—used their technical expertise and capital reserves to conquer the airwaves. They acquired licenses to local stations and eliminated their few independent competitors. The refusal of the Federal Communication Commission (FCC) to issue any new licenses between 1948 and 1955 was a de facto endorsement of the big three's stranglehold on the market.

In addition to replicating radio's organizational structure, television also looked to radio for content. Many of the early programs were adaptations of popular radio variety and comedy shows, including *The Ed Sullivan Show* and *Milton Berle's Texaco Star Theater*. These were accompanied by live plays, dramas, sports, and situation comedies. Because of the cost and difficulty of recording, most programs were broadcast live, forcing stations across the country to air shows at the same time. And since audiences had a limited number of channels to choose from, viewing experiences were broadly shared. More than two thirds of television-owning households, for instance, watched popular shows such as *I Love Lucy*.

The limited number of channels and programs meant that networks selected programs that appealed to the widest possible audience to draw viewers and advertisers, television's greatest financers. By the mid-1950s, an hour of primetime programming cost about $150,000 (about $1.5 million in today's dollars) to produce. This proved too expensive for most commercial sponsors, who began turning to a joint financing model of thirty-second spot ads. The need to appeal to as many people as possible

Advertising was everywhere in the 1950s, including on TV shows such as the quiz show *Twenty One*, sponsored by Geritol, a dietary supplement. Library of Congress.

promoted the production of noncontroversial shows aimed at the entire family. Programs such as *Father Knows Best* and *Leave it to Beaver* featured light topics, humor, and a guaranteed happy ending the whole family could enjoy.[22]

Television's broad appeal, however, was about more than money and entertainment. Shows of the 1950s, such as *Father Knows Best* and *I Love Lucy*, idealized the nuclear family, "traditional" gender roles, and white, middle-class domesticity. *Leave It to Beaver*, which became the prototypical example of the 1950s television family, depicted its breadwinner father and homemaker mother guiding their children through life lessons. Such shows, and Cold War America more broadly, reinforced a popular consensus that such lifestyles were not only beneficial but the most effective way to safeguard American prosperity against communist threats and social "deviancy."

Postwar prosperity facilitated, and in turn was supported by, the ongoing postwar baby boom. From 1946 to 1964, American fertility experienced an unprecedented spike. A century of declining birth rates abruptly reversed. Although popular memory credits the cause of the baby boom to the return of virile soldiers from battle, the real story is more nuanced. After years of economic depression, families were now wealthy enough to support larger families and had homes large enough to accommodate them, while women married younger and American culture celebrated the ideal of a large, insular family.

Underlying this "reproductive consensus" was the new cult of professionalism that pervaded postwar American culture, including the professionalization of homemaking. Mothers and fathers alike flocked to the experts for their opinions on marriage, sexuality, and, most especially, child-rearing. Psychiatrists held an almost mythic status as people took their opinions and prescriptions, as well as their vocabulary, into their everyday life. Books like Dr. Spock's *Baby and Child Care* (1946) were diligently studied by women who took their career as housewife as just that: a career, complete with all the demands and professional trappings of job development and training. And since most women had multiple children roughly the same age as their neighbors' children, a cultural obsession with kids flourished throughout the era. Women bore the brunt of this pressure, chided if they did not give enough of their time to the children—especially if it was because of a career—yet cautioned that spending too much time would lead to "Momism," producing "sissy" boys who would be incapable of contributing to society and extremely susceptible to the communist threat.

A new youth culture exploded within the greater American popular culture. On the one hand, the anxieties of the atomic age hit America's youth particularly hard. Keenly aware of the discontent bubbling beneath the surface of the Affluent Society, many youth embraced rebellion. The 1955 film *Rebel Without a Cause* demonstrated the restlessness and emotional incertitude of the postwar generation raised in increasing affluence yet increasingly unsatisfied with their comfortable lives. At the same time, perhaps yearning for something beyond the "massification" of American culture yet having few other options to turn to beyond popular culture, American youth embraced rock 'n' roll. They listened to Little Richard, Buddy Holly, and especially Elvis Presley (whose sexually suggestive hip movements were judged subversive).

The popularity of rock 'n' roll had not yet blossomed into the countercultural musical revolution of the coming decade, but it provided a magnet for teenage restlessness and rebellion. "Television and Elvis," the musician Bruce Springsteen recollected, "gave us full access to a new language, a new form of communication, a new way of being, a new way

While many Black musicians such as Chuck Berry helped pioneer rock 'n' roll, white artists such as Elvis Presley brought it into the mainstream American culture. Elvis's good looks, sensual dancing, and sonorous voice stole the hearts of millions of American teenage girls, who were at that moment becoming a central segment of the consumer population. Wikimedia.

of looking, a new way of thinking; about sex, about race, about identity, about life; a new way of being an American, a human being; and a new way of hearing music." American youth had seen so little of Elvis's energy and sensuality elsewhere in their culture. "Once Elvis came across the airwaves," Springsteen said, "once he was heard and seen in action, you could not put the genie back in the bottle. After that moment, there was yesterday, and there was today, and there was a red hot, rockabilly forging of a new tomorrow, before your very eyes."[23]

Other Americans took larger steps to reject the expected conformity of the Affluent Society. The writers, poets, and musicians of the Beat Generation, disillusioned with capitalism, consumerism, and traditional gender roles, sought a deeper meaning in life. Beats traveled across the country, studied Eastern religions, and experimented with drugs, sex, and art.

Behind the scenes, Americans were challenging sexual mores. The gay rights movement, for instance, stretched back into the Affluent Society. While the country proclaimed homosexuality a mental disorder, gay men established the Mattachine Society in Los Angeles and gay women formed the Daughters of Bilitis in San Francisco as support groups. They held meetings, distributed literature, provided legal and counseling services, and formed chapters across the country. Much of their work, however, remained secretive because homosexuals risked arrest and abuse if discovered.[24]

Society's "consensus," on everything from the consumer economy to gender roles, did not go unchallenged. Much discontent was channeled through the machine itself: advertisers sold rebellion no less than they sold baking soda. And yet others were rejecting the old ways, choosing new lifestyles, challenging old hierarchies, and embarking on new paths.

VI. Politics and Ideology in the Affluent Society

Postwar economic prosperity and the creation of new suburban spaces inevitably shaped American politics. In stark contrast to the Great Depression, the new prosperity renewed belief in the superiority of capitalism, cultural conservatism, and religion.

In the 1930s, the economic ravages of the international economic catastrophe knocked the legs out from under the intellectual justifications for keeping government out of the economy. And yet pockets of true believers kept alive the gospel of the free market. The single most important was the National Association of Manufacturers (NAM). In the midst of the depression, NAM reinvented itself and went on the offensive, initiating advertising campaigns supporting "free enterprise" and "The American Way of Life."[25] More importantly, NAM became a node for business leaders, such as J. Howard Pew of Sun Oil and Jasper Crane of DuPont Chemical Co., to network with like-minded individuals and take the message of free enterprise to the American people. The network of business leaders that NAM brought together in the midst of the Great Depression formed the financial, organizational, and ideological underpinnings of the free market advocacy groups that emerged and found ready adherents in America's new suburban spaces in the postwar decades.

One of the most important advocacy groups that sprang up after the war was Leonard Read's Foundation for Economic Education (FEE). Read founded FEE in 1946 on the premise that "The American Way of Life" was essentially individualistic and that the best way to protect and promote that individualism was through libertarian economics. Libertarianism took as its core principle the promotion of individual liberty, property rights, and an economy with a minimum of government regulation. FEE, whose advisory board and supporters came mostly from the NAM network of Pew and Crane, became a key ideological factory, supplying businesses, service clubs, churches, schools, and universities with a steady stream of libertarian literature, much of it authored by Austrian economist Ludwig von Mises.[26]

Shortly after FEE's formation, Austrian economist and libertarian intellectual Friedrich Hayek founded the Mont Pelerin Society (MPS) in 1947. The MPS brought together libertarian intellectuals from both sides of the Atlantic to challenge Keynesian economics—the dominant notion that government fiscal and monetary policy were necessary economic tools—in academia. University of Chicago economist Milton Friedman became its president. Friedman (and his Chicago School of Economics) and the MPS became some of the most influential free market advocates in the world and helped legitimize for many the libertarian ideology so successfully evangelized by FEE, its descendant organizations, and libertarian popularizers such as the novelist Ayn Rand.[27]

Libertarian politics and evangelical religion were shaping the origins of a new conservative, suburban constituency. Suburban communities' distance from government and other top-down community-building mechanisms—despite relying on government subsidies and government programs—left a social void that evangelical churches eagerly filled. More often than not the theology and ideology of these churches reinforced socially conservative views while simultaneously reinforcing congregants' belief in economic individualism. Novelist Ayn Rand, meanwhile, whose novels *The Fountainhead* (1943) and *Atlas Shrugged* (1957) were two of the decades' best sellers, helped move the ideas of individualism, "rational self-interest," and "the virtue of selfishness" outside the halls of business and academia and into suburbia. The ethos of individualism became the building blocks for a new political movement. And yet, while

Undated portrait of President Harry S. Truman. National Archives.

the growing suburbs and their brewing conservative ideology eventually proved immensely important in American political life, their impact was not immediately felt. They did not yet have a champion.

In the post–World War II years the Republican Party faced a fork in the road. Its complete lack of electoral success since the Depression led to a battle within the party about how to revive its electoral prospects. The more conservative faction, represented by Ohio senator Robert Taft (son of former president William Howard Taft) and backed by many party activists and financiers such as J. Howard Pew, sought to take the party further to the right, particularly in economic matters, by rolling back New Deal programs and policies. On the other hand, the more moderate wing of the party, led by men such as New York governor Thomas Dewey and Nelson Rockefeller, sought to embrace and reform New Deal programs and policies. There were further disagreements among party members about how involved the United States should be in the world. Issues such as foreign aid, collective security, and how best to fight communism divided the party.

Initially, the moderates, or "liberals," won control of the party with the nomination of Thomas Dewey in 1948. Dewey's shocking loss to Truman, however, emboldened conservatives, who rallied around Taft as the 1952 presidential primaries approached. With the conservative banner riding high in the party, General Dwight Eisenhower ("Ike"), most recently North Atlantic Treaty Organization (NATO) supreme commander, felt obliged to join the race in order to beat back the conservatives and "prevent one of our great two Parties from adopting a course which could lead to national suicide." In addition to his fear that Taft and the conservatives would undermine collective security arrangements such as NATO, he also berated the "neanderthals" in his party for their anti–New Deal stance. Eisenhower felt that the best way to stop communism was to undercut its appeal by alleviating the conditions under which it was most attractive. That meant supporting New Deal programs. There was also a political calculus to Eisenhower's position. He observed, "Should any political party attempt to abolish social security, unemployment insurance, and eliminate labor laws and farm programs, you would not hear of that party again in our political history."[28]

The primary contest between Taft and Eisenhower was close and controversial. Taft supporters claimed that Eisenhower stole the nomination from Taft at the convention. Eisenhower, attempting to placate the conservatives in his party, picked California congressman and virulent anticommunist Richard Nixon as his running mate. With the Republican nomination sewn up, the immensely popular Eisenhower swept to victory in the 1952 general election, easily besting Truman's hand-picked successor, Adlai Stevenson. Eisenhower's popularity boosted Republicans across the country, leading them to majorities in both houses of Congress.

The Republican sweep in the 1952 election, owing in part to Eisenhower's popularity, translated into few tangible legislative accomplishments. Within two years of his election, the moderate Eisenhower saw his legislative proposals routinely defeated by an unlikely alliance of conservative Republicans, who thought Eisenhower was going too far, and liberal Democrats, who thought he was not going far enough. For example, in 1954 Eisenhower proposed a national healthcare plan that would have provided federal support for increasing healthcare coverage across the nation without getting the government directly involved in regulating the healthcare industry. The proposal was defeated in the house by a 238–134 vote with a swing bloc of seventy-five conservative Republicans joining liberal Democrats voting against the plan.[29] Eisenhower's proposals in education and agriculture often suffered similar defeats. By the end of his presidency, Ike's domestic legislative achievements were largely limited to expanding social security; making Health, Education and Welfare (HEW) a cabinet position; passing the National Defense Education Act; and bolstering federal support to education, particularly in math and science.

As with any president, however, Eisenhower's impact was bigger than just legislation. Ike's "middle of the road" philosophy guided his foreign policy as much as his domestic agenda. He sought to keep the United States from direct interventions abroad by bolstering anticommunist and procapitalist allies. Ike funneled money to the French in Vietnam fighting the Ho Chi Minh–led communists, walked a tight line between helping Chiang Kai-Shek's Taiwan without overtly provoking Mao Zedong's China, and materially backed groups that destabilized "unfriendly" governments in Iran and Guatemala. The centerpiece of Ike's Soviet policy, meanwhile, was the threat of "massive retaliation," or the threat of nuclear force in the face of communist expansion, thereby checking Soviet expansion without direct American involvement. While Ike's "mainstream" "middle way" won broad popular support, his own party was slowly moving away from his positions. By 1964 the party had moved far enough to the right to nominate Arizona senator Barry Goldwater, the most conservative candidate in a generation. The political moderation of the Affluent Society proved little more than a way station on the road to liberal reforms and a more distant conservative ascendancy.

VII. Conclusion

The postwar American "consensus" held great promise. Despite the looming threat of nuclear war, millions experienced an unprecedented prosperity and an increasingly proud American identity. Prosperity seemed to promise ever higher standards of living. But things fell apart, and the center could not hold: wracked by contradiction, dissent, discrimination, and inequality, the Affluent Society stood on the precipice of revolution.

VIII. Reference Material

This chapter was edited by James McKay, with content contributions by Edwin C. Breeden, Aaron Cowan, Elsa Devienne, Maggie Flamingo, Destin Jenkins, Kyle Livie, Jennifer Mandel, James McKay, Laura Redford, Ronny Regev, and Tanya Roth.

Recommended citation: Edwin C. Breeden et al., "The Affluent Society," James McKay, ed., in *The American Yawp*, eds. Joseph Locke and Ben Wright (Stanford, CA: Stanford University Press, 2019).

NOTES TO CHAPTER 26

1. John Kenneth Galbraith, *The Affluent Society* (New York: Houghton Mifflin, 1958), 129.

2. See, for example, Claudia Goldin and Robert A. Margo, "The Great Compression: The Wage Structure in the United States at Mid-Century," *Quarterly Journal of Economics* 107 (February 1992): 1–34.

3. Price Fishback, Jonathan Rose, and Kenneth Snowden, *Well Worth Saving: How the New Deal Safeguarded Home Ownership* (Chicago: University of Chicago Press, 2013).

4. Leo Schnore, "The Growth of Metropolitan Suburbs," *American Sociological Review* 22 (April 1957): 169.

5. Lizabeth Cohen, *A Consumers' Republic: The Politics of Mass Consumption in Postwar America* (New York: Random House, 2002), 202.

6. Elaine Tyler May, *Homeward Bound: American Families in the Cold War Era* (New York, Basic Books, 1999), 152.

7. Leo Fishman, *The American Economy* (Princeton, NJ: Van Nostrand, 1962), 560.

8. John P. Diggins, *The Proud Decades: America in War and in Peace, 1941–1960* (New York: Norton, 1989), 219.

9. David Kushner, *Levittown: Two Families, One Tycoon, and the Fight for Civil Rights in America's Legendary Suburb* (New York: Bloomsbury Press, 2009), 17.

10. Thomas Sugrue, *The Origins of the Urban Crisis: Race and Inequality in Postwar Detroit* (Princeton, NJ: Princeton University Press, 2005).

11. Becky M. Nicolaides, *My Blue Heaven: Life and Politics in the Working–Class Suburbs of Los Angeles, 1920–1965* (Chicago: University of Chicago Press, 2002), 193.

12. Adam W. Rome, *The Bulldozer in the Countryside: Suburban Sprawl and the Rise of American Environmentalism* (Cambridge: Cambridge University Press, 2001), 7.

13. See also J. R. McNeill and Peter Engelke, *The Great Acceleration: An Environmental History of the Anthropocene* (Cambridge, MA: Harvard University Press, 2016); Andrew Needham, *Power Lines: Phoenix and the Making of the Modern Southwest* (Princeton: Princeton University Press, 2014); and Ted Steinberg, *Down to Earth: Nature's Role in American History* (New York: Oxford University Press, 2002).

14. *Oliver Brown, et al. v. Board of Education of Topeka, et al.*, 347 U.S. 483 (1954).

15. James T. Patterson and William W. Freehling, *Brown v. Board of Education: A Civil Rights Milestone and Its Troubled Legacy* (New York: Oxford University Press, 2001), 25; Pete Daniel, *Standing at the Crossroads: Southern Life in the Twentieth Century* (Baltimore: Johns Hopkins University Press, 1996), 161–164.

16. Patterson and Freehling, *Brown v. Board*, xxv.

17. Charles T. Clotfelter, *After Brown: The Rise and Retreat of School Desegregation* (Princeton, NJ: Princeton University Press, 2011), 6.

18. William Bradford Huie, "The Shocking Story of Approved Killing in Mississippi," *Look* (January 24, 1956), 46–50.

19. Lewis L. Gould, *Watching Television Come of Age: The New York Times Reviews by Jack Gould* (Austin: University of Texas Press, 2002), 186.

20. Gary Edgerton, *Columbia History of American Television* (New York: Columbia University Press, 2009), 90.

21. Ibid., 178.

22. Christopher H. Sterling and John Michael Kittross, *Stay Tuned: A History of American Broadcasting* (New York: Routledge, 2001), 364.

23. Bruce Springsteen, "SXSW Keynote Address," *Rolling Stone* (March 28, 2012), http://www.rollingstone.com/music/news/exclusive-the-complete-text-of -bruce-springsteens-sxsw-keynote-address-20120328.

24. John D'Emilio, *Sexual Politics, Sexual Communities*, 2nd ed. (Chicago: University of Chicago Press, 2012), 102–103.

25. See Richard Tedlow, "The National Association of Manufacturers and Public Relations During the New Deal," *Business History Review* 50 (Spring 1976), 25–45; and Wendy Wall, *Inventing the "American Way": The Politics of Consensus from the New Deal to the Civil Rights Movement* (New York: Oxford University Press, 2008).

26. Gregory Eow, "Fighting a New Deal: Intellectual Origins of the Reagan Revolution, 1932–1952," PhD diss., Rice University, 2007; Brian Doherty, *Radicals for Capitalism: A Freewheeling History of the Modern American Libertarian Movement* (New York: Public Affairs, 2007); and Kim Phillips Fein, *Invisible*

Hands: The Businessmen's Crusade Against the New Deal (New York: Norton, 2009), 43–55.

27. Angus Burgin, *The Great Persuasion: Reinventing Free Markets Since the Depression* (Cambridge, MA: Harvard University Press, 2012); Jennifer Burns, *Goddess of the Market: Ayn Rand and the American Right* (New York: Oxford University Press, 2009).

28. Allan J. Lichtman, *White Protestant Nation: The Rise of the American Conservative Movement* (New York: Atlantic Monthly Press, 2008), 180, 201, 185.

29. Steven Wagner, *Eisenhower Republicanism Pursuing the Middle Way* (DeKalb: Northern Illinois University Press, 2006), 15.

RECOMMENDED READING

Boyle, Kevin. *The UAW and the Heyday of American Liberalism, 1945–1968.* Ithaca, NY: Cornell University Press, 1995.

Branch, Taylor. *Parting the Waters: America in the King Years, 1954–1963.* New York: Simon and Schuster, 1988.

Brown, Kate. *Plutopia: Nuclear Families, Atomic Cities, and the Great Soviet and American Plutonium Disasters.* New York: Oxford University Press, 2013.

Brown-Nagin, Tomiko. *Courage to Dissent: Atlanta and the Long History of the Civil Rights Movement.* New York: Oxford University Press, 2011.

Cohen, Lizabeth. *A Consumer's Republic: The Politics of Mass Consumption in Postwar America.* New York: Knopf, 2003.

Coontz, Stephanie. *The Way We Never Were: American Families and the Nostalgia Trap.* New York: Basic Books, 1993.

Dudziak, Mary. *Cold War Civil Rights: Race and the Image of American Democracy.* Princeton, NJ: Princeton University Press, 2002.

Fried, Richard M. *Nightmare in Red: The McCarthy Era in Perspective.* New York: Oxford University Press, 1990.

Grisinger, Joanna. *The Unwieldy American State: Administrative Politics Since the New Deal.* Cambridge, UK: Cambridge University Press, 2012.

Hernández, Kelly Lytle. *Migra! A History of the U.S. Border Patrol.* Berkeley: University of California Press, 2010.

Horowitz, Daniel. *Betty Friedan and the Making of the Feminine Mystique: The American Left, the Cold War, and Modern Feminism.* Amherst: University of Massachusetts Press, 1998.

Jackson, Kenneth T. *Crabgrass Frontier: The Suburbanization of the United States.* New York: Oxford University Press, 1985.

Jumonville, Neil. *Critical Crossings: The New York Intellectuals in Postwar America.* Berkeley: University of California Press, 1991.

Levenstein, Lisa. *A Movement Without Marches: African American Women and the Politics of Poverty in Postwar Philadelphia.* Chapel Hill: University of North Carolina Press, 2009.

May, Elaine Tyler. *Homeward Bound: American Families in the Cold War Era.* New York: Basic Books, 1988.

McGirr, Lisa. *Suburban Warriors: The Origins of the New American Right.* Princeton, NJ: Princeton University Press, 2001.

Ngai, Mae. *Impossible Subjects: Illegal Aliens and the Making of Modern America.* Princeton, NJ: Princeton University Press, 2003.

Patterson, James T. *Grand Expectations: The United States, 1945–1974.* New York: Oxford University Press, 1996.

Roberts, Gene, and Hank Klibanoff. *The Race Beat: The Press, the Civil Rights Struggle, and the Awakening of a Nation.* New York: Knopf, 2006.

Self, Robert. *American Babylon: Race and the Struggle for Postwar Oakland.* Princeton, NJ: Princeton University Press, 2005.

Sugrue, Thomas. *The Origins of the Urban Crisis: Race and Inequality in Postwar Detroit.* Princeton, NJ: Princeton University Press, 2005.

Von Eschen, Penny. *Satchmo Blows Up the World: Jazz Ambassadors Play the Cold War.* Cambridge, MA: Harvard University Press, 2004.

Wagnleitner, Reinhold. *Coca-Colonization and the Cold War: The Cultural Mission of the United States in Austria After the Second World War.* Chapel Hill: University of North Carolina Press, 1994.

Wall, Wendy. *Inventing the "American Way": The Politics of Consensus from the New Deal to the Civil Rights Movement.* New York: Oxford University Press, 2008.

Whitfield, Stephen. *The Culture of the Cold War.* Baltimore: Johns Hopkins University Press, 1991.

27

The Sixties

I. Introduction

Perhaps no decade is so immortalized in American memory as the 1960s. Couched in the colorful rhetoric of peace and love, complemented by stirring images of the civil rights movement, and fondly remembered for its music, art, and activism, the decade brought many people hope for a more inclusive, forward-thinking nation. But the decade was also plagued by strife, tragedy, and chaos. It was the decade of the Vietnam War, inner-city riots, and assassinations that seemed to symbolize the crushing of a new generation's idealism. A decade of struggle and disillusionment rocked by social, cultural, and political upheaval, the 1960s are remembered because so much changed, and because so much did not.

Demonstrators march from Selma to Montgomery, Alabama, in 1965 to champion African American civil rights. Library of Congress.

II. Kennedy and Cuba

The decade's political landscape began with a watershed presidential election. Americans were captivated by the 1960 race between Republican vice president Richard Nixon and Democratic senator John F. Kennedy, two candidates who pledged to move the nation forward and invigorate an economy experiencing the worst recession since the Great Depression. Kennedy promised to use federal programs to strengthen the economy and address pockets of longstanding poverty, while Nixon called for a reliance on private enterprise and reduction of government spending. Both candidates faced criticism as well; Nixon had to defend Dwight Eisenhower's domestic policies, while Kennedy, who was attempting to become the first Catholic president, had to counteract questions about his faith and convince voters that he was experienced enough to lead.

One of the most notable events of the Nixon-Kennedy presidential campaign was their televised debate in September, the first of its kind between major presidential candidates. The debate focused on domestic policy and provided Kennedy with an important moment to present himself as a composed, knowledgeable statesman. In contrast, Nixon, an experienced debater who faced higher expectations, looked sweaty and defensive. Radio listeners famously thought the two men performed equally well, but the TV audience was much more impressed by Kennedy, giving him an advantage in subsequent debates. Ultimately, the election was extraordinarily close; in the largest voter turnout in American history up to that point, Kennedy bested Nixon by less than one percentage point (34,227,096 to 34,107,646 votes). Although Kennedy's lead in electoral votes was more comfortable at 303 to 219, the Democratic Party's victory did not translate in Congress, where Democrats lost a few seats in both houses. As a result, Kennedy entered office in 1961 without the mandate necessary to achieve the ambitious agenda he would refer to as the New Frontier.

Kennedy also faced foreign policy challenges. The United States entered the 1960s unaccustomed to stark foreign policy failures, having emerged from World War II as a global superpower before waging a Cold War against the Soviet Union in the 1950s. In the new decade, unsuccessful conflicts in Cuba and Vietnam would yield embarrassment, fear, and tragedy, stunning a nation that expected triumph and altering the way many thought of America's role in international affairs.

On January 8, 1959, Fidel Castro and his revolutionary army initiated a new era of Cuban history. Having ousted the corrupt Cuban president Fulgencio Batista, who had fled Havana on New Year's Eve, Castro and his rebel forces made their way triumphantly through the capital city's streets. The United States, which had long propped up Batista's corrupt regime, had withdrawn support and, initially, expressed sympathy for Castro's new government, which was immediately granted diplomatic recognition. But President Dwight Eisenhower and members of his administration were wary. The new Cuban government soon instituted leftist economic policies centered on agrarian reform, land redistribution, and the nationalization of private enterprises. Cuba's wealthy and middle-class citizens fled the island in droves. Many settled in Miami, Florida, and other American cities.

The relationship between Cuba and the United States deteriorated rapidly. On October 19, 1960, the United States instituted a near-total trade embargo to economically isolate the Cuban regime, and in January 1961, the two nations broke off formal diplomatic relations. The Central Intelligence Agency (CIA), acting under the mistaken belief that the Castro government lacked popular support and that Cuban citizens would revolt if given the opportunity, began to recruit members of the exile community to participate in an invasion of the island. On April 16, 1961, an invasion force consisting primarily of Cuban émigrés landed on Girón Beach at the Bay of Pigs. Cuban soldiers and civilians quickly overwhelmed the exiles, many of whom were taken prisoner. The Cuban government's success at thwarting the Bay of Pigs invasion did much to legitimize the new regime and was a tremendous embarrassment for the Kennedy administration.

As the political relationship between Cuba and the United States disintegrated, the Castro government became more closely aligned with the Soviet Union. This strengthening of ties set the stage for the Cuban Missile Crisis, perhaps the most dramatic foreign policy crisis in the history of the United States. In 1962, in response to the United States' longtime maintenance of a nuclear arsenal in Turkey and at the invitation of the Cuban government, the Soviet Union deployed nuclear missiles in Cuba. On October 14, 1962, American spy planes detected the construction of missile launch sites, and on October 22, President Kennedy addressed the American people to alert them to this threat. Over the course of the next several days, the world watched in horror as the United States and the Soviet Union hovered on the brink of nuclear war. Finally, on October 28,

The Cuban Missile Crisis was a time of great anxiety in America. Eight hundred women demonstrated outside the United Nations Building in 1962 to promote peace. Library of Congress.

the Soviet Union agreed to remove its missiles from Cuba in exchange for a U.S. agreement to remove its missiles from Turkey and a formal pledge that the United States would not invade Cuba, and the crisis was resolved peacefully.

Though the Cuban Missile Crisis temporarily halted the flow of Cuban refugees into the United States, emigration began again in earnest in the mid-1960s. In 1965, the Johnson administration and the Castro government brokered a deal that facilitated the reunion of families that had been separated by earlier waves of migration, opening the door for thousands to leave the island. In 1966 President Lyndon B. Johnson signed the Cuban Adjustment Act, a law allowing Cuban refugees to become permanent residents. Over the course of the 1960s, hundreds of thousands of Cubans left their homeland and built new lives in America.

III. The Civil Rights Movement Continues

So much of the energy and character of the sixties emerged from the civil rights movement, which won its greatest victories in the early years of the decade. The movement itself was changing. Many of the civil rights activists pushing for school desegregation in the 1950s were middle-class and middle-aged. In the 1960s, a new student movement arose whose members wanted swifter changes in the segregated South. Confrontational protests, marches, boycotts, and sit-ins accelerated.[1]

The tone of the modern U.S. civil rights movement changed at a North Carolina department store in 1960, when four African American students participated in a sit-in at a whites-only lunch counter. The 1960 Greensboro sit-ins were typical. Activists sat at segregated lunch counters in an act of defiance, refusing to leave until being served and willing to be ridiculed, attacked, and arrested if they were not. This tactic drew resistance but forced the desegregation of Woolworth's department stores. It prompted copycat demonstrations across the South. The protests offered evidence that student-led direct action could enact social change. Increasingly disenchanted with the seemingly distant, professionalized civil rights leadership of older southern ministers, Ella Baker left King's Southern Christian Leadership Conference and helped organize the Student Non-Violent Coordinating Committee (SNCC, often pronounced "snick") that year. She embraced the direct, grassroots action of student activists such as Julian Bond, Stokely Carmichael, Diane Nash, John Lewis, and countless others who would push the civil rights movement in a new, more confrontational direction.[2]

In the following year, 1961, civil rights advocates attempted a bolder variation of a sit-in when they participated in the Freedom Rides. Activists in the Congress of Racial Equality (CORE) organized interstate bus rides following a Supreme Court decision outlawing segregation on public buses and trains. The rides intended to test the court's ruling, which many southern states had ignored. An interracial group of Freedom Riders boarded buses in Washington, D.C., with the intention of sitting in integrated patterns on the buses as they traveled through the Deep South. On the initial rides in May 1961, the riders encountered fierce resistance in Alabama. Angry mobs composed of KKK members attacked riders in Birmingham, burning one of the buses and beating the activists who escaped. Additional Freedom Rides launched through the summer and generated national attention amid additional violent resistance. Ultimately, the Interstate Commerce Commission enforced integrated interstate buses and trains in November 1961.[3]

In the fall of 1961, civil rights activists descended on Albany, a small city in southwest Georgia. Known for entrenched segregation and racial violence, Albany seemed an unlikely place for Black Americans to rally and demand change. The activists there, however, formed the Albany

Movement, a coalition of civil rights organizers that included members of the Student Nonviolent Coordinating Committee (SNCC), the Southern Christian Leadership Conference (SCLC), and the NAACP. But the movement was stymied by Albany police chief Laurie Pritchett, who launched mass arrests but refused to engage in police brutality and bailed out leading officials to avoid negative media attention. It was a peculiar scene, and a lesson for southern activists.[4]

The Albany Movement included elements of a Christian commitment to social justice in its platform, with activists stating that all people were "of equal worth" in God's family and that "no man may discriminate against or exploit another." In many instances in the 1960s, Black Christianity propelled civil rights advocates to action and demonstrated the significance of religion to the broader civil rights movement. King's rise to prominence underscored the role that African American religious figures played in the 1960s civil rights movement. Protesters sang hymns and spirituals as they marched. Preachers rallied the people with messages of justice and hope. Churches hosted meetings, prayer vigils, and conferences on nonviolent resistance. The moral thrust of the movement strengthened African American activists and confronted white society by framing segregation as a moral evil.[5]

James Meredith, accompanied by U.S. Marshals, walks to class at the University of Mississippi in 1962. Meredith was the first African American student admitted to the segregated university. Library of Congress.

As the civil rights movement garnered more followers and more attention, white resistance stiffened. In October 1962, James Meredith became the first African American student to enroll at the University of Mississippi. Meredith's enrollment sparked riots on the Oxford campus, prompting President John F. Kennedy to send in U.S. Marshals and National Guardsmen to maintain order. On an evening known infamously as the Battle of Ole Miss, segregationists clashed with troops in the middle of campus, resulting in two deaths and hundreds of injuries. Violence served as a reminder of the strength of white resistance to the civil rights movement, particularly in the realm of education.[6]

The following year, 1963, was perhaps the decade's most eventful year for civil rights. In April and May, the SCLC organized the Birmingham Campaign, a broad campaign of direct action aiming to topple segregation in Alabama's largest city. Activists used business boycotts, sit-ins, and peaceful marches as part of the campaign. SCLC leader Martin Luther King Jr. was jailed, prompting his famous handwritten letter urging not only his nonviolent approach but active confrontation to directly challenge injustice. The campaign further added to King's national reputation and featured powerful photographs and video footage of white police officers using fire hoses and attack dogs on young African American protesters. It also yielded an agreement to desegregate public accommodations in the city: activists in Birmingham scored a victory for civil rights and drew international praise for the nonviolent approach in the face of police-sanctioned violence and bombings.[7]

White resistance intensified. While much of the rhetoric surrounding the 1960s focused on a younger, more liberal generation's progressive ideas, conservatism maintained a strong presence on the American political scene. Few political figures in the decade embodied the working-class, conservative views held by millions of white Americans quite like George Wallace. Wallace's vocal stance on segregation was immortalized in his 1963 inaugural address as Alabama governor with the phrase: "Segregation now, segregation tomorrow, segregation forever!" Just as the civil rights movement began to gain unprecedented strength, Wallace became the champion of the many white southerners opposed to the movement. Consequently, Wallace was one of the best examples of the very real opposition civil rights activists faced in the late twentieth century.[8]

As governor, Wallace loudly supported segregation. His efforts were symbolic, but they earned him national recognition as a political figure

Alabama governor George Wallace stands defiantly at the door of the University of Alabama, blocking the attempted integration of the school. Wallace became the most notorious pro-segregation politician of the 1960s, proudly proclaiming, in his 1963 inaugural address, "Segregation now, segregation tomorrow, segregation forever." Library of Congress.

willing to fight for what many southerners saw as their traditional way of life. In June 1963, just five months after becoming governor, in his "Stand in the Schoolhouse Door," Wallace famously stood in the door of Foster Auditorium to protest integration at the University of Alabama. President Kennedy addressed the nation that evening, criticizing Wallace and calling for a comprehensive civil rights bill. A day later, civil rights leader Medgar Evers was assassinated at his home in Jackson, Mississippi.

That summer, civil rights leaders organized the August 1963 March on Washington. The march called for, among other things, civil rights legislation, school integration, an end to discrimination by public and private employers, job training for the unemployed, and a raise in the minimum wage. On the steps of the Lincoln Memorial, King delivered his famous "I Have a Dream" speech, an internationally renowned call for civil rights that raised the movement's profile to new heights and put unprecedented pressure on politicians to pass meaningful civil rights legislation.[9]

Kennedy offered support for a civil rights bill, but southern resistance was intense and Kennedy was unwilling to expend much political

This photograph shows Martin Luther King Jr. and other Black civil rights leaders arm-in-arm with leaders of the Jewish community during the March on Washington on August 28, 1963. Wikimedia.

capital on it. And so the bill stalled in Congress. Then, on November 22, 1963, President Kennedy was assassinated in Dallas. The nation's youthful, popular president was gone. Vice President Lyndon Johnson lacked Kennedy's youth, his charisma, his popularity, and his aristocratic upbringing, but no one knew Washington better and no one before or since fought harder and more successfully to pass meaningful civil rights legislation. Raised in poverty in the Texas Hill Country, Johnson scratched and clawed his way up the political ladder. He was both ruthlessly ambitious and keenly conscious of poverty and injustice. He idolized Franklin Roosevelt whose New Deal had brought improvements for the impoverished central Texans Johnson grew up with.

President Lyndon Johnson, then, an old white southerner with a thick Texas drawl, embraced the civil rights movement. He took Kennedy's stalled civil rights bill, ensured that it would have teeth, and navigated it through Congress. The following summer he signed the Civil Rights Act of 1964, widely considered to be among the most important pieces of civil rights legislation in American history. The comprehensive act barred segregation in public accommodations and outlawed discrimination based on race, ethnicity, gender, and national or religious origin.

The civil rights movement created space for political leaders to pass legislation, and the movement continued pushing forward. Direct action continued through the summer of 1964, as student-run organizations like SNCC and the Congress of Racial Equality (CORE) helped with the Freedom Summer in Mississippi, a drive to register African American voters in a state with an ugly history of discrimination. Freedom Summer campaigners set up schools for African American children. Even with progress, intimidation and violent resistance against civil rights continued, particularly in regions with longstanding traditions of segregation. Three young CORE activists, James Chaney, Michael Schwerner, and Andrew Goodman, were murdered by local law enforcement officers and Klan members in Neshoba County, outside of Philadelphia, Mississippi.[10] In August, over 2,000 Black Mississippians assembled in Jackson and formed the Mississippi Freedom Democratic Party. They demanded that their delegates be seated at the Democratic National Convention. Denied anything more than two at-large seats, the Party protested. "I question

Lyndon B. Johnson consults with civil rights leaders in the White House. One of Johnson's greatest legacies would be his staunch support of civil rights legislation. Wikimedia.

America," co-founder Fannie Lou Hamer said in a nationally televised address. "Is this America?" she asked.

Activists kept fighting. In March 1965, activists attempted to march from Selma to Montgomery, Alabama, on behalf of local African American voting rights. In a narrative that had become familiar, "Bloody Sunday" featured peaceful protesters attacked by white law enforcement with batons and tear gas. After they were turned away violently a second time, marchers finally made the fifty-mile trek to the state capitol later in the month. Coverage of the first march prompted President Johnson to present the bill that became the Voting Rights Act of 1965, an act that abolished voting discrimination in federal, state, and local elections. In two consecutive years, landmark pieces of legislation had assaulted de jure (by law) segregation and disenfranchisement.[11]

Johnson gives Senator Richard Russell the famous "Johnson Treatment." Yoichi R. Okamoto, Photograph of Lyndon B. Johnson pressuring Senator Richard Russell, December 17, 1963. Wikimedia.

IV. Lyndon Johnson's Great Society

On a May morning in 1964, President Johnson laid out a sweeping vision for a package of domestic reforms known as the Great Society. Speaking before that year's graduates of the University of Michigan, Johnson called for "an end to poverty and racial injustice" and challenged both

Five leaders of the civil rights movement in 1965. From left: Bayard Rustin, Andrew Young, N.Y. Congressman William Ryan, James Farmer, and John Lewis. Library of Congress.

the graduates and American people to "enrich and elevate our national life, and to advance the quality of our American civilization." At its heart, he promised, the Great Society would uplift racially and economically disfranchised Americans, too long denied access to federal guarantees of equal democratic and economic opportunity, while simultaneously raising all Americans' standards and quality of life.[12]

The Great Society's legislation was breathtaking in scope, and many of its programs and agencies are still with us today. The Civil Rights Act of 1964 and the Voting Rights Act of 1965 codified federal support for many of the civil rights movement's goals by prohibiting job discrimination, abolishing the segregation of public accommodations, and providing vigorous federal oversight of southern states' election laws in order to guarantee minority access to the ballot. Ninety years after Reconstruction, these measures effectively ended Jim Crow. Moreover, the Immigration and Nationality Act of 1965—or the Hart-Celler Act—abolished the quota regime established by the 1924 Reed-Johnson Act. American immigration, which had for more than four decades effectively barred legal immigration to the United States from anywhere other than Northern and Western Europe, finally opened the United States up to the world and forever reshaped the demographics of the nation.

In addition to civil rights, the Great Society took on a range of quality-of-life concerns that seemed suddenly solvable in a society of such affluence. It established the first federal food stamp program. Medicare and Medicaid would ensure access to quality medical care for the aged and poor. In 1965, the Elementary and Secondary Education Act was the first sustained and significant federal investment in public education, totaling more than $1 billion. Significant funds were poured into colleges and universities. The Great Society also established the National Endowment for the Arts and the National Endowment for the Humanities, federal investments in arts and letters that fund American cultural expression to this day.

While these programs persisted and even thrived, in the years immediately following this flurry of legislative activity, the national conversation surrounding Johnson's domestic agenda largely focused on the $3 billion spent on War on Poverty programming within the Great Society's Economic Opportunity Act (EOA) of 1964. No EOA program was more controversial than Community Action, considered the cornerstone antipoverty program. Johnson's antipoverty planners felt that the key to uplifting disfranchised and impoverished Americans was involving poor and marginalized citizens in the actual administration of poverty programs, what they called "maximum feasible participation." Community Action Programs would give disfranchised Americans a seat at the table in planning and executing federally funded programs that were meant to benefit them—a significant sea change in the nation's efforts to confront poverty, which had historically relied on local political and business elites or charitable organizations for administration.[13]

In fact, Johnson himself had never conceived of poor Americans running their own poverty programs. While the president's rhetoric offered a stirring vision of the future, he had singularly old-school notions for how his poverty policies would work. In contrast to "maximum feasible participation," the president imagined a second New Deal: local elite-run public works camps that would instill masculine virtues in unemployed young men. Community Action almost entirely bypassed local administrations and sought to build grassroots civil rights and community advocacy organizations, many of which had originated in the broader civil rights movement. Despite widespread support for most Great Society programs, the War on Poverty increasingly became the focal point of domestic criticisms from the left and right. On the left, frustrated Americans recognized the president's resistance to further empowering poor minority communities and also assailed the growing war in Vietnam, the cost of which undercut domestic poverty spending. As racial unrest and violence swept across urban centers, critics from the right lambasted federal spending for "unworthy" citizens.

Johnson had secured a series of meaningful civil rights laws, but then things began to stall. Days after the ratification of the Voting Rights Act, race riots broke out in the Watts neighborhood of Los Angeles. Rioting in Watts stemmed from local African American frustrations with residential segregation, police brutality, and racial profiling. Waves of riots rocked American cities every summer thereafter. Particularly destructive riots occurred in 1967—two summers later—in Newark and Detroit. Each resulted in deaths, injuries, arrests, and millions of dollars in property damage. In spite of Black achievements, problems persisted for many African Americans. The phenomenon of "white flight"—when whites in metropolitan areas fled city centers for the suburbs—often resulted in resegregated residential patterns. Limited access to economic and social opportunities in urban areas bred discord. In addition to reminding the nation that the civil rights movement was a complex, ongoing event without a concrete endpoint, the unrest in northern cities reinforced the notion that the struggle did not occur solely in the South. Many Americans also viewed the riots as an indictment of the Great Society, President Johnson's sweeping agenda of domestic programs that sought to remedy inner-city ills by offering better access to education, jobs, medical care, housing, and other forms of social welfare. The civil rights movement was never the same.[14]

The Civil Rights Acts, the Voting Rights Acts, and the War on Poverty provoked conservative resistance and were catalysts for the rise of Republicans in the South and West. However, subsequent presidents and Congresses have left intact the bulk of the Great Society, including Medicare and Medicaid, food stamps, federal spending for arts and literature, and Head Start. Even Community Action Programs, so fraught during their few short years of activity, inspired and empowered a new generation of minority and poverty community activists who had never before felt, as one put it, that "this government is with us."[15]

V. The Origins of the Vietnam War

American involvement in the Vietnam War began during the postwar period of decolonization. The Soviet Union backed many nationalist movements across the globe, but the United States feared the expansion of communist influence and pledged to confront any revolutions aligned against Western capitalism. The Domino Theory—the idea that if a country fell to communism, then neighboring states would soon follow—governed American foreign policy. After the communist takeover of China in 1949, the United States financially supported the French military's effort to retain control over its colonies in Vietnam, Cambodia, and Laos.

Between 1946 and 1954, France fought a counterinsurgency campaign against the nationalist Viet Minh forces led by Ho Chi Minh. The United States assisted the French war effort with funds, arms, and advisors, but it was not enough. On the eve of the Geneva Peace Conference in 1954, Viet Minh forces defeated the French army at Dien Bien Phu. The conference temporarily divided Vietnam into two separate states until UN-monitored elections occurred. But the United States feared a communist electoral victory and blocked the elections. The temporary partition became permanent. The United States established the Republic of Vietnam, or South Vietnam, with the U.S.-backed Ngo Dinh Diem as prime minister. Diem, who had lived in the United States, was a committed anticommunist.

Diem's government, however, and its Army of the Republic of Vietnam (ARVN) could not contain the communist insurgency seeking the reunification of Vietnam. The Americans provided weapons and support, but despite a clear numerical and technological advantage, South Vietnam stumbled before insurgent Vietcong (VC) units. Diem, a corrupt leader propped up by the American government with little domestic support, was assassinated in 1963. A merry-go-round of military dictators followed as the situation in South Vietnam continued to deteriorate. The American public, though, remained largely unaware of Vietnam in the early 1960s, even as President John F. Kennedy deployed some sixteen thousand military advisors to help South Vietnam suppress a domestic communist insurgency.[16]

This all changed in 1964. On August 2, the USS *Maddox* reported incoming fire from North Vietnamese ships in the Gulf of Tonkin. Although the details of the incident are controversial, the Johnson administration exploited the event to provide a pretext for escalating American involvement in Vietnam. Congress passed the Gulf of Tonkin Resolution, granting President Johnson the authority to deploy the American military to defend South Vietnam. U.S. Marines landed in Vietnam in March 1965, and the American ground war began.

American forces under General William Westmoreland were tasked with defending South Vietnam against the insurgent VC and the regular North Vietnamese Army (NVA). But no matter how many troops the Americans sent or how many bombs they dropped, they could not win. This was a different kind of war. Progress was not measured by cities won or territory taken but by body counts and kill ratios. Although American officials like Westmoreland and secretary of defense Robert McNamara claimed a communist defeat was on the horizon, by 1968 half a million American troops were stationed in Vietnam, nearly twenty thousand had been killed, and the war was still no closer to being won. Protests, which would provide the backdrop for the American counterculture, erupted across the country.

VI. Culture and Activism

Epitomizing the folk music and protest culture of 1960s youth, Joan Baez and Bob Dylan are pictured here singing together at the March on Washington in 1963. Wikimedia.

The 1960s wrought enormous cultural change. The United States that entered the decade looked and sounded little like the one that left it. Rebellion rocked the supposedly hidebound conservatism of the 1950s as the youth counterculture became mainstream. Native Americans, Chicanos, women, and environmentalists participated in movements demonstrating that rights activism could be applied to ethnicity, gender, and nature. Even established religious institutions such as the Catholic Church underwent transformations, emphasizing freedom and tolerance. In each

instance, the decade brought substantial progress and evidence that activism remained fluid and unfinished.

Much of the counterculture was filtered through popular culture and consumption. The fifties consumer culture still saturated the country, and advertisers continued to appeal to teenagers and the expanding youth market. During the 1960s, though, advertisers looked to a growing counterculture to sell their products. Popular culture and popular advertising in the 1950s had promoted an ethos of "fitting in" and buying products to conform. The new countercultural ethos touted individuality and rebellion. Some advertisers were subtle; ads for Volkswagens (VWs) acknowledged the flaws and strange look of their cars. One ad read, "Presenting America's slowest fastback," which "won't go over 72 mph even though the speedometer shows a wildly optimistic top speed of 90." Another stated, "And if you run out of gas, it's easy to push." By marketing the car's flaws and reframing them as positive qualities, the advertisers commercialized young people's resistance to commercialism, while simultaneously positioning the VW as a car for those wanting to stand out in a crowd. A more obviously countercultural ad for the VW Bug showed two cars: one black and one painted multicolor in the hippie style; the contrasting captions read, "We do our thing," and "You do yours."

Companies marketed their products as countercultural in and of themselves. One of the more obvious examples was a 1968 ad from Columbia Records, a hugely successful record label since the 1920s. The ad pictured a group of stock rebellious characters—a shaggy-haired white hippie, a buttoned-up Beat, two biker types, and a Black jazz man sporting an Afro—in a jail cell. The counterculture had been busted, the ad states, but "the man can't bust our music." Merely buying records from Columbia was an act of rebellion, one that brought the buyer closer to the counterculture figures portrayed in the ad.[17]

But it wasn't just advertising: the culture was changing and changing rapidly. Conservative cultural norms were falling everywhere. The dominant style of women's fashion in the 1950s, for instance, was the poodle skirt and the sweater, tight-waisted and buttoned up. The 1960s ushered in an era of much less restrictive clothing. Capri pants became popular casual wear. Skirts became shorter. When Mary Quant invented the miniskirt in 1964, she said it was a garment "in which you could move, in which you could run and jump."[18] By the late 1960s, the hippies' more androgynous look became trendy. Such trends bespoke the new popular ethos of the 1960s: freedom, rebellion, and individuality.

In a decade plagued by social and political instability, the American counterculture also sought psychedelic drugs as its remedy for alienation. For middle-class white teenagers, society had become stagnant and bureaucratic. The New Left, for instance, arose on college campuses frustrated with the lifeless bureaucracies that they believed strangled true freedom. Lysergic acid diethylamide (LSD) began its life as a drug used primarily in psychological research before trickling down into college campuses and out into society at large. The counterculture's notion that American stagnation could be remedied by a spiritual-psychedelic experience drew heavily from psychologists and sociologists. The popularity of these drugs also spurred a political backlash. By 1966, enough incidents had been connected to LSD to spur a Senate hearing on the drug, and newspapers were reporting that hundreds of LSD users had been admitted to psychiatric wards.

The counterculture conquered popular culture. Rock 'n' roll, liberalized sexuality, an embrace of diversity, recreational drug use, unalloyed idealism, and pure earnestness marked a new generation. Criticized by conservatives as culturally dangerous and by leftists as empty narcissism, the youth culture nevertheless dominated headlines and steered American culture. Perhaps one hundred thousand youth descended on San Francisco for the utopic promise of 1967's Summer of Love. 1969's Woodstock concert in New York became shorthand for the new youth culture and its mixture of politics, protest, and personal fulfillment. While the ascendance of the hippies would be both exaggerated and short-lived, and while Vietnam and Richard Nixon shattered much of its idealism, the counterculture's liberated social norms and its embrace of personal fulfillment still define much of American culture.

VII. Beyond Civil Rights

Despite substantial legislative achievements, frustrations with the slow pace of change grew. Tensions continued to mount in cities, and the tone of the civil rights movement changed yet again. Activists became less conciliatory in their calls for progress. Many embraced the more militant message of the burgeoning Black Power Movement and Malcolm X, a Nation of Islam (NOI) minister who encouraged African Americans to pursue freedom, equality, and justice by "any means necessary." Prior to his death in 1965, Malcolm X and the NOI emerged as the radical alternative to the racially integrated, largely Protestant approach of Martin Luther King Jr. Malcolm advocated armed resistance in defense of the safety

and well-being of Black Americans, stating, "I don't call it violence when it's self-defense, I call it intelligence." For his part, King and leaders from more mainstream organizations like the NAACP and the Urban League criticized both Malcolm X and the NOI for what they perceived to be racial demagoguery. King believed Malcolm X's speeches were a "great disservice" to Black Americans, claiming that they lamented the problems of African Americans without offering solutions. The differences between King and Malcolm X represented a core ideological tension that would inhabit Black political thought throughout the 1960s and 1970s.[19]

By the late 1960s, SNCC, led by figures such as Stokely Carmichael, had expelled its white members and shunned the interracial effort in the rural South, focusing instead on injustices in northern urban areas. After President Johnson refused to take up the cause of the Black delegates in the Mississippi Freedom Democratic Party at the 1964 Democratic National Convention, SNCC activists became frustrated with institutional tactics and turned away from the organization's founding principle of nonviolence. This evolving, more aggressive movement called for African Americans to play a dominant role in cultivating Black institutions and articulating Black interests rather than relying on interracial, moderate approaches. At a June 1966 civil rights march, Carmichael told the crowd, "What we gonna start saying now is black power!"[20] The slogan not only

Like Booker T. Washington and W. E. B. Du Bois before them, Martin Luther King Jr. and Malcom X, pictured here in 1964, represented different strategies to achieve racial justice. Library of Congress.

The Black Panther Party used radical and incendiary tactics to bring attention to the continued oppression of Black Americans. This 1970 poster captures their outlook. Wikimedia.

resonated with audiences, it also stood in direct contrast to King's "Freedom Now!" campaign. The political slogan of Black power could encompass many meanings, but at its core it stood for the self-determination of Black people in political, economic, and social organizations.

Carmichael asserted that "black power means black people coming together to form a political force."[21] To others it also meant violence. In 1966, Huey Newton and Bobby Seale formed the Black Panther Party in Oakland, California. The Black Panthers became the standard-bearers for direct action and self-defense, using the concept of decolonization in their drive to liberate Black communities from white power structures. The revolutionary organization also sought reparations and exemptions for Black men from the military draft. Citing police brutality and racist governmental policies, the Black Panthers aligned themselves with the "other people of color in the world" against whom America was fighting abroad. Although it was perhaps most well known for its open display of weapons, military-style dress, and Black nationalist beliefs, the party's 10-Point Plan also included employment, housing, and education. The Black Panthers worked in local communities to run "survival programs" that provided food, clothing, medical treatment, and drug rehabilitation.

They focused on modes of resistance that empowered Black activists on their own terms.[22]

But African Americans weren't the only Americans struggling to assert themselves in the 1960s. The successes of the civil rights movement and growing grassroots activism inspired countless new movements. In the summer of 1961, for instance, frustrated Native American university students founded the National Indian Youth Council (NIYC) to draw attention to the plight of Indigenous Americans. In the Pacific Northwest, the council advocated for tribal fisherman to retain immunity from conservation laws on reservations and in 1964 held a series of "fish-ins": activists and celebrities cast nets and waited for the police to arrest them.[23] The NIYC's militant rhetoric and use of direct action marked the beginning of what was called the Red Power movement, an intertribal movement designed to draw attention to Native issues and to protest discrimination. The American Indian Movement (AIM) and other activists staged dramatic demonstrations. In November 1969, dozens began a year-and-a-half-long occupation of the abandoned Alcatraz Island in San Francisco Bay. In 1973, hundreds occupied the town of Wounded Knee, South Dakota, site of the infamous 1890 massacre, for several months.[24]

Meanwhile, the Chicano movement in the 1960s emerged out of the broader Mexican American civil rights movement of the post–World War II era. The word *Chicano* was initially considered a derogatory term for Mexican immigrants, until activists in the 1960s reclaimed the term and used it as a catalyst to campaign for political and social change among Mexican Americans. The Chicano movement confronted discrimination in schools, politics, agriculture, and other formal and informal institutions. Organizations like the Mexican American Political Association (MAPA) and the Mexican American Legal Defense Fund (MALDF) buoyed the Chicano movement and patterned themselves after similar influential groups in the African American civil rights movement.[25]

Cesar Chavez became the most well-known figure of the Chicano movement, using nonviolent tactics to campaign for workers' rights in the grape fields of California. Chavez and activist Dolores Huerta founded the National Farm Workers Association, which eventually merged and became the United Farm Workers of America (UFWA). The UFWA fused the causes of Chicano and Filipino activists protesting the subpar working conditions of California farmers on American soil. In addition to embarking on a hunger strike and a boycott of table grapes, Chavez led a three-hundred-mile march in March and April 1966 from Delano, California, to the state capital of Sacramento. The pro-labor campaign garnered the national spotlight and the support of prominent political figures such as Robert Kennedy. Today, Chavez's birthday (March 31) is observed as a federal holiday in California, Colorado, and Texas.

Rodolfo "Corky" Gonzales was another activist whose calls for Chicano self-determination resonated long past the 1960s. A former boxer and Denver native, Gonzales founded the Crusade for Justice in 1966, an organization that would establish the first annual Chicano Liberation Day at the National Chicano Youth Conference. The conference also yielded the Plan Espiritual de Aztlán, a Chicano nationalist manifesto that reflected Gonzales's vision of Chicanos as a unified, historically grounded, all-encompassing group fighting against discrimination in the United States. By 1970, the Texas-based La Raza Unida political party had a strong foundation for promoting Chicano nationalism and continuing the campaign for Mexican American civil rights.[26]

The feminist movement also grew in the 1960s. Women were active in both the civil rights movement and the labor movement, but their increasing awareness of gender inequality did not find a receptive audience among male leaders in those movements. In the 1960s, then, many of these women began to form a movement of their own. Soon the country experienced a groundswell of feminist consciousness.

An older generation of women who preferred to work within state institutions figured prominently in the early part of the decade. When John F. Kennedy established the Presidential Commission on the Status of Women in 1961, former first lady Eleanor Roosevelt headed the effort. The commission's official report, a self-declared "invitation to action," was released in 1963. Finding discriminatory provisions in the law and practices of industrial, labor, and governmental organizations, the commission advocated for "changes, many of them long overdue, in the conditions of women's opportunity in the United States."[27] Change was recommended in areas of employment practices, federal tax and benefit policies affecting women's income, labor laws, and services for women as wives, mothers, and workers. This call for action, if heeded, would ameliorate the types of discrimination primarily experienced by middle-class and elite white working women, all of whom were used to advocating through institutional structures like government agencies and unions.[28] The specific concerns of poor and nonwhite women lay largely beyond the scope of the report.

Betty Friedan's *The Feminine Mystique* hit bookshelves the same year the commission released its report. Friedan had been active in the union movement and was by this time a mother in the new suburban landscape of postwar America. In her book, Friedan labeled the "problem that has no name," and in doing so helped many white middle-class American women come to see their dissatisfaction as housewives not as something "wrong with [their] marriage, or [themselves]," but instead as a social problem experienced by millions of American women. Friedan observed that there was a "discrepancy between the reality of our lives as women and the image to which we were trying to conform, the image I call the feminine mystique." No longer would women allow society to blame the "problem that has no name" on a loss of femininity, too much education, or too much female independence and equality with men.[29]

The 1960s also saw a different group of women pushing for change in government policy. Mothers on welfare began to form local advocacy groups in addition to the National Welfare Rights Organization, founded in 1966. Mostly African American, these activists fought for greater benefits and more control over welfare policy and implementation. Women like Johnnie Tillmon successfully advocated for larger grants for school clothes and household equipment in addition to gaining due process and fair administrative hearings prior to termination of welfare entitlements.

Yet another mode of feminist activism was the formation of consciousness-raising groups. These groups met in women's homes and at women's centers, providing a safe environment for women to discuss everything from experiences of gender discrimination to pregnancy, from relationships with men and women to self-image. The goal of consciousness-raising was to increase self-awareness and validate the experiences of women. Groups framed such individual experiences as examples of society-wide sexism, and claimed that "the personal is political."[30] Consciousness-raising groups created a wealth of personal stories that feminists could use in other forms of activism and crafted networks of women from which activists could mobilize support for protests.

The end of the decade was marked by the Women's Strike for Equality, celebrating the fiftieth anniversary of women's right to vote. Sponsored by the National Organization for Women (NOW), the 1970 protest focused on employment discrimination, political equality, abortion, free childcare, and equality in marriage. All of these issues foreshadowed the backlash against feminist goals in the 1970s. Not only would feminism face opposition from other women who valued the traditional homemaker role to which feminists objected, the feminist movement would also fracture internally as minority women challenged white feminists' racism and lesbians vied for more prominence within feminist organizations.

American environmentalism's significant gains during the 1960s emerged in part from Americans' recreational use of nature. Postwar

The women's movement stalled during the 1930s and 1940s, but by the 1960s it was back in full force. Inspired by the civil rights movement and fed up with gender discrimination, women took to the streets to demand their rights as American citizens. Here, women march during the "Women's Strike for Equality," a nationwide protest launched on the 50th anniversary of women's suffrage. Photograph, August 26, 1970. Library of Congress.

Americans backpacked, went to the beach, fished, and joined birding organizations in greater numbers than ever before. These experiences, along with increased formal education, made Americans more aware of threats to the environment and, consequently, to themselves. Many of these threats increased in the postwar years as developers bulldozed open space for suburbs and new hazards emerged from industrial and nuclear pollutants.

By the time that biologist Rachel Carson published her landmark book, *Silent Spring*, in 1962, a nascent environmentalism had emerged in America. *Silent Spring* stood out as an unparalleled argument for the interconnectedness of ecological and human health. Pesticides, Carson argued, also posed a threat to human health, and their overuse threatened the ecosystems that supported food production. Carson's argument was compelling to many Americans, including President Kennedy, but was virulently opposed by chemical industries that suggested the book was the product of an emotional woman, not a scientist.[31]

After *Silent Spring*, the social and intellectual currents of environmentalism continued to expand rapidly, culminating in the largest demonstration in history, Earth Day, on April 22, 1970, and in a decade of lawmaking that significantly restructured American government. Even before the massive gathering for Earth Day, lawmakers from the local to the federal level had pushed for and achieved regulations to clean up the air and water. President Richard Nixon signed the National Environmental Policy Act into law in 1970, requiring environmental impact statements for any project directed or funded by the federal government. He also created the Environmental Protection Agency, the first agency charged with studying, regulating, and disseminating knowledge about the environment. A raft of laws followed that were designed to offer increased protection for air, water, endangered species, and natural areas.

The decade's activism manifested across the world. It even affected the Catholic Church. The Second Vatican Council, called by Pope John XXIII to modernize the church and bring it in closer dialogue with the non-Catholic world, operated from 1962 to 1965, when it proclaimed multiple reforms, including the vernacular mass (mass in local languages, rather than in Latin) and a greater role for laypeople, and especially women, in the Church. Many Catholic churches adopted more informal, contemporary styles. Many conservative Catholics recoiled at what they perceived as rapid and dangerous changes, but Vatican II's reforms in many ways created the modern Catholic Church.

VIII. Conclusion

In 1969, Americans hailed the moon landing as a profound victory in the space race against the Soviet Union. This landmark achievement fulfilled the promise of the late John F. Kennedy, who had declared in 1961 that the United States would put a man on the moon by the end of the decade. But while Neil Armstrong said his steps marked "one giant leap for mankind," and Americans marveled at the achievement, the brief moment of wonder only punctuated years of turmoil. The Vietnam War disillusioned a generation, riots rocked cities, protests hit campuses, and assassinations robbed the nation of many of its leaders. The forward-thinking spirit of a complex decade had waned. Uncertainty loomed.

IX. Reference Material

This chapter was edited by Samuel Abramson, with content contributions by Samuel Abramson, Marsha Barrett, Brent Cebul, Michell Chresfield, William Cossen, Jenifer Dodd, Michael Falcone, Leif Fredrickson, Jean-Paul de Guzman,

Jordan Hill, William Kelly, Lucie Kyrova, Maria Montalvo, Emily Prifogle, Ansley Quiros, Tanya Roth, and Robert Thompson.

Recommended citation: Samuel Abramson et al., "The Sixties," Samuel Abramson, ed., in *The American Yawp*, eds. Joseph Locke and Ben Wright (Stanford, CA: Stanford University Press, 2019).

NOTES TO CHAPTER 27

1. For the major events of the civil rights movement, see Taylor Branch, *Parting the Waters: America in the King Years, 1954–63* (New York: Simon and Schuster, 1988); Taylor Branch, *Pillar of Fire: America in the King Years, 1963–65* (New York: Simon and Schuster, 1998); and Taylor Branch, *At Canaan's Edge: America in the King Years, 1965–68* (New York: Simon and Schuster, 2007).

2. Branch, *Parting the Waters*.

3. Raymond Arsenault, *Freedom Riders: 1961 and the Struggle for Racial Justice* (New York: Oxford University Press, 2006).

4. Clayborne Carson, *In Struggle: SNCC and the Black Awakening of the 1960s* (Cambridge, MA: Harvard University Press, 1980); Adam Fairclough, *To Redeem the Soul of America: The Southern Christian Leadership Conference & Martin Luther King* (Athens: University of Georgia Press, 1987).

5. David L. Chappell, *A Stone of Hope: Prophetic Religion and the Death of Jim Crow* (Chapel Hill: University of North Carolina Press, 2005).

6. Branch, *Parting the Waters*.

7. Ibid.

8. Dan T. Carter, *The Politics of Rage: George Wallace, the Origins of the New Conservatism, and the Transformation of American Politics* (Baton Rouge: LSU Press, 2000).

9. Branch, *Parting the Waters*.

10. Branch, *Pillar of Fire*.

11. Branch, *At Canaan's Edge*.

12. Lyndon Baines Johnson, "Remarks at the University of Michigan," May 22, 1964, *Public Papers of the Presidents of the United States: Lyndon B. Johnson, 1964* (Washington, DC: U.S. Government Printing Office, 1965), 704.

13. See, for instance, Wesley G. Phelps, *A People's War on Poverty: Urban Politics and Grassroots Activists in Houston* (Athens: University of Georgia Press, 2014).

14. Ibid.

15. Guian A. McKee, "'This Government is with Us': Lyndon Johnson and the Grassroots War on Poverty," in *The War on Poverty: A New Grassroots History, 1964–1980*, ed. Annelise Orleck and Lisa Gayle Hazirjian (Athens: University of Georgia Press, 2011).

16. Michael P. Sullivan, *The Vietnam War: A Study in the Making of American Foreign Policy* (Lexington: University Press of Kentucky, 1985), 58.

17. Thomas Frank, *The Conquest of Cool: Business Culture, Counterculture, and the Rise of Hip Consumerism* (Chicago: University of Chicago Press, 1998), 7.

18. Brenda Polan and Roger Tredre, *The Great Fashion Designers* (New York: Berg, 2009), 103–104.

19. Manning Marable, *Malcolm X: A Life of Reinvention* (New York: Penguin, 2011).

20. Peniel E. Joseph, ed., *The Black Power Movement: Rethinking the Civil Rights–Black Power Era* (New York: Routledge, 2013), 2.

21. Gordon Parks, "Whip of Black Power," *Life* (May 19, 1967), 82.

22. Joshua Bloom and Waldo E. Martin Jr., *Black Against Empire: The History and Politics of the Black Panther Party* (Berkeley: University of California Press, 2012).

23. In 1974, fishing rights activists and tribal leaders reached a legal victory in *United States v. Washington*, otherwise known as the Boldt Decision, which declared that Native Americans were entitled to up to 50 percent of the fish caught in the "usual and accustomed places," as stated in 1850s treaties.

24. Paul Chaat Smith and Robert Allen Warrior, *Like a Hurricane: The Indian Movement from Alcatraz to Wounded Knee* (New York: New Press, 1997).

25. See, for instance, Juan Gómez-Quiñones and Irene Vásquez, *Making Aztlán: Ideology and Culture of the Chicana and Chicano Movement, 1966–1977* (Albuquerque: University of New Mexico Press, 2014).

26. Armando Navarro, *Mexican American Youth Organization: Avant-Garde of the Movement in Texas* (Austin: University of Texas Press, 1995); Ignacio M. Garcia, *United We Win: The Rise and Fall of La Raza Unida Party* (Tucson: University of Arizona Mexican American Studies Research Center, 1989).

27. *American Women: Report of the President's Commission the Status of Women* (U.S. Department of Labor: 1963), 2, https://www.dol.gov/wb/American %20Women%20Report.pdf, accessed June 7, 2018.

28. Flora Davis, *Moving the Mountain: The Women's Movement in America Since 1960* (Champaign: University of Illinois Press, 1999); Cynthia Ellen Harrison, *On Account of Sex: The Politics of Women's Issues, 1945–1968* (Berkeley: University of California Press, 1988).

29. Betty Friedan, *The Feminine Mystique* (New York: Norton, 1963), 50.

30. Carol Hanisch, "The Personal Is Political," in *Notes from the Second Year: Women's Liberation*, ed. Shulamith Firestone and Anne Koedt (New York: Radical Feminism, 1970).

31. Rachel Carson, *Silent Spring* (New York: Houghton Mifflin, 1962; Linda Lear, *Rachel Carson: Witness for Nature* (New York: Holt, 1997).

RECOMMENDED READING

Branch, Taylor. *Parting the Waters: America in the King Years, 1954–1963.* New York: Simon and Schuster, 1988.

———. *Pillar of Fire: America in the King Years, 1963–65.* New York: Simon and Schuster, 1998.

Breines, Winifred. *The Trouble Between Us: An Uneasy History of White and Black Women in the Feminist Movement.* New York: Oxford University Press, 2006.

Brick, Howard. *The Age of Contradictions: American Thought and Culture in the 1960s*. Ithaca, NY: Cornell University Press, 2000.

Brown-Nagin, Tomiko. *Courage to Dissent: Atlanta and the Long History of the Civil Rights Movement*. New York: Oxford University Press, 2011.

Carson, Clayborne. *In Struggle: SNCC and the Black Awakening of the 1960s*. Cambridge, MA: Harvard University Press, 1981.

Chafe, William. *Civilities and Civil Rights: Greensboro, North Carolina, and the Black Struggle for Freedom*. New York: Oxford University Press, 1980.

Dallek, Robert. *Flawed Giant: Lyndon Johnson and His Times, 1961–1973*. New York: Oxford University Press, 1993.

D'Emilio, John. *Sexual Politics, Sexual Communities: The Making of a Homosexual Minority in the United States, 1940–1970*. Chicago: University of Chicago Press, 1983.

Echols, Alice. *Daring to Be Bad: Radical Feminism in America, 1967–1975*. Minneapolis: University of Minnesota Press, 1989.

Gitlin, Todd. *The Sixties: Years of Hope, Days of Rage*. New York: Bantam Books, 1987.

Hall, Jacquelyn Dowd. "The Long Civil Rights Movement and the Political Uses of the Past." *Journal of American History* 91 (March 2005): 1233–1263.

Isserman, Maurice. *If I Had a Hammer: The Death of the Old Left and the Birth of the New Left*. Champaign: University of Illinois Press, 1987.

Johnson, Troy R. *The American Indian Occupation of Alcatraz Island: Red Power and Self-Determination*. Lincoln: University of Nebraska Press, 2008.

Joseph, Peniel. *Waiting 'til the Midnight Hour: A Narrative History of Black Power in America*. New York: Holt, 2006.

Kazin, Michael, and Maurice Isserman. *America Divided: The Civil War of the 1960s*. New York: Oxford University Press, 2007.

McGirr, Lisa. *Suburban Warriors: The Origins of the New American Right*. Princeton, NJ: Princeton University Press, 2001.

Orleck, Annelise. *Storming Caesar's Palace: How Black Mothers Fought Their Own War on Poverty*. New York: Beacon Books, 2005.

Patterson, James T. *America's Struggle Against Poverty in the Twentieth Century*. Cambridge, MA: Harvard University Press, 1981.

Patterson, James T. *Grand Expectations: The United States, 1945–1974*. New York: Oxford University Press, 1996.

Perlstein, Rick. *Before the Storm: Barry Goldwater and the Unmaking of the American Consensus*. New York: Hill and Wang, 2001.

Ransby, Barbara. *Ella Baker and the Black Freedom Movement: A Radical Democratic Vision*. Chapel Hill: University of North Carolina Press, 2000.

Robnett, Belinda. *How Long? How Long?: African American Women in the Struggle for Civil Rights*. New York: Oxford University Press, 2000.

Sugrue, Thomas. *The Origins of the Urban Crisis: Race and Inequality in Postwar Detroit*. Princeton, NJ: Princeton University Press, 2005.

28

The Unraveling

I. Introduction

On December 6, 1969, an estimated three hundred thousand people converged on the Altamont Motor Speedway in Northern California for a massive free concert headlined by the Rolling Stones and featuring some of the era's other great rock acts.[1] Only four months earlier, Woodstock had shown the world the power of peace and love and American youth. Altamont was supposed to be "Woodstock West."[2]

But Altamont was a disorganized disaster. Inadequate sanitation, a horrid sound system, and tainted drugs strained concertgoers. To save money, the Hells Angels biker gang was paid $500 in beer to be the show's "security team." The crowd grew progressively angrier throughout the day. Fights broke out. Tensions rose. The Angels, drunk and high, armed themselves with sawed-off pool cues and indiscriminately

Abandoned Packard automotive plant in Detroit, Michigan. Wikimedia.

beat concertgoers who tried to come on the stage. The Grateful Dead refused to play. Finally, the Stones came on stage.[3]

The crowd's anger was palpable. Fights continued near the stage. Mick Jagger stopped in the middle of playing "Sympathy for the Devil" to try to calm the crowd: "Everybody be cool now, c'mon," he pleaded. Then, a few songs later, in the middle of "Under My Thumb," eighteen-year-old Meredith Hunter approached the stage and was beaten back. Pissed off and high on methamphetamines, Hunter brandished a pistol, charged again, and was stabbed and killed by an Angel. His lifeless body was stomped into the ground. The Stones just kept playing.[4]

If the more famous Woodstock music festival captured the idyll of the sixties youth culture, Altamont revealed its dark side. There, drugs, music, and youth were associated not with peace and love but with anger, violence, and death. While many Americans in the 1970s continued to celebrate the political and cultural achievements of the previous decade, a more anxious, conservative mood grew across the nation. For some, the United States had not gone nearly far enough to promote greater social equality; for others, the nation had gone too far, unfairly trampling the rights of one group to promote the selfish needs of another. Onto these brewing dissatisfactions, the 1970s dumped the divisive remnants of a failed war, the country's greatest political scandal, and an intractable economic crisis. It seemed as if the nation was ready to unravel.

II. The Strain of Vietnam

Perhaps no single issue contributed more to public disillusionment than the Vietnam War. As the war deteriorated, the Johnson administration escalated American involvement by deploying hundreds of thousands of troops to prevent the communist takeover of the south. Stalemates, body counts, hazy war aims, and the draft catalyzed an antiwar movement and triggered protests throughout the United States and Europe. With no end in sight, protesters burned draft cards, refused to pay income taxes, occupied government buildings, and delayed trains loaded with war materials. By 1967, antiwar demonstrations were drawing hundreds of thousands. In one protest, hundreds were arrested after surrounding the Pentagon.[5]

Vietnam was the first "living room war."[6] Television, print media, and open access to the battlefield provided unprecedented coverage of the conflict's brutality. Americans confronted grisly images of casualties and atrocities. In 1965, *CBS Evening News* aired a segment in which

Vietnam War protesters at the March on the Pentagon. Lyndon B. Johnson Library via Wikimedia.

U.S. Marines burned the South Vietnamese village of Cam Ne with little apparent regard for the lives of its occupants, who had been accused of aiding Vietcong guerrillas. President Johnson berated the head of CBS, yelling over the phone, "Your boys just shat on the American flag."[7]

While the U.S. government imposed no formal censorship on the press during Vietnam, the White House and military nevertheless used press briefings and interviews to paint a deceptive image of the war. The United States was winning the war, officials claimed. They cited numbers of enemies killed, villages secured, and South Vietnamese troops trained. However, American journalists in Vietnam quickly realized the hollowness of such claims (the press referred to afternoon press briefings in Saigon as "the Five o'Clock Follies").[8] Editors frequently toned down their reporters' pessimism, often citing conflicting information received from their own sources, who were typically government officials. But the evidence of a stalemate mounted.

Stories like CBS's Cam Ne piece exposed a credibility gap, the yawning chasm between the claims of official sources and the increasingly evident reality on the ground in Vietnam.[9] Nothing did more to expose this gap than the 1968 Tet Offensive. In January, communist forces attacked more than one hundred American and South Vietnamese sites throughout South Vietnam, including the American embassy in Saigon. While U.S. forces repulsed the attack and inflicted heavy casualties on the Vietcong, Tet demonstrated that despite the repeated claims of administration officials, the enemy could still strike at will anywhere in the country, even after years of war. Subsequent stories and images eroded public trust even further. In 1969, investigative reporter Seymour Hersh revealed that U.S. troops had raped and/or massacred hundreds of civilians in the village of My Lai.[10] Three years later, Americans cringed at Nick Ut's wrenching photograph of a naked Vietnamese child fleeing a South Vietnamese napalm attack. More and more American voices came out against the war.

Reeling from the war's growing unpopularity, on March 31, 1968, President Johnson announced on national television that he would not seek reelection.[11] Eugene McCarthy and Robert F. Kennedy unsuccessfully battled against Johnson's vice president, Hubert Humphrey, for the Democratic Party nomination (Kennedy was assassinated in June). At the Democratic Party's national convention in Chicago, local police brutally assaulted protesters on national television.

For many Americans, the violent clashes outside the convention hall reinforced their belief that civil society was unraveling. Republican challenger Richard Nixon played on these fears, running on a platform of "law and order" and a vague plan to end the war. Well aware of domestic pressure to wind down the war, Nixon sought, on the one hand, to appease antiwar sentiment by promising to phase out the draft, train South Vietnamese forces to assume more responsibility for the war effort, and gradually withdraw American troops. Nixon and his advisors called it "Vietnamization."[12] At the same time, Nixon appealed to the so-called silent majority of Americans who still supported the war (and opposed the antiwar movement) by calling for an "honorable" end to U.S. involvement—what he later called "peace with honor."[13] He narrowly edged out Humphrey in the fall's election.

Public assurances of American withdrawal, however, masked a dramatic escalation of conflict. Looking to incentivize peace talks, Nixon pursued a "madman strategy" of attacking communist supply lines across Laos and Cambodia, hoping to convince the North Vietnamese that he would do anything to stop the war.[14] Conducted without public knowledge or congressional approval, the bombings failed to spur the peace process, and talks stalled before the American-imposed November

1969 deadline. News of the attacks renewed antiwar demonstrations. Police and National Guard troops killed six students in separate protests at Jackson State University in Mississippi, and, more famously, Kent State University in Ohio in 1970.

Another three years passed—and another twenty thousand American troops died—before an agreement was reached.[15] After Nixon threatened to withdraw all aid and guaranteed to enforce a treaty militarily, the North and South Vietnamese governments signed the Paris Peace Accords in January 1973, marking the official end of U.S. force commitment to the Vietnam War. Peace was tenuous, and when war resumed North Vietnamese troops quickly overwhelmed southern forces. By 1975, despite nearly a decade of direct American military engagement, Vietnam was united under a communist government.

The Vietnam War profoundly influenced domestic politics. Moreover, it poisoned many Americans' perceptions of their government and its role in the world. And yet, while the antiwar demonstrations attracted considerable media attention and stand today as a hallmark of the sixties counterculture, many Americans nevertheless continued to regard the war as just. Wary of the rapid social changes that reshaped American society in the 1960s and worried that antiwar protests threatened an already tenuous civil order, a growing number of Americans turned to conservatism.

III. Racial, Social, and Cultural Anxieties

The civil rights movement looked dramatically different at the end of the 1960s than it had at the beginning. The movement had never been monolithic, but prominent, competing ideologies had fractured the movement in the 1970s. The rise of the Black Power movement challenged the integrationist dreams of many older activists as the assassinations of Martin Luther King Jr. and Malcolm X fueled disillusionment and many alienated activists recoiled from liberal reformers.

The political evolution of the civil rights movement was reflected in American culture. The lines of race, class, and gender ruptured American "mass" culture. The monolith of popular American culture, pilloried in the fifties and sixties as exclusively white, male-dominated, conservative, and stifling, finally shattered and Americans retreated into ever smaller, segmented subcultures. Marketers now targeted particular products to ever smaller pieces of the population, including previously neglected

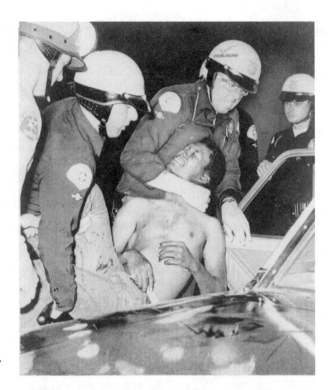

Los Angeles police violently arrest a man during the Watts riot on August 12, 1965. Wikimedia.

groups such as African Americans.[16] Subcultures often revolved around certain musical styles, whether pop, disco, hard rock, punk rock, country, or hip-hop. Styles of dress and physical appearance likewise aligned with cultures of choice.

If the popular rock acts of the sixties appealed to a new counter-culture, the seventies witnessed the resurgence of cultural forms that appealed to a white working class confronting the social and political upheavals of the 1960s. Country hits such as Merle Haggard's "Okie from Muskogee" evoked simpler times and places where people "still wave Old Glory down at the courthouse" and they "don't let our hair grow long and shaggy like the hippies out in San Francisco." (Haggard would claim the song was satirical, but it nevertheless took hold.) A popular television sitcom, *All in the Family*, became an unexpected hit among "middle America." The show's main character, Archie Bunker, was designed to mock reactionary middle-aged white men, but audiences embraced him. "Isn't anyone interested in upholding standards?" he lamented in an episode dealing with housing integration. "Our world is coming crumbling down. The coons are coming!"[17]

As Bunker knew, African Americans were becoming much more visible in American culture. While Black cultural forms had been prominent

The cast of CBS's *All in the Family* in 1973. Wikimedia.

throughout American history, they assumed new popular forms in the 1970s. Disco offered a new, optimistic, racially integrated pop music. Musicians such as Aretha Franklin, Andraé Crouch, and "fifth Beatle" Billy Preston brought their background in church performance to their own recordings as well as to the work of white artists like the Rolling Stones, with whom they collaborated. By the end of the decade, African American musical artists had introduced American society to one of the most significant musical innovations in decades: the Sugarhill Gang's 1979 record, *Rapper's Delight*. A lengthy paean to Black machismo, it became the first rap single to reach the Top 40.[18]

Just as rap represented a hypermasculine Black cultural form, Hollywood popularized its white equivalent. Films such as 1971's *Dirty Harry* captured a darker side of the national mood. Clint Eastwood's titular character exacted violent justice on clear villains, working within the sort of brutally simplistic ethical standard that appealed to Americans anxious about a perceived breakdown in "law and order." ("The film's moral position is fascist," said critic Roger Ebert, who nevertheless gave it three out of four stars.[19])

Perhaps the strongest element fueling American anxiety over "law and order" was the increasingly visible violence associated with the civil rights movement. No longer confined to the anti-Black terrorism that struck the southern civil rights movement in the 1950s and 1960s, publicly visible violence now broke out among Black Americans in urban riots and among whites protesting new civil rights programs. In the mid-1970s, for instance, protests over the use of busing to overcome residential segregation and truly integrate public schools in Boston washed the city in racial violence. Stanley Forman's Pulitzer Prize–winning photo, *The Soiling of Old Glory*, famously captured a Black civil rights attorney, Ted Landsmark, being attacked by a mob of anti-busing protesters, one of whom wielded an American flag as a weapon.[20]

Urban riots, though, rather than anti-integration violence, tainted many white Americans' perception of the civil rights movement and urban life in general. Civil unrest broke out across the country, but the riots in Watts/Los Angeles (1965), Newark (1967), and Detroit (1967) were the most shocking. In each, a physical altercation between white police officers and African Americans spiraled into days of chaos and destruction. Tens of thousands participated in urban riots. Many looted and destroyed white-owned business. There were dozens of deaths, tens of millions of dollars in property damage, and an exodus of white capital that only further isolated urban poverty.[21]

In 1967, President Johnson appointed the Kerner Commission to investigate the causes of America's riots. Their report became an unexpected best seller.[22] The commission cited Black frustration with the hopelessness of poverty as the underlying cause of urban unrest. As the head of the Black National Business League testified, "It is to be more than naïve—indeed, it is a little short of sheer madness—for anyone to expect the very poorest of the American poor to remain docile and content in their poverty when television constantly and eternally dangles the opulence of our affluent society before their hungry eyes."[23] A Newark rioter who looted several boxes of shirts and shoes put it more simply: "They tell us about that pie in the sky but that pie in the sky is too damn high."[24] But white conservatives blasted the conclusion that white racism and economic hopelessness were to blame for the violence. African Americans wantonly destroying private property, they said, was not a symptom of America's intractable racial inequalities but the logical outcome of a liberal culture of permissiveness that tolerated—even encouraged—nihilistic civil disobedience. Many white moderates and liberals, meanwhile, saw the explosive violence as a sign that African Americans had rejected the nonviolence of the earlier civil rights movement.

The unrest of the late sixties did, in fact, reflect a real and growing disillusionment among African Americans with the fate of the civil rights crusade. In the still-moldering ashes of Jim Crow, African Americans in Watts and other communities across the country bore the burdens of lifetimes of legally sanctioned discrimination in housing, employment, and credit. Segregation survived the legal dismantling of Jim Crow. The perseverance into the present day of stark racial and economic segregation in nearly all American cities destroyed any simple distinction between southern de jure segregation and nonsouthern de facto segregation. Black neighborhoods became traps that too few could escape.

Political achievements such as the 1964 Civil Rights Act and the 1965 Voting Rights Act were indispensable legal preconditions for social and political equality, but for most, the movement's long (and now often forgotten) goal of economic justice proved as elusive as ever. "I worked to get these people the right to eat cheeseburgers," Martin Luther King Jr. supposedly said to Bayard Rustin as they toured the devastation in Watts some years earlier, "and now I've got to do something . . . to help them get the money to buy it."[25] What good was the right to enter a store without money for purchases?

IV. The Crisis of 1968

To Americans in 1968, the country seemed to be unraveling. Martin Luther King Jr. was killed on April 4, 1968. He had been in Memphis to support striking sanitation workers. (Prophetically, he had reflected on his own mortality in a rally the night before. Confident that the civil rights movement would succeed without him, he brushed away fears of death. "I've been to the mountaintop," he said, "and I've seen the promised land."). The greatest leader in the American civil rights movement was lost. Riots broke out in over a hundred American cities. Two months later, on June 6, Robert F. Kennedy was killed campaigning in California. He had represented the last hope of liberal idealists. Anger and disillusionment washed over the country.

As the Vietnam War descended ever deeper into a brutal stalemate and the Tet Offensive exposed the lies of the Johnson administration, students shut down college campuses and government facilities. Protests enveloped the nation.

Protesters converged on the Democratic National Convention in Chicago at the end of August 1968, when a bitterly fractured Democratic

Party gathered to assemble a passable platform and nominate a broadly acceptable presidential candidate. Demonstrators planned massive protests in Chicago's public spaces. Initial protests were peaceful, but the situation quickly soured as police issued stern threats and young people began to taunt and goad officials. Many of the assembled students had protest and sit-in experiences only in the relative safe havens of college campuses and were unprepared for Mayor Richard Daley's aggressive and heavily armed police force and National Guard troops in full riot gear. Attendees recounted vicious beatings at the hands of police and Guardsmen, but many young people—convinced that much public sympathy could be won via images of brutality against unarmed protesters—continued stoking the violence. Clashes spilled from the parks into city streets, and eventually the smell of tear gas penetrated the upper floors of the opulent hotels hosting Democratic delegates. Chicago's brutality overshadowed the convention and culminated in an internationally televised, violent standoff in front of the Hilton Hotel. "The whole world is watching," the protesters chanted. The Chicago riots encapsulated the growing sense that chaos now governed American life.

For many sixties idealists, the violence of 1968 represented the death of a dream. Disorder and chaos overshadowed hope and progress. And for conservatives, it was confirmation of all of their fears and hesitations. Americans of 1968 turned their back on hope. They wanted peace. They wanted stability. They wanted "law and order."

V. The Rise and Fall of Richard Nixon

Beleaguered by an unpopular war, inflation, and domestic unrest, President Johnson opted against reelection in March 1968—an unprecedented move in modern American politics. The forthcoming presidential election was shaped by Vietnam and the aforementioned unrest as much as by the campaigns of Democratic nominee Vice President Hubert Humphrey, Republican Richard Nixon, and third-party challenger George Wallace, the infamous segregationist governor of Alabama. The Democratic Party was in disarray in the spring of 1968, when senators Eugene McCarthy and Robert Kennedy challenged Johnson's nomination and the president responded with his shocking announcement. Nixon's candidacy was aided further by riots that broke out across the country after the assassination of Martin Luther King Jr. and the shock and dismay experienced after the slaying of Robert Kennedy in June. The Republican nominee's

campaign was defined by shrewd maintenance of his public appearances and a pledge to restore peace and prosperity to what he called "the silent center; the millions of people in the middle of the political spectrum." This campaign for the "silent majority" was carefully calibrated to attract suburban Americans by linking liberals with violence and protest and rioting. Many embraced Nixon's message; a September 1968 poll found that 80 percent of Americans believed public order had "broken down."

Richard Nixon campaigns in Philadelphia during the 1968 presidential election. National Archives.

Meanwhile, Humphrey struggled to distance himself from Johnson and maintain working-class support in northern cities, where voters were drawn to Wallace's appeals for law and order and a rejection of civil rights. The vice president had a final surge in northern cities with the aid of union support, but it was not enough to best Nixon's campaign. The final tally was close: Nixon won 43.3 percent of the popular vote (31,783,783), narrowly besting Humphrey's 42.7 percent (31,266,006). Wallace, meanwhile, carried five states in the Deep South, and his 13.5 percent (9,906,473) of the popular vote constituted an impressive showing for a third-party candidate. The Electoral College vote was more decisive for Nixon; he earned 302 electoral votes, while Humphrey and Wallace received only 191 and 45 votes, respectively. Although Republicans won a few seats, Democrats retained control of both the House and Senate and made Nixon the first president in 120 years to enter office with the opposition party controlling both houses.

Once installed in the White House, Richard Nixon focused his energies on American foreign policy, publicly announcing the Nixon Doctrine in 1969. On the one hand, Nixon asserted the supremacy of American democratic capitalism and conceded that the United States would continue supporting its allies financially. However, he denounced previous administrations' willingness to commit American forces to Third World conflicts and warned other states to assume responsibility for their own defense. He was turning America away from the policy of active, anti-communist containment, and toward a new strategy of détente.[26]

Promoted by national security advisor and eventual secretary of state Henry Kissinger, détente sought to stabilize the international system by thawing relations with Cold War rivals and bilaterally freezing arms levels. Taking advantage of tensions between communist China and the Soviet Union, Nixon pursued closer relations with both in order to de-escalate tensions and strengthen the United States' position relative to each. The strategy seemed to work. In 1972, Nixon became the first American president to visit communist China and the first since Franklin Roosevelt to visit the Soviet Union. Direct diplomacy and cultural exchange programs with both countries grew and culminated with the formal normalization of U.S.-Chinese relations and the signing of two U.S.-Soviet arms agreements: the antiballistic missile (ABM) treaty and the Strategic Arms Limitations Treaty (SALT I). By 1973, after almost thirty years of Cold War tension, peaceful coexistence suddenly seemed possible.

Soon, though, a fragile calm gave way again to Cold War instability. In November 1973, Nixon appeared on television to inform Americans that energy had become "a serious national problem" and that the United States was "heading toward the most acute shortages of energy since World War II."[27] The previous month Arab members of the Organization of the Petroleum Exporting Countries (OPEC), a cartel of the world's leading oil producers, embargoed oil exports to the United States in retaliation for American intervention in the Middle East. The embargo launched the first U.S. energy crisis. By the end of 1973, the global price of oil had quadrupled.[28] Drivers waited in line for hours to fill up their cars. Individual gas stations ran out of gas. American motorists worried that oil could run out at any moment. A Pennsylvania man died when his emergency stash of gasoline ignited in his trunk and backseat.[29] OPEC rescinded its embargo in 1974, but the economic damage had been done. The crisis extended into the late 1970s.

Like the Vietnam War, the oil crisis showed that small countries could still hurt the United States. At a time of anxiety about the nation's future, Vietnam and the energy crisis accelerated Americans' disenchantment with the United States' role in the world and the efficacy and quality of its leaders. Furthermore, government scandals in the 1970s and early 1980s sapped trust in America's public institutions. In 1971, the Nixon administration tried unsuccessfully to sue the *New York Times* and the *Washington Post* to prevent the publication of the Pentagon Papers, a confidential and damning history of U.S. involvement in Vietnam commissioned by the Defense Department and later leaked. The papers showed how presidents from Truman to Johnson repeatedly deceived the public on the war's scope and direction.[30] Nixon faced a rising tide of congressional opposition to the war, and Congress asserted unprecedented oversight of American war spending. In 1973, it passed the War Powers Resolution, which dramatically reduced the president's ability to wage war without congressional consent.

However, no scandal did more to unravel public trust than Watergate. On June 17, 1972, five men were arrested inside the offices of the Democratic National Committee (DNC) in the Watergate Complex in downtown Washington, D.C. After being tipped off by a security guard, police found the men attempting to install sophisticated bugging equipment. One of those arrested was a former CIA employee then working as a security aide for the Nixon administration's Committee to Re-elect the President (lampooned as "CREEP").

While there is no direct evidence that Nixon ordered the Watergate break-in, he had been recorded in conversation with his chief of staff requesting that the DNC chairman be illegally wiretapped to obtain the names of the committee's financial supporters. The names could then be given to the Justice Department and the Internal Revenue Service (IRS) to conduct spurious investigations into their personal affairs. Nixon was also recorded ordering his chief of staff to break into the offices of the Brookings Institution and take files relating to the war in Vietnam, saying, "Goddammit, get in and get those files. Blow the safe and get it."[31]

Whether or not the president ordered the Watergate break-in, the White House launched a massive cover-up. Administration officials ordered the CIA to halt the FBI investigation and paid hush money to the burglars and White House aides. Nixon distanced himself from the incident publicly and went on to win a landslide election victory in November 1972. But, thanks largely to two persistent journalists at the *Washington Post*, Bob Woodward and Carl Bernstein, information continued to surface that tied the burglaries ever closer to the CIA, the FBI, and the White House. The Senate held televised hearings. Citing executive privilege,

Nixon refused to comply with orders to produce tapes from the White House's secret recording system. In July 1974, the House Judiciary Committee approved a bill to impeach the president. Nixon resigned before the full House could vote on impeachment. He became the first and only American president to resign from office.[32]

Vice President Gerald Ford was sworn in as his successor and a month later granted Nixon a full presidential pardon. Nixon disappeared from public life without ever publicly apologizing, accepting responsibility, or facing charges.

VI. Deindustrialization and the Rise of the Sunbelt

American workers had made substantial material gains throughout the 1940s and 1950s. During the so-called Great Compression, Americans of all classes benefited from postwar prosperity. Segregation and discrimination perpetuated racial and gender inequalities, but unemployment continually fell and a highly progressive tax system and powerful unions lowered general income inequality as working-class standards of living nearly doubled between 1947 and 1973.

But general prosperity masked deeper vulnerabilities. Perhaps no case better illustrates the decline of American industry and the creation of an intractable urban crisis than Detroit. Detroit boomed during World War II. When auto manufacturers like Ford and General Motors converted their assembly lines to build machines for the American war effort, observers dubbed the city the "arsenal of democracy."

Abandoned Youngstown factory. Stuart Spivack, via Flickr.

After the war, however, automobile firms began closing urban factories and moving to outlying suburbs. Several factors fueled the process. Some cities partly deindustrialized themselves. Municipal governments in San Francisco, St. Louis, and Philadelphia banished light industry to make room for high-rise apartments and office buildings. Mechanization also contributed to the decline of American labor. A manager at a newly automated Ford engine plant in postwar Cleveland captured the interconnections between these concerns when he glibly noted to United Automobile Workers (UAW) president Walter Reuther, "You are going to have trouble collecting union dues from all of these machines."[33] More importantly, however, manufacturing firms sought to reduce labor costs by automating, downsizing, and relocating to areas with "business friendly" policies like low tax rates, anti-union right-to-work laws, and low wages.

Detroit began to bleed industrial jobs. Between 1950 and 1958, Chrysler, which actually kept more jobs in Detroit than either Ford or General Motors, cut its Detroit production workforce in half. In the years between 1953 and 1960, East Detroit lost ten plants and over seventy-one thousand jobs.[34] Because Detroit was a single-industry city, decisions made by the Big Three automakers reverberated across the city's industrial landscape. When auto companies mechanized or moved their operations, ancillary suppliers like machine tool companies were cut out of the supply chain and likewise forced to cut their own workforce. Between 1947 and 1977, the number of manufacturing firms in the city dropped from over three thousand to fewer than two thousand. The labor force was gutted. Manufacturing jobs fell from 338,400 to 153,000 over the same three decades.[35]

Industrial restructuring decimated all workers, but deindustrialization fell heaviest on the city's African Americans. Although many middle-class Black Detroiters managed to move out of the city's ghettos, by 1960, 19.7 percent of Black autoworkers in Detroit were unemployed, compared to just 5.8 percent of whites.[36] Overt discrimination in housing and employment had for decades confined African Americans to segregated neighborhoods where they were forced to pay exorbitant rents for slum housing. Subject to residential intimidation and cut off from traditional sources of credit, few could afford to follow industry as it left the city for the suburbs and other parts of the country, especially the South. Segregation and discrimination kept them stuck where there were fewer and fewer jobs. Over time, Detroit devolved into a mass of unemployment, crime, and crippled municipal resources. When riots rocked Detroit in

1967, 25 to 30 percent of Black residents between ages eighteen and twenty-four were unemployed.[37]

Deindustrialization in Detroit and elsewhere also went hand in hand with the long assault on unionization that began in the aftermath of World War II. Lacking the political support they had enjoyed during the New Deal years, labor organizations such as the CIO and the UAW shifted tactics and accepted labor-management accords in which cooperation, not agitation, was the strategic objective.

This accord held mixed results for workers. On the one hand, management encouraged employee loyalty through privatized welfare systems that offered workers health benefits and pensions. Grievance arbitration and collective bargaining also provided workers official channels through which to criticize policies and push for better conditions. At the same time, bureaucracy and corruption increasingly weighed down unions and alienated them from workers and the general public. Union management came to hold primary influence in what was ostensibly a "pluralistic" power relationship. Workers—though still willing to protest—by necessity pursued a more moderate agenda compared to the union workers of the 1930s and 1940s. Conservative politicians meanwhile seized on popular suspicions of Big Labor, stepping up their criticism of union leadership and positioning themselves as workers' true ally.

While conservative critiques of union centralization did much to undermine the labor movement, labor's decline also coincided with ideological changes within American liberalism. Labor and its political concerns undergirded Roosevelt's New Deal coalition, but by the 1960s, many liberals had forsaken working-class politics. More and more saw poverty as stemming not from structural flaws in the national economy, but from the failure of individuals to take full advantage of the American system. Roosevelt's New Deal might have attempted to rectify unemployment with government jobs, but Johnson's Great Society and its imitators funded government-sponsored job training, even in places without available jobs. Union leaders in the 1950s and 1960s typically supported such programs and philosophies.

Internal racism also weakened the labor movement. While national CIO leaders encouraged Black unionization in the 1930s, white workers on the ground often opposed the integrated shop. In Detroit and elsewhere after World War II, white workers participated in "hate strikes" where they walked off the job rather than work with African Americans. White workers similarly opposed residential integration, fearing, among other things, that Black newcomers would lower property values.[38]

By the mid-1970s, widely shared postwar prosperity leveled off and began to retreat. Growing international competition, technological inefficiency, and declining productivity gains stunted working- and middle-class wages. As the country entered recession, wages decreased and the pay gap between workers and management expanded, reversing three decades of postwar contraction. At the same time, dramatic increases in mass incarceration coincided with the deregulation of prison labor to allow more private companies access to cheaper inmate labor, a process that, whatever its aggregate impact, impacted local communities where free jobs were moved into prisons. The tax code became less progressive and labor lost its foothold in the marketplace. Unions represented a third of the workforce in the 1950s, but only one in ten workers belonged to one as of 2015.[39]

Geography dictated much of labor's fall, as American firms fled pro-labor states in the 1970s and 1980s. Some went overseas in the wake of new trade treaties to exploit low-wage foreign workers, but others turned to anti-union states in the South and West stretching from Virginia to Texas to Southern California. Factories shuttered in the North and Midwest, leading commentators by the 1980s to dub America's former industrial heartland the Rust Belt. With this, they contrasted the prosperous and dynamic Sun Belt.

Urban decay confronted Americans of the 1960s and 1970s. As the economy sagged and deindustrialization hit much of the country, Americans increasingly associated major cities with poverty and crime. In this 1973 photo, two subway riders sit amid a graffitied subway car in New York City. National Archives (8464439).

Coined by journalist Kevin Phillips in 1969, the term *Sun Belt* refers to the swath of southern and western states that saw unprecedented economic, industrial, and demographic growth after World War II.[40] During the New Deal, President Franklin D. Roosevelt declared the American South "the nation's No. 1 economic problem" and injected massive federal subsidies, investments, and military spending into the region. During the Cold War, Sun Belt politicians lobbied hard for military installations and government contracts for their states.[41]

Meanwhile, southern states' hostility toward organized labor beckoned corporate leaders. The Taft-Hartley Act in 1947 facilitated southern states' frontal assault on unions. Thereafter, cheap, nonunionized labor, low wages, and lax regulations pulled northern industries away from the Rust Belt. Skilled northern workers followed the new jobs southward and westward, lured by cheap housing and a warm climate slowly made more tolerable by modern air conditioning.

The South attracted business but struggled to share their profits. Middle-class whites grew prosperous, but often these were recent transplants, not native southerners. As the cotton economy shed farmers and laborers, poor white and Black southerners found themselves mostly excluded from the fruits of the Sun Belt. Public investments were scarce. White southern politicians channeled federal funding away from primary and secondary public education and toward high-tech industry and university-level research. The Sun Belt inverted Rust Belt realities: the South and West had growing numbers of high-skill, high-wage jobs but lacked the social and educational infrastructure needed to train native poor and middle-class workers for those jobs.

Regardless, more jobs meant more people, and by 1972, southern and western Sun Belt states had more electoral votes than the Northeast and Midwest. This gap continues to grow.[42] Though the region's economic and political ascendance was a product of massive federal spending, New Right politicians who constructed an identity centered on "small government" found their most loyal support in the Sun Belt. These business-friendly politicians successfully synthesized conservative Protestantism and free market ideology, creating a potent new political force. Housewives organized reading groups in their homes, and from those reading groups sprouted new organized political activities. Prosperous and mobile, old and new suburbanites gravitated toward an individualistic vision of free enterprise espoused by the Republican Party. Some, especially those most vocally anticommunist, joined groups like the Young

Americans for Freedom and the John Birch Society. Less radical suburban voters, however, still gravitated toward the more moderate brand of conservatism promoted by Richard Nixon.

VII. The Politics of Love, Sex, and Gender

The sexual revolution continued into the 1970s. Many Americans—feminists, gay men, lesbians, and straight couples—challenged strict gender roles and rejected the rigidity of the nuclear family. Cohabitation without marriage spiked, straight couples married later (if at all), and divorce levels climbed. Sexuality, decoupled from marriage and procreation, became for many not only a source of personal fulfillment but a worthy political cause.

At the turn of the decade, sexuality was considered a private matter yet rigidly regulated by federal, state, and local law. Statutes typically defined legitimate sexual expression within the confines of patriarchal, procreative marriage. Interracial marriage, for instance, was illegal in many states until 1967 and remained largely taboo long after. Same-sex intercourse and cross-dressing were criminalized in most states, and gay

Demonstrators opposed to the Equal Rights Amendment protest in front of the White House in 1977. Library of Congress.

men, lesbians, and transgender people were vulnerable to violent police enforcement as well as discrimination in housing and employment.

Two landmark legal rulings in 1973 established the battle lines for the "sex wars" of the 1970s. First, the Supreme Court's 7–2 ruling in *Roe v. Wade* (1973) struck down a Texas law that prohibited abortion in all cases when a mother's life was not in danger. The Court's decision built on precedent from a 1965 ruling that, in striking down a Connecticut law prohibiting married couples from using birth control, recognized a constitutional "right to privacy."[43] In *Roe*, the Court reasoned that "this right of privacy . . . is broad enough to encompass a woman's decision whether or not to terminate her pregnancy."[44] The Court held that states could not interfere with a woman's right to an abortion during the first trimester of pregnancy and could only fully prohibit abortions during the third trimester.

Other Supreme Court rulings, however, found that sexual privacy could be sacrificed for the sake of "public" good. *Miller v. California* (1973), a case over the unsolicited mailing of sexually explicit advertisements for illustrated "adult" books, held that the First Amendment did not protect "obscene" material, defined by the Court as anything with sexual appeal that lacked, "serious literary, artistic, political, or scientific value."[45] The ruling expanded states' abilities to pass laws prohibiting materials like hard-core pornography. However, uneven enforcement allowed pornographic theaters and sex shops to proliferate despite whatever laws states had on the books. Americans debated whether these represented the pinnacle of sexual liberation or, as poet and lesbian feminist Rita Mae Brown suggested, "the ultimate conclusion of sexist logic."[46]

Of more tangible concern for most women, though, was the right to equal employment access. Thanks partly to the work of Black feminists like Pauli Murray, Title VII of the 1964 Civil Rights Act banned employment discrimination based on sex, in addition to race, color, religion, and national origin. "If sex is not included," she argued in a memorandum sent to members of Congress, "the civil rights bill would be including only half of the Negroes."[47] Like most laws, Title VII's full impact came about slowly, as women across the nation cited it to litigate and pressure employers to offer them equal opportunities compared to those they offered to men. For one, employers in the late sixties and seventies still viewed certain occupations as inherently feminine or masculine. NOW organized airline workers against a major company's sexist ad campaign that showed female flight attendants wearing buttons that read, "I'm Debbie,

Fly Me" or "I'm Cheryl, Fly Me." Actual female flight attendants were required to wear similar buttons.[48] Other women sued to gain access to traditionally male jobs like factory work. Protests prompted the Equal Employment Opportunity Commission (EEOC) to issue a more robust set of protections between 1968 and 1971. Though advancement came haltingly and partially, women used these protections to move eventually into traditional male occupations, politics, and corporate management.

The battle for sexual freedom was not just about the right to get *into* places, though. It was also about the right to get out of them—specifically, unhappy households and marriages. Between 1959 and 1979, the American divorce rate more than doubled. By the early 1980s, nearly half of all American marriages ended in divorce.[49] The stigma attached to divorce evaporated and a growing sense of sexual and personal freedom motivated individuals to leave abusive or unfulfilling marriages. Legal changes also promoted higher divorce rates. Before 1969, most states required one spouse to prove that the other was guilty of a specific offense, such as adultery. The difficulty of getting a divorce under this system encouraged widespread lying in divorce courts. Even couples desiring an amicable split were sometimes forced to claim that one spouse had cheated on the other even if neither (or both) had. Other couples temporarily relocated to states with more lenient divorce laws, such as Nevada.[50] Widespread recognition of such practices prompted reforms. In 1969, California adopted the first no-fault divorce law. By the end of the 1970s, almost every state had adopted some form of no-fault divorce. The new laws allowed for divorce on the basis of "irreconcilable differences," even if only one party felt that he or she could not stay in the marriage.[51]

Gay men and women, meanwhile, negotiated a harsh world that stigmatized homosexuality as a mental illness or an immoral depravity. Building on postwar efforts by gay rights organizations to bring homosexuality into the mainstream of American culture, young gay activists of the late sixties and seventies began to challenge what they saw as the conservative gradualism of the "homophile" movement. Inspired by the burgeoning radicalism of the Black Power movement, the New Left protests of the Vietnam War, and the counterculture movement for sexual freedom, gay and lesbian activists agitated for a broader set of sexual rights that emphasized an assertive notion of liberation rooted not in mainstream assimilation but in pride of sexual difference.

Perhaps no single incident did more to galvanize gay and lesbian activism than the 1969 uprising at the Stonewall Inn in New York City's

The window under the Stonewall Inn sign reads: "We homosexuals plead with our people to please help maintain peaceful and quiet conduct on the streets of the Village–Mattachine." Photograph, 1969. Wikimedia.

Greenwich Village. Police regularly raided gay bars and hangouts. But when police raided the Stonewall in June 1969, the bar patrons protested and sparked a multiday street battle that catalyzed a national movement for gay liberation. Seemingly overnight, calls for homophile respectability were replaced with chants of "Gay Power!"[52]

In the following years, gay Americans gained unparalleled access to private and public spaces. Gay activists increasingly attacked cultural norms that demanded they keep their sexuality hidden. Citing statistics that sexual secrecy contributed to stigma and suicide, gay activists urged people to come out and embrace their sexuality. A step towards the normalization of homosexuality occurred in 1973, when the American Psychiatric Association stopped classifying homosexuality as a mental illness. Pressure mounted on politicians. In 1982, Wisconsin became the first state to ban discrimination based on sexual orientation. More than eighty cities and nine states followed suit over the following decade.

But progress proceeded unevenly, and gay Americans continued to suffer hardships from a hostile culture.

Like all social movements, the sexual revolution was not free of division. Transgender people were often banned from participating in Gay Pride rallies and lesbian feminist conferences. They, in turn, mobilized to fight the high incidence of rape, abuse, and murder of transgender people. A 1971 newsletter denounced the notion that transgender people were mentally ill and highlighted the particular injustices they faced in and out of the gay community, declaring, "All power to Trans Liberation."[53]

As events in the 1970s broadened sexual freedoms and promoted greater gender equality, so too did they generate sustained and organized opposition. Evangelical Christians and other moral conservatives, for instance, mobilized to reverse gay victories. In 1977, activists in Dade County, Florida, used the slogan "Save Our Children" to overturn an ordinance banning discrimination based on sexual orientation.[54] A leader of the ascendant religious right, Jerry Falwell, said in 1980, "It is now time to take a stand on certain moral issues. . . . We must stand against the Equal Rights Amendment, the feminist revolution, and the homosexual revolution. We must have a revival in this country."[55]

Much to Falwell's delight, conservative Americans did, in fact, stand against and defeat the Equal Rights Amendment (ERA), their most stunning social victory of the 1970s. Versions of the amendment—which declared, "Equality of rights under the law shall not be denied or abridged by the United States or any state on account of sex"—were introduced to Congress each year since 1923. It finally passed amid the upheavals of the sixties and seventies and went to the states for ratification in March 1972.[56] With high approval ratings, the ERA seemed destined to pass swiftly through state legislatures and become the Twenty-Seventh Amendment. Hawaii ratified the amendment the same day it cleared Congress. Within a year, thirty states had done so. But then the amendment stalled. It took years for more states to pass it. In 1977, Indiana became the thirty-fifth and final state to ratify.[57]

By 1977, anti-ERA forces had successfully turned the political tide against the amendment. At a time when many women shared Betty Friedan's frustration that society seemed to confine women to the role of homemaker, Phyllis Schlafly's STOP ERA organization ("Stop Taking Our Privileges") trumpeted the value and advantages of being a homemaker and mother.[58] Marshaling the support of evangelical Christians and other religious conservatives, Schlafly worked tirelessly to stifle the

ERA. She lobbied legislators and organized counter-rallies to ensure that Americans heard "from the millions of happily married women who believe in the laws which protect the family and require the husband to support his wife and children."[59] The amendment needed only three more states for ratification. It never got them. In 1982, the time limit for ratification expired—and along with it, the amendment.[60]

The failed battle for the ERA uncovered the limits of the feminist crusade. And it illustrated the women's movement's inherent incapacity to represent fully the views of 50 percent of the country's population, a population riven by class differences, racial disparities, and cultural and religious divisions.

VIII. The Misery Index

Although Nixon eluded prosecution, Watergate continued to weigh on voters' minds. It netted big congressional gains for Democrats in the 1974 midterm elections, and Ford's pardon damaged his chances in 1976. Former Georgia governor Jimmy Carter, a nuclear physicist and peanut farmer who represented the rising generation of younger, racially liberal

Supporters rally with pumpkins carved in the likeness of President Jimmy Carter in Polk County, Florida, in October 1980. State Library and Archives of Florida via Flickr.

"New South" Democrats, captured the Democratic nomination. Carter did not identify with either his party's liberal or conservative wing; his appeal was more personal and moral than political. He ran on no great political issues, letting his background as a hardworking, honest, southern Baptist navy man ingratiate him to voters around the country, especially in his native South, where support for Democrats had wavered in the wake of the civil rights movement. Carter's wholesome image was painted in direct contrast to the memory of Nixon, and by association with the man who pardoned him. Carter sealed his party's nomination in June and won a close victory in November.[61]

When Carter took the oath of office on January 20, 1977, however, he became president of a nation in the midst of economic turmoil. Oil shocks, inflation, stagnant growth, unemployment, and sinking wages weighed down the nation's economy. Some of these problems were traceable to the end of World War II when American leaders erected a complex system of trade policies to help rebuild the shattered economies of Western Europe and Asia. After the war, American diplomats and politicians used trade relationships to win influence and allies around the globe. They saw the economic health of their allies, particularly West Germany

The 1979 energy crisis panicked consumers who remembered the 1973 oil shortage, prompting Americans to buy oil in huge quantities. Library of Congress.

and Japan, as a crucial bulwark against the expansion of communism. Americans encouraged these nations to develop vibrant export-oriented economies and tolerated restrictions on U.S. imports.

This came at great cost to the United States. As the American economy stalled, Japan and West Germany soared and became major forces in the global production for autos, steel, machine tools, and electrical products. By 1970, the United States began to run massive trade deficits. The value of American exports dropped and the prices of its imports skyrocketed. Coupled with the huge cost of the Vietnam War and the rise of oil-producing states in the Middle East, growing trade deficits sapped the United States' dominant position in the global economy.

American leaders didn't know how to respond. After a series of negotiations with leaders from France, Great Britain, West Germany, and Japan in 1970 and 1971, the Nixon administration allowed these rising industrial nations to continue flouting the principles of free trade. They maintained trade barriers that sheltered their domestic markets from foreign competition while at the same time exporting growing amounts of goods to the United States. By 1974, in response to U.S. complaints and their own domestic economic problems, many of these industrial nations overhauled their protectionist practices but developed even subtler methods (such as state subsidies for key industries) to nurture their economies.

The result was that Carter, like Ford before him, presided over a hitherto unimagined economic dilemma: the simultaneous onset of inflation and economic stagnation, a combination popularized as *stagflation*.[62] Neither Ford nor Carter had the means or ambition to protect American jobs and goods from foreign competition. As firms and financial institutions invested, sold goods, and manufactured in new rising economies like Mexico, Taiwan, Japan, Brazil, and elsewhere, American politicians allowed them to sell their often cheaper products in the United States.

As American officials institutionalized this new unfettered global trade, many American manufacturers perceived only one viable path to sustained profitability: moving overseas, often by establishing foreign subsidiaries or partnering with foreign firms. Investment capital, especially in manufacturing, fled the United States looking for overseas investments and hastened the decline in the productivity of American industry.

During the 1976 presidential campaign, Carter had touted the "misery index," the simple addition of the unemployment rate to the inflation rate, as an indictment of Gerald Ford and Republican rule. But Carter failed to slow the unraveling of the American economy, and the stubborn and confounding rise of both unemployment and inflation damaged his presidency.

Just as Carter failed to offer or enact policies to stem the unraveling of the American economy, his idealistic vision of human rights–based foreign policy crumbled. He had not made human rights a central theme in his campaign, but in May 1977 he declared his wish to move away from a foreign policy in which "inordinate fear of communism" caused American leaders to "adopt the flawed and erroneous principles and tactics of our adversaries." Carter proposed instead "a policy based on constant decency in its values and on optimism in our historical vision."[63]

Carter's human rights policy achieved real victories: the United States either reduced or eliminated aid to American-supported right-wing dictators guilty of extreme human rights abuses in places like South Korea, Argentina, and the Philippines. In September 1977, Carter negotiated the return to Panama of the Panama Canal, which cost him enormous political capital in the United States.[64] A year later, in September 1978, Carter negotiated a peace treaty between Israeli prime minister Menachem Begin and Egyptian president Anwar Sadat. The Camp David Accords—named for the president's rural Maryland retreat, where thirteen days of secret negotiations were held—represented the first time an Arab state had recognized Israel, and the first time Israel promised Palestine self-government. The accords had limits, for both Israel and the Palestinians, but they represented a major foreign policy coup for Carter.[65]

And yet Carter's dreams of a human rights–based foreign policy crumbled before the Cold War and the realities of American politics. The United States continued to provide military and financial support for dictatorial regimes vital to American interests, such as the oil-rich state of Iran. When the President and First Lady Rosalynn Carter visited Tehran, Iran, in January 1978, the president praised the nation's dictatorial ruler, Shah Reza Pahlavi, and remarked on the "respect and the admiration and love" Iranians had for their leader.[66] When the shah was deposed in November 1979, revolutionaries stormed the American embassy in Tehran and took fifty-two Americans hostage. Americans not only experienced another oil crisis as Iran's oil fields shut down, they watched America's news programs, for 444 days, remind them of the hostages and America's new global impotence. Carter couldn't win their release. A failed rescue mission only ended in the deaths of eight American servicemen. Already beset with a punishing economy, Carter's popularity plummeted.

Carter's efforts to ease the Cold War by achieving a new nuclear arms control agreement disintegrated under domestic opposition from conservative Cold War hawks such as Ronald Reagan, who accused Carter of weakness. A month after the Soviets invaded Afghanistan in December 1979, a beleaguered Carter committed the United States to defending its "interests" in the Middle East against Soviet incursions, declaring that "an assault [would] be repelled by any means necessary, including military force." The Carter Doctrine not only signaled Carter's ambivalent commitment to de-escalation and human rights, it testified to his increasingly desperate presidency.[67]

The collapse of American manufacturing, the stubborn rise of inflation, the sudden impotence of American foreign policy, and a culture ever more divided: the sense of unraveling pervaded the nation. "I want to talk to you right now about a fundamental threat to American democracy," Jimmy Carter said in a televised address on July 15, 1979. "The threat is nearly invisible in ordinary ways. It is a crisis of confidence. It is a crisis that strikes at the very heart and soul and spirit of our national will."

IX. Conclusion

Though American politics moved right after Lyndon Johnson's administration, Nixon's 1968 election was no conservative counterrevolution. American politics and society remained in flux throughout the 1970s. American politicians on the right and the left pursued relatively moderate courses compared to those in the preceding and succeeding decades. But a groundswell of anxieties and angers brewed beneath the surface. The world's greatest military power had floundered in Vietnam and an American president stood flustered by Middle Eastern revolutionaries. The cultural clashes from the sixties persisted and accelerated. While cities burned, a more liberal sexuality permeated American culture. The economy crashed, leaving America's cities prone before poverty and crime and its working class gutted by deindustrialization and globalization. American weakness was everywhere. And so, by 1980, many Americans—especially white middle- and upper-class Americans—felt a nostalgic desire for simpler times and simpler answers to the frustratingly complex geopolitical, social, and economic problems crippling the nation. The appeal of Carter's soft drawl and Christian humility had signaled this yearning, but his utter failure to stop the unraveling of American power and confidence opened the way for a new movement, one with new personalities and a new conservatism—one that promised to undo the damage and restore the United States to its own nostalgic image of itself.

X. Reference Material

This chapter was edited by Edwin Breeden, with content contributions by Seth Anziska, Jeremiah Bauer, Edwin Breeden, Kyle Burke, Brent Cebul, Alexandra Evans, Sean Fear, Anne Gray Fischer, Destin Jenkins, Matthew Kahn, Suzanne Kahn, Brooke Lamperd, Katherine McGarr, Matthew Pressman, Adam Parsons, Emily Prifogle, John Rosenberg, Brandy Thomas Wells, and Naomi R. Williams.

Recommended citation: Seth Anziska et al., "The Unraveling," Edwin Breeden, ed., in *The American Yawp*, eds. Joseph Locke and Ben Wright (Stanford, CA: Stanford University Press, 2019).

NOTES TO CHAPTER 28

1. Acts included Santana; Jefferson Airplane; Crosby, Stills, Nash & Young; and the Flying Burrito Brothers. The Grateful Dead were scheduled but refused to play.

2. Bruce J. Schulman, *The Seventies: The Great Shift in American Culture, Society, and Politics* (Cambridge, MA: Da Capo Press, 2002), 18.

3. Allen J. Matusow, *The Unraveling of America: A History of Liberalism in the 1960s*, updated ed. (Athens: University of Georgia Press, 2009), 304–305.

4. Owen Gleibman, "Altamont at 45: The Most Dangerous Rock Concert," BBC, December 5, 2014, http://www.bbc.com/culture/story/20141205-did-altamont-end-the-60s.

5. Jeff Leen, "The Vietnam Protests: When Worlds Collided," *Washington Post*, September 27, 1999, http://www.washingtonpost.com/wp-srv/local/2000/vietnam092799.htm.

6. Michael J. Arlen, *Living-Room War* (New York: Viking, 1969).

7. Tom Engelhardt, *The End of Victory Culture: Cold War America and the Disillusioning of a Generation*, revised ed. (Amherst: University of Massachusetts Press, 2007), 190.

8. Mitchel P. Roth, *Historical Dictionary of War Journalism* (Westport, CT: Greenwood, 1997), 105.

9. David L. Anderson, *The Columbia Guide to the Vietnam War* (New York: Columbia University Press, 2002), 109.

10. Guenter Lewy, *America in Vietnam* (New York: Oxford University Press, 1978), 325–326.

11. Lyndon B. Johnson, "Address to the Nation Announcing Steps to Limit the War in Vietnam and Reporting His Decision Not to Seek Reelection," March 31, 1968, Lyndon Baines Johnson Library, http://www.lbjlib.utexas.edu/johnson/archives.hom/speeches.hom/680331.asp.

12. Lewy, *America in Vietnam*, 164–169; Henry Kissinger, *Ending the Vietnam War: A History of America's Involvement in and Extrication from the Vietnam War* (New York: Simon and Schuster, 2003), 81–82.

13. Richard Nixon, "Address to the Nation Announcing Conclusion of an Agreement on Ending the War and Restoring Peace in Vietnam," January 23, 1973, *American Presidency Project*, http://www.presidency.ucsb.edu/ws/?pid=3808.

14. Richard Nixon, quoted in Walter Isaacson, *Kissinger: A Biography* (New York: Simon and Schuster, 2005), 163–164.

15. Geneva Jussi Hanhimaki, *The Flawed Architect: Henry Kissinger and American Foreign Policy* (New York: Oxford University Press, 2004), 257.

16. Cohen, *Consumer's Republic*.

17. Quotes from "Lionel Moves into the Neighborhood," *All in the Family*, season 1, episode 8 (1971), http://www.tvrage.com/all-in-the-family/episodes /5587.

18. Jim Dawson and Steve Propes, *45 RPM: The History, Heroes and Villains of a Pop Music Revolution* (San Francisco: Backbeat Books, 2003), 120.

19. Roger Ebert, "Review of *Dirty Harry*," January 1, 1971, http://www .rogerebert.com/reviews/dirty-harry-1971.

20. Ronald P. Formisano, *Boston Against Busing: Race, Class, and Ethnicity in the 1960s and 1970s* (Chapel Hill: University of North Carolina Press, 1991).

21. Michael W. Flamm, *Law and Order: Street Crime, Civil Unrest, and the Crisis of Liberalism in the 1960s* (New York: Columbia University Press, 2005), 58–59, 85–93.

22. Thomas J. Sugrue, *Sweet Land of Liberty: The Forgotten Struggle for Civil Rights in the North* (New York: Random House, 2008), 348.

23. Cohen, *Consumer's Republic*, 373.

24. Ibid., 376.

25. Martin Luther King, quoted in David J. Garrow, *Bearing the Cross: Martin Luther King Jr. and the Southern Christian Leadership Conference* (New York: Morrow, 1986), 439.

26. Richard M. Nixon, "Address to the Nation on the War in Vietnam," November 3, 1969, *American Experience*, http://www.pbs.org/wgbh/american experience/features/primary-resources/nixon-vietnam/.

27. Richard Nixon, "Address to the Nation about Policies to Deal with Energy Shortages," November 7, 1973, *American Presidency Project*, http://www .presidency.ucsb.edu/ws/?pid=4034.

28. Office of the Historian, "Oil Embargo, 1973–1974," U.S. Department of State, https://history.state.gov/milestones/1969-1976/oil-embargo.

29. "Gas Explodes in Man's Car," Uniontown (PA) *Morning Herald*, December 5, 1973, p. 12.

30. Larry H. Addington, *America's War in Vietnam: A Short Narrative History* (Bloomington: Indiana University Press, 2000), 140–141.

31. Schulman, *Seventies*, 44.

32. "Executive Privilege," in John J. Patrick, Richard M. Pious, and Donald A. Ritchie, "Executive Privilege," *The Oxford Guide to the United States Government* (New York: Oxford University Press, 2001), 227; Schulman, *The Seventies*, 44–48.

33. Sugrue, *Origins of the Urban Crisis*, 132.

34. Ibid., 136, 149.

35. Ibid., 144.

36. Ibid., 144.

37. Ibid., 261.

38. Jefferson Cowie and Nick Salvatore, "The Long Exception: Rethinking the Place of the New Deal in American History," *International Labor and Working-Class History* 74 (Fall 2008): 1–32, esp. 9.

39. Quoctrung Bui, "50 Years of Shrinking Union Membership in One Map," February 23, 2015, NPR, http://www.npr.org/sections/money/2015/02/23/385843576/50–years-of-shrinking-union-membership-in-one-map.

40. Kevin P. Phillips, *The Emerging Republic Majority* (New Rochelle, NY: Arlington House, 1969), 17.

41. Bruce J. Schulman, *From Cotton Belt to Sunbelt: Federal Policy, Economic Development, and the Transformation of the South, 1938–1980*, 3rd printing (Durham, NC: Duke University Press, 2007), 3.

42. William H. Frey, "The Electoral College Moves to the Sun Belt," research brief, Brookings Institution, May 2005.

43. *Griswold v. Connecticut*, 381 U.S. 479, June 7, 1965.

44. *Roe v. Wade*, 410 U.S. 113, January 22, 1973.

45. *Miller v. California*, 413 U.S. 15, June 21, 1973.

46. Rita Mae Brown, quoted in David Allyn, *Make Love, Not War—The Sexual Revolution: An Unfettered History* (New York: Routledge, 2001), 239.

47. Nancy MacLean, *Freedom Is Not Enough: The Opening of the American Workplace* (Cambridge, MA: Harvard University Press), 121.

48. Ibid., 129.

49. Arland Thornton, William G. Axinn, and Yu Xie, *Marriage and Cohabitation* (Chicago: University of Chicago Press, 2007), 57.

50. Glenda Riley, *Divorce: An American Tradition* (New York: Oxford University Press, 1991), 135–139.

51. Ibid., 161–165; Mary Ann Glendon, *The Transformation of Family Law: State, Law, and Family in the United States and Western Europe* (Chicago: University of Chicago Press, 1989), 188–189.

52. David Carter, *Stonewall: The Riots That Sparked the Gay Revolution* (New York: St. Martin's Press, 2004), 147.

53. *Trans Liberation Newsletter*, in Susan Styker, *Transgender History* (Berkeley, CA: Seal Press, 2008), 96–97.

54. William N. Eskridge, *Dishonorable Passions: Sodomy Laws in America, 1861–2003* (New York: Viking, 2008), 209–212.

55. Jerry Falwell, *Listen, America!* (Garden City, NY: Doubleday), 19.

56. Donald Critchlow, *Phyllis Schlafly and Grassroots Conservatism: A Woman's Crusade* (Princeton, NJ: Princeton University Press, 2005), 213–216.

57. Ibid., 218–219; Joel Krieger, ed., *The Oxford Companion to the Politics of the World*, 2nd ed. (New York: Oxford University Press, 2001), 256.

58. Critchlow, *Phyllis Schlafly and Grassroots Conservatism*, 219.

59. Phyllis Schlafly, quoted in Christine Stansell, *The Feminist Promise: 1792 to the Present* (New York: Modern Library, 2010), 340.

60. Critchlow, *Phyllis Schlafly and Grassroots Conservatism*, 281.

61. Sean Wilentz, *The Age of Reagan: A History, 1974–2008* (New York: HarperCollins, 2008), 69–72.

62. Ibid., 75.

63. Jimmy Carter, "University of Notre Dame—Address at the Commencement Exercises at the University," May 22, 1977, *American Presidency Project*, http://www.presidency.ucsb.edu/ws/?pid=7552.

64. Wilentz, *Age of Reagan*, 100–102.

65. Harvey Sicherman, *Palestinian Autonomy, Self-Government, and Peace* (Boulder, CO: Westview Press, 1993), 35.

66. Jimmy Carter, "Tehran, Iran Toasts of the President and the Shah at a State Dinner," December 31, 1977, *American Presidency Project*, http://www.presidency.ucsb.edu/ws/?pid=7080.

67. Jimmy Carter, "The State of the Union Address," January 23, 1980, *American Presidency Project*, http://www.presidency.ucsb.edu/ws/?pid=33079.

RECOMMENDED READING

Carter, Dan T. *The Politics of Rage: George Wallace, the Origins of the New Conservatism, and the Transformation of American Politics.* Baton Rouge: LSU Press, 1995.

Cowie, Jefferson R. *Stayin' Alive: The 1970s and the Last Days of the Working Class.* New York: New Press, 2010.

Evans, Sara. *Personal Politics: The Roots of Women's Liberation in the Civil Rights Movement and the New Left.* New York: Vintage Books, 1979.

Flamm, Michael W. *Law and Order: Street Crime, Civil Unrest, and the Crisis of Liberalism in the 1960s.* New York: Columbia University Press, 2005.

Formisano, Ronald P. *Boston Against Busing: Race, Class, and Ethnicity in the 1960s and 1970s.* Chapel Hill: University of North Carolina Press, 1991.

Greenberg, David. *Nixon's Shadow: The History of an Image.* New York: Norton, 2004.

Harvey, David. *The Condition of Postmodernity: An Enquiry into the Origins of Cultural Change.* Cambridge, UK: Blackwell, 1989.

Jenkins, Philip. *Decade of Nightmares: The End of the Sixties and the Making of Eighties America.* New York: Oxford University Press, 2008.

Kalman, Laura. *Right Star Rising: A New Politics, 1974–1980.* New York: Norton, 2010.

Lassiter, Matthew D. *The Silent Majority: Suburban Politics in the Sunbelt South.* Princeton, NJ: Princeton University Press, 2006.

MacLean, Nancy. *Freedom Is Not Enough: The Opening of the American Workplace.* Cambridge, MA: Harvard University Press, 2008.

Marable, Manning. *Malcolm X: A Life of Reinvention.* New York: Viking, 2011.

Matusow, Allen J. *The Unraveling of America: A History of Liberalism in the 1960s.* New York: Harper and Row, 1984.

Murch, Donna Jean. *Living for the City: Migration, Education, and the Rise of the Black Panther Party in Oakland, California*. Durham: University of North Carolina Press, 2010.

Patterson, James T. *Grand Expectations: The United States, 1945–1974*. New York: Oxford University Press, 1996.

Perlstein, Rick. *Nixonland: The Rise of a President and the Fracturing of America*. New York: Norton, 2003.

Phelps, Wesley. *A People's War on Poverty: Urban Politics, Grassroots Activists, and the Struggle for Democracy in Houston, 1964–1976*. Athens: University of Georgia Press, 2014.

Rodgers, Daniel T. *Age of Fracture*. Cambridge, MA: Belknap Press, 2011.

Roth, Benita. *Separate Roads to Feminism: Black, Chicana, and White Feminist Movements in America's Second Wave*. New York: Cambridge University Press, 2004.

Sargent, Daniel J. *A Superpower Transformed: The Remaking of American Foreign Relations in the 1970s*. Oxford, UK: Oxford University Press, 2015.

Schulman, Bruce J. *The Seventies: The Great Shift in American Culture, Society, and Politics*. New York: Free Press, 2001.

Springer, Kimberly. *Living for the Revolution: Black Feminist Organizations, 1968–1980*. Durham, NC: Duke University Press, 2005.

Stein, Judith. *Pivotal Decade: How the United States Traded Factories for Finance in the 1970s*. New Haven, CT: Yale University Press, 2010.

Thompson, Heather Ann. *Blood in the Water: The Attica Prison Uprising of 1971 and Its Legacy*. New York: Pantheon Books, 2016.

Zaretsky, Natasha. *No Direction Home: The American Family and the Fear of National Decline*. Chapel Hill: University of North Carolina Press, 2007.

29

The Triumph of the Right

I. Introduction

Speaking to Detroit autoworkers in October 1980, Republican presidential candidate Ronald Reagan described what he saw as the American Dream under Democratic president Jimmy Carter. The family garage may have still held two cars, cracked Reagan, but they were "both Japanese and they're out of gas."[1] The charismatic former governor of California suggested that a once-proud nation was running on empty. But Reagan held out hope for redemption. Stressing the theme of "national decline," he nevertheless promised to make the United States once again a glorious "city upon a hill."[2] In November, Reagan's vision triumphed.

Reagan rode the wave of a powerful political movement referred to by historians as the New Right. More libertarian in its economics and more politically forceful in its conservative religious principles than the moderate brand of conservatism popular after World War II, the New

Activist Phyllis Schlafly campaigns against the Equal Rights Amendment in 1977. Library of Congress.

Right had by the 1980s evolved into the most influential wing of the Republican Party. And it could claim increasing credit for Republican electoral successes. Building on the gradual unraveling of the New Deal political order in the 1960s and 1970s (see Chapter 28), the conservative movement not only enjoyed the guidance of skilled politicians like Reagan but drew tremendous energy from a broad range of grassroots activists. Countless ordinary citizens—newly mobilized Christian conservatives, in particular—helped the Republican Party steer the country rightward. Enduring conflicts over race, economic policy, sexual politics, and foreign affairs fatally fractured the liberal consensus that had dominated American politics since the presidency of Franklin Roosevelt, and the New Right attracted support from Reagan Democrats, blue-collar voters who had lost faith in the old liberal creed.

The rise of the right affected Americans' everyday lives in numerous ways. The Reagan administration's embrace of free markets dispensed with the principles of active income redistribution and social welfare spending that had animated the New Deal and Great Society in the 1930s and 1960s. As American liberals increasingly embraced a "rights" framework directed toward African Americans, Latinos, women, lesbians and gays, and other marginalized groups, conservative policy makers targeted the regulatory and legal landscape of the United States. Critics complained that Reagan's policies served the interests of corporations and wealthy individuals and pointed to the sudden widening of economic inequality. But the New Right harnessed popular distrust of regulation, taxes, and bureaucrats, and conservative activists celebrated the end of hyperinflation and substantial growth in GDP.

In many ways, however, the rise of the right promised more than it delivered. Battered but intact, the social welfare programs of the New Deal and Great Society (for example, social security, Medicaid, and Aid to Families with Dependent Children) survived the 1980s. Despite Republican vows of fiscal discipline, both the federal government and the national debt ballooned. At the end of the decade, conservative Christians viewed popular culture as more vulgar and hostile to their values than ever before. And in the near term, the New Right registered only partial victories on a range of public policies and cultural issues. Yet from a long-term perspective, conservatives achieved a subtler and more enduring transformation of American politics and society. In the words of one historian, the conservative movement successfully "changed the terms of debate and placed its opponents on the defensive."[3] Liberals and their programs and policies did not disappear, but they increasingly fought battles on terrain chosen by the New Right.

II. Conservative Ascendance

The Reagan Revolution marked the culmination of a long process of political mobilization on the American right. In the first two decades after World War II the New Deal seemed firmly embedded in American electoral politics and public policy. Even two-term Republican president Dwight D. Eisenhower declined to roll back the welfare state. To be sure, William F. Buckley tapped into a deep vein of elite conservatism in 1955 by announcing in the first issue of *National Review* that his magazine "stands athwart history yelling Stop."[4] Senator Joseph McCarthy and John Birch Society founder Robert Welch stirred anticommunist fervor. But in general, the far right lacked organizational cohesion. Following Lyndon Johnson's resounding defeat of Republican Barry Goldwater— "Mr. Conservative"—in the 1964 presidential election, many observers declared American conservatism finished. *New York Times* columnist James Reston wrote that Goldwater had "wrecked his party for a long time to come."[5]

Despite these dire predictions, conservatism not only persisted, it prospered. Its growing appeal had several causes. The expansive social and economic agenda of Johnson's Great Society reminded anticommunists of Soviet-style central planning and deficits alarmed fiscal conservatives. Race also drove the creation of the New Right. The civil rights movement, along with the Civil Rights Act and the Voting Rights Act, challenged the racial hierarchy of the Jim Crow South. All of these occurred under Democratic leadership, pushing white southerners toward the Republican Party. In the late 1960s and early 1970s, Black Power, affirmative action, and court-ordered busing of children between schools to achieve racial balance brought "white backlash" in the North, often in cities previously known for political liberalism. To many white Americans, the urban rebellions, antiwar protests, and student uprisings of the late 1960s signaled social chaos. At the same time, slowing wage growth, rising prices, and growing tax burdens threatened many working- and middle-class citizens who long formed the core of the New Deal coalition. Liberalism no longer seemed to offer the great mass of white Americans a road map to prosperity, so they searched for new political solutions.

Former Alabama governor and conservative Democrat George Wallace masterfully exploited the racial, cultural, and economic resentments of working-class whites during his presidential runs in 1968 and 1972. Wallace's record as a staunch segregationist made him a hero in the Deep South, where he won five states as a third-party candidate in the 1968 general election. Wallace's populist message also resonated with blue-collar voters in the industrial North who felt left behind by the rights revolution. On the campaign stump, the fiery candidate lambasted hippies, antiwar protesters, and government bureaucrats. He assailed female welfare recipients for "breeding children as a cash crop" and ridiculed "over-educated, ivory-tower" intellectuals who "don't know how to park a bicycle straight."[6] Wallace also advanced progressive proposals for federal job training programs, a minimum wage hike, and legal protections for collective bargaining. Running as a Democrat in 1972, Wallace captured the Michigan primary and polled second in the industrial heartland of Wisconsin, Pennsylvania, and Indiana. In May 1972, an assassin's bullet left Wallace paralyzed and ended his campaign. Nevertheless, his amalgamation of older, New Deal–style proposals and conservative populism represented the rapid reordering of party loyalties in the late 1960s and early 1970s. Richard Nixon similarly harnessed the New Right's sense of grievance through his rhetoric about "law and order" and the "silent majority."[7] But Nixon and his Republican successor, Gerald Ford, continued to accommodate the politics of the New Deal order. The New Right remained without a major public champion.

Christian conservatives also felt themselves under siege from liberalism. In the early 1960s, Supreme Court decisions prohibiting teacher-led prayer (*Engel v. Vitale*) and Bible reading in public schools (*Abington v. Schempp*) led some on the right to conclude that a liberal judicial system threatened Christian values. In the following years, the counterculture's celebration of sex and drugs, along with relaxed obscenity and pornography laws, intensified the conviction that "permissive" liberalism encouraged immorality in private life. Evangelical Protestants—Christians who professed a personal relationship with Jesus Christ, upheld the Bible as an infallible source of truth, and felt a duty to convert, or evangelize, nonbelievers—composed the core of the so-called religious right.

With increasing assertiveness in the 1960s and 1970s, Christian conservatives mobilized to protect the "traditional" family. Women composed a striking number of the religious right's foot soldiers. In 1968 and 1969 a group of newly politicized mothers in Anaheim, California, led a sustained protest against sex education in public schools.[8] Catholic activist Phyllis Schlafly marshaled opposition to the ERA, while evangelical pop singer Anita Bryant drew national headlines for her successful fight to repeal Miami's gay rights ordinance in 1977. In 1979, Beverly LaHaye (whose husband, Tim—an evangelical pastor in San Diego—later coauthored the wildly popular *Left Behind* Christian book series) founded Concerned Women for America, which linked small groups of local activists opposed to the ERA, abortion, homosexuality, and no-fault divorce.

Activists like Schlafly and LaHaye valorized motherhood as women's highest calling. Abortion therefore struck at the core of their female identity. More than perhaps any other issue, abortion drew different segments of the religious right—Catholics and Protestants, women and men—together. The Supreme Court's 1973 *Roe v. Wade* ruling outraged many devout Catholics and evangelicals (who had been less universally opposed to the procedure than their Catholic counterparts). Christian author Francis Schaeffer cultivated evangelical opposition to abortion through the 1979 documentary film *Whatever Happened to the Human Race?*, arguing that the "fate of the unborn is the fate of the human race."[9] With abortion framed in stark, existential terms, many evangelicals felt compelled to combat the procedure through political action.

Grassroots passion drove anti-abortion activism, but a set of religious and secular institutions turned the various strands of the New Right into a sophisticated movement. In 1979 Jerry Falwell—a Baptist minister and religious broadcaster from Lynchburg, Virginia—founded the Moral Majority, an explicitly political organization dedicated to advancing a "pro-life, pro-family, pro-morality, and pro-American" agenda. The Moral Majority skillfully wove together social and economic appeals to make itself a force in Republican politics. Secular, business-oriented institutions also joined the attack on liberalism, fueled by stagflation and by the federal government's creation of new regulatory agencies like the Environmental Protection Agency and the Occupational Safety and Health Administration. Conservative business leaders bankrolled new "think tanks" like the Heritage Foundation and the Cato Institute. These organizations provided grassroots activists with ready-made policy prescriptions. Other business leaders took a more direct approach by hiring Washington lobbyists and creating political action committees (PACs) to press their agendas in the halls of Congress and federal agencies. Between 1976 and 1980 the number of corporate PACs rose from under three hundred to over twelve hundred.

Grassroots activists and business leaders received unlikely support from a circle of neoconservatives—disillusioned intellectuals who had rejected liberalism and the Left and become Republicans. Irving Kristol, a former Marxist who went on to champion free-market capitalism as a *Wall Street Journal* columnist, defined a neoconservative as a "liberal who has been mugged by reality."[10] Neoconservative journals like *Commentary* and *Public Interest* argued that the Great Society had proven counterproductive, perpetuating the poverty and racial segregation that it aimed to cure. By the middle of the 1970s, neoconservatives felt mugged by foreign affairs as well. As ardent Cold Warriors, they argued that Nixon's policy of détente left the United States vulnerable to the Soviet Union.

In sum, several streams of conservative political mobilization converged in the late 1970s. Each wing of the burgeoning New Right—disaffected northern blue-collar workers, white southerners, evangelicals and devout Catholics, business leaders, disillusioned intellectuals, and Cold War hawks—turned to the Republican Party as the most effective vehicle for their political counterassault on liberalism and the New Deal political order. After years of mobilization, the domestic and foreign policy storms of the Carter administration provided the tailwinds that brought the conservative movement to shore.

III. The Conservatism of the Carter Years

The election of Jimmy Carter in 1976 brought a Democrat to the White House for the first time since 1969. Large Democratic majorities in Congress provided the new president with an opportunity to move aggressively on the legislative front. With the infighting of the early 1970s behind them, many Democrats hoped the Carter administration would update and expand the New Deal. But Carter won the presidency on a wave of post-Watergate disillusionment with government that did not translate into support for liberal ideas.

In its early days, the Carter administration embraced several policies backed by liberals. It pushed an economic stimulus package containing $4 billion for public works, extended food stamp benefits to 2.5 million new recipients, enlarged the Earned Income Tax Credit for low-income households, and expanded the Nixon-era Comprehensive Employment and Training Act (CETA).[11] But the White House quickly realized that Democratic control of Congress did not guarantee support for its initially left-leaning economic proposals. Many of the Democrats elected to Congress in the aftermath of Watergate were more moderate than their predecessors, who had been trained in the New Deal gospel. These conservative Democrats sometimes partnered with congressional Republicans to oppose Carter, most notably in response to the administration's proposal for a federal office of consumer protection.

Events outside Carter's control certainly helped discredit liberalism, but the president's own temperamental and philosophical conservatism hamstrung the administration and pushed national politics further to the right. In his 1978 State of the Union address, Carter lectured Americans that "government cannot solve our problems . . . it cannot eliminate poverty, or provide a bountiful economy, or reduce inflation, or save our cities, or cure illiteracy, or provide energy."[12] The statement neatly captured the ideological transformation of the county. Rather than leading a resurgence of American liberalism, Carter became, as one historian put it, "the first president to govern in a post–New Deal framework."[13] Organized labor felt abandoned by Carter, who remained cool to several of their highest legislative priorities. The president offered tepid support for a national health insurance proposal and declined to lobby aggressively for a package of modest labor law reforms. The business community rallied to defeat the latter measure, in what AFL-CIO chief George Meany described as "an attack by every anti-union group in America to kill the labor movement."[14] In 1977 and 1978, liberal Democrats rallied behind the Humphrey-Hawkins Full Employment and Training Act, which promised to end unemployment through extensive government planning. The bill aimed not only to guarantee a job to every American but also to reunite the interracial, working-class Democratic coalition that had been fractured by deindustrialization and affirmative action.[15] But Carter's lack of enthusiasm for the proposal allowed conservatives from both parties to water the bill down to a purely symbolic gesture. Liberals, like labor leaders, came to regard the president as an unreliable ally.

Carter also came under fire from Republicans, especially the religious right. His administration incurred the wrath of evangelicals in 1978 when the IRS established new rules revoking the tax-exempt status of racially segregated, private Christian schools. The rules only strengthened a policy instituted by the Nixon administration; however, the religious right accused Carter of singling out Christian institutions. Republican activist Richard Viguerie described the IRS controversy as the "spark that ignited the religious right's involvement in real politics."[16] Race sat just below the surface of the IRS fight. After all, many of the schools had been founded to circumvent court-ordered desegregation. But the IRS ruling allowed the New Right to rain down fire on big government interference while downplaying the practice of segregation at the heart of the case.

While the IRS controversy flared, economic crises multiplied. Unemployment reached 7.8 percent in May 1980, up from 6 percent at the start of Carter's first term.[17] Inflation (the rate at which the cost of goods and services increases) jumped from 6 percent in 1978 to a staggering 20 percent by the winter of 1980.[18] In another bad omen, the iconic Chrysler Corporation appeared close to bankruptcy. The administration responded to these challenges in fundamentally conservative ways. First, Carter proposed a tax cut for the upper middle class, which Congress passed in 1978. Second, the White House embraced a longtime goal of the conservative movement by deregulating the airline and trucking industries in 1978 and 1980, respectively. Third, Carter proposed balancing the federal budget—much to the dismay of liberals, who would have preferred that he use deficit spending to finance a *new* New Deal. Finally, to halt inflation, Carter's appointed chair of the Federal Reserve, Paul Volcker, raised interest rates and tightened the money supply—policies designed to reduce inflation in the long run but which increased unemployment in the short run. Liberalism was on the run.

The decade's second "energy crisis," which witnessed another spike in oil prices and oil shortages across the country, brought out the southern Baptist moralist in Carter. On July 15, 1979, the president delivered a nationally televised speech on energy policy in which he attributed the country's economic woes to a "crisis of confidence." Carter lamented that "too many of us now tend to worship self-indulgence and consumption."[19] The country initially responded favorably to the push for energy conservation, yet Carter's emphasis on discipline and sacrifice and his spiritual diagnosis for economic hardship sidestepped deeper questions of large-scale economic change and downplayed the harsh toll inflation had taken on regular Americans.

IV. The Election of 1980

These domestic challenges, combined with the Soviet invasion of Afghanistan and the hostage crisis in Iran, hobbled Carter heading into his 1980 reelection campaign. Many Democrats were dismayed by his policies. The president of the International Association of Machinists dismissed

Carter as "the best Republican President since Herbert Hoover."[20] Angered by the White House's refusal to back national health insurance, Massachusetts senator Ted Kennedy challenged Carter in the Democratic primaries. Running as the party's liberal standard-bearer and heir to the legacy of his slain older brothers, Kennedy garnered support from key labor unions and left-wing Democrats. Carter ultimately vanquished Kennedy, but the close primary tally exposed the president's vulnerability.

Carter's opponent in the general election was Ronald Reagan, a former Hollywood actor who had served two terms as governor of California. Reagan ran as a staunch fiscal conservative and a Cold War hawk, vowing to reduce government spending and shrink the federal bureaucracy. Reagan also accused his opponent of failing to confront the Soviet Union and vowed steep increases in military spending. Carter responded by calling Reagan a warmonger, but the Soviet invasion of Afghanistan and the confinement of 52 American hostages in Iran discredited Carter's foreign policy in the eyes of many Americans.

The incumbent fared no better on domestic affairs. Unemployment remained at nearly 8 percent.[21] Meanwhile the Federal Reserve's anti-inflation measures pushed interest rates to an unheard-of 18.5 percent.[22] Reagan seized on these bad economic trends. On the campaign trail he brought down the house by proclaiming: "A recession is when your neighbor loses his job, and a depression is when you lose your job." Reagan would then pause before concluding, "And a recovery is when Jimmy Carter loses his job."[23]

Social and cultural issues presented yet another challenge for the president. Although a self-proclaimed "born-again" Christian and Sunday school teacher, Carter struggled to court the religious right. Carter scandalized devout Christians by admitting to lustful thoughts during an interview with *Playboy* magazine in 1976, telling the reporter he had "committed adultery in my heart many times."[24] Although Reagan was only a nominal Christian and rarely attended church, the religious right embraced him. Reverend Jerry Falwell directed the full weight of the Moral Majority behind Reagan. The organization registered an estimated two million new voters in 1980. Reagan also cultivated the religious right by denouncing abortion and endorsing prayer in school. The IRS tax exemption issue resurfaced as well, with the 1980 Republican platform vowing to "halt the unconstitutional regulatory vendetta launched by Mr. Carter's IRS commissioner against independent schools."[25] Early in the primary season, Reagan condemned the policy during a speech at

Jerry Falwell, a wildly popular TV evangelist, founded the Moral Majority in the late 1970s. Decrying the demise of the nation's morality, the organization gained a massive following and helped to cement the status of the New Christian Right in American politics. Wikimedia.

South Carolina's Bob Jones University, which had recently sued the IRS after the school's ban on interracial dating led to the loss of its tax-exempt status.

Reagan's campaign appealed subtly but unmistakably to the racial hostilities of white voters. The candidate held his first post–nominating convention rally at the Neshoba County Fair near Philadelphia, Mississippi, the town where three civil rights workers had been murdered in 1964. In his speech, Reagan championed the doctrine of states' rights, which had been the rallying cry of segregationists in the 1950s and 1960s. In criticizing the welfare state, Reagan had long employed thinly veiled racial stereotypes about a "welfare queen" in Chicago who drove a Cadillac while defrauding the government or a "strapping young buck" purchasing T-bone steaks with food stamps.[26] Like George Wallace before him, Reagan exploited the racial and cultural resentments of struggling white working-class voters. And like Wallace, he attracted blue-collar workers in droves.

With the wind at his back on almost every issue, Reagan only needed to blunt Carter's characterization of him as an angry extremist. Reagan did so during their only debate by appearing calm and amiable. "Are you better off than you were four years ago?" he asked the American people at the conclusion of the debate.[27] The American people answered no. Reagan won the election with 51 percent of the popular vote to Carter's 41 percent. (Independent John Anderson captured 7 percent.)[28] Despite capturing only a slim majority, Reagan scored a decisive 489–49 victory in the Electoral College.[29] Republicans gained control of the Senate for the first time since 1955 by winning twelve seats. Liberal Democrats George McGovern, Frank Church, and Birch Bayh went down in defeat, as did liberal Republican Jacob Javits. The GOP picked up thirty-three House seats, narrowing the Democratic advantage in the lower chamber.[30] The New Right had arrived in Washington, D.C.

Ronald Reagan secured the presidency by appealing to the growing conservatism of much of the country. Here, Ronald Reagan and his wife, Nancy Reagan, wave from a limousine during the inaugural parade in Washington, D.C., in 1981. Wikimedia.

V. The New Right in Power

In his first inaugural address Reagan proclaimed that "government is not the solution to the problem, government is the problem."[31] In reality, Reagan focused less on eliminating government than on redirecting gov-

ernment to serve new ends. In line with that goal, his administration embraced supply-side economic theories that had recently gained popularity among the New Right. While the postwar gospel of Keynesian economics had focused on stimulating consumer demand, supply-side economics held that lower personal and corporate tax rates would encourage greater private investment and production. Supply-side advocates promised that the resulting wealth would reach—or "trickle down" to, in the words of critics—lower-income groups through job creation and higher wages. Conservative economist Arthur Laffer predicted that lower tax rates would generate so much economic activity that federal tax revenues would actually increase. The administration touted the so-called Laffer Curve as justification for the tax cut plan that served as the cornerstone of Reagan's first year in office. Republican congressman Jack Kemp, an early supply-side advocate and co-sponsor of Reagan's tax bill, promised that it would unleash the "creative genius that has always invigorated America."[32]

The tax cut faced early skepticism from Democrats and even some Republicans. Vice president George H. W. Bush had belittled supply-side

The Iranian hostage crisis ended literally during President Reagan's inauguration speech. The Reagan administration received credit for bringing the hostages home. This group photograph shows the former hostages in the hospital in 1981 before being released back to the United States. Wikimedia.

theory as "voodoo economics" during the 1980 Republican primaries.[33] But a combination of skill and serendipity pushed the bill over the top. Reagan aggressively and effectively lobbied individual members of Congress for support on the measure. Then on March 30, 1981, Reagan survived an assassination attempt by a mentally unstable young man named John Hinckley. Public support swelled for the hospitalized president. Congress ultimately approved a $675 billion tax cut in July 1981 with significant Democratic support. The bill reduced overall federal taxes by more than one quarter and lowered the top marginal rate from 70 percent to 50 percent, with the bottom rate dropping from 14 percent to 11 percent. It also slashed the rate on capital gains from 28 percent to 20 percent.[34] The next month, Reagan scored another political triumph in response to a strike called by the Professional Air Traffic Controllers Organization (PATCO). During the 1980 campaign, Reagan had wooed organized labor, describing himself as "an old union man" (he had led the Screen Actors Guild from 1947 to 1952) who still held Franklin Roosevelt in high regard.[35] PATCO had been one of the few labor unions to endorse Reagan. Nevertheless, the president ordered the union's striking air traffic controllers back to work and fired more than eleven thousand who refused. Reagan's actions crippled PATCO and left the American labor movement reeling. For the rest of the 1980s the economic terrain of the United States—already unfavorable to union organizing—shifted decisively in favor of employers. The unionized portion of the private-sector workforce fell from 20 percent in 1980 to 12 percent in 1990.[36] Reagan's tax bill and the defeat of PATCO not only enhanced the economic power of corporations and high-income households, they confirmed that a new conservative age had dawned in American life.

The new administration appeared to be flying high in the fall of 1981, but developments challenged the rosy economic forecasts emanating from the White House. As Reagan ratcheted up tension with the Soviet Union, Congress approved his request for $1.2 trillion in new military spending.[37] The combination of lower taxes and higher defense budgets caused the national debt to balloon. By the end of Reagan's first term it equaled 53 percent of GDP, as opposed to 33 percent in 1981.[38] The increase was staggering, especially for an administration that had promised to curb spending. Meanwhile, Federal Reserve chairman Paul Volcker continued his policy from the Carter years of combating inflation by maintaining high interest rates, which surpassed 20 percent in June 1981.[39] The Fed's action increased the cost of borrowing money and stifled economic activity.

As a result, the United States experienced a severe economic recession in 1981 and 1982. Unemployment rose to nearly 11 percent, the highest figure since the Great Depression.[40] Reductions in social welfare spending heightened the impact of the recession on ordinary people. Congress had followed Reagan's lead by reducing funding for food stamps and Aid to Families with Dependent Children and removed a half million people from the Supplemental Social Security program for the physically disabled.[41] The cuts exacted an especially harsh toll on low-income communities of color. The head of the NAACP declared that the administration's budget cuts had rekindled "war, pestilence, famine, and death."[42] Reagan also received bipartisan rebuke in 1981 after proposing cuts to social security benefits for early retirees. The Senate voted unanimously to condemn the plan, and Democrats framed it as a heartless attack on the elderly. Confronted with recession and harsh public criticism, a chastened White House worked with Democratic House Speaker Tip O'Neill in 1982 on a bill that restored $98 billion of the previous year's tax cuts.[43] Despite compromising with the administration on taxes, Democrats railed against the so-called Reagan Recession, arguing that the president's economic policies favored the most fortunate Americans. This appeal, which Democrats termed the "fairness issue," helped them win twenty-six House seats in the autumn congressional races.[44] The New Right appeared to be in trouble.

VI. Morning in America

Reagan nimbly adjusted to the political setbacks of 1982. Following the rejection of his social security proposals, Reagan appointed a bipartisan panel to consider changes to the program. In early 1983, the commission recommended a onetime delay in cost-of-living increases, a new requirement that government employees pay into the system, and a gradual increase in the retirement age from sixty-five to sixty-seven. The commission also proposed raising state and federal payroll taxes, with the new revenue poured into a trust fund that would transform social security from a pay-as-you-go system to one with significant reserves.[45] Congress quickly passed the recommendations into law, allowing Reagan to take credit for strengthening a program cherished by most Americans. The president also benefited from an economic rebound. Real disposable income rose 2.5 percent in 1983 and 5.8 percent the following year.[46] Unemployment dropped to 7.5 percent in 1984.[47] Meanwhile, the "harsh medicine" of high interest rates helped reduce inflation to 3.5 percent.[48]

President Ronald Reagan, a master of the photo op, appears here with a row of American flags at his back at a 1982 rally for Senator David Durenberger in Minneapolis, Minnesota. National Archives (198527).

While campaigning for reelection in 1984, Reagan pointed to the improving economy as evidence that it was "morning again in America."[49] His personal popularity soared. Most conservatives ignored the debt increase and tax hikes of the previous two years and rallied around the president.

The Democratic Party, on other hand, stood at an ideological crossroads in 1984. The favorite to win the party's nomination was Walter Mondale, a staunch ally of organized labor and the civil rights movement as a senator during the 1960s and 1970s. He later served as Jimmy Carter's vice president. Mondale's chief rivals were civil rights activist Jesse Jackson and Colorado senator Gary Hart, one of the young Democrats elected to Congress in 1974 following Nixon's downfall. Hart and other "Watergate babies" still identified themselves as liberals but rejected their party's faith in activist government and embraced market-based approaches to policy issues. In so doing, they conceded significant political ground to supply-siders and conservative opponents of the welfare state. Many Democrats, however, were not prepared to abandon their New Deal heritage, and so the ideological tension within the party played out in the 1984 primary campaign. Jackson offered a largely progressive program but won only two states. Hart's platform—economically moderate but socially liberal—inverted the political formula of Mondale's New Deal–style liberalism. Throughout the primaries, Hart contrasted his "new ideas" with Mondale's "old-fashioned" politics. Mondale eventually secured his party's nomination but suffered a crushing defeat in the general election. Reagan captured forty-nine of fifty states, winning 58.8 percent of the popular vote.[50]

Mondale's loss seemed to confirm that the new breed of moderate Democrats better understood the mood of the American people. The future of the party belonged to post–New Deal liberals like Hart and to the constituency that supported him in the primaries: upwardly mobile, white professionals and suburbanites. In February 1985, a group of centrists formed the Democratic Leadership Council (DLC) as a vehicle for distancing the party from organized labor and Keynesian economics while cultivating the business community. Jesse Jackson dismissed the DLC as "Democrats for the Leisure Class," but the organization included many of the party's future leaders, including Arkansas governor Bill Clinton.[51] The formation of the DLC illustrated the degree to which to the New Right had transformed American politics: New Democrats looked a lot like old Republicans.

Reagan entered his second term with a much stronger mandate than in 1981, but the Grand Old Party (GOP) makeover of Washington, D.C., stalled. The Democrats regained control of the Senate in 1986, and Democratic opposition prevented Reagan from eliminating means-tested social welfare programs, although Congress failed to increase benefit levels for welfare programs or raise the minimum wage, decreasing the real value of those benefits. Democrats and Republicans occasionally fashioned legislative compromises, as with the Tax Reform Act of 1986. The bill lowered the top corporate tax rate from 46 percent to 34 percent and reduced the highest marginal income tax rate from 50 percent to 28 percent, while also simplifying the tax code and eliminating numerous loopholes.[52] The steep cuts to the corporate and individual rates certainly benefited wealthy individuals, but the legislation made virtually no net change to federal revenues. In 1986, Reagan also signed into law the Immigration Reform and Control Act. American policy makers hoped to do two things: deal with the millions of undocumented immigrants already in the United States while simultaneously choking off future unsanctioned migration. The former goal was achieved (nearly three million undocumented workers received legal status) but the latter proved elusive.

One of Reagan's most far-reaching victories occurred through judicial appointments. He named 368 district and federal appeals court judges during his two terms.[53] Observers noted that almost all of the appointees were white men. (Seven were African American, fifteen were Latino, and two were Asian American.) Reagan also appointed three Supreme Court justices: Sandra Day O'Connor, who to the dismay of the religious right turned out to be a moderate; Anthony Kennedy, a solidly conservative Catholic who occasionally sided with the court's liberal wing; and archconservative Antonin Scalia. The New Right's transformation of the judiciary had limits. In 1987, Reagan nominated Robert Bork to fill a vacancy on the Supreme Court. Bork, a federal judge and former Yale University law professor, was a staunch conservative. He had opposed the 1964 Civil Rights Act, affirmative action, and the *Roe v. Wade* decision. After acrimonious confirmation hearings, the Senate rejected Bork's nomination by a vote of 58–42.[54]

VII. African American Life in Reagan's America

African Americans read Bork's nomination as another signal of the conservative movement's hostility to their social, economic, and political aspirations. Indeed, Ronald Reagan's America presented African Americans with a series of contradictions. Black Americans achieved significant

Jesse Jackson, pictured here in 1983, was only the second African American to mount a national campaign for the presidency. His work as a civil rights activist garnered him a significant following in the African American community but never enough to secure the Democratic nomination. Library of Congress.

advances in politics, culture, and socioeconomic status. A trend from the late 1960s and 1970s continued and Black politicians gained control of major municipal governments across the country during the 1980s. In 1983, voters in Philadelphia and Chicago elected Wilson Goode and Harold Washington, respectively, as their cities' first Black mayors. At the national level, civil rights leader Jesse Jackson became the first African American man to run for president when he campaigned for the Democratic Party's nomination in 1984 and 1988. Propelled by chants of "Run, Jesse, run," Jackson achieved notable success in 1988, winning nine state primaries and finishing second with 29 percent of the vote.[55]

The excitement created by Jackson's campaign mirrored the acclaim received by a few prominent African Americans in media and entertainment. Comedian Eddie Murphy rose to stardom on television's *Saturday Night Live* and achieved box office success with movies like *48 Hours* and *Beverly Hills Cop*. In 1982, pop singer Michael Jackson released *Thriller*, the best-selling album of all time. Oprah Winfrey began her phenomenally successful nationally syndicated talk show in 1985. Comedian Bill Cosby's sitcom about an African American doctor and lawyer raising their four children drew the highest ratings on television for most of the decade. The popularity of *The Cosby Show* revealed how class informed perceptions of race in the 1980s. Cosby's fictional TV family represented a growing number of Black middle-class professionals in the United States. Indeed, income for the top fifth of African American households increased faster than that of white households for most of the decade. Middle-class African Americans found new doors open to them in the 1980s, but the poor and working-class faced continued challenges. During Reagan's last year in office the African American poverty rate stood at 31.6 percent, as opposed to 10.1 percent for whites.[56] Black unemployment remained double that of whites throughout the decade.[57] By 1990, the median income for Black families was $21,423, or 42 percent below the median income for white households.[58] The Reagan administration failed to address such disparities and in many ways intensified them.

New Right values threatened the legal principles and federal policies of the Great Society and the "rights revolution." Reagan's appointment of conservatives to agencies such as the Justice Department and the Equal Employment Opportunity Commission took aim at key policy achievements of the civil rights movement. When the 1965 Voting Rights Act came up for renewal during Reagan's first term, the Justice Department pushed the president to oppose any extension. Only the intervention of more moderate congressional Republicans saved the law.

The administration also initiated a plan to rescind federal affirmative action rules. In 1986, a broad coalition of groups—including the NAACP, the Urban League, the AFL-CIO, and even the National Association of Manufacturers—compelled the administration to abandon the effort. Despite the conservative tenor of the country, diversity programs were firmly entrenched in the corporate world by the end of the decade.

Americans increasingly embraced racial diversity as a positive value but most often approached the issue through an individualistic—not a systemic—framework. Certain federal policies disproportionately affected racial minorities. Spending cuts enacted by Reagan and congressional Republicans shrank Aid to Families with Dependent Children, Medicaid, food stamps, school lunch programs, and job training programs that provided crucial support to African American households. In 1982, the National Urban League's annual "State of Black America" report concluded that "never [since the first report in 1976] . . . has the state of Black America been more vulnerable. Never in that time have black economic rights been under such powerful attack."[59] African American communities, especially in urban areas, also bore the stigma of violence and criminality. Homicide was the leading cause of death for Black males between ages fifteen and twenty-four, occurring at a rate six times that of other groups.[60] Although African Americans were most often the victims of violent crime, sensationalist media reports incited fears about Black-on-white crime in big cities. Ironically, such fear could by itself spark violence. In December 1984 a thirty-seven-year-old white engineer, Bernard Goetz, shot and seriously wounded four Black teenagers on a New York City subway car. The so-called Subway Vigilante suspected that the young men—armed with screwdrivers—planned to rob him. Pollsters found that 90 percent of white New Yorkers sympathized with Goetz.[61] Echoing the law-and-order rhetoric (and policies) of the 1960s and 1970s, politicians—both Democratic and Republican—and law enforcement agencies implemented more aggressive policing of minority communities and mandated longer prison sentences for those arrested. The explosive growth of mass incarceration exacted a heavy toll on African American communities long into the twenty-first century.

VIII. Bad Times and Good Times

Working- and middle-class Americans, especially those of color, struggled to maintain economic equilibrium during the Reagan years. The

growing national debt generated fresh economic pain. The federal government borrowed money to finance the debt, raising interest rates to
heighten the appeal of government bonds. Foreign money poured into
the United States, raising the value of the dollar and attracting an influx of goods from overseas. The imbalance between American imports
and exports grew from $36 billion in 1980 to $170 billion in 1987.[62]
Foreign competition battered the already anemic manufacturing sector.
The appeal of government bonds likewise drew investment away from
American industry.

Continuing an ongoing trend, many steel and automobile factories
in the industrial Northeast and Midwest closed or moved overseas during the 1980s. Bruce Springsteen, the self-appointed bard of blue-collar
America, offered eulogies to Rust Belt cities in songs like "Youngstown"
and "My Hometown," in which the narrator laments that his "foreman
says these jobs are going, boys / and they ain't coming back."[63] Competition from Japanese carmakers spurred a "Buy American" campaign.
Meanwhile, a "farm crisis" gripped the rural United States. Expanded
world production meant new competition for American farmers, while
soaring interest rates caused the already sizable debt held by family farms
to mushroom. Farm foreclosures skyrocketed during Reagan's tenure. In
September 1985, prominent musicians including Neil Young and Willie
Nelson organized Farm Aid, a benefit concert at the University of Illinois's football stadium designed to raise money for struggling farmers.

At the other end of the economic spectrum, wealthy Americans thrived
under the policies of the New Right. The financial industry found new
ways to earn staggering profits during the Reagan years. Wall Street bro-
kers like junk bond king Michael Milken reaped fortunes selling high-
risk, high-yield securities. Reckless speculation helped drive the stock
market steadily upward until the crash of October 19, 1987. On Black
Friday, the market plunged eight hundred points, erasing 13 percent of
its value. Investors lost more than $500 billion.[64] An additional financial
crisis loomed in the savings and loan (S&L) industry, and Reagan's de-
regulatory policies bore significant responsibility. In 1982 Reagan signed
a bill increasing the amount of federal insurance available to savings and
loan depositors, making those financial institutions more popular with
consumers. The bill also allowed S&Ls to engage in high-risk loans and
investments for the first time. Many such deals failed catastrophically,
while some S&L managers brazenly stole from their institutions. In the
late 1980s, S&Ls failed with regularity, and ordinary Americans lost

precious savings. The 1982 law left the government responsible for bail-
ing out S&Ls out at an eventual cost of $132 billion.[65]

IX. Culture Wars of the 1980s

Popular culture of the 1980s offered another venue in which conservatives and liberals waged a battle of ideas. The militarism and patriotism
of Reagan's presidency pervaded movies like *Top Gun* and the *Rambo*
series, starring Sylvester Stallone as a Vietnam War veteran haunted by
his country's failure to pursue victory in Southeast Asia. In contrast, director Oliver Stone offered searing condemnations of the war in *Platoon*
and *Born on the Fourth of July*. Television shows like *Dynasty* and *Dallas* celebrated wealth and glamour, reflecting the pride in conspicuous
consumption that emanated from the White House and corporate boardrooms during the decade. At the same time, films like *Wall Street* and
novels like Bret Easton Ellis's *Less Than Zero* skewered the excesses of
the rich.

The most significant aspect of much popular culture in the 1980s,
however, was its lack of politics altogether. Steven Spielberg's *E.T.: The
Extra-Terrestrial* and his Indiana Jones adventure trilogy topped the box
office. Cinematic escapism replaced the social films of the 1970s. Quint-
essential Hollywood leftist Jane Fonda appeared frequently on television
but only to peddle exercise videos. Television viewership—once dominated by the big three networks of NBC, ABC, and CBS—fragmented
with the rise of cable channels catering to particularized tastes. Few cable
channels so captured the popular imagination as MTV, which debuted in
1981. Telegenic artists like Madonna, Prince, and Michael Jackson skillfully used MTV to boost their reputations and album sales. Conservatives condemned music videos for corrupting young people with vulgar,
anti-authoritarian messages, but the medium only grew in stature. Critics
of MTV targeted Madonna in particular. Her 1989 video "Like a Prayer"
drew protests for what some people viewed as sexually suggestive and
blasphemous scenes. The religious right increasingly perceived popular
culture as hostile to Christian values.

The Apple II computer, introduced in 1977, was the first successful
mass-produced microcomputer meant for home use. Cultural battles were
even more heated in the realm of gender and sexual politics. American
women pushed further into male-dominated spheres during the 1980s.
By 1984, women in the workforce outnumbered those who worked at

home.[66] That same year, New York representative Geraldine Ferraro became the first woman to run on a major party's presidential ticket when Democratic candidate Walter Mondale named her his running mate. Yet the triumph of the right placed fundamental questions about women's rights near the center of American politics—particularly in regard to abortion. The issue increasingly divided Americans. Pro-life Democrats and pro-choice Republicans grew rare, as the National Abortion Rights Action League enforced pro-choice orthodoxy on the left and the National Right to Life Commission did the same with pro-life orthodoxy on the right. Religious conservatives took advantage of the Republican takeover of the White House and Senate in 1980 to push for new restrictions on abortion—with limited success. Senators Jesse Helms of North Carolina and Orrin Hatch of Utah introduced versions of a Human Life Amendment to the U.S. Constitution that defined life as beginning at conception. Both efforts failed.[67] Reagan, more interested in economic issues than social ones, provided only lukewarm support for the anti-abortion movement. He further outraged anti-abortion activists by appointing

The Apple II was the smallest and sleekest personal computer model yet introduced. Indeed, it revolutionized both the substance and design of personal computers. Wikimedia.

Sandra Day O'Connor, a supporter of abortion rights, to the Supreme Court. Despite these setbacks, anti-abortion forces succeeded in defunding some abortion providers. The 1976 Hyde Amendment prohibited the use of federal funds to pay for abortions; by 1990 almost every state had its own version of the Hyde Amendment. Yet some anti-abortion activists demanded more. In 1988 evangelical activist Randall Terry founded Operation Rescue, an organization that targeted abortion clinics and prochoice politicians with confrontational—and sometimes violent—tactics. Operation Rescue demonstrated that the fight over abortion would grow only more heated in the 1990s.

The emergence of a deadly new illness, acquired immunodeficiency syndrome (AIDS), simultaneously devastated, stigmatized, and energized the nation's homosexual community. When AIDS appeared in the early 1980s, most of its victims were gay men. For a time the disease was known as GRID—gay-related immune deficiency. The epidemic rekindled older pseudoscientific ideas about the inherently diseased nature of homosexual bodies. The Reagan administration met the issue with indifference, leading liberal congressman Henry Waxman to rage that "if the same disease had appeared among Americans of Norwegian descent . . . rather than among gay males, the response of both the government and the medical community would be different."[68] Some religious figures seemed to relish the opportunity to condemn homosexual activity; Catholic columnist Patrick Buchanan remarked that "the sexual revolution has begun to devour its children."[69]

Homosexuals were left to forge their own response to the crisis. Some turned to confrontation—like New York playwright Larry Kramer. Kramer founded the Gay Men's Health Crisis, which demanded a more proactive response to the epidemic. Others sought to humanize AIDS victims; this was the goal of the AIDS Memorial Quilt, a commemorative project begun in 1985. By the middle of the decade the federal government began to address the issue haltingly. Surgeon General C. Everett Koop, an evangelical Christian, called for more federal funding on AIDS-related research, much to the dismay of critics on the religious right. By 1987 government spending on AIDS-related research reached $500 million—still only 25 percent of what experts advocated.[70] In 1987 Reagan convened a presidential commission on AIDS; the commission's report called for antidiscrimination laws to protect people with AIDS and for more federal spending on AIDS research. The shift encouraged activists. Nevertheless, on issues of abortion and gay rights—as with the push

The AIDS epidemic hit gay and African American communities particularly hard in the 1980s,
prompting widespread social stigmatization,
but also prompting awareness campaigns, such
as this poster featuring singer Patti LaBelle.
Wikimedia.

for racial equality—activists spent the 1980s preserving the status quo
rather than building on previous gains. This amounted to a significant
victory for the New Right.

X. The New Right Abroad

The conservative movement gained ground on gender and sexual politics, but it captured the entire battlefield on American foreign policy in
the 1980s, at least for a time. Ronald Reagan entered office a committed Cold Warrior. He held the Soviet Union in contempt, denouncing it
in a 1983 speech as an "evil empire."[71] And he never doubted that the
Soviet Union would end up "on the ash heap of history," as he said in a
1982 speech to the British Parliament.[72] Indeed, Reagan believed it was
the duty of the United States to speed the Soviet Union to its inevitable
demise. His Reagan Doctrine declared that the United States would supply aid to anticommunist forces everywhere in the world.[73] To give this

doctrine force, Reagan oversaw an enormous expansion in the defense budget. Federal spending on defense rose from $171 billion in 1981 to $229 billion in 1985, the highest level since the Vietnam War.[74] He described this as a policy of "peace through strength," a phrase that appealed to Americans who, during the 1970s, feared that the United States was losing its status as the world's most powerful nation. Yet the irony is that Reagan, for all his militarism, helped bring the Cold War to an end through negotiation, a tactic he had once scorned.

Reagan's election came at a time when many Americans feared their country was in an irreversible decline. American forces withdrew in disarray from South Vietnam in 1975. The United States returned control of the Panama Canal to Panama in 1978, despite protests from conservatives. Pro-American dictators were toppled in Iran and Nicaragua in 1979. The Soviet Union invaded Afghanistan that same year, leading conservatives to warn about American weakness in the face of Soviet expansion. Reagan spoke to fears of decline and warned, in 1976, that "this nation has become Number Two in a world where it is dangerous—if not fatal—to be second best."[75]

The Reagan administration made Latin America a showcase for its newly assertive policies. Jimmy Carter had sought to promote human

Margaret Thatcher and Ronald Reagan, pictured here at Camp David in December 1984, led two of the world's most powerful countries and formed an alliance that benefited both throughout their tenures in office. Wikimedia.

rights in the region, but Reagan and his advisors scrapped this approach and instead focused on fighting communism—a term they applied to all Latin American left-wing movements. And so when communists with ties to Cuba overthrew the government of the Caribbean nation of Grenada in October 1983, Reagan dispatched the U.S. Marines to the island. Dubbed Operation Urgent Fury, the Grenada invasion overthrew the leftist government after less than a week of fighting. Despite the relatively minor nature of the mission, its success gave victory-hungry Americans something to cheer about after the military debacles of the previous two decades.

Grenada was the only time Reagan deployed the American military in Latin America, but the United States also influenced the region by supporting right-wing, anticommunist movements there. From 1981 to 1990, the United States gave more than $4 billion to the government of El Salvador in a largely futile effort to defeat the guerrillas of the Farabundo Martí National Liberation Front (FMLN).[76] Salvadoran security forces equipped with American weapons committed numerous atrocities, including the slaughter of almost one thousand civilians at the village of El Mozote in December 1981.

Operation Urgent Fury, the U.S. invasion of Grenada, was broadly supported by the U.S. public. This photograph shows the deployment of U.S. Army Rangers into Grenada. Photograph, October 25, 1983. Wikimedia.

The Reagan administration took a more cautious approach in the Middle East, where its policy was determined by a mix of anticommunism and hostility toward the Islamic government of Iran. When Iraq invaded Iran in 1980, the United States supplied Iraqi dictator Saddam Hussein with military intelligence and business credits—even after it became clear that Iraqi forces were using chemical weapons. Reagan's greatest setback in the Middle East came in 1982, when, shortly after Israel invaded Lebanon, he dispatched Marines to the Lebanese city of Beirut to serve as a peacekeeping force. On October 23, 1983, a suicide bomber killed 241 Marines stationed in Beirut. Congressional pressure and anger from the American public forced Reagan to recall the Marines from Lebanon in March 1984. Reagan's decision demonstrated that, for all his talk of restoring American power, he took a pragmatic approach to foreign policy. He was unwilling to risk another Vietnam by committing American troops to Lebanon.

Though Reagan's policies toward Central America and the Middle East aroused protest, his policy on nuclear weapons generated the most controversy. Initially Reagan followed the examples of presidents Nixon, Ford, and Carter by pursuing arms limitation talks with the Soviet Union. American officials participated in the Intermediate-range Nuclear Force (INF) Talks that began in 1981 and the Strategic Arms Reduction Talks (START) in 1982. But the breakdown of these talks in 1983 led Reagan to proceed with plans to place Pershing II nuclear missiles in Western Europe to counter Soviet SS-20 missiles in Eastern Europe. Reagan went a step further in March 1983, when he announced plans for a Strategic Defense Initiative (SDI), a space-based system that could shoot down incoming Soviet missiles. Critics derided the program as a "Star Wars" fantasy, and even Reagan's advisors harbored doubts. "We don't have the technology to do this," secretary of state George Shultz told aides.[77] These aggressive policies fed a growing nuclear freeze movement throughout the world. In the United States, organizations like the Committee for a Sane Nuclear Policy organized protests that culminated in a June 1982 rally that drew almost a million people to New York City's Central Park.

Protests in the streets were echoed by resistance in Congress. Congressional Democrats opposed Reagan's policies on the merits; congressional Republicans, though they supported Reagan's anticommunism, were wary of the administration's fondness for circumventing Congress. In 1982, the House voted 411–0 to approve the Boland Amendment, which barred the United States from supplying funds to the contras, a

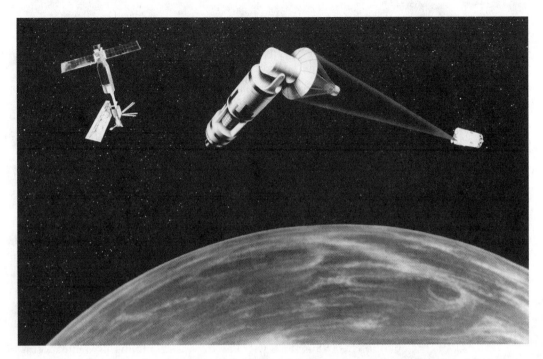

President Reagan proposed new space- and ground-based defense systems to protect the United States from nuclear missiles in his 1984 Strategic Defense Initiative (SDI). Scientists argued that it was technologically unfeasible, and it was lambasted in the media as the "Star Wars" program. Wikimedia.

right-wing insurgency fighting the leftist Sandinista government in Nicaragua. Reagan, overlooking the contras' brutal tactics, hailed them as the "moral equivalent of the Founding Fathers."[78] The Reagan administration's determination to flout these amendments led to a scandal that almost destroyed Reagan's presidency. Robert MacFarlane, the president's national security advisor, and Oliver North, a member of the National Security Council, raised money to support the contras by selling American missiles to Iran and funneling the money to Nicaragua. When their scheme was revealed in 1986, it was hugely embarrassing for Reagan. The president's underlings had not only violated the Boland Amendment but had also, by selling arms to Iran, made a mockery of Reagan's declaration that "America will never make concessions to the terrorists." But while the Iran-Contra affair generated comparisons to the Watergate scandal, investigators were never able to prove Reagan knew about the operation. Without such a "smoking gun," talk of impeaching Reagan remained simply talk.

Though the Iran-Contra scandal tarnished the Reagan administration's image, it did not derail Reagan's most significant achievement: easing tensions with the Soviet Union. This would have seemed impossible in Reagan's first term, when the president exchanged harsh words with a rapid succession of Soviet leaders—Leonid Brezhnev, Yuri Andropov, and Konstantin Chernenko. In 1985, however, the aged Chernenko's death handed leadership of the Soviet Union to Mikhail Gorbachev, who, while a true believer in socialism, nonetheless realized that the Soviet Union desperately needed to reform itself. He instituted a program of *perestroika*, which referred to the restructuring of the Soviet system, and of *glasnost*, which meant greater transparency in government. Gorbachev also reached out to Reagan in hopes of negotiating an end to the arms race, which was bankrupting the Soviet Union. Reagan and Gorbachev met in Geneva, Switzerland, in 1985 and Reykjavik, Iceland, in 1986. The summits failed to produce any concrete agreements, but the two leaders developed a relationship unprecedented in the history of U.S.-Soviet relations. This trust made possible the Intermediate Nuclear Forces Treaty of 1987, which committed both sides to a sharp reduction in their nuclear arsenal.

By the late 1980s the Soviet empire was crumbling. Reagan successfully combined anticommunist rhetoric (such as his 1987 speech at the Berlin Wall, where he declared, "General Secretary Gorbachev, if you seek peace . . . tear down this wall!") with a willingness to negotiate with Soviet leadership.[79] But the most significant causes of collapse lay within the Soviet empire itself. Soviet-allied governments in Eastern Europe tottered under pressure from dissident organizations like Poland's Solidarity and East Germany's Neues Forum. Some of these countries, such as Poland, were also pressured from within by the Roman Catholic Church, which had turned toward active anticommunism under Pope John Paul II. When Gorbachev made it clear that he would not send the Soviet military to prop up these regimes, they collapsed one by one in 1989—in Poland, Hungary, Czechoslovakia, Romania, Bulgaria, and East Germany. Within the Soviet Union, Gorbachev's proposed reforms unraveled the decaying Soviet system rather than bringing stability. By 1991 the Soviet Union itself had vanished, dissolving into a Commonwealth of Independent States.

XI. Conclusion

Reagan left office in 1988 with the Cold War waning and the economy booming. Unemployment had dipped to 5 percent by 1988.[80] Between 1981 and 1986, gas prices fell from $1.38 per gallon to 95¢.[81] The stock market recovered from the crash, and the Dow Jones Industrial

Average—which stood at 950 in 1981—reached 2,239 by the end of Reagan's second term.[82] Yet the economic gains of the decade were unequally distributed. The top fifth of households enjoyed rising incomes while the rest stagnated or declined.[83] In constant dollars, annual chief executive officer (CEO) pay rose from $3 million in 1980 to roughly $12 million during Reagan's last year in the White House.[84] Between 1985 and 1989 the number of Americans living in poverty remained steady at thirty-three million.[85] Real per capita money income grew at only 2 percent per year, a rate roughly equal to the Carter years.[86] The American economy saw more jobs created than lost during the 1980s, but half of the jobs eliminated were in high-paying industries.[87] Furthermore, half of the new jobs failed to pay wages above the poverty line. The economic divide was most acute for African Americans and Latinos, one third of whom qualified as poor.

The triumph of the right proved incomplete. The number of government employees actually increased under Reagan. With more than 80 percent of the federal budget committed to defense, entitlement programs, and interest on the national debt, the right's goal of deficit elimination floundered for lack of substantial areas to cut.[88] Between 1980 and 1989 the national debt rose from $914 billion to $2.7 trillion.[89] Despite steep tax cuts for corporations and the wealthy, the overall tax burden of the American public basically remained unchanged. Moreover, so-called regressive taxes on payroll and certain goods actually *increased* the tax burden on low- and middle-income Americans. Finally, Reagan slowed but failed to vanquish the five-decade legacy of liberal economics. Most New Deal and Great Society programs proved durable. Government still offered its neediest citizens a safety net, if a now continually shrinking one.

Yet the discourse of American politics had irrevocably changed. The preeminence of conservative political ideas grew ever more pronounced, even when Democrats controlled Congress or the White House. In response to the conservative mood of the country, the Democratic Party adapted its own message to accommodate many of the Republicans' Reagan-era ideas and innovations. The United States was on a rightward path.

XII. Reference Material

This chapter was edited by Richard Anderson and William J. Schultz, with content contributions by Richard Anderson, Laila Ballout, Marsha Barrett, Seth Bartee, Eladio Bobadilla, Kyle Burke, Andrew Chadwick, Aaron Cowan, Jennifer

Donnally, Leif Fredrickson, Kori Graves, Karissa A. Haugeberg, Jonathan Hunt, Stephen Koeth, Colin Reynolds, William J. Schultz, and Daniel Spillman.

Recommended citation: Richard Anderson et al., "The Triumph of the Right," Richard Anderson and William J. Schultz, eds., in *The American Yawp*, eds. Joseph Locke and Ben Wright (Stanford, CA: Stanford University Press, 2019).

NOTES TO CHAPTER 29

1. Ronald Reagan, quoted in Steve Neal, "Reagan Assails Carter On Auto Layoffs," *Chicago Tribune*, October 20, 1980, 5.

2. Ronald Reagan, quoted in James T. Patterson, *Restless Giant: The United States from Watergate to Bush v. Gore* (New York: Oxford University Press, 2005), 152.

3. Robert Self, *All in the Family: The Realignment of American Democracy Since the 1960s* (New York: Hill and Wang, 2012), 369.

4. William F. Buckley Jr., "Our Mission Statement," *National Review*, November 19, 1955. http://www.nationalreview.com/article/223549/our-mission -statement-william-f-buckley-jr.

5. James Reston, "What Goldwater Lost: Voters Rejected His Candidacy, Conservative Cause and the G.O.P.," *New York Times*, November 4, 1964, 23.

6. George Wallace, quoted in William Chafe, *The Unfinished Journey: America Since World War II* (New York: Oxford University Press, 1991), 377.

7. James Patterson, *Grand Expectations: The United States, 1945–1974* (New York: Oxford University Press, 1996), 735–736.

8. Lisa McGirr, *Suburban Warriors: The Origins of the New American Right* (Princeton, NJ: Princeton University Press, 2001), 227–231.

9. Francis Schaeffer, quoted in *Whatever Happened to the Human Race?* (Episode I), Film, directed by Franky Schaeffer, (1979, USA, Franky Schaeffer V Productions). https://www.youtube.com/watch?v=UQAyIwi5l6E.

10. Walter Goodman, "Irving Kristol: Patron Saint of the New Right," *New York Times Magazine*, December 6, 1981. http://www.nytimes.com/1981/12/06 /magazine/irving-kristol-patron-saint-of-the-new-right.html.

11. Patterson, *Restless Giant*, 113.

12. Jimmy Carter, 1978 State of the Union Address, January 19, 1978, Jimmy Carter Presidential Library and Museum, http://www.jimmycarterlibrary .gov/documents/speeches/su78jec.phtml.

13. Jefferson Cowie, *Stayin' Alive: The 1970s and the Last Days of the Working Class* (New York: New Press, 2010), 12.

14. George Meany, quoted in ibid., 293.

15. Ibid., 268.

16. Richard Viguerie, quoted in Joseph Crespino, "Civil Rights and the Religious Right," in *Rightward Bound: Making America Conservative in the 1970s*, ed. Bruce J. Schulman and Julian Zelizer (Cambridge, MA: Harvard University Press, 2008), 91.

17. Patterson, *Restless Giant*, 148.

18. Judith Stein, *Pivotal Decade: How the United States Traded Factories for Finance in the Seventies* (New Haven, CT: Yale University Press, 2010), 231.

19. Jimmy Carter, quoted in Chafe, *Unfinished Journey*, 453.

20. William Winpisinger, quoted in Cowie, *Stayin' Alive*, 261.

21. Patterson, *Restless Giant*, 148.

22. Ibid.

23. Ibid.

24. Jimmy Carter, quoted in "Carter Tells of 'Adultery in His Heart,'" *Los Angeles Times*, September 21, 1976, B6.

25. Crespino, "Civil Rights and the Religious Right," 103.

26. Patterson, *Restless Giant*, 163; Jon Nordheimer, "Reagan Is Picking His Florida Spots: His Campaign Aides Aim for New G.O.P. Voters in Strategic Areas," *New York Times*, February 5, 1976, 24.

27. Sean Wilentz, *The Age of Reagan: A History, 1974–2008* (New York: HarperCollins, 2008), 124.

28. Meg Jacobs and Julian Zelizer, *Conservatives in Power: The Reagan Years, 1981–1989: A Brief History with Documents* (Boston: Bedford St. Martin's, 2011), 2.

29. Patterson, *Restless Giant*, 150.

30. Ibid.

31. Ronald Reagan, quoted in Jacobs and Zelizer, *Conservatives in Power*, 20.

32. Jack Kemp, quoted in Jacobs and Zelizer, *Conservatives in Power*, 21.

33. Wilentz, *Age of Reagan*, 121.

34. Jacobs and Zelizer, *Conservatives in Power*, 25–26.

35. Ronald Reagan, quoted in Neal, "Reagan Assails Carter," 5.

36. Stein, *Pivotal Decade*, 267.

37. Chafe, *Unfinished Journey*, 474.

38. Patterson, *Restless Giant*, 159.

39. Gil Troy, *Morning in America: How Ronald Reagan Invented the 1980s* (Princeton, NJ: Princeton University Press, 2005), 67.

40. Chafe, *Unfinished Journey*, 476.

41. Ibid., 474.

42. Margaret Bush Wilson, quoted in Troy, *Morning in America*, 93.

43. Ibid., 210.

44. Ibid., 110.

45. Patterson, *Restless Giant*, 163–164.

46. Troy, *Morning in America*, 208.

47. Chafe, *Unfinished Journey*, 477.

48. Patterson, *Restless Giant*, 162. Many people used the term *harsh medicine* to describe Volcker's action on interest rates; see Art Pine, "Letting Harsh Medicine Work," *Washington Post*, October 14, 1979, G1.

49. Patterson, *Restless Giant*, 189.

50. Ibid.

51. Ibid., 190–191.

52. Troy, *Morning in America*, 210; Patterson, *Restless Giant*, 165.

53. Patterson, *Restless Giant*, 173–174.

54. Ibid., 171.

55. 1988 Democratic Primaries, CQ *Voting and Elections Collection*, database accessed June 30, 2015.

56. *The State of Black America, 1990* (New York: National Urban League, 1990), 34.

57. Andrew Hacker, *Two Nations: Black and White, Separate, Hostile, Unequal* (New York: Scribner, 1992), 102.

58. Ibid., 94.

59. Troy, *Morning in America*, 91.

60. American Social History Project, *Who Built America? Vol. Two: Since 1877* (New York: Bedford St. Martin's, 2000), 723.

61. Patterson, *Restless Giant*, 172–173.

62. Chafe, *Unfinished Journey*, 487.

63. Bruce Springsteen, "My Hometown," *Born in the USA* (Columbia Records: New York, 1984).

64. Chafe, *Unfinished Journey*, 489.

65. Patterson, *Restless Giant*, 175.

66. Ruth Rosen, *The World Split Open: How the Modern Women's Movement Changed America* (New York: Penguin, 2000), 337.

67. Self, *All in the Family*, 376–377.

68. Ibid., 387–388.

69. Ibid., 384.

70. Ibid., 389.

71. Wilentz, *Age of Reagan*, 163.

72. Lou Cannon, "President Calls for 'Crusade': Reagan Proposes Plan to Counter Soviet Challenge," *Washington Post*, June 9, 1982, A1.

73. Conservative newspaper columnist Charles Krauthammer coined the phrase. See Wilentz, *Age of Reagan*, 157.

74. Patterson, *Restless Giant*, 205.

75. Laura Kalman, *Right Star Rising: A New Politics, 1974–1980* (New York: Norton, 2010), 166–167.

76. Ronald Reagan, "Address to the Nation on United States Policy in Central America," May 9, 1984. http://www.reagan.utexas.edu/archives/speeches /1984/50984h.htm.

77. Frances Fitzgerald, *Way out There in the Blue: Reagan, Star Wars, and the End of the Cold War* (New York: Simon and Schuster, 2000), 205.

78. Ronald Reagan, "Remarks at the Annual Dinner of the Conservative Political Action Conference," March 1, 1985. http://www.presidency.ucsb.edu /ws/?pid=38274.

79. Lou Cannon, "Reagan Challenges Soviets to Dismantle Berlin Wall: Aides Disappointed at Crowd's Lukewarm Reception," *Washington Post*, June 13, 1987, A1.

80. Patterson, *Restless Giant*, 163.

81. Ibid.

82. Patterson, *Restless Giant.*

83. Jacobs and Zelizer, *Conservatives in Power,* 32.

84. Patterson, *Restless Giant,* 186.

85. Ibid., 164.

86. Ibid., 166.

87. Chafe, *Unfinished Journey,* 488.

88. Jacobs and Zelizer, *Conservatives in Power,* 31.

89. Patterson, *Restless Giant,* 158.

RECOMMENDED READING

Brier, Jennifer. *Infectious Ideas: U.S. Political Responses to the AIDS Crisis.* Chapel Hill: University of North Carolina Press, 2009.

Carter, Dan T. *The Politics of Rage: George Wallace, the Origins of the New Conservatism, and the Transformation of American Politics.* Baton Rouge: LSU Press, 1995.

Chappell, Marisa. *The War on Welfare: Family, Poverty, and Politics in Modern America.* Philadelphia: University of Pennsylvania Press, 2009.

Crespino, Joseph. *In Search of Another Country: Mississippi and the Conservative Counterrevolution.* Princeton, NJ: Princeton University Press, 2007.

Critchlow, Donald. *The Conservative Ascendancy: How the GOP Right Made Political History.* Cambridge, MA: Harvard University Press, 2007.

Dallek, Matthew. *The Right Moment: Ronald Reagan's First Victory and the Decisive Turning Point in American Politics.* New York: Free Press, 2000.

Hinton, Elizabeth. *From the War on Poverty to the War on Crime.* Cambridge, MA: Harvard University Press, 2016.

Hunter, James D. *Culture Wars: The Struggle to Define America.* New York: Basic Books, 1992.

Kalman, Laura. *Right Star Rising: A New Politics, 1974–1980.* New York: Norton, 2010.

Kruse, Kevin M. *White Flight: Atlanta and the Making of Modern Conservatism.* Princeton, NJ: Princeton University Press, 2005.

Lassiter, Matthew D. *The Silent Majority: Suburban Politics in the Sunbelt South.* Princeton, NJ: Princeton University Press, 2006.

MacLean, Nancy. *Freedom Is Not Enough: The Opening of the American Workplace.* Cambridge, MA: Harvard University Press, 2008.

Moreton, Bethany. *To Serve God and Walmart: The Making of Christian Free Enterprise.* Cambridge, MA: Harvard University Press, 2009.

Nadasen, Premilla. *Welfare Warriors: The Welfare Rights Movement in the United States.* New York: Routledge, 2005.

Nickerson, Michelle M. *Mothers of Conservatism: Women and the Postwar Right.* Princeton, NJ: Princeton University Press, 2012.

Patterson, James T. *Restless Giant: The United States from Watergate to Bush v. Gore.* New York: Oxford University Press, 2005.

Phillips-Fein, Kim. *Invisible Hands: The Businessmen's Crusade Against the New Deal.* New York: Norton, 2010.

Rodgers, Daniel T. *Age of Fracture.* Cambridge: Belknap Press, 2011.

Schoenwald, Jonathan. *A Time for Choosing: The Rise of Modern American Conservatism.* New York: Oxford University Press, 2001.

Self, Robert O. *All in the Family: The Realignment of American Democracy Since the 1960s.* New York: Hill and Wang, 2012.

Troy, Gil. *Morning in America: How Ronald Reagan Invented the 1980s.* Princeton, NJ: Princeton University Press, 2005.

Westad, Odd Arne. *The Global Cold War: Third World Interventions and the Making of Our Times.* New York: Cambridge University Press, 2005.

Wilentz, Sean. *The Age of Reagan: A History, 1974–2008.* New York: HarperCollins, 2008.

Williams, Daniel K. *God's Own Party: The Making of the Christian Right.* New York: Oxford University Press, 2007.

Zaretsky, Natasha. *No Direction Home: The American Family and the Fear of National Decline.* Chapel Hill: University of North Carolina Press, 2007.

30

The Recent Past

I. Introduction

The U.S. Capitol was stormed on January 6, 2021. Thousands of right-wing protesters, fueled by an onslaught of lies, fabrications, and conspiracy theories surrounding the November 2020 elections, rallied that morning in front of the White House to "Stop the Steal." Repeating a familiar litany of lies and distortions, the sitting president of the United States then urged them to march on the Capitol and stop the certification of the November electoral vote. "You'll never take back our country with weakness," he said. "Fight like hell," he said. "If you don't fight like hell, you're not going to have a country anymore."[1] And so they did. They marched on the Capitol, armed themselves with metal pipes, baseball bats, hockey sticks, pepper spray, stun guns, and flagpoles, and attacked the police officers barricading the building.

Supporters of defeated U.S. president Donald Trump cheer the breaching of the U.S. Capitol on January 6, 2021. Via Wikimedia.

"It was like something from a medieval battle," Capitol Police Officer Aquilino Gonell recalled.[2] The mob pulled D.C. Metropolitan Police Officer Michael Fanone into the crowd, beat him with flagpoles, and tasered him. "Kill him with his own gun," Fanone remembered the mob shouting just before he lost consciousness. "I can still hear those words in my head today," he testified six months later.[3]

The mob breached the barriers and poured into the building, marking perhaps the greatest domestic assault on the American federal government since the Civil War. But the events of January 6 were rooted in history.

Revolutionary technological change, unprecedented global flows of goods and people and capital, an amorphous and decades-long War on Terror, accelerating inequality, growing diversity, a changing climate, political stalemate: our present is not an island of circumstance but a product of history. Time marches forever on. The present becomes the past but, as William Faulkner famously put it, "The past is never dead. It's not even past."[4] The last several decades of American history have culminated in the present, an era of innovation and advancement but also of stark partisan division, racial and ethnic tension, protests over gender divides, uneven economic growth, widening inequalities, military interventions, bouts of mass violence, and pervasive anxieties about the present and future of the United States. Through boom and bust, national tragedy, foreign wars, bouts of mass violence, and the maturation of a new generation, a new chapter of American history is busily being written.

II. American Politics Before September 11, 2001

The conservative Reagan Revolution lingered over the presidential election of 1988. At stake was the legacy of a newly empowered conservative movement, a movement that would move forward with Reagan's vice president, George H. W. Bush, who triumphed over Massachusetts governor Michael Dukakis with a promise to continue the conservative work that had commenced in the 1980s.

The son of a U.S. senator from Connecticut, George H. W. Bush was a World War II veteran, president of a successful oil company, chair of the Republican National Committee, director of the CIA, and member of the House of Representatives from Texas. After failing to best Reagan in the 1980 Republican primaries, he was elected as his vice president in 1980 and again in 1984. In 1988, Michael Dukakis, a proud liberal from Massachusetts, challenged Bush for the White House.

Dukakis ran a weak campaign. Bush, a Connecticut aristocrat who had never been fully embraced by movement conservatism, particularly the newly animated religious right, nevertheless hammered Dukakis with moral and cultural issues. Bush said Dukakis had blocked recitation of the Pledge of Allegiance in Massachusetts schools and that he was a "card-carrying member" of the ACLU. Bush meanwhile dispatched his eldest son, George W. Bush, as his ambassador to the religious right.[5] Bush also infamously released a political ad featuring the face of Willie Horton, a Black Massachusetts man and convicted murderer who raped a woman after being released through a prison furlough program during Dukakis's tenure as governor. "By the time we're finished," Bush's campaign manager, Lee Atwater, said, "they're going to wonder whether Willie Horton is Dukakis' running mate."[6] Liberals attacked conservatives for perpetuating the ugly "code word" politics of the old Southern Strategy—the underhanded appeal to white racial resentments perfected by Richard Nixon in the aftermath of civil rights legislation.[7] Buoyed by such attacks, Bush won a large victory and entered the White House.

Bush's election signaled Americans' continued embrace of Reagan's conservative program and further evidenced the utter disarray of the Democratic Party. American liberalism, so stunningly triumphant in the 1960s, was now in full retreat. It was still, as one historian put it, the "Age of Reagan."[8]

The Soviet Union collapsed during Bush's tenure. Devastated by a stagnant economy, mired in a costly and disastrous war in Afghanistan, confronted with dissident factions in Eastern Europe, and rocked by internal dissent, the Soviet Union crumbled. Soviet leader and reformer Mikhail Gorbachev loosened the Soviet Union's tight personal restraints and censorship (*glasnost*) and liberalized the Soviet political machinery (*perestroika*). Eastern Bloc nations turned against their communist organizations and declared their independence from the Soviet Union. Gorbachev let them go. Soon, Soviet Union unraveled. On December 25, 1991, Gorbachev resigned his office, declaring that the Soviet Union no longer existed. At the Kremlin—Russia's center of government—the new tricolor flag of the Russian Federation was raised.[9]

The dissolution of the Soviet Union left the United States as the world's only remaining superpower. Global capitalism seemed triumphant. Observers wondered if some final stage of history had been reached, if the old battles had ended and a new global consensus built around peace and open markets would reign forever. "What we may be witnessing is not just the end of the Cold War, or the passing of a particular period of post-

During the Gulf War, the Iraqi military set fire to Kuwait's oil fields, many of which burned for months. March 21, 1991. Wikimedia.

war history, but the end of history as such," wrote Francis Fukuyama in his much-talked-about 1989 essay, "The End of History?"[10] Assets in Eastern Europe were privatized and auctioned off as newly independent nations introduced market economies. New markets were rising in Southeast Asia and Eastern Europe. India, for instance, began liberalizing its economic laws and opening itself up to international investment in 1991. China's economic reforms, advanced by Chairman Deng Xiaoping and his handpicked successors, accelerated as privatization and foreign investment proceeded.

The post–Cold War world was not without international conflicts, however. When Iraq invaded the small but oil-rich nation of Kuwait in 1990, Congress granted President Bush approval to intervene. The United States laid the groundwork for intervention (Operation Desert Shield) in August and commenced combat operations (Operation Desert Storm) in January 1991. With the memories of Vietnam still fresh, many Americans were hesitant to support military action that could expand into a protracted war or long-term commitment of troops. But the Gulf War was a swift victory for the United States. New technologies—including laser-guided precision bombing—amazed Americans, who could now watch twenty-four-hour live coverage of the war on the Cable News Network (CNN). The Iraqi army disintegrated after only a hundred hours of ground combat. President Bush and his advisors opted not to pursue the war into Baghdad and risk an occupation and insurgency. And so the war was won. Many wondered if the "ghosts of Vietnam" had been exorcised.[11] Bush won enormous popular support. Gallup polls showed a job approval rating as high as 89 percent in the weeks after the end of the war.[12]

President Bush's popularity seemed to suggest an easy reelection in 1992, but Bush had still not won over the New Right, the aggressively conservative wing of the Republican Party, despite his attacks on Dukakis, his embrace of the flag and the pledge, and his promise, "Read my lips: no new taxes." He faced a primary challenge from political commentator Patrick Buchanan, a former Reagan and Nixon White House advisor, who cast Bush as a moderate, as an unworthy steward of the conservative movement who was unwilling to fight for conservative Americans in the nation's ongoing culture war. Buchanan did not defeat Bush in the Republican primaries, but he inflicted enough damage to weaken his candidacy.[13]

Still thinking that Bush would be unbeatable in 1992, many prominent Democrats passed on a chance to run, and the Democratic Party nominated a relative unknown, Arkansas governor Bill Clinton. Dogged by charges of marital infidelity and draft dodging during the Vietnam War, Clinton was a consummate politician with enormous charisma and a skilled political team. He framed himself as a New Democrat, a centrist open to free trade, tax cuts, and welfare reform. Twenty-two years younger than Bush, he was the first baby boomer to make a serious run at the presidency. Clinton presented the campaign as a generational choice. During the campaign he appeared on MTV, played the saxophone on *The Arsenio Hall Show*, and told voters that he could offer the United States a new way forward.

Bush ran on his experience and against Clinton's moral failings. The GOP convention in Houston that summer featured speeches from Pat Buchanan and religious leader Pat Robertson decrying the moral decay plaguing American life. Clinton was denounced as a social liberal who would weaken the American family through both his policies and his individual moral character. But Clinton was able to convince voters that his moderated southern brand of liberalism would be more effective than the moderate conservatism of George Bush. Bush's candidacy, of course, was perhaps most damaged by a sudden economic recession. As Clinton's political team reminded the country, "It's the economy, stupid."

Clinton won the election, but the Reagan Revolution still reigned. Clinton and his running mate, Tennessee senator Albert Gore Jr., both moderate southerners, promised a path away from the old liberalism of the 1970s and 1980s (and the landslide electoral defeats of the 1980s). They were Democrats, but conservative Democrats, so-called New Democrats. In his first term, Clinton set out an ambitious agenda that included an economic stimulus package, universal health insurance, a continuation of the Middle East peace talks initiated by Bush's secretary of state James A. Baker III, welfare reform, and a completion of the North American Free Trade Agreement (NAFTA) to abolish trade barriers between the United States, Mexico, and Canada. His moves to reform welfare, open trade, and deregulate financial markets were particular hallmarks of Clinton's Third Way, a new Democratic embrace of heretofore conservative policies.[14]

With NAFTA, Clinton reversed decades of Democratic opposition to free trade and opened the nation's northern and southern borders to the free flow of capital and goods. Critics, particularly in the Midwest's Rust Belt, blasted the agreement for opening American workers to competition by low-paid foreign workers. Many American factories relocated and set up shops—*maquilas*—in northern Mexico that took advantage of Mexico's low wages. Thousands of Mexicans rushed to the *maquilas*. Thousands more continued on past the border.

If NAFTA opened American borders to goods and services, people still navigated strict legal barriers to immigration. Policy makers believed that free trade would create jobs and wealth that would incentivize Mexican workers to stay home, and yet multitudes continued to leave for opportunities in *el norte*. The 1990s proved that prohibiting illegal migration was, if not impossible, exceedingly difficult. Poverty, political corruption, violence, and hopes for a better life in the United States—or simply higher wages—continued to lure immigrants across the border. Between 1990 and 2010, the proportion of foreign-born individuals in the United States grew from 7.9 percent to 12.9 percent, and the number of undocumented immigrants tripled from 3.5 million to 11.2. While large numbers continued to migrate to traditional immigrant destinations—California, Texas, New York, Florida, New Jersey, and Illinois—the 1990s also witnessed unprecedented migration to the American South. Among the fastest-growing immigrant destination states were Kentucky, Tennessee, Arkansas, Georgia, and North Carolina, all of which had immigration growth rates in excess of 100 percent during the decade.[15]

In response to the continued influx of immigrants and the vocal complaints of anti-immigration activists, policy makers responded with such initiatives as Operation Gatekeeper and Hold the Line, which attempted to make crossing the border more prohibitive. The new strategy "funneled" immigrants to dangerous and remote crossing areas. Immigration officials hoped the brutal natural landscape would serve as a natural deterrent. It wouldn't. By 2017, hundreds of immigrants died each year of drowning, exposure, and dehydration.[16]

Clinton, meanwhile, sought to carve out a middle ground in his domestic agenda. In his first weeks in office, Clinton reviewed Department of Defense policies restricting homosexuals from serving in the armed forces. He pushed through a compromise plan, Don't Ask, Don't Tell, that removed any questions about sexual orientation in induction interviews but also required that gay military personnel keep their sexual orientation private. The policy alienated many. Social conservatives were outraged and his credentials as a conservative southerner suffered, while many liberals recoiled at continued antigay discrimination.

In his first term, Clinton also put forward universal healthcare as a major policy goal, and first lady Hillary Rodham Clinton played a major role in the initiative. But the push for a national healthcare law collapsed on itself. Conservatives revolted, the healthcare industry flooded the airwaves with attack ads, Clinton struggled with congressional Democrats, and voters bristled. A national healthcare system was again repulsed.

The midterm elections of 1994 were a disaster for the Democrats, who lost the House of Representatives for the first time since 1952. Congressional Republicans, led by Georgia congressman Newt Gingrich and Texas congressman Dick Armey, offered a policy agenda they called the Contract with America. Republican candidates from around the nation gathered on the steps of the Capitol to pledge their commitment to a conservative legislative blueprint to be enacted if the GOP won control of the House. The strategy worked.

Social conservatives were mobilized by an energized group of religious activists, especially the Christian Coalition, led by Pat Robertson and Ralph Reed. Robertson was a television minister and entrepreneur whose 1988 long shot run for the Republican presidential nomination brought him a massive mailing list and a network of religiously motivated voters around the country. From that mailing list, the Christian Coalition organized around the country, seeking to influence politics on the local and national level.

In 1996 the generational contest played out again when the Republicans nominated another aging war hero, Senator Bob Dole of Kansas, but Clinton again won the election, becoming the first Democrat to serve back-to-back terms since Franklin Roosevelt. He was aided in part by the amelioration of conservatives by his signing of welfare reform legislation, the Personal Responsibility and Work Opportunity Reconciliation Act of 1996, which decreased welfare benefits, restricted eligibility, and turned over many responsibilities to states. Clinton said it would "break the cycle of dependency."[17]

Clinton presided over a booming economy fueled by emergent computing technologies. Personal computers had skyrocketed in sales, and the Internet became a mass phenomenon. Communication and commerce were never again the same. The tech boom was driven by business, and the 1990s saw robust innovation and entrepreneurship. Investors scrambled to find the next Microsoft or Apple, suddenly massive computing companies. But it was the Internet that sparked a bonanza. The dot-com boom fueled enormous economic growth and substantial financial speculation to find the next Google or Amazon.

Republicans, defeated at the polls in 1996 and 1998, looked for other ways to undermine Clinton's presidency. Political polarization seemed unprecedented and a sensation-starved, post-Watergate media demanded scandal. The Republican Congress spent millions on investigations hoping to uncover some shred of damning evidence to sink Clinton's presidency, whether it be real estate deals, White House staffing, or adultery. Rumors of sexual misconduct had always swirled around Clinton. The press, which had historically turned a blind eye to such private matters, saturated the media with Clinton's sex scandals. Congressional investigations targeted the allegations and Clinton denied having "sexual relations" with Monica Lewinsky before a grand jury and in a statement to the American public. Republicans used the testimony to allege perjury. In December 1998, the House of Representatives voted to impeach the president. It was a wildly unpopular step. Two thirds of Americans disapproved, and a majority told Gallup pollsters that Republicans had abused their constitutional authority. Clinton's approval rating, meanwhile, jumped to 78 percent.[18] In February 1999, Clinton was acquitted by the Senate by a vote that mostly fell along party lines.

The 2000 election pitted Vice President Albert Gore Jr. against George W. Bush, the twice-elected Texas governor and son of the former president. Gore, wary of Clinton's recent impeachment despite Clinton's enduring approval ratings, distanced himself from the president and eight years of relative prosperity. Instead, he ran as a pragmatic, moderate liberal. Bush, too, ran as a moderate, claiming to represent a compassionate conservatism and a new faith-based politics. Bush was an outspoken evangelical. In a presidential debate, he declared Jesus Christ his favorite political philosopher. He promised to bring church leaders into government, and his campaign appealed to churches and clergy to get out the vote. Moreover, he promised to bring honor, dignity, and integrity to the Oval Office, a clear reference to Clinton. Utterly lacking the political charisma that had propelled Clinton, Gore withered under Bush's attacks. Instead of trumpeting the Clinton presidency, Gore found himself answering the media's questions about whether he was sufficiently an alpha male and whether he had invented the Internet.

Few elections have been as close and contentious as the 2000 election, which ended in a deadlock. Gore had won the popular vote by 500,000 votes, but the Electoral College hinged on a contested Florida election. On election night the media called Florida for Gore, but then Bush made late gains and news organizations reversed themselves by declaring the state for Bush—and Bush the probable president-elect. Gore conceded privately to Bush, then backpedaled as the counts edged back toward Gore yet again. When the nation awoke the next day, it was unclear who had been elected president. The close Florida vote triggered an automatic recount.

Lawyers descended on Florida. The Gore campaign called for manual recounts in several counties. Local election boards, Florida Secretary of State Kathleen Harris, and the Florida Supreme Court all weighed in until the U.S. Supreme Court stepped in and, in an unprecedented 5–4 decision in *Bush v. Gore*, ruled that the recount had to end. Bush was awarded Florida by a margin of 537 votes, enough to win him the state and give him a majority in the Electoral College. He had won the presidency.

In his first months in office, Bush fought to push forward enormous tax cuts skewed toward America's highest earners. The bursting of the dot-com bubble weighed down the economy. Old political and cultural fights continued to be fought. And then the towers fell.

III. September 11 and the War on Terror

On the morning of September 11, 2001, nineteen operatives of the al-Qaeda terrorist organization hijacked four passenger planes on the East Coast. American Airlines Flight 11 crashed into the North Tower of the World Trade Center in New York City at 8:46 a.m. Eastern Daylight Time (EDT). United Airlines Flight 175 crashed into the South Tower at 9:03. American Airlines Flight 77 crashed into the western façade of the Pentagon at 9:37. At 9:59, the South Tower of the World Trade Center collapsed. At 10:03, United Airlines Flight 93 crashed in a field outside Shanksville, Pennsylvania, brought down by passengers who had received news of the earlier hijackings. At 10:28, the North Tower collapsed. In less than two hours, nearly three thousand Americans had been killed.

The attacks stunned Americans. Late that night, Bush addressed the nation and assured the country that "the search is under way for those who are behind these evil acts." At Ground Zero three days later, Bush thanked first responders for their work. A worker said he couldn't hear him. "I can hear you," Bush shouted back, "The rest of the world hears you. And the people who knocked these buildings down will hear all of us soon."

American intelligence agencies quickly identified the radical Islamic militant group al-Qaeda, led by the wealthy Saudi Osama bin Laden, as the perpetrators of the attack. Sheltered in Afghanistan by the Taliban, the country's Islamic government, al-Qaeda was responsible for a 1993 bombing of the World Trade Center and a string of attacks at U.S. embassies and military bases across the world. Bin Laden's Islamic radicalism and his anti-American aggression attracted supporters across the region and, by 2001, al-Qaeda was active in over sixty countries.

Ground Zero six days after the September 11 attacks. Wikimedia.

Although in his presidential campaign Bush had denounced foreign nation-building, he populated his administration with neoconservatives, firm believers in the expansion of American democracy and American interests abroad. Bush advanced what was sometimes called the Bush Doctrine, a policy in which the United States would have the right to unilaterally and preemptively make war on any regime or terrorist organization that posed a threat to the United States or to U.S. citizens. It would lead the United States into protracted conflicts in Afghanistan and Iraq and entangle the United States in nations across the world. Journalist Dexter Filkins called it a Forever War, a perpetual conflict waged against an amorphous and undefeatable enemy.[19] The geopolitical realities of the twenty-first-century world were forever transformed.

The United States, of course, had a history in Afghanistan. When the Soviet Union invaded Afghanistan in December 1979 to quell an insurrection that threatened to topple Kabul's communist government, the United States financed and armed anti-Soviet insurgents, the Mujahideen. In 1981, the Reagan administration authorized the CIA to provide the Mujahideen with weapons and training to strengthen the insurgency. An independent wealthy young Saudi, Osama bin Laden, also fought with and funded the Mujahideen. And they began to win. Afghanistan bled the Soviet Union dry. The costs of the war, coupled with growing instability at home, convinced the Soviets to withdraw from Afghanistan in 1989.[20]

President Bush addresses rescue workers at Ground Zero. 2001. FEMA Photo Library.

Osama bin Laden relocated al-Qaeda to Afghanistan after the country fell to the Taliban in 1996. Under Bill Clinton, the United States launched cruise missiles at al-Qaeda camps in Afghanistan in retaliation for al-Qaeda bombings on American embassies in Africa.

After September 11, with a broad authorization of military force, Bush administration officials made plans for military action against al-Qaeda and the Taliban. What would become the longest war in American history began with the launching of Operation Enduring Freedom in October 2001. Air and missile strikes hit targets across Afghanistan. U.S. Special Forces joined with fighters in the anti-Taliban Northern Alliance. Major Afghan cities fell in quick succession. The capital, Kabul, fell on November 13. Bin Laden and al-Qaeda operatives retreated into the rugged mountains along the border of Pakistan in eastern Afghanistan. The American occupation of Afghanistan continued.

As American troops struggled to contain the Taliban in Afghanistan, the Bush administration set its sights on Iraq. After the conclusion of the Gulf War in 1991, American officials established economic sanctions, weapons inspections, and no-fly zones. By mid-1991, American warplanes were routinely patrolling Iraqi skies and coming under periodic fire from Iraqi missile batteries. The overall cost to the United States of maintaining the two no-fly zones over Iraq was roughly $1 billion a year. Related military activities in the region added almost another $500 million to the annual bill. On the ground in Iraq, meanwhile, Iraqi authorities clashed with UN weapons inspectors. Iraq had suspended its program for weapons of mass destruction, but Saddam Hussein fostered ambiguity about the weapons in the minds of regional leaders to forestall any possible attacks against Iraq.

In 1998, a standoff between Hussein and the United Nations over weapons inspections led President Bill Clinton to launch punitive strikes aimed at debilitating what was thought to be a developed chemical weapons program. Attacks began on December 16, 1998. More than two hundred cruise missiles fired from U.S. Navy warships and Air Force B-52 bombers flew into Iraq, targeting suspected chemical weapons storage facilities, missile batteries, and command centers. Airstrikes continued for three more days, unleashing in total 415 cruise missiles and 600 bombs against 97 targets. The number of bombs dropped was nearly double the number used in the 1991 conflict.

The United States and Iraq remained at odds throughout the 1990s and early 2000, when Bush administration officials began championing "regime change." The administration publicly denounced Saddam Hussein's regime and its alleged weapons of mass destruction. After the ad-

ministration deceptively tied Saddam Hussein to international terrorists, a majority of Americans linked Hussein to the 9/11 attacks.[21] The administration's push for war was in full swing. Protests broke out across the country and all over the world, but majorities of Americans supported military action. On October 16, Congress passed the Authorization for Use of Military Force Against Iraq resolution, giving Bush the power to make war in Iraq. Iraq began cooperating with UN weapons inspectors in late 2002, but the Bush administration pressed on. On February 6, 2003, Secretary of State Colin Powell, who had risen to public prominence as chairman of the Joint Chiefs of State during the Persian Gulf War in 1991, presented allegations of a robust Iraqi weapons program to the UN. Protests continued.

The first American bombs hit Baghdad on March 20, 2003. Several hundred thousand troops moved into Iraq and Hussein's regime quickly collapsed. Baghdad fell on April 9. On May 1, 2003, aboard the USS *Abraham Lincoln*, beneath a banner reading *Mission Accomplished*, George W. Bush announced that "major combat operations in Iraq have ended."[22] No evidence of weapons of mass destruction were ever found. And combat operations had not ended, not really. The Iraqi insurgency

Despite George W. Bush's ill-conceived photo op under a "Mission Accomplished" banner in May 2003, combat operations in Iraq continued for years. Wikimedia.

had begun, and the United States would spend the next ten years struggling to contain it.

Efforts by various intelligence gathering agencies led to the capture
of Saddam Hussein, hidden in an underground compartment near his
hometown, on December 13, 2003. The new Iraqi government found
him guilty of crimes against humanity and he was hanged on December
30, 2006. But the war in Iraq was not over.

IV. The End of the Bush Years

The War on Terror was a centerpiece in the race for the White House in
2004. The Democratic ticket, headed by Massachusetts senator John F.
Kerry, a Vietnam War hero who entered the public consciousness for his
subsequent testimony against it, attacked Bush for the ongoing inability to
contain the Iraqi insurgency or to find weapons of mass destruction, the
revelation and photographic evidence that American soldiers had abused
prisoners at the Abu Ghraib prison outside Baghdad, and the inability to
find Osama bin Laden. Moreover, many enemy combatants who had been
captured in Iraq and Afghanistan were "detained" indefinitely at a military
prison in Guantanamo Bay in Cuba. "Gitmo" became infamous for its
harsh treatment, indefinite detentions, and torture of prisoners. Bush defended the War on Terror, and his allies attacked critics for failing to "support the troops." Moreover, Kerry had voted for the war—he had to attack
the very thing that he had authorized. Bush won a close but clear victory.

The second Bush term saw the continued deterioration of the wars in
Iraq and Afghanistan, but Bush's presidency would take a bigger hit from
his perceived failure to respond to the domestic tragedy that followed
Hurricane Katrina's devastating hit on the Gulf Coast. Katrina had been
a category 5 hurricane. It was, the *New Orleans Times-Picayune* reported, "the storm we always feared."[23]

New Orleans suffered a direct hit, the levees broke, and the bulk of the
city flooded. Thousands of refugees flocked to the Superdome, where supplies and medical treatment and evacuation were slow to come. Individuals
died in the heat. Bodies wasted away. Americans saw poor Black Americans abandoned. Katrina became a symbol of a broken administrative system, a devastated coastline, and irreparable social structures that allowed
escape and recovery for some and not for others. Critics charged that Bush
had staffed his administration with incompetent supporters and had further ignored the displaced poor and Black residents of New Orleans.[24]

Hurricane Katrina was one of the deadliest and more destructive hurricanes to hit American soil in U.S. history. It nearly destroyed New Orleans, Louisiana, as well as cities, towns, and rural areas across the Gulf Coast. It sent hundreds of thousands of refugees to nearby cities such as Houston, Texas, where they temporarily resided in massive structures like the Astrodome. Photograph, September 1, 2005. Wikimedia.

Immigration, meanwhile, had become an increasingly potent political issue. The Clinton administration had overseen the implementation of several anti-immigration policies on the U.S.-Mexico border, but hunger and poverty were stronger incentives than border enforcement policies were deterrents. Illegal immigration continued, often at great human cost, but nevertheless fanned widespread anti-immigration sentiment among many American conservatives. But George W. Bush used the issue to win re-election, and Republicans used it in the 2006 midterms, passing legislation—with bipartisan support—that provided for a border "fence." Seven hundred miles of towering steel barriers sliced through border towns and deserts. Many immigrants and their supporters tried to fight back. The spring and summer of 2006 saw waves of massive protests across the country. Hundreds of thousands marched in Chicago, New York, and Los Angeles, and tens of thousands marched in smaller cities around the country. Legal change, however, went nowhere. Moderate conservatives feared upsetting business interests' demand for cheap, exploitable labor and alienating large voting blocs by stifling immigration, and moderate liberals feared upsetting anti-immigrant groups by pushing too hard for liberalization of immigration laws. The fence was built and the border was tightened.

At the same time, Iraq descended further into chaos as insurgents battled against American troops and groups such as Abu Musab al-Zarqawi's al-Qaeda in Iraq bombed civilians and released video recordings of beheadings. In 2007, twenty-seven thousand additional U.S. forces deployed to Iraq under the command of General David Petraeus. The effort, "the surge," employed more sophisticated anti-insurgency strategies and, combined with Sunni efforts, pacified many of Iraq's cities and provided cover for the withdrawal of American forces. On December 4, 2008, the Iraqi government approved the U.S.-Iraq Status of Forces Agreement, and U.S. combat forces withdrew from Iraqi cities before June 30, 2009. The last U.S. combat forces left Iraq on December 18, 2011. Violence and instability continued to rock the country.

Afghanistan, meanwhile, had also continued to deteriorate. In 2006, the Taliban reemerged, as the Afghan government proved both highly corrupt and incapable of providing social services or security for its citizens. The Taliban began re-acquiring territory. Money and American troops continued to prop up the Afghanistan government until American forces withdrew hastily in August 2021. The Taliban immediately took over the remainder of the country, outlasting America's twenty-year occupation.

V. The Great Recession

The Great Recession began, as most American economic catastrophes began, with the bursting of a speculative bubble. Throughout the 1990s and into the new millennium, home prices continued to climb, and financial services firms looked to cash in on what seemed to be a safe but lucrative investment. After the dot-com bubble burst, investors searched for a secure investment rooted in clear value, rather than in trendy technological speculation. What could be more secure than real estate? But mortgage companies began writing increasingly risky loans and then bundling them together and selling them over and over again, sometimes so quickly that it became difficult to determine exactly who owned what.

Decades of financial deregulation had rolled back Depression-era restraints and again allowed risky business practices to dominate the world of American finance. It was a bipartisan agenda. In the 1990s, for instance, Bill Clinton signed the Gramm-Leach-Bliley Act, repealing provisions of the 1933 Glass-Steagall Act separating commercial and investment banks, and the Commodity Futures Modernization Act, which exempted credit-default swaps—perhaps the key financial mechanism behind the crash—from regulation.

Mortgages had been so heavily leveraged that when American homeowners began to default on their loans, the whole system collapsed. Major financial services firms such as Bear Stearns and Lehman Brothers disappeared almost overnight. In order to prevent the crisis from spreading, President Bush signed the Emergency Economic Stabilization Act, and the federal government immediately began pouring billions of dollars into the industry, propping up hobbled banks. Massive giveaways to bankers created shock waves of resentment throughout the rest of the country, contributing to Barack Obama's 2008 election. But Obama oversaw the program after his inauguration. Thereafter, conservative members of the Tea Party decried the cronyism of an incoming Obama administration filled with former Wall Street executives. The same energies also motivated the Occupy Wall Street movement, as mostly young left-leaning New Yorkers protested an American economy that seemed overwhelmingly tilted toward "the one percent."[25]

The Great Recession only magnified already rising income and wealth inequalities. According to the chief investment officer at JPMorgan Chase, the largest bank in the United States, "profit margins have reached levels not seen in decades," and "reductions in wages and benefits explain the majority of the net improvement."[26] A study from the Congressional Budget Office (CBO) found that since the late 1970s, after-tax benefits of the wealthiest 1 percent grew by over 300 percent. The "average" American's after-tax benefits had grown 35 percent. Economic trends have disproportionately and objectively benefited the wealthiest Americans. Still, despite political rhetoric, American frustration failed to generate anything like the social unrest of the early twentieth century. A weakened labor movement and a strong conservative bloc continue to stymie serious attempts at reversing or even slowing economic inequalities. Occupy Wall Street managed to generate a fair number of headlines and shift public discussion away from budget cuts and toward inequality, but its membership amounted to only a fraction of the far more influential and money-driven Tea Party. Its presence on the public stage was fleeting.

The Great Recession, however, was not. While American banks quickly recovered and recaptured their steady profits, and the American stock market climbed again to new heights, American workers continued to lag. Job growth was slow and unemployment rates would remain stubbornly high for years. Wages froze, meanwhile, and well-paying full-time jobs that were lost were too often replaced by low-paying, part-time work. A generation of workers coming of age within the crisis, more-over, had been savaged by the economic collapse. Unemployment among young Americans hovered for years at rates nearly double the national average.

VI. The Obama Years

By the 2008 election, with Iraq still in chaos, Democrats were ready to embrace the antiwar position and sought a candidate who had consistently opposed military action in Iraq. Senator Barack Obama had only been a member of the Illinois state senate when Congress debated the war actions, but he had publicly denounced the war, predicting the sectarian violence that would ensue, and remained critical of the invasion through his 2004 campaign for the U.S. Senate. He began running for president almost immediately after arriving in Washington.

A former law professor and community activist, Obama became the first African American candidate to ever capture the nomination of a major political party.[27] During the election, Obama won the support of an increasingly antiwar electorate. When an already fragile economy finally collapsed in 2007 and 2008, Bush's policies were widely blamed.

In 2008, Barack Obama became the first African American elected to the presidency. In this official White House photo from May 2009, five-year-old Jacob Philadelphia said, "I want to know if my hair is just like yours." The White House, via Flickr.

Obama's opponent, Republican senator John McCain, was tied to those policies and struggled to fight off the nation's desire for a new political direction. Obama won a convincing victory in the fall and became the nation's first African American president.

President Obama's first term was marked by domestic affairs, especially his efforts to combat the Great Recession and to pass a national healthcare law. Obama came into office as the economy continued to deteriorate. He continued the bank bailout begun under his predecessor and launched a limited economic stimulus plan to provide government spending to reignite the economy.

Despite Obama's dominant electoral victory, national politics fractured, and a conservative Republican firewall quickly arose against the Obama administration. *The Tea Party* became a catch-all term for a diffuse movement of fiercely conservative and politically frustrated American voters. Typically whiter, older, and richer than the average American, flush with support from wealthy backers, and clothed with the iconography of the Founding Fathers, Tea Party activists registered their deep suspicions of the federal government.[28] Tea Party protests dominated the public eye in 2009 and activists steered the Republican Party far to the right, capturing primary elections all across the country.

Obama's most substantive legislative achievement proved to be a national healthcare law, the Patient Protection and Affordable Care Act (Obamacare). Presidents since Theodore Roosevelt had striven to pass national healthcare reform and failed. Obama's plan forsook liberal models of a national healthcare system and instead adopted a heretofore conservative model of subsidized private care (similar plans had been put forward by Republicans Richard Nixon, Newt Gingrich, and Obama's 2012 opponent, Mitt Romney). Beset by conservative protests, Obama's healthcare reform narrowly passed through Congress. It abolished pre-existing conditions as a cause for denying care, scrapped junk plans, provided for state-run healthcare exchanges (allowing individuals without healthcare to pool their purchasing power), offered states funds to subsidize an expansion of Medicaid, and required all Americans to provide proof of a health insurance plan that measured up to government-established standards (those who did not purchase a plan would pay a penalty tax, and those who could not afford insurance would be eligible for federal subsidies). The number of uninsured Americans remained stubbornly high, however, and conservatives spent most of the next decade attacking the bill.

Meanwhile, in 2009, President Barack Obama deployed seventeen thousand additional troops to Afghanistan as part of a counterinsurgency

Former Taliban fighters surrender their arms to the government of the Islamic Republic of Afghanistan during a reintegration ceremony at the provincial governor's compound in May 2012. Wikimedia.

campaign that aimed to "disrupt, dismantle, and defeat" al-Qaeda and the Taliban. Meanwhile, U.S. Special Forces and CIA drones targeted al-Qaeda and Taliban leaders. In May 2011, U.S. Navy Sea, Air and Land Forces (SEALs) conducted a raid deep into Pakistan that led to the killing of Osama bin Laden. The United States and NATO began a phased withdrawal from Afghanistan in 2011, with an aim of removing all combat troops by 2014. Although weak militarily, the Taliban remained politically influential in south and eastern Afghanistan. Al-Qaeda remained active in Pakistan but shifted its bases to Yemen and the Horn of Africa. As of December 2013, the war in Afghanistan had claimed the lives of 3,397 U.S. service members.

VII. Stagnation

In 2012, Barack Obama won a second term by defeating Republican Mitt Romney, the former governor of Massachusetts. However, Obama's inability to control Congress and the ascendancy of Tea Party Republicans stunted the passage of meaningful legislation. Obama was a lame duck before he ever won reelection, and gridlocked government came to represent an acute sense that much of American life—whether in politics, economics, or race relations—had grown stagnant.

The economy continued its halfhearted recovery from the Great Recession. The Obama administration campaigned on little to specifically address the crisis and, faced with congressional intransigence, accomplished even less. While corporate profits climbed and stock markets soared, wages stagnated and employment sagged for years after the Great Recession. By 2016, the statistically average American worker had not received a raise in almost forty years. The average worker in January 1973 earned $4.03 an hour. Adjusted for inflation, that wage was about two dollars per hour more than the average American earned in 2014. Working Americans were losing ground. Moreover, most income gains in the economy had been largely captured by a small number of wealthy earners. Between 2009 and 2013, 85 percent of all new income in the United States went to the top 1 percent of the population.[29]

But if money no longer flowed to American workers, it saturated American politics. In 2000, George W. Bush raised a record $172 million for his campaign. In 2008, Barack Obama became the first presidential candidate to decline public funds (removing any applicable caps to his total fund-raising) and raised nearly three quarters of a billion dollars for his campaign. The average House seat, meanwhile, cost about $1.6 million, and the average Senate Seat over $10 million.[30] The Supreme Court, meanwhile, removed barriers to outside political spending. In 2002, Senators John McCain and Russ Feingold had crossed party lines to pass the Bipartisan Campaign Reform Act, bolstering campaign finance laws passed in the aftermath of the Watergate scandal in the 1970s. But political organizations—particularly PACs—exploited loopholes to raise large sums of money and, in 2010, the Supreme Court ruled in *Citizens United v. FEC* that no limits could be placed on political spending by corporations, unions, and nonprofits. Money flowed even deeper into politics.

The influence of money in politics only heightened partisan gridlock, further blocking bipartisan progress on particular political issues. Climate change, for instance, has failed to transcend partisan barriers. In the 1970s and 1980s, experts substantiated the theory of anthropogenic (human-caused) global warming. Eventually, the most influential of these panels, the UN's Intergovernmental Panel on Climate Change (IPCC) concluded in 1995 that there was a "discernible human influence on global climate."[31] This conclusion, though stated conservatively, was by that point essentially a scientific consensus. By 2007, the IPCC considered the evidence "unequivocal" and warned that "unmitigated climate change would, in the long term, be likely to exceed the capacity of natural, managed and human systems to adapt."[32]

Climate change became a permanent and major topic of public discussion and policy in the twenty-first century. Fueled by popular coverage, most notably, perhaps, the documentary *An Inconvenient Truth*, based on Al Gore's book and presentations of the same name, addressing climate change became a plank of the American left and a point of denial for the American right. American public opinion and political action still lagged far behind the scientific consensus on the dangers of global warming. Conservative politicians, conservative think tanks, and energy companies waged war to sow questions in the minds of Americans, who remain divided on the question, and so many others.

Much of the resistance to addressing climate change is economic. As Americans looked over their shoulder at China, many refused to sacrifice immediate economic growth for long-term environmental security. Twenty-first-century relations with China remained characterized by contradictions and interdependence. After the collapse of the Soviet Union, China reinvigorated its efforts to modernize its country. By liberating and subsidizing much of its economy and drawing enormous foreign investments, China has posted massive growth rates during the last several decades. Enormous cities rise by the day. In 2000, China had a GDP around an eighth the size of U.S. GDP. Based on growth rates and trends, analysts suggest that China's economy will bypass that of the United States soon. American concerns about China's political system have persisted, but money sometimes matters more to Americans. China has become one of the country's leading trade partners. Cultural exchange has increased, and more and more Americans visit China each year, with many settling down to work and study.

VIII. American Carnage

By 2016, American voters were fed up. In that year's presidential race, Republicans spurned their political establishment and nominated a real estate developer and celebrity billionaire, Donald Trump, who, decrying the tyranny of political correctness and promising to Make America Great Again, promised to build a wall to keep out Mexican immigrants and bar Muslim immigrants. The Democrats, meanwhile, flirted with the candidacy of Senator Bernie Sanders, a self-described democratic socialist from Vermont, before ultimately nominating Hillary Clinton, who, after eight years as first lady in the 1990s, had served eight years in the Senate and four more as secretary of state. Voters despaired: Trump and Clinton were the most unpopular nominees in modern American history. Majorities of Americans viewed each candidate unfavorably and majorities in both parties said, early in the election season, that they were motivated more by voting *against* their rival candidate than *for* their own.[33] With

Donald Trump speaking at a 2018 rally. Photo by Gage Skidmore. Via Wikimedia.

incomes frozen, politics gridlocked, race relations tense, and headlines full of violence, such frustrations only channeled a larger sense of stagnation, which upset traditional political allegiances. In the end, despite winning nearly three million more votes nationwide, Clinton failed to carry key Midwestern states where frustrated white, working-class voters abandoned the Democratic Party—a Republican president hadn't carried Wisconsin, Michigan, or Pennsylvania, for instance, since the 1980s—and swung their support to the Republicans. Donald Trump won the presidency.

Political divisions only deepened after the election. A nation already deeply split by income, culture, race, geography, and ideology continued to come apart. Trump's presidency consumed national attention. Traditional print media and the consumers and producers of social media could not help but throw themselves at the ins and outs of Trump's norm-smashing first years while seemingly refracting every major event through the prism of the Trump presidency. Robert Mueller's investigation of Russian election-meddling and the alleged collusion of campaign officials in that effort produced countless headlines. New policies, meanwhile, enflamed widening cultural divisions. Border apprehensions and deportations reached record levels under the Obama administration, but Trump pushed even farther. He pushed for a massive wall along the border to supplement the fence built under the Bush administration. He began ordering the deportation of so-called Dreamers—students who were born elsewhere but grew up in the United States—and immigration officials separated refugee-status-seeking parents and children at the border. Trump's border policies heartened his base and aggravated his opponents.

In his inaugural address, Donald Trump promised to end what he called "American carnage"—a nation ravaged, he said, by illegal immigrants, crime, and foreign economic competition. But, under his presidency, the nation only spiraled deeper into cultural and racial divisions, domestic unrest, and growing anxiety about the nation's future. Trump represented an aggressive, pugilistic anti-liberalism, and, as president, he never missed an opportunity to fuel the fires of right-wing rage. Refusing to settle for the careful statement or defer to bureaucrats, Trump smashed many of the norms of the presidency and raged on his personal Twitter account. And he refused to be governed by the truth.

Few Americans, especially after the Johnson and Nixon administrations, believed that presidents never lied. But perhaps no president ever lied so boldly or so often as Donald Trump, who made, according to one accounting, an untrue statement every day for the first forty days of his presidency.[34] By the latter years of his presidency, only about a third of Americans counted him as trustworthy.[35] And that compulsive dishonesty led directly to January 6, 2021.

In November 2020, Joseph R. Biden, a longtime senator from Delaware and former vice president under Barack Obama, running alongside Kamala Harris, a California senator who would become the nation's first female vice president, convincingly defeated Donald Trump at the polls: Biden won the popular vote by a margin of four percent and the electoral vote by a margin of 74 votes, marking the first time an incumbent president had been defeated in twenty-eight years. But Trump refused to concede the election. He said it had been stolen. He said votes had been manufactured. He said it was all rigged. The claims were easily debunked, but it didn't seem to matter: months after the election, somewhere between one-half and two-thirds of self-identified Republicans judged the election stolen.[36] So when, on the afternoon of January 6, 2021, the president again articulated a litany of lies about the election and told the crowd of angry conspiracy-minded protesters to march to the Capitol and "fight like hell," they did just that.

Thousands of Trump's followers converged on the Capitol. Roughly one in seven of the more than five hundred rioters later arrested were affiliated with extremist groups organized around conspiracy theories, white supremacy, and the right-wing militia movement.[37] They waved

American and Confederate flags, displayed conspiracy theory slogans and white supremacist icons, carried Christian iconography, and, above all, bore flags, hats, shirts, and other emblazoned with the name of Donald Trump.[38] Arming themselves for hand-to-hand combat, they pushed past barriers and battled barricaded police officers. The Capitol attackers injured about 150 of them.[39] Officers suffered concussions, burns, bruises, stab wounds, and broken bones.[40] One suffered a non-fatal heart attack after being shocked repeatedly by a stun gun. Capitol Police Officer Brian D. Sicknick was killed, either by repeated attacks with a fire extinguisher or from mace or bear spray. Four other officers later died by suicide.

As the rioters breached the building, officers inside the House chamber moved furniture to barricade the doors as House members huddled together on the floor, waiting for a breach. Ashli Babbitt, a thirty-five-year-old Air Force veteran consumed by social-media conspiracy theories and wearing a Trump flag around her neck, was shot and killed by a Capitol Police officer when she attempted to storm the chamber. The House chamber held, but attackers breached the Senate Chamber on the opposite end of the building. Lawmakers had already been evacuated.

The rioters held the Capitol for several hours before the National Guard cleared it that evening. Congress, refusing to back down, stayed that evening to certify the results of the election. And yet, despite everything that had happened that day, the president's unfounded claims of election fraud kept their grip on on Republican lawmakers. Eleven Republican senators and 150 of the House's 212 Republicans lodged objections to the certification. And a little more than a month later, they refused to convict Donald Trump during his quickly organized second impeachment trial, this time for "incitement of insurrection."

IX. The Pandemic

In the winter of 2019 and 2020, a new respiratory virus, Covid-19, emerged in Wuhan, China. It was a coronavirus, named after its spiky, crown-like appearance under a microscope. Other coronaviruses had been identified and contained in previous years, but, by December 2019, Chinese doctors were treating dozens of cases, and, by January, hundreds. Wuhan shut down to contain the outbreak, but the virus escaped. In January 2020, the United States confirmed its first case. Deaths were reported in the Philippines and in France. Outbreaks struck Italy and Iran. And American case counts grew. Countries began locking down. Air travel slowed.

The virus was highly contagious and could be spread before the onset of symptoms. Many who had the virus were asymptomatic: they didn't exhibit any symptoms at all. But others, especially the elderly and those with "comorbidities," were struck down. The virus attacked their airways, suffocating them. Doctors didn't know what they were battling. They struggled to procure oxygen and respirators and inoculated the worst cases with what they had. But the deaths piled up.

The virus hit New York City in the spring. The city was devastated. Hospitals overflowed as doctors struggled to treat a disease they barely understood. By April, thousands of patients were dying every day. The city couldn't keep up with the bodies. Dozens of "mobile morgues" were set up to house bodies that wouldn't be processed for months.[41]

With medical-grade masks in short supply, Americans made their own homemade cloth masks. Many right-wing Americans notably refused to wear them at all, further exposing workers and family members to the virus.

Failing to contain the outbreak, the country shut down. Flights stopped. Schools and restaurants closed. White-collar workers transitioned to working from home when offices shut down. But others weren't so lucky. By April, 10 million Americans had lost their jobs.[42]

But shutdowns were scattered and incomplete. States were left to fend for themselves, setting their own policies and competing with one another to acquire scarce personal protective equipment (PPE). Many workers couldn't stay home. Hourly workers, lacking paid sick leave, often had to choose between a paycheck and reporting to work having been exposed or even when presenting symptoms. Mask-wearing, meanwhile, was politicized. By May, 100,000 Americans were dead. A new wave of cases hit the South in July and August, overwhelming hospitals across much of the region. But the worst came in the winter, when the outbreak went fully national. Hundreds of thousands tested positive for the virus every day and nearly three thousand Americans died every day throughout January and much of February.

The outbreak retreated in the spring, and pharmaceutical labs, flush with federal dollars, released new, cutting-edge vaccines. By late spring, Americans were getting vaccinated by the millions. The virus looked like it could be defeated. But many Americans, variously swayed by conspiracy theories peddled on social media or simply politically radicalized into associating vaccinations with anti-Trump politics, refused them. By late summer, barely a majority of those eligible for vaccines were fully vaccinated. More contagious and elusive strains evolved and spread, and the virus continued churning through the population, sending many, especially the elderly, chronically ill, and unvaccinated, to hospitals and to early deaths. By the end of the summer of 2021, according to official counts, over 600,000 Americans had died from Covid-19. By May 2022, the official death toll in the United States crossed one million.

X. New Horizons

Americans looked anxiously to the future, and yet also, often, to a new generation busy discovering, perhaps, that change was not impossible. Much public commentary in the early twenty-first century concerned "Millennials" and "Generation Z," the generations that came of age during the new millennium. Commentators, demographers, and political prognosticators continued to ask what the new generation will bring. *Time*'s May 20, 2013, cover, for instance, read *Millennials Are Lazy, Entitled Narcissists Who Still Live with Their Parents: Why They'll Save Us All*. Pollsters focused on features that distinguish millennials from older Americans: millennials, the pollsters said, were more diverse, more liberal, less religious, and wracked by economic insecurity. "They are," as one Pew report read, "relatively unattached to organized politics and religion, linked by social media, burdened by debt, distrustful of people, in no rush to marry—and optimistic about the future."[43]

Millennial attitudes toward homosexuality and gay marriage reflected one of the most dramatic changes in the popular attitudes of recent years. After decades of advocacy, American attitudes shifted rapidly. In 2006, a majority of Americans still told Gallup pollsters that "gay or lesbian relations" was "morally wrong."[44] But prejudice against homosexuality plummeted and greater public acceptance of coming out opened the culture—in 2001, 73 percent of Americans said they knew someone who was gay, lesbian, or bisexual; in 1983, only 24 percent did. Gay characters—and in particular, gay characters with depth and complexity—could be found across the cultural landscape. Attitudes shifted such that, by the 2010s, polls registered majority support for the legalization of gay marriage. A writer for the *Wall Street Journal* called it "one of the fastest-moving changes in social attitudes of this generation."[45]

Such change was, in many respects, a generational one: on average, younger Americans supported gay marriage in higher numbers than older Americans. The Obama administration, meanwhile, moved tentatively. Refusing to push for national interventions on the gay marriage front, Obama did, however, direct a review of Defense Department policies that repealed the Don't Ask, Don't Tell policy in 2011. Without the support of national politicians, gay marriage was left to the courts. Beginning in Massachusetts in 2003, state courts had begun slowly ruling against gay marriage bans. Then, in June 2015, the Supreme Court ruled 5–4 in *Obergefell v. Hodges* that same-sex marriage was a constitutional right. Nearly two thirds of Americans supported the position.[46]

While liberal social attitudes marked the younger generation, perhaps nothing defined young Americans more than the embrace of technology. The Internet in particular, liberated from desktop modems, shaped more of daily life than ever before. The release of the Apple iPhone in 2007 popularized the concept of smartphones for millions of consumers and, by 2011, about a third of Americans owned a mobile computing device. Four years later, two thirds did.[47]

Together with the advent of social media, Americans used their smartphones and their desktops to stay in touch with old acquaintances, chat with friends, share photos, and interpret the world—as newspaper and magazine subscriptions dwindled, Americans increasingly turned to their social media networks for news and information.[48] Ambitious new online media companies, hungry for clicks and the ad revenue they represented, churned out provocatively titled, easy-to-digest stories that could be linked and tweeted and shared widely among like-minded online communities,[49] but even traditional media companies, forced to downsize their newsrooms to accommodate shrinking revenues, fought to adapt to their new online consumers.

The ability of individuals to share stories through social media apps revolutionized the media landscape—smartphone technology and the democratization of media reshaped political debates and introduced new political questions. The easy accessibility of video capturing and the ability for stories to go viral outside traditional media, for instance, brought new attention to the tense and often violent relations between municipal police officers and African Americans. The 2014 death of Michael Brown in Ferguson, Missouri, sparked protests and focused the issue. It perhaps became a testament to the power of social media platforms, such as Twitter, that a hashtag, #blacklivesmatter, became a rallying cry for protesters, and counterhashtags, #alllivesmatter and #bluelivesmatter, for critics.[50] But a relentless number of videos documenting the deaths of Black men at the hands of police officers continued to circulate across social media networks. The deaths of Eric Garner, twelve-year-old Tamir Rice, Philando Castile, and others were captured on cell phone cameras

and went viral. So too did the stories of Breonna Taylor and Botham Jean. "Say their names," a popular chant at Black Lives Matters marches went. And then George Floyd was murdered.

On May 25, 2020, a teenager, Darnella Frazier, filmed Minneapolis police officer Derek Chauvin with his knee on the neck of George Floyd. "I can't breathe," Floyd said. Despite his pleas, and those of bystanders, Chauvin kept his knee on Floyd's neck for nine minutes. Floyd's body had long since gone limp. The horrific footage shocked much of the country. Despite state and local lockdowns to slow the spread of Covid-19, spontaneous demonstrations broke out across the country. Protests erupted not only in major cities but in small towns and rural communities. The demonstrations dwarfed, in raw numbers, any comparable protest in American history. Taken together, as many as 25 million Americans may have participated in racial justice demonstrations that summer.[51] And yet, despite the marches, no great national policy changes quickly followed. The "system" resisted calls to address "systemic racism." Localities made efforts, of course. Criminal justice reformers won elections as district attorneys. Police departments mandated their officers carry body cameras. As cries of "defund the police" sounded among left-wing Americans, some cities experimented with alternative emergency services that emphasized mediation and mental health. Meanwhile, at a symbolic level, Democratic-leaning towns and cities in the South pulled down their Confederate iconography. But the intractable racial injustices

George Floyd's murder in 2020 sparked the largest protests in American history. Here, crowds holding homemade signs protest in New York City. Via Wikimedia.

embedded deeply within American life had not been uprooted, and racial disparities in wealth, education, health, and other measures persevered, as they already had, in the United States, for hundreds of years.

As the Black Lives Matter movement captured national attention, another social media phenomenon, the #MeToo movement, began as the magnification of and outrage toward the past sexual crimes of notable male celebrities before injecting a greater intolerance toward those accused of sexual harassment and violence into much of the rest of American society. The sudden zero tolerance reflected the new political energies of many American women, sparked in large part by the candidacy and presidency of Donald Trump. The day after Trump's inauguration, between five hundred thousand and one million people descended on Washington, D.C., for the Women's March, and millions more demonstrated in cities and towns around the country to show a broadly defined commitment toward the rights of women and others in the face of the Trump presidency. And with three appointments to the Supreme Court, Donald Trump's legacy would persist past his presidency. On June 24, 2022, the new conservative majority decided *Dobbs v. Jackson*, overturning *Roe v. Wade* (1973) and *Planned Parenthood v. Casey* (1992), cases that established a constitutional right to abortion. Meanwhile, other avenues of sexual politics opened across the country. By the 2020s, the broader American culture increasingly featured transgender individuals in media, and many Americans began making their preferred pronouns explicit—as well as deploying "they" as a gender-neutral pronoun—to undermine fixed notions of gender. Many conservatives, however, fought back. State legislators around the country sponsored "bathroom bills" to keep transgender individuals out of the bathroom of their identified gender, alleging that they posed a violent sexual risk. In Texas, Attorney General Ken Paxton declared pediatric gender-affirming care to be child abuse.

As issues of race and gender captured much public discussion, immigration continued on as a potent political issue. Even as anti-immigrant initiatives like California's Proposition 187 (1994) and Arizona's SB1070 (2010) reflected the anxieties of many white Americans, younger Americans proved far more comfortable with immigration and diversity (which makes sense, given that they are the most diverse American generation in living memory). Since Lyndon Johnson's Great Society liberalized immigration laws in the 1960s, the demographics of the United States have been transformed. In 2012, nearly one quarter of all Americans were immigrants or the sons and daughters of immigrants. Half came from Latin

America. The ongoing Hispanicization of the United States and the ever-shrinking proportion of non-Hispanic whites have been the most talked about trends among demographic observers. By 2013, 17 percent of the nation was Hispanic. In 2014, Latinos surpassed non-Latino whites to become the largest ethnic group in California. In Texas, the image of a white cowboy hardly captures the demographics of a minority-majority state in which Hispanic Texans will soon become the largest ethnic group. For the nearly 1.5 million people of Texas's Rio Grande Valley, for instance, where most residents speak Spanish at home, a full three fourths of the population is bilingual.[52] Political commentators often wonder what political transformations these populations will bring about when they come of age and begin voting in larger numbers.

XI. Conclusion

The collapse of the Soviet Union brought neither global peace nor stability, and the attacks of September 11, 2001, plunged the United States into interminable conflicts around the world. At home, economic recession, a slow recovery, stagnant wage growth, and general pessimism infected American life as contentious politics and cultural divisions poisoned social harmony, leading directly to the January 6, 2021, attack on the U.S. Capitol. And yet the stream of history changes its course. Trends shift, things change, and events turn. New generations bring with them new perspectives, and they share new ideas. Our world is not foreordained. It is the product of history, the ever-evolving culmination of a longer and broader story, of a larger history, of a raw, distinctive, American Yawp.

XI. Reference Material

This chapter was edited by Michael Hammond, with content contributions by Eladio Bobadilla, Andrew Chadwick, Zach Fredman, Leif Fredrickson, Michael Hammond, Richara Hayward, Joseph Locke, Mark Kukis, Shaul Mitelpunkt, Michelle Reeves, Elizabeth Skilton, Bill Speer, and Ben Wright.

Recommended citation: Eladio Bobadilla et al., "The Recent Past," Michael Hammond, ed., in *The American Yawp*, eds. Joseph Locke and Ben Wright (Stanford, CA: Stanford University Press, 2019).

NOTES TO CHAPTER 30
1. Calvin Woodward, "AP FACT CHECK: Trump's Team Glosses over His Jan. 6 Tirade," Associated Press, February 12, 2021. https://apnews.com/

article/ap-fact-check-donald-trump-capitol-siege-violence-elections-507f4feb
badecb84e1637e55999ac0ea

2. Peter Hermann, "'We Got to Hold This Door': How Battered D.C. Police
Made a Stand against the Capitol Mob," *Washington Post*, January 14, 2021.
https://www.washingtonpost.com/dc-md-va/2021/01/14/dc-police-capitol-riot/.

3. Luke Broadwater and Nicholas Fandos, "'A Hit Man Sent Them': Police
at the Capitol Recount the Horrors of Jan. 6 as the Inquiry Begins," *New York
Times*, July 27, 2021. https://www.nytimes.com/2021/07/27/us/jan-6-inquiry
.html.

4. William Faulker, *Requiem for a Nun* (New York: Random House,
1954), 73.

5. Bill Minutaglio, *First Son: George W. Bush and the Bush Family Dynasty*
(New York: Random House, 1999), 210–224.

6. Roger Simon, "How a Murderer and Rapist Became the Bush Campaign's
Most Valuable Player," *Baltimore Sun*, November 11, 1990.

7. See especially Dan T. Carter, *From George Wallace to Newt Gingrich:
Race in the Conservative Counterrevolution, 1963–1994* (Baton Rouge: LSU
Press, 1996), 72–80.

8. Sean Wilentz, *The Age of Reagan: A History, 1974–2008* (New York:
HarperCollins, 2008).

9. James F. Clarity, "End of the Soviet Union," *New York Times*, December
26, 1991.

10. Francis Fukuyama, "The End of History?" *National Interest* (Summer
1989).

11. William Thomas Allison, *The Gulf War, 1990–91* (New York: Palgrave
Macmillan, 2012), 145, 165.

12. Charles W. Dunn, *The Presidency in the Twenty-first Century* (Lexington: University Press of Kentucky, 2011), 152.

13. Robert M. Collins, *Transforming America: Politics and Culture During
the Reagan Years* (New York: Columbia University Press, 2009), 171, 172.

14. For Clinton's presidency and the broader politics of the 1990s, see James
T. Patterson, *Restless Giant: The United States from Watergate to Bush v. Gore*
(New York: Oxford University Press, 2005); and Wilentz, *Age of Reagan*.

15. Patterson, *Restless Giant*, 298–299.

16. United Nations International Organization for Migration, "Migrant
Deaths Remain High Despite Sharp Fall in US-Mexico Border Crossings in 2017,"
press release, February 6, 2018. https://news.un.org/en/story/2018/02/1002101.

17. Carolyn Skorneck, "Final Welfare Bill Written," *Washington Post*, July
30, 1996, A1.

18. Frank Newport, "Clinton Receives Record High Job Approval Rating,"
Gallup, December 24, 1998. http://news.gallup.com/poll/4111/clinton-receives
-record-high-job-approval-rating-after-impeachment-vot.aspx.

19. Dexter Filkins, *The Forever War* (New York: Vintage Books, 2009).

20. See, for instance, Lawrence Wright, *The Looming Tower: Al Qaeda and
the Road to 9/11* (New York: Knopf, 2006).

21. https://www.washingtonpost.com/archive/politics/2003/09/06/hussein-link-to-911-lingers-in manyminds/7cd31079-21d1-42cf-8651-b67e93350fde/.))
—the Bush administration began pushing for a "pre-emptive" war in the fall of 2002. The administration alleged that Hussein was trying to acquire uranium and that it had aluminum tubes used for nuclear centrifuges. Public opinion was divided. George W. Bush said in October, "Facing clear evidence of peril, we cannot wait for the final proof—the smoking gun—that could come in the form of a mushroom cloud." (Thomas R. Mockaitis, *The Iraq War: A Documentary and Reference Guide* (Santa Barbara, CA: ABC-Clio, 2012), 26.

22. Judy Keen, "Bush to Troops: Mission Accomplished," *USA Today*, June 5, 2003.

23. Bruce Nolan, "Katrina: The Storm We've Always Feared," *New Orleans Times-Picayune*, August 30, 2005.

24. Douglas Brinkley, *The Great Deluge: Hurricane Katrina, New Orleans, and the Mississippi Gulf Coast* (New York: HarperCollins, 2006).

25. On the Great Recession, see Joseph Stiglitz, *Freefall: America, Free Markets, and the Sinking of the World Economy* (New York: Norton, 2010); and Michael Lewis, *The Big Short: Inside the Doomsday Machine* (New York: Norton: 2010).

26. Harold Meyerson, "Corporate America's Chokehold on Wages," *Washington Post*, July 19, 2011.

27. Thomas J. Sugrue, *Not Even Past: Barack Obama and the Burden of Race Book* (Princeton, NJ: Princeton University Press, 2012).

28. Kate Zernike and Megan Thee-Brenan, "Poll Finds Tea Party Backers Wealthier and More Educated," *New York Times*, April 14, 2010; Jill Lepore, *The Whites of Their Eyes: The Tea Party's Revolution and the Battle over American History* (Princeton, NJ: Princeton University Press, 2011).

29. Kerry Close, "The 1% Pocketed 85% of Post-Recession Income Growth," *Time*, June 16, 2016. http://time.com/money/4371332/income-inequality-recession/. See also Justin Wolfers, "The Gains from the Economic Recovery Are Still Limited to the Top One Percent," *New York Times*, January 27, 2015. http://www.nytimes.com/2015/01/28/upshot/gains-from-economic-recovery-still-limited-to-top-one-percent.html.

30. Julia Queen and Christian Hilland, "2008 Presidential Campaign Financial Activity Summarized: Receipts Nearly Double 2004 Total," Federal Election Commission, June 8, 2009. http://www.fec.gov/press/press2009/20090608PresStat.shtml; Andre Tartar and Eric Benson, "The Forever Campaign," *New York Magazine* (October 14, 2012). http://nymag.com/news/politics/elections-2012/timeline-2012-10/.

31. Intergovernmental Panel on Climate Change, *Climate Change 2013: The Physical Science Basis* (Cambridge, UK: Cambridge University Press, 2014).

32. Intergovernmental Panel on Climate Change, *Climate Change 2014: Impacts, Adaptation and Vulnerability: Global and Sectoral Aspects* (Cambridge, UK: Cambridge University Press, 2014).

33. Philip Bump, "A Quarter of Americans Dislike Both Major-Party Presidential Candidates," *Washington Post*, July 14, 2016. https://www.washingtonpost.com/news/the-fix/wp/2016/07/14/a-quarter-of-americans-dislike-both-major-party-presidential-candidates/?tid=a_inl; Aaron Zitner and Julia Wolfe, "Trump and Clinton's Popularity Problem," *Wall Street Journal*, May 24, 2016. http://graphics.wsj.com/elections/2016/donald-trump-and-hillary-clintons-popularity-problem/.

34. David Leonhardt and Stuart A. Thompson, "Trump's Lies," *New York Times*, December 14, 2017, updated November 11, 2017. https://www.nytimes.com/interactive/2017/06/23/opinion/trumps-lies.html.

35. Megan Brenan, "Americans' Views of Trump's Character Firmly Established," Gallup, June 18, 2020. https://news.gallup.com/poll/312737/americans-views-trump-character-firmly-established.aspx.

36. See, for instance, https://www.ipsos.com/sites/default/files/ct/news/documents/202104/topline_write_up_reuters_ipsos_trump_coattails_poll_-_april_02_2021.pdf.

37. Clare Hymes, Cassidy McDonald, and Eleanor Watson, "What We Know about the "Unprecedented" Capitol Riot Arrests," CBS News, August 11, 2021. https://www.cbsnews.com/news/us-capitol-riot-arrests-latest/.

38. Matthew Rosenberg and Ainara Tiefenthäler, "Decoding the Far-Right Symbols at the Capitol Riot," *New York Times*, January 13, 2021. https://www.nytimes.com/2021/01/13/video/extremist-signs-symbols-capitol-riot.html

39. "Capitol Police Officer Brian D. Sicknick Dies After Suffering Injuries During U.S. Capitol Riot," CBS News, January 8, 2021. https://www.cbsnews.com/baltimore/news/capitol-riot-officer-injured-hospitalized-latest/.

40. Michael S. Schmidt and Luke Broadwater, "Officers' Injuries, Including Concussions, Show Scope of Violence at Capitol Riot," *New York Times*, February 11, 2021. https://www.nytimes.com/2021/02/11/us/politics/capitol-riot-police-officer-injuries.html.

41. Alan Feuer and Andrea Salcedo, "New York City Deploys 45 Mobile Morgues as Virus Strains Funeral Homes," *New York Times*, April 2, 2020. https://www.nytimes.com/2020/04/02/nyregion/coronavirus-new-york-bodies.html.

42. Derrick Bryson Taylor, "A Timeline of the Coronavirus Pandemic," *New York Times*, March 17, 2021. https://www.nytimes.com/article/coronavirus-timeline.html.

43. Paul Taylor, *The Next America: Boomers, Millennials, and the Looming Generational Showdown* (New York: Public Affairs, 2014).

44. "Gay and Lesbian Rights," Gallup, December 5–7, 2003. http://www.gallup.com/poll/1651/gay-lesbian-rights.aspx.

45. Janet Hook, "Support for Gay Marriage Hits All-Time High," *Wall Street Journal*, March 9, 2015.

46. Ibid.

47. Monica Anders, "Technology Device Ownership: 2015," Pew Research Center, October 29, 2015. http://www.pewglobal.org/2016/02/22/smartphone-ownership-and-internet-usage-continues-to-climb-in-emerging-economies/.

48. Monica Anderson and Andrea Caumont, "How Social Media Is Reshaping News," Pew Research Center, September 24, 2014. http://www.pewresearch.org/fact-tank/2014/09/24/how-social-media-is-reshaping-news/.

49. See, for instance, Nicholas G. Carr's 2010 *The Shallows: What the Internet Is Doing to Our Brains*, a 2011 Pulitzer Prize finalist.

50. Bijan Stephen, "Social Media Helps Black Lives Matter Fight the Power," *Wired* (November 2015). http://www.wired.com/2015/10/how-black-lives-matter-uses-social-media-to-fight-the-power/.

51. Larry Buchanan, Quoctrung Bui, and Jugal K. Patel, "Black Lives Matter May Be the Largest Movement in U.S. History," *New York Times*, July 3, 2020. https://www.nytimes.com/interactive/2020/07/03/us/george-floyd-protests-crowd-size.html.

52. U.S. Census Bureau, 2016 American Community Survey 1-Year Estimates. https://factfinder.census.gov/bkmk/table/1.0/en/ACS/16_1YR/S1601/0500000US48061|0500000US48215.

RECOMMENDED READING

Alexander, Michelle. *The New Jim Crow: Mass Incarceration in the Age of Colorblindness*. New York: New Press, 2012.

Canaday, Margot. *The Straight State: Sexuality and Citizenship in Twentieth-Century America*. Princeton, NJ: Princeton University Press, 2011.

Carter, Dan T. *From George Wallace to Newt Gingrich: Race in the Conservative Counterrevolution, 1963–1994*. Baton Rouge: LSU Press, 1996.

Cowie, Jefferson. *Capital Moves: RCA's 70-Year Quest for Cheap Labor*. New York: New Press, 2001.

Ehrenreich, Barbara. *Nickel and Dimed: On (Not) Getting By in America*. New York: Metropolitan, 2001.

Evans, Sara. *Tidal Wave: How Women Changed America at Century's End*. New York: Free Press, 2003.

Gardner, Lloyd C. *The Long Road to Baghdad: A History of U.S. Foreign Policy from the 1970s to the Present*. New York: Free Press, 2008.

Hinton, Elizabeth. *From the War on Poverty to the War on Crime*. Cambridge, MA: Harvard University Press, 2016.

Hollinger, David. *Postethnic America: Beyond Multiculturalism*. New York: Basic Books, 1995.

Hunter, James D. *Culture Wars: The Struggle to Define America*. New York: Basic Books, 1992.

Meyerowitz, Joanne. *How Sex Changed: A History of Transsexuality in the United States*. Cambridge, MA: Harvard University Press, 2004.

Mittelstadt, Jennifer. *The Rise of the Military Welfare State*. Cambridge, MA: Harvard University Press, 2015.

Moreton, Bethany. *To Serve God and Walmart: The Making of Christian Free Enterprise*. Cambridge, MA: Harvard University Press, 2009.

Nadasen, Premilla. *Welfare Warriors: The Welfare Rights Movement in the United States*. New York: Routledge, 2005.

Osnos, Evan. *Age of Ambition: Chasing Fortune, Truth and Faith in the New China*. New York: Farrar, Straus and Giroux, 2014.

Packer, George. *The Unwinding: An Inner History of the New America*. New York: Farrar, Straus and Giroux, 2013.

Patterson, James T. *Restless Giant: The United States from Watergate to Bush v. Gore*. New York: Oxford University Press, 2005.

Piketty, Thomas. *Capital in the Twenty-First Century*. Translated from the French by Arthur Goldhammer. Cambridge, MA: Belknap Press, 2013.

Ricks, Thomas E. *Fiasco: The American Military Adventure in Iraq*. New York: Penguin, 2006.

Schlosser, Eric. *Fast Food Nation: The Dark Side of the All-American Meal*. New York: Houghton Mifflin Harcourt, 2001.

Stiglitz, Joseph. *Freefall: America, Free Markets, and the Sinking of the World Economy*. New York: Norton, 2010.

Taylor, Paul. *The Next America: Boomers, Millennials, and the Looming Generational Showdown*. New York: Public Affairs, 2014.

Wilentz, Sean. *The Age of Reagan: A History, 1974–2008*. New York: HarperCollins, 2008.

Williams, Daniel K. *God's Own Party: The Making of the Christian Right*. New York: Oxford University Press, 2007.

Wright, Lawrence. *The Looming Tower: Al Qaeda and the Road to 9/11*. New York: Knopf, 2006.

Contributors

Kyle Roberts, Loyola University Chicago
Jentery Sayers, University of Victoria
Kelly Schrum, George Mason University
Lisa Spiro, Rice University
Erik Steiner, Stanford University
Mark Tebeau, Arizona State University
Lauren Tilton, Yale University
Kathryn Tomasek, Wheaton College
Andrew J. Torget, University of North Texas
William J. Turkel, University of Western
    Ontario
Lauren Tilton, Yale University
Kathryn Tomasek, Wheaton College
Andrew J. Torget, University of North Texas
William J. Turkel, University of Western Ontario

CHAPTER EDITORS
Samuel Abramson, Rice University
Ellen Adams, Alice T. Miner Museum
Richard Anderson, Princeton University
Lauren Brand, Southern Nazarene University
Edwin Breeden, Old Exchange Building and Old
    Slave Mart Museum
Emily Conroy-Krutz, Michigan State University
Ari Cushner, San Jose State University
Matthew Downs, University of Mobile
Angela Esco Elder, Converse College
Jesse Gant, University of Wisconsin
Jane Fiegen Green, American Historical
    Association
Paula Fortier, Independent Researcher
Nathaniel Green, Northern Virginia Community
    College
Michael Hammond, Taylor University
Michael Hattem, Yale University
Mary Anne Henderson, University of
    Washington
David Hochfelder, University at Albany, SUNY
Daniel Johnson, Bilkent University
Amy Kohout, Colorado College
Gregg Lightfoot, The Girls Preparatory School
James McKay, University of Wisconsin
William Schultz, Princeton University
Nora Slonimsky, Iona College
Tara Strauch, College of Wooster
David Thomson, Sacred Heart University

Nicole Turner, Virginia Commonwealth
    University
Andrew Wegmann, Delta State University
Brandy Thomas Wells, Augusta College
Jonathan Wilfred Wilson, University of Scranton
    and Marywood University

IMAGE CURATORS
Erin Holmes, University of South Carolina
Katherine Lennard, Stanford University
Jo-Ann Morgan, Western Illinois University
Christina Regelski, Rice University
Amy Sopcak-Joseph, University of Connecticut
Whitney Stewart, University of Texas at Dallas
Colleen Tripp, California State University,
    Northridge

CONTRIBUTORS
Christopher L. Abernathy, University of
    Oklahoma
Gregory Ablavsky, Stanford Law School
Sam Abramson, Rice University
Ellen Adams, William and Mary
Alvita Akiboh, Northwestern University
Jim Ambuske, University of Virginia
Richard A. Anderson, Princeton University
Seth Anziska, University College London
Kelly B. Arehart, William and Mary
Carolyn Arena, Omohundro Institute of Early
    American History and Culture
Emily Arendt, Montana State University
    Billings
Jeffrey Bain-Conkin, Notre Dame University
Andrew Baker, Texas A&M University–
    Commerce
Thomas Balcerski, Eastern Connecticut State
    University
Simon Balto, Ball State University
Laila Ballout, Northwestern University
Seth Bartee, Guilford Technical Community
    College
Marco Basile, Harvard University
Jeremiah Bauer, University of Nebraska
Joshua Beatty, SUNY Plattsburgh
Amanda Bellows, The New School
Jacob Betz, Harvard University

Marsha Barrett, University of Illinois at Urbana-Champaign

Ian Beamish, Johns Hopkins University

Myles Beaupre, Notre Dame University

Ethan R. Bennett, Washington University in St. Louis

Daniel Birge, Boston University

William Black, Rice University

John Blanton, The City College of New York

Drew Bledsoe, Lee University

Cameron Blevins, Northeastern University

Nicholas Blood, Emory University

Eladio Bobadilla, Duke University

Lauren Brand, Southern Nazarene University

Edwin Breeden, Old Exchange Building and Old Slave Mart Museum

Michael Brenes, Yale University

Marjorie Brown, Houston Community College

Kyle Burke, Northwestern University

L. D. Burnett, Tarleton State University

Alexander Burns, Ball State University

Carole Butcher, North Dakota State University

Matthew A. Byron, Young Harris College

Michael T. Caires, University of Virginia

Christina Carrick, Boston University

Michelle Cassidy, Central Michigan University

Peter Catapano, New York City College of Technology

Steffi Cerato, Johns Hopkins University

Andrew Chadwick, University of Maryland

Tizoc Chavez, Vanderbilt University

Christopher Childers, Pittsburg State University

Micah Childress, Grand Valley State University

Mary Beth Basile Chopas, University of North Carolina

Frank Cirillo, University of Virginia

Justin Clark, Nanyang Technological University

Dana Cochran, Virginia Tech

Kristin Condotta Lee, Washington University in St. Louis

Emily Conroy-Krutz, Michigan State University

Christopher Consolino, Johns Hopkins University

Adam Constanzo, Texas A&M Corpus Christi

Wiliam Cossen, Penn State University

Aaron Cowan, Slippery Rock University

Mari Crabtree, College of Charleston

Michell Cresfield, Vanderbilt University

Ari Cushner, San Jose State University

Lori Daggar, Ursinus College

Andrew David, Boston University

Morgan Deane, Brigham Young University-Idaho

Jenifer Dodd, Vanderbilt University

Jean-Paul de Guzman, University of California, Los Angeles

Matthew Downs, University of Mobile

Jennifer Donnally, University of North Carolina

Mary Draper, Midwestern State University

Dan Du, University of Georgia

Blake Earle, Southern Methodist University

Ashton Ellett, University of Georgia

Angela Esco Elder, Converse College

Alexandra Evans, University of Virginia

Sean Fear, University of Leeds

Maggie Flamingo, University of Wisconsin

Paula Fortier, University of New Orleans

Jeff Fortnoy, University of Oklahoma

Michael Franczak, Boston College

Leif Fredrickson, University of Virginia

Zach Fredman, Dartmouth College

Stephanie Gamble, Johns Hopkins University

Jesse Gant, University of Wisconsin

Josh Garrett-Davis, Autry Museum of the American West

Zach P. Gastellum, University of Oklahoma

Jamie Goodall, Stevenson University

Jonathan Grandage, Florida State University

Larry A. Grant, The Citadel

Anne Gray Fischer, Brown University

Kori Graves, University at Albany, SUNY

Jane Fiegen Green, American Historical Association

Nathaniel Green, Northern Virginia Community College

Robert Gudmestad, Colorado State University

Joseph Haker, University of Minnesota

Blaine Hamilton, Rice University

Tracey Hanshew, Washington State University

Caroline Bunnell Harris, University of California, Los Angeles

Michael Hattem, Yale University

Karissa Haugeberg, Tulane University

Chris Hayashida-Knight, Penn State University

Richara Leona Hayward, University of Pennsylvania

Timothy C. Hemmis, Texas A&M University– Central Texas

Mary Anne Henderson, University of Washington

Mariah Hepworth, Northwestern University

Jordan Hill, Virginia Tech University

Hidetaka Hirota, Columbia University

David Hochfelder, University at Albany, SUNY

Nicolas Hoffmann, Oak Mountain Academy

Lilian Hoodes, Northwestern University

Rebecca Howard, University of Arkansas

Amanda Hughett, Duke University

Kylie A. Hulbert, Texas A&M University– Kingsville

Matthew C. Hulbert, University of Georgia

Jonathan Hunt, Stanford University

Jun Suk Hyun University of Georgia

Hendrick Isom, Brown University

Zachary Jacobson, Northwestern University

Destin Jenkins, University of Chicago

Nathan Jérémie-Brink, New Brunswick Theological Seminary

D. Andrew Johnson, Rice University

Daniel Johnson, Bilkent University

Christopher C. Jones, Brigham Young University

Matthew Kahn, Northwestern University

Suzanne Kahn, Columbia University

Micki Kaufman, CUNY Graduate Center

Lindsay Keiter, Penn State Altoona

William Kelly, Rutgers University

Brenden Kennedy, University of Montana Western

S. Wright Kennedy, Rice University

William Kerrigan, Muskingum University

Krista Kinslow, Boston University

Jonathan Koefoed, Belhaven University

Gerard Koeppel, Independent Scholar

Stephn M. Koeth, Columbia University

Amy Kohout, Colorado College

Erin Bonuso Kramer, University of Wisconsin

Dale Kretz, Texas Tech University

Matthew Kruer, University of Chicago

Mark Kukis, Keck Graduate Institute

Lucie Kyrova, Charles University

Guy Lancaster, Central Arkansas Library System

Allison Lange, Wentworth Institute of Technology

Kathryn Knowles Lasdow, Columbia University

Brooke Lamperd, Brown University

Scott Libson, Emory University

Gregg Lightfoot, The Girls Preparatory School

Matthew Linton, Brandeis University

Kyle Livie, Oholone College

Jennifer Mandel, Mount Washington College

John Garrison Marks, American Association for State and Local History

Dawn Marsh, Purdue University

Valerie A. Martinex, University of Texas

Paul Matzko, Penn State University

Ashley Mays, University of North Carolina

Lisa Mercer, University of Illinois at Urbana-Champaign

Spencer McBride, Louisiana State University

Keith D. McCall, Rice University

Charles McCrary, Florida State University

Katherine J. McGarr, University of Wisconsin

James McKay, University of Wisconsin

José Juan Pérez Meléndez, University of California, Davis

Ryan T. Menath, U.S. Air Force Academy

Samantha Miller, University of Pennsylvania

Shaul Mitelpunkt, University of York

Elisa Minoff, University of South Florida

Maria Montalvo, Tulane University

Celeste Day Moore, Hamilton College

Erik A. Moore, University of Oklahoma

Gregory Moore, Notre Dame College

Jessica Parker Moore, Texas Christian University

Joseph Moore, Gardner-Webb University

Isabella Morales, Princeton University

Felicia Moralez, University of Notre Dame

Melissa Morris, Bridgewater State University

Christen Mucher, Smith College

Andrea Nero, University at Buffalo, SUNY

Christopher Null, University of California, Los Angeles

James Owen, University of Georgia

Brooke Palmieri, University College London

R. Joseph Parrott, The Ohio State University

Adam Parsons, Syracuse University

Ryan Poe, Duke University

Matthew Pressman, Seton Hall University

Emily Alise Prifogle, Princeton University

Bradley Proctor, University of North Carolina

Ansley Quiros, University of North Alabama

Laura Redford, UCLA

Michelle Reeves, US Naval War College

Ronny Regev, The Hebrew University of Jerusalem

Emily Remus, University of Notre Dame

Colin Reynolds, Emory University

Leah Richier, University of Georgia

Julie Richter, William and Mary

Bryan Rindfleisch, Marquette University

Angela Riotto, University of Akron

John P. Riley, Binghamton University, SUNY

James Risk, University of South Carolina

Andrew Robichaud, Stanford University

Michael Robinson, University of Mobile

Cara Rogers, Rice University

Katherine Rohrer, University of North Georgia

Emily Romeo, Depaul University

Nick Rowland, University of Texas

Brent Ruswick, West Chester University

Matthew K. Saionz, University of Florida

John Saillant, Western Michigan University

Christopher Paul Sawula, Emory University

Ian Saxine, Northwestern University

David Schley, Hong Kong Baptist University

John Schmitz, Northern Virginia Community College

Kristopher Shields, Rutgers University

Evgenia Shnayder Shoop, University of Pennsylvania

Cameron Shriver, Ohio State University

Matt Simmons, University of Florida

Donna Sinclair, University of Central Michigan

Phillip Luke Sinitiere, College of Biblical Studies

William E. Skidmore, Rice University

Elizabeth Skilton, University of Louisiana at Lafayette

Nora Slonimsky, Iona College

Katherine Smoak, Johns Hopkins University

Christopher Sparshott, Northwestern University in Qatar

Bill Speer, American Military University

Daniel Spillman, Oklahoma Baptist University

Kate Sohasky, Johns Hopkins University

Marie Stango, California State University, Bakersfield

Megan Stanton, University of Wisconsin

Rowan Steinecker, University of Central Oklahoma

Colin Stephenson, Ohio State University

Gregory N. Stern, Florida State University

Whitney Stewart, University of Texas at Dallas

Tara Strauch, University of South Carolina

Joseph Super, University of West Virginia

Jordan Taylor, Indiana University

Michael Harrison Taylor, University of Georgia

Emma Teitelman, University of Pennsylvania

Chris Thomas, Reynolds Community College

Susan Thomas, University of North Carolina at Greensboro

Robert John Thompson III, Southern Mississippi

David Thomson, Sacred Heart University

Patrick Troester, University of Akron

Ann Tucker, University of North Georgia

Nicole Turner, Virginia Commonwealth University

Ashley Rose Young, Smithsonian Institution

Caitlin Verboon, Yale University

Alyce Vigil, Northern Oklahoma College

James Wainwright, Prince George's Community College

Kevin Waite, Durham University

Kaylynn Washnock, University of Georgia

C. Ruth Watterson, Harvard University

Benjamin Weber, Harvard University

Kelly B. Weber, Rice University

Andrew Wegmann, Delta State University

James Wellborn, Georgia College

Brandy Thomas Wells, Augusta College

Benjamin Wetzel, University of Notre Dame

Luke Willert, Harvard University

Mason B. Williams, Williams College

Naomi R. Williams, The College at Brockport, SUNY

Jonathan Wilfred Wilson, University of Scranton and Marywood University

Kevin Wisniewski, University of Maryland, Baltimore County

Nicholas Wood, Spring Hill College

Michael E. Woods, Marshall University

Garrett Wright, University of North Carolina

Nathan Wuertenberg, Ball State University

Charlton Yingling, University of Louisville

Kevin Young, University of Georgia

Rebecca Zimmer, University of Southern Mississippi